Understanding Trade-Based Laundering

Trade-Based Money Laundering (TBML) is a global threat that has emerged as one of the most sophisticated financial crimes that exploits global trade systems to conceal illicit funds. *Understanding Trade-Based Money Laundering: A Practical Guide* provides unique in-depth analysis of different types, techniques, and case studies, along with tools and strategies for prevention and detection. It explores how TBML distorts economies, undermines fair competition, and facilitates criminal activities, such as terrorism, drug trafficking, and human trafficking.

Providing a comprehensive overview of the mechanisms and techniques used in TBML, this book explores the global regulatory framework, underground financial systems, virtual currencies, and gold trade, among other topics. Drawing on a comparative study of anti-money laundering regulations in the Islamic banking systems of the UAE, Malaysia, Sudan, and Pakistan, it offers strategies for future preparedness and a framework for action in the technological era. Readers will gain an understanding of the challenges faced by law enforcement and the importance of international cooperation in addressing this global issue.

This book is an essential resource for students and practitioners with an interest in understanding the practical aspects of money laundering, as well as policymakers, law enforcement agencies, financial regulators, and researchers concerned with combating financial crimes that threaten global development and security.

Syed Zubair Ahmed, PhD, is an academic author and practitioner with over 25 years of professional experience, specializing in accounting, auditing, compliance, and anti-fraud.

"The book delivers a timely framework that helps companies improve transparency in their financial reporting and regulatory compliance. It is an essential resource for auditors to understand and reduce the practical risks of trade-based money laundering."

Shafqat Reza, *FCA, FCIS, CPA, M.Com, LLB. Principal Partner,*
Raza Siddiqui & Co., Chartered Accountants

"The book provides a practical framework to help people address one of the most difficult challenges in international trade. The book bridges theoretical concepts with practical applications, making it a must-have for professionals fighting financial crime internationally in the business field."

Muhammad Rauf Khatri, *CIMA, CGM, CAUAE, MBA (Finance);*
Manager, GL Ports Cluster, Abu Dhabi Ports, United Arab Emirates

"Ahmed's work provides practical insights that help management accountants achieve compliance through their strategic decision-making. The tool establishes essential international finance professional requirements through its ability to link regulatory knowledge with business outcomes."

Ikhtiar Ahmed Khoso, *PhD (Finance), Director,*
Center for Entrepreneurial Leadership & Incubation,
Sukkur IBA University, Sindh, Pakistan

Understanding Trade-Based Money Laundering

A Practical Guide

Syed Zubair Ahmed

Routledge
Taylor & Francis Group
LONDON AND NEW YORK

Designed cover image: © Getty Images / alexsl

First published 2027
by Routledge
4 Park Square, Milton Park, Abingdon, Oxon OX14 4RN

and by Routledge
605 Third Avenue, New York, NY 10158

Routledge is an imprint of the Taylor & Francis Group, an informa business

British Library Cataloguing-in-Publication Data
A catalogue record for this book is available from the British Library

Library of Congress Cataloging-in-Publication Data
Names: Ahmed, Syed Zubair author
Title: Understanding trade-based money laundering : a practical guide /
Syed Zubair Ahmed.
Description: Abingdon, Oxon ; New York, NY : Routledge, 2027. | Includes
bibliographical references and index.
Identifiers: LCCN 2026009460 | ISBN 9781032762234 hardback |
ISBN 9781032762210 paperback | ISBN 9781003477631 ebook
Subjects: LCSH: Money laundering | International trade—Moral and ethical
aspects | Fraud—Prevention
Classification: LCC HV6768 .A395 2027 | DDC 364.46/8—dc23/eng/20260605
LC record available at https://lccn.loc.gov/2026009460

ISBN: 978-1-032-76223-4 (hbk)
ISBN: 978-1-032-76221-0 (pbk)
ISBN: 978-1-003-47763-1 (ebk)

DOI: 10.4324/9781003477631

Typeset in Times New Roman
by codeMantra

Access the Support Material: www.routledge.com/9781032762210

In memory of my father, Syed Nabi Ahmed, whose solid support, steadfast guidance, and inspiration have always been a model for me. He defined my journey, and this book would not have been possible without him.

Contents

Figures

Tables

Cases

Section

About the Author

Syed Zubair Ahmed is a highly accomplished and experienced professional with over 25 years of progressive experience in accounting, internal and external audit, and anti-fraud. He has a proven track record of representing a diverse range of internal and external clients in the private sector. He is skilled in working with multiple layers of management in numerous sectors to increase productivity and knowledge.

Zubair began his professional journey at Hyder Bhimji & Co. Chartered Accountants in Karachi, Pakistan, a prominent audit firm that offers a wide range of services, including external and internal audit assurance, corporate compliance, regulatory standards, tax practices, and consulting services accredited by the Institute of Chartered Accountants of Pakistan. During his four-year tenure with the firm, he audited financial, manufacturing, and banking institutions.

In addition to his professional work, Zubair is a dedicated and self-motivated writer, editor, and educator. He has written on a wide range of topics for newspapers and magazines, has served as an editor for a newspaper, and has contributed to scientific journals. He is also a freelance writer for blogs and websites.

Zubair's passion as an educator is to ignite critical and creative thinking in his students. He has designed and developed undergraduate and graduate-level courses, including financial management, corporate finance, investment, forensic accounting, and fraud examination and investigation.

Zubair's educational qualifications encompass a comprehensive range of disciplines, including a Bachelor of Commerce (B.Com), a Master of Commerce (M.Com), an Executive Master of Business Administration (EMBA), and a Ph.D. in Forensic Accounting. His certification as a member of the Association of Certified Fraud Examiners (ACFE) underscores his active involvement in the surveillance and mitigation of financial crime. Zubair's domain expertise encompasses accounting, finance, and anti-fraud practices, fortified by substantial practical experience. His competencies in budgeting, systems management, feasibility analysis, and financial crime investigation substantiate his profound contribution to his field.

Preface

As the night descends upon the city, the shadows take on their own life. In the obscure corners of the back alleys, a group of ominous figures huddle together, their faces hidden by the veil of darkness. They are the puppet masters of a nefarious plot, cunningly designed to conceal the profits of their unlawful deeds through the guise of legitimate trade. Such is the disturbing world of trade-based money laundering (TBML)—a looming menace that poses an immediate and existential threat to our global economy and the fabric of our society, transcending borders and affecting us all.

Understanding Trade-Based Money Laundering: A Practical Guide is not just a book but also a comprehensive and indispensable guide to understanding and combating the growing threat of TBML. As criminal organizations become more proficient in their methods, law enforcement, banks, and businesses must stay ahead of the obnoxious game. This book examines the inner workings of TBML, from its use in laundering money through intricate international trade to the specific techniques and typologies employed by criminals. This book also provides an overview of the global regulatory framework for TBML and examines the robust management of financial systems within the global economy.

This book examines the tactics of money launderers, ranging from the misuse of the international gold trade to the exploitation of free trade zones. It also examines the global issue of illicit financial flows and the crucial role that money laundering plays in facilitating criminal activity. With an in-depth analysis of the various typologies of TBML, this guide provides essential strategies for identifying and neutralizing the risk indicators of this threat.

This book also explores various typologies of TBML and offers strategies for identifying risk indicators through customer, transaction, shipment, and payment red flags. It examines the international regulatory framework for TBML and the sanctions regime, as well as the significance of knowing your customer (KYC) and combating the financing of terrorism (CFT) in the banking industry.

As the clock ticks and the criminal masterminds continue to perfect their schemes, we must stay one step ahead. This book concludes with a powerful call to arms, outlining strategies for future preparedness in the ongoing battle against TBML. From the latest technological advancements to a revolutionary alternative remittance system using blockchain-based digital currency, this book leaves no stone unturned in the quest for solutions. Appendices delve even more profoundly, exploring the intersection of TBML and the technological era and providing a comprehensive overview of the EU's anti-money laundering directive. Refrain from being caught off guard—take charge and arm yourself with the information you need to emerge victorious in this battle. With determination and the right resources, you can stay ahead of the game and protect our economy from those who seek to undermine the entire system.

Knowledge is a powerful tool in the battle against TBML. Moreover, with *Understanding Trade-Based Money Laundering: A Practical Guide*, you will have the most potent weapon in your arsenal. This groundbreaking book offers up-to-date analysis, real-world case studies, and practical strategies to combat TBML. As the old saying goes, "Knowledge is power." This book is unarguably a driving force of knowledge and is the best anchor in troubled waters. With each page, you will gain a deeper understanding of the insidious tactics and shocking cover-ups exploited by TBML masterminds, and you will be equipped with the tools to protect the global economy from their damaging schemes. So do not just sit on the sidelines—join the fight against TBML with *Understanding Trade-Based Money Laundering: A Practical Guide*.

Glossary of Abbreviations

Abbreviation	*Full Form*	*Context/Notes*
1MDB	1Malaysia Development Berhad	Malaysian sovereign wealth fund case
6AMLD	Sixth EU Money Laundering Directive	EU regulatory framework
ABC	Agricultural Bank of China	Financial institution
ABF	Australian Border Force	Enforcement agency
ABI	Italian Banking Association	Industry body
ACAMS	Association of Certified Anti-Money Laundering Specialists	Professional association
AI	Artificial Intelligence	Technology in AML/KYC
AML	Anti-Money Laundering	Core compliance regime
AMLA	Anti-Money Laundering Act of 2020	U.S. legislation
AMLSCU	Anti-Money Laundering and Suspicious Transactions Unit	Regulatory unit
AMLU	Anti-Money Laundering Unit	Enforcement unit
APG	Asia/Pacific Group on Money Laundering	FATF-style regional body
ASGM	Artisanal and Small-Scale Gold Mining	Sector risk
AU	African Union	Regional organization
BBC	British Broadcasting Corporation	Media
BICG	Brazilian Institute of Corporate Governance	Governance body
BIS	Bureau of Industry and Security (U.S. Department of Commerce)	Export controls
BIoG	Basel Institute on Governance	Research institute
BMPE	Black-Market Peso Exchange	TBML method
BNM	Bank Negara Malaysia	Central bank
BRI	Belt and Road Initiative	Geopolitical/economic program
BSA	Bank Secrecy Act	U.S. AML law
BaFin	Federal Financial Supervisory Authority (Germany)	Regulator
CBDC	Central Bank Digital Currency	Emerging financial technology
CBJ	Central Bank of Jordan	Central bank
CBM	Central Bank of Malaysia	Central bank
CBRC	China Banking Regulatory Commission	Regulator
CDD	Customer Due Diligence	Standard AML/KYC process requiring verification of customer identity and risk assessment.
CET	Combating the Financing of Terrorism	Preferred regulatory term for countering terrorist financing; aligns with AML/CFT frameworks.

(*Continued*)

Abbreviation	*Full Form*	*Context/Notes*
CFT	Countering the Financing of Terrorism	Used in FATF and IMF documents; often paired with AML (AML/CFT). (Note: Use 'CET'—Combating the Financing of Terrorism—in academic/regulatory contexts unless quoting sources.)
CFTC	Commodity Futures Trading Commission	U.S. regulator
CIA	Central Intelligence Agency	U.S. intelligence
CNTC	China National Tobacco Corporation	State enterprise
COMEX	New York Commodity Exchange	Market
CRS	Common Reporting Standard	OECD tax transparency
CTA	Corporate Transparency Act	U.S. legislation (Note: Clarify whether this refers to the Corporate Transparency Act or Commodity Trading Advisor in context.)
CTA (alt.)	Commodity Trading Advisor	Distinct context—clarify in text
CTR	Currency Transaction Report	AML reporting
DEA	Drug Enforcement Administration	U.S. federal agency responsible for combating drug trafficking and related financial crimes.
DeFi	Decentralized Finance	Blockchain/crypto
DEX	Decentralized Exchange	Blockchain/crypto
DFSA	Dubai Financial Services Authority	Regulator
DHS	Department of Homeland Security	U.S. agency
DOJ	U.S. Department of Justice	Federal agency enforcing laws, including AML, sanctions, and financial crime prosecutions.
DTO	Drug Trafficking Organization	Criminal networks
EDD	Enhanced Due Diligence	Additional scrutiny is applied to high-risk customers or transactions.
EFIU	European Financial Intelligence Unit	FIU
EMC	European Monitoring Center on Money Laundering	EU body
EU	European Union	Regional bloc
Egmont Group	International network of Financial Intelligence Units (FIUs)	Facilitates cooperation and information exchange among FIUs worldwide.
Europol	European Union Agency for Law Enforcement Cooperation	Enforcement
FATCA	Foreign Account Tax Compliance Act	U.S. tax law
FATF	Financial Action Task Force	An intergovernmental body setting global AML/CFT standards.
FATF Rec. 24	Financial Action Task Force Recommendation 24 (Beneficial Ownership Transparency)	Requires countries to ensure transparency of beneficial ownership to prevent misuse of legal persons for money laundering or terrorist financing.
FBI	Federal Bureau of Investigation	U.S. law enforcement
FCA	Financial Conduct Authority (UK)	Independent regulator overseeing financial markets and firms; enforces AML/CFT compliance in the UK.
FDI	Foreign Direct Investment	Economic term
FFI	Foreign Financial Institution	FATCA context
FININT	Financial Intelligence	Intelligence discipline
FINRA	Financial Industry Regulatory Authority	U.S. regulator
FIU	Financial Intelligence Unit	National agency responsible for receiving, analyzing, and disseminating suspicious transaction reports.

(*Continued*)

Abbreviation	*Full Form*	*Context/Notes*
FSOC	Financial Stability Oversight Council	U.S. regulator
FT	Financial Times	Media
FTZs	Free Trade Zones	Trade context
FinCEN	Financial Crimes Enforcement Network	U.S. FIU
Fintech	Financial Technology	Industry
GAO	Government Accountability Office	U.S. oversight
GDP	Gross Domestic Product	Economic measure of the total value of goods and services produced; often impacted by sanctions and financial crime.
GDPR	General Data Protection Regulation	EU privacy law
GENIUS Act	Legislative title	Not abbreviation—exclude
GFI	Global Financial Integrity	NGO
GTO	Geographic Targeting Order	AML reporting
HKMA	Hong Kong Monetary Authority	Regulator
ICC	International Chamber of Commerce	Trade body
ICE	Intercontinental Exchange	Market
ICE (alt.)	U.S. Immigration and Customs Enforcement	Enforcement
ICIJ	International Consortium of Investigative Journalists	Media
IEEPA	International Emergency Economic Powers Act	U.S. law
IFF	Illicit Financial Flows	Economic crime
IGA	Intergovernmental Agreement	FATCA context
IOU	I Owe You	An informal financial instrument acknowledging debt, framed as a simple credit mechanism relevant to informal value-transfer systems.
IRS	Internal Revenue Service	U.S. tax authority; enforces FATCA and monitors compliance with tax-related AML/CFT obligations.
ITA	International Trade Administration	U.S. agency promoting trade and enforcing compliance with export regulations.
IoT	Internet of Things	Network of connected devices; relevant in compliance contexts for monitoring financial transactions and cybersecurity risks.
KRA	Kenya Revenue Authority	Tax authority
KYC	Know Your Customer	Core AML process requiring financial institutions to verify customer identity and assess risk.
KYCC	Know Your Customer's Customer	Extended due diligence
LBMA	London Bullion Market Association	Market
MENAFATF	Middle East & North Africa FATF	Regional body
ML	Machine Learning	Technology
MPA	Maritime and Port Authority (Singapore)	Regulator
MiCA	Markets in Crypto-Assets (EU Regulation)	EU law
NAO	National Audit Office (China)	Oversight
NBER	National Bureau of Economic Research	Research institute
NDAA	National Defense Authorization Act	U.S. law
OAS	Organization of American States	Regional body
OCCRP	Organized Crime and Corruption Reporting Project	NGO

(*Continued*)

Abbreviation	*Full Form*	*Context/Notes*
OCR	Optical Character Recognition	Technology used to digitize and analyze documents; relevant for compliance monitoring and transaction screening.
OECD	Organization for Economic Cooperation and Development	International body
OFAC	Office of Foreign Assets Control (U.S. Treasury)	Administers and enforces U.S. economic and trade sanctions.
PEP	Politically Exposed Person	AML risk category
PEPO	European Public Prosecutor's Office	EU body
POC	Proof of Concept	Technology
PRA	Prudential Regulation Authority (UK)	Regulates banks, insurers, and major investment firms; enforces AML/CFT compliance.
RFI	Red Flag Indicator	Warning signs used by financial institutions to detect suspicious activity, including TBML and AML risks.
RPM	Resale Price Method	Transfer pricing
RSN	Regulated Settlement Network	Blockchain/crypto
SAR	Suspicious Activity Report	AML reporting
SBP	State Bank of Pakistan	Central bank
SDN	Specially Designated Nationals	OFAC designation
SDN List	Specially Designated Nationals and Blocked Persons List	OFAC
SEC	U.S. Securities and Exchange Commission	Regulates securities markets; enforces compliance with AML/CFT and financial reporting standards.
SGE	Shanghai Gold Exchange	Market
SMEs	Small and Medium-sized Enterprises	Business (Note: Use plural form consistently.)
SSA	Singapore Shipping Association	Industry
STRs	Suspicious Transaction Reports	AML reporting
SWIFT	Society for Worldwide Interbank Financial Telecommunication	Messaging network
StAR	Stolen Asset Recovery Initiative	World Bank/UNODC
TBML	Trade-Based Money Laundering	AML typology
TJN	Tax Justice Network	NGO
UBO	Ultimate Beneficial Owner	AML/KYC
UCC	Uniform Commercial Code	U.S. law
UCP	Uniform Customs and Practice for Documentary Credits	Trade finance
UN	United Nations	International body
UNCECOC	UN Convention on the Use of Electronic Communications in International Contracts	Treaty
UNCITRAL	UN Commission on International Trade Law	UN body
UNCTAD	UN Conference on Trade and Development	UN body
UNODC	UN Office on Drugs and Crime	UN body
UNSC	United Nations Security Council	Imposes global sanctions and maintains international peace and security.
UNTOC	UN Convention against Transnational Organized Crime	Treaty

(*Continued*)

Abbreviation	*Full Form*	*Context/Notes*
USA PATRIOT Act	Uniting and Strengthening America by Providing Appropriate Tools Required to Intercept and Obstruct Terrorism Act	U.S. law
VASPs	Virtual Asset Service Providers	Crypto
WCO	World Customs Organization	International body
WGC	World Gold Council	Industry
WMD	Weapons of Mass Destruction	Security
WTO	World Trade Organization	International body
e-BDN	e-Bunker Delivery Note	Digital documentation used in maritime shipping to record fuel delivery; relevant in TBML contexts.

Key Notes

- CFT vs. CET: Standardize to CET – Combating the Financing of Terrorism in academic/regulatory contexts. Avoid "CTF" unless quoting a source verbatim.
- StAR vs. SARI: Use StAR consistently.
- IOU: Expand on first use as *IOU (I Owe You)*.
- CTA: Clarify context (Corporate Transparency Act vs. Commodity Trading Advisor) in text.
- SMEs: Use plural form consistently.
- hawala: Not an abbreviation; use lowercase except at sentence start.

Introduction

Unveiling the Thrilling World of Trade-Based Money Laundering

Money laundering is a sophisticated and widespread issue that plagues economies across the world. Criminals are constantly seeking ways to conceal the proceeds of their illegal activities, and trade-based money laundering (TBML) has emerged as one of the most prevalent methods. Through TBML, criminals can exploit the global trading system to mask the origin of illicit funds, making it highly challenging for authorities to detect and prevent such activities. In this discussion, we will take a deep dive into the world of TBML, examining its significance, impact, and intriguing key facets. Join us on this journey as we uncover the dark side of global trade and unravel the mysteries of TBML.

What Is TBML and Why Is It Crucial?

TBML is a sophisticated and complex financial crime that has become increasingly prevalent in the modern era. At its core, TBML involves utilizing trade transactions to launder illicit funds across international borders. Criminals engage in a range of deceptive tactics, including over- and under-invoicing, to manipulate the value and volume of goods in these transactions, thereby disguising the origin and destination of the funds involved. The sheer scale of TBML is staggering, with some experts estimating that up to $2 trillion is laundered through trade annually. This makes it a critical issue for governments, financial institutions, and law enforcement agencies worldwide to address as they combat economic crime and ensure the integrity of the global financial ecosystem.

The danger posed by TBML cannot be overstated. Failure to study and prevent this insidious practice can have dire consequences. As the profits from illicit activities are concealed through trade transactions, criminals can fund even more nefarious activities such as terrorism and drug trafficking. TBML also has a far-reaching impact on the global economy. It distorts trade statistics, undermines international trade relationships, and erodes trust in the financial system. As the saying goes, "Eternal vigilance is the price of liberty." We must remain watchful in our fight against TBML to protect our society and our economy.

The Fascinating Aspect of TBML:
The most fascinating aspect of TBML is its complexity and adaptability. TBML is a captivating subject for those interested in the ever-evolving world of financial crime. What sets TBML apart from other forms of money laundering is its multifaceted nature, with criminals constantly devising new methods to conceal the illicit origin of their funds.

The challenge for law enforcement agencies is to keep pace with these innovative schemes, which require continuous research, collaboration, and innovation. It is a global problem that demands a global response.

DOI: 10.4324/9781003477631-1

TBML's adaptability is what makes it so compelling. Criminals use a variety of techniques, such as over- or under-invoicing, misdescribing goods, multiple invoicing, and transfer pricing, to manipulate trade transactions and launder their illicit funds. They also leverage the complexity of global supply chains and cross-border trade to their advantage.

As a result, the fight against TBML requires a multidisciplinary approach that involves experts from finance, law enforcement, trade, and technology. This approach must be complemented by a coordinated effort between governments, international organizations, and the private sector to share information and best practices.

How TBML Schemes Are Used to Bust?

The fight against TBML requires collaboration among law enforcement, financial regulators, and international organizations. The use of data analytics, artificial intelligence, and machine learning has been instrumental in identifying suspicious trade transactions and patterns. For example, Operation Darkness Falls in 2018 was a joint investigation by U.S. Immigration and Customs Enforcement (ICE) and Homeland Security Investigations (HSI) that resulted in the indictment of 36 individuals and entities involved in TBML schemes.

Estimated Loss Impact on the Global Economy:
The estimated impact of TBML on the global economy is difficult to quantify due to the complexity of TBML schemes. However, the Financial Action Task Force (FATF) estimates that TBML could account for up to 87% of global illicit financial flows, with a significant impact on economic development and stability.

Specific Merits and Limitations of TBML:
One key advantage of TBML is its potential to drive legitimate economic activity and trade. However, this potential is often overshadowed by TBML's negative impact on the global economy. A major limitation of TBML is the lack of transparency in international trade, making it difficult to detect and investigate suspicious activities.

Expected Changes and Opportunities:
The fight against TBML requires a coordinated effort from various stakeholders, including policymakers, regulators, academics, and industry practitioners. Students can contribute by pursuing research and developing innovative solutions to combat TBML. Practitioners and analysts will be better equipped to identify and prevent TBML in their respective fields. Businessmen can take steps to protect themselves from reputational and legal risks associated with TBML. Policymakers and regulators can strengthen international cooperation and develop effective policies and regulations to prevent TBML.

The field of TBML prevention and detection offers numerous opportunities for professionals across industries. One area where TBML presents a significant opportunity is in the field of data analytics. As the volume of data generated by businesses continues to grow, data analytics professionals can apply their skills to develop more sophisticated techniques to identify and prevent TBML.

In addition to data analytics, financial technology (fintech) offers significant opportunities for TBML prevention and detection. As fintech continues to revolutionize the financial industry, it also creates new opportunities for criminals to engage in money laundering activities. Fintech professionals can leverage their expertise to develop new technologies and tools to detect and prevent TBML.

Another opportunity in TBML prevention and detection is regulatory technology (regtech). Regtech signifies the use of technology to facilitate compliance with regulatory requirements. As governments worldwide continue to crack down on money laundering, demand for regtech solutions is likely to grow. Professionals in regtech can leverage their expertise to develop new solutions to prevent and detect TBML.

Finally, international trade offers significant opportunities for those interested in TBML prevention and detection. As global trade continues to grow, criminals have increasingly turned to TBML as a means of laundering money. Professionals in international trade can apply their expertise to develop new tools and techniques to identify and impede TBML.

Companies that specialize in TBML prevention and detection also offer significant opportunities for those interested in pursuing a career in this field. As the threat of TBML continues to grow, companies that specialize in TBML prevention and detection will be in high demand. These companies can offer a broad range of services, from training and education to technology development, including machine learning algorithms and artificial intelligence tools.

In summary, TBML is a significant issue that poses an enormous threat to the global economy and security. Its impact can be devastating, with estimated losses of billions of dollars. The study of TBML is crucial for spotting and impeding this type of financial crime. With a better understanding of TBML, policymakers, regulators, analysts, practitioners, and business leaders can take measures to mitigate TBML and protect their respective fields from reputational and legal risks. The study of TBML also presents opportunities for growth and innovation in various fields. As former U.S. Treasury Under Secretary for Terrorism and Financial Intelligence David Cohen said, “Trade-based money laundering is a serious problem that demands our attention and resources. We must work together to understand and combat this illicit activity, which undermines legitimate commerce and threatens our national security.” (Cohen, 2013)

Insight

An Analysis of the Scope and Characteristics of Global TBML and Its Implications for Development

The report, “Trade-Based Money Laundering: A Global Challenge,” was published in February 2023 by Global Financial Integrity (GFI), Fedesarrollo, Transparency International Kenya, and the Advocates Coalition for Development and Environment (ACODE). This report analyzes the reach, methods, and impacts of global TBML on development, security, and innovation.

Understanding TBML: Definition and Overview

TBML involves disguising the illicit origin of funds through trade transactions, such as over- or under-invoicing of goods, using false descriptions or misrepresentations of goods or services, and manipulating customs declarations. Criminal organizations and individuals use TBML to move large sums of money across borders while evading detection by law enforcement agencies.

The Scale of TBML: How Big Is the Problem?

TBML is a major and growing global issue, with annual costs estimated at \$1.4–\$3.5 trillion. This staggering figure represents 10% to 30% of all illicit financial flows globally (Egmont Group, 2021, and FATF, 2020).

TBML involves disguising the origins of illicit proceeds by moving value through international trade transactions. Common methods include over- or under-invoicing goods, misrepresenting shipped items, and using informal value transfer systems. The most frequently targeted products are cars, metals, minerals, agricultural goods, and textiles (FATF, 2020).

Scope of TBML: Industries and Countries Most Affected

The most vulnerable sectors include textiles, electronics, pharmaceuticals, precious metals and stones, and second-hand goods (FATF, 2020). These industries are targeted due to their wide pricing margins, extended trade cycles, and susceptibility to gaps in customer due diligence processes across jurisdictions (FATF, 2020).

High-risk regions for TBML include Asia, Africa, and Latin America, where the practice is most prevalent (FATF, 2020). The United States, Mexico, Colombia, China, and Hong Kong are among the countries most impacted by TBML. The predicate offenses generating the laundered funds are predominantly drug trafficking (43%), tax evasion (18%), fraud (7%), and corruption (6%) (Egmont Group, 2021). These nations experience substantial losses in tax and customs revenues due to trade misinvoicing, a common TBML technique (Egmont Group, 2021).

The impact of TBML is substantial, with estimates suggesting a global value gap of $8.7 trillion between export and import declarations of developing and advanced economies from 2008 to 2017 (Kellermann, 2021). This figure underscores the significant economic repercussions of TBML, especially for countries that lose substantial tax and customs revenues to trade misinvoicing (Kellermann, 2021).

Financial institutions engaged in trade finance are also heavily affected by TBML, as they risk facilitating money laundering and incurring regulatory penalties, reputational damage, and the loss of correspondent banking relationships if they fail to implement effective TBML control frameworks (International Finance Corporation, 2024). From 2019 to 2020, the number and dollar value of AML and know-your-customer (KYC) fines nearly doubled, from $5.7 billion to $10.4 billion (Alessa, 2021).

Challenges of TBML:

The report underscores that TBML poses complex and intimidating challenges for law enforcement and undermines global development. TBML disguises the proceeds of crime by moving value through legitimate trade transactions. The most common TBML methodologies include over- and under-invoicing of goods, misrepresentation of goods shipped, multiple invoicing of goods, over- and under-shipment, phantom shipments, black-market peso exchange, and informal value transfer systems. Misinvoicing was the most common method, accounting for 63% of cases. The report highlights challenges in identifying and preventing TBML, including a lack of transparency in global supply chains, limited law enforcement resources, and the complexity of trade transactions. The report suggests that cooperation among government agencies, financial institutions, and the private sector is crucial to combat TBML effectively.

Principal Findings and Impact on Global Trade:
Despite a comprehensive mapping of known TBML cases from 2011 to 2021 revealing only $60 billion laundered (Global Financial Integrity, 2023), estimates suggest the true scope of TBML activity is much larger, reaching hundreds of billions or even trillions of dollars annually (Global Financial Integrity, 2023; International Finance Corporation, 2024). This underscores a critical gap: unchecked TBML fuels criminal activities, corruption, and tax evasion, ultimately harming economies and societies (Global Financial Integrity, 2023).

The think tank Global Financial Integrity estimated the gap between export and import declarations of developing and advanced economies at $8.7 trillion for 2008–2017, indicating the approximate extent of TBML in the global economy (International Finance Corporation, 2024). Another study estimated the annual average scale of TBML from $1.4 trillion to $3.5 trillion, representing 10% to 30% of all illicit financial flows worldwide (Egmont Group, 2021; Financial Action Task Force, 2020).

The most affected nations by TBML were the United States, Mexico, Colombia, China, and Hong Kong. The report also found that almost any type of merchandise can be procured to launder illicit proceeds from TBML schemes, including cars/transport vehicles, metals and minerals, agricultural products, and textiles.

TBML undermines fair competition, distorts trade flows, and facilitates the financing of illicit activities, including terrorism, human trafficking, and drug smuggling. The report concludes that addressing TBML is critical to protecting the integrity of the global financial system and ensuring sustainable economic growth.

Purpose and Benefits of the Report:
The report aims to achieve several key objectives:

a Raising Awareness: It seeks to amplify awareness about TBML and its risk factors.
b Interagency Collaboration: It encourages collaboration among various agencies to combat TBML effectively.
c Beneficial Ownership Registries: Execution of national beneficial ownership registries is recommended.
d Technological Assessment: It utilizes new technologies to evaluate trade transaction pricing.
e Free Trade Zone Supervision: It fortifies supervision over free trade zones.
f Anti-Corruption Strategies: It ensures that national anti-corruption strategies cover international trade and ports.
g Resource Allocation: Offering customs agencies with adequate financial, human, and technological resources.
h Curbing Illicit Flows: By tackling TBML, the report aims to reduce illicit financial flows.
i Awareness Promotion: It also seeks to raise awareness about this issue.
j Expertise Promotion: Promoting expertise among civil society, governments, and international organizations.

Main Takeaways:
The report's main takeaways are that TBML poses intimidating challenges for law enforcement, financial intelligence units, and regulatory bodies; undermines global development; and affects economies and societies by perpetuating criminal activities, corruption, and tax evasion. Tackling TBML requires a multi-pronged approach:

i Raising awareness and educating stakeholders
ii Establishing interagency task forces for coordination
iii Implementing beneficial ownership registries
iv Ensuring real-time information exchange between countries
v Leveraging technology to appraise trade pricing
vi Reinforcing oversight of free trade zones
vii Offering customs agencies with adequate resources (FATF, 2020).

By taking these measures, nations can combat the pernicious effects of TBML, which include perpetuating criminal activities, corruption, and tax evasion. Ultimately, curbing TBML is crucial for promoting economic development, good governance, and the worldwide rule of law.

Case 0.1 Operation Darkness Falls: Dismantling a Major TBML Scheme

In August 2018, the U.S. Department of Justice (DOJ) announced the results of "Operation Darkness Falls," a major law enforcement operation targeting one of the world's most prolific darknet fentanyl vendors, Pharmville. This operation not only disrupted the illegal drug trade but also uncovered a sophisticated TBML scheme that had been siphoning millions of dollars from the U.S. economy. As part of this joint operation led by the Department of Homeland Security Investigations (HSI), Internal Revenue Service (IRS), United States Postal Inspection Service, and Federal Bureau of Investigation (FBI), a major TBML scheme was uncovered, resulting in the arrest of 11 individuals and the seizure of over $3.5 million in assets (U.S. Department of Justice, 2018).

Background

Criminal organizations use TBML to obscure the illicit origin of funds by integrating them into international trade transactions (Financial Action Task Force, 2006). This involves misrepresenting the price, quantity, or quality of goods traded, making illicit funds appear as legitimate business proceeds.

Key elements/points of the case:

i The TBML scheme involved utilizing Chinese goods, primarily clothing and textiles, that were shipped to the United States and sold through online marketplaces such as Amazon and eBay.
ii The individuals involved in the scheme created fraudulent invoices that overstated the value of the goods and applied fake identities to receive payments from U.S.-based companies.
iii The proceeds from the sale of the goods were then transferred to Chinese bank accounts, where they were converted to cryptocurrency and sent back to the United States to procure additional goods.
iv The individuals involved in the scheme utilized a network of shell companies and bank accounts to launder the money and avoid detection by law enforcement.
v The total value of the scheme was estimated to be around $700 million, making it one of the largest TBML schemes ever uncovered in the United States.

The importance of the case:
Operation Darkness Falls was a tremendous victory against drug trafficking and financial crimes (U.S. Department of Justice, 2018). It underlined the growing threat of darknet drug markets and the sophisticated techniques criminal organizations employ to launder their proceeds. Such schemes pose massive challenges for law enforcement due to their sophistication and ability to move large sums of money across borders undetected.

Parties involved:
The primary target was Pharmville, a darknet fentanyl vendor considered one of the most prolific globally (U.S. Department of Justice, 2018). The investigation also revealed the involvement of a Mexican national supplying precursor chemicals to the Cártel de Jalisco Nueva Generación (CJNG) for manufacturing controlled substances.

Agencies involved:
Operation Darkness Falls was a joint effort encompassing:

i U.S. Department of Justice (DOJ),
ii Drug Enforcement Administration (DEA), and
iii Internal Revenue Service (IRS).

These agencies collaborated with information to gather intelligence, conduct surveillance, and ultimately disrupt Pharmville's operations and its network associates (U.S. Department of Justice, 2018).

How the Scam Was Busted

While detailed methods of uncovering and dismantling the TBML scheme are not fully disclosed, it likely involved a combination of financial intelligence, undercover operations, and international cooperation (Financial Action Task Force, 2006). Suspicious transaction reports and bank records often disclose crucial clues, while undercover agents infiltrate criminal organizations to gather corroborative evidence. International cooperation is essential because illicit funds and goods often cross borders.

Impact of Loss on the Industry and Economy

The TBML scheme uncovered in Operation Darkness Falls siphoned millions of dollars from the U.S. economy through the over-invoicing of imported goods (U.S. Department of Justice, 2018). Such schemes distort markets, undercut prices, and create an uneven playing field for legitimate businesses. This results in lost revenue, reduced investment, and job losses across affected industries. In addition, the proceeds from drug trafficking laundered through TBML schemes can fund further criminal enterprises, perpetuating a cycle of detriment to society.

The Role of the Courts

The courts played a pivotal role in Operation Darkness Falls by ensuring that justice was served to those involved in the darknet fentanyl trafficking and the TBML scheme. Legal proceedings were initiated against Pharmville's operators, leading to multiple indictments and arrests. The courts examined extensive evidence collected during the investigation, including financial records, undercover operations, and intelligence reports. These proceedings resulted in significant penalties and sentences for the perpetrators, which served as a deterrent to other potential offenders.

For instance, individuals found guilty of participating in the TBML scheme encountered substantial fines and lengthy prison sentences. These sentences not only punished the criminals but also sent a clear, forceful message about the consequences of participating in such illegal activities. The judicial system's involvement was crucial to dismantling the criminal network and averting similar crimes in the future (U.S. Department of Justice, 2018).

Lessons Learned from the Case

Operation Darkness Falls afforded various important lessons for law enforcement, regulatory agencies, and the public:

a Collaboration Is Key: The operation's success was mainly due to the collaboration between multiple agencies, encompassing the DOJ, DEA, and IRS. This joint endeavor demonstrated the effectiveness of sharing intelligence, resources, and expertise in countering intricate criminal operations.

b Financial Intelligence Is Crucial: Using financial intelligence, such as suspicious transaction reports and detailed financial records, was instrumental in uncovering the TBML scheme. This case underscored the value of monitoring financial operations and using data analytics to spot potential money laundering activities.

c Need for International Cooperation: Given the global nature of TBML, international cooperation was essential in tracing and spotting the movement of illicit funds and goods. The case underscored the necessity for cross-border collaboration and information sharing to tackle transnational crimes effectively.

d Regulatory Oversight: Strengthening regulatory oversight in international trade and financial systems is essential to thwart TBML activities. Enhanced scrutiny and stricter enforcement of trade regulations can minimize the opportunities for criminals to exploit these systems.

Major Takeaways from the Case

i Disruption of Criminal Networks: Operation Darkness Falls successfully disrupted a major darknet fentanyl vendor and its associated TBML scheme, demonstrating that targeting the financial infrastructure of criminal organizations can effectively weaken their operations.

ii Economic Impact: The TBML scheme had a colossal economic impact, siphoning millions of dollars from the U.S. economy. Such schemes distort markets, create unfair competition, and undermine legitimate businesses. Tackling TBML is crucial for maintaining the integrity of the financial system and ensuring a level playing field for all businesses.

iii Role of Technology: Using technology in both facilitating and combating TBML was quite evident. Darknet marketplaces and encrypted communications were tools utilized by criminals, while advanced financial analytics and digital surveillance were employed by law enforcement to track and dismantle illegal operations.

iv Legal Precedents: The legal actions taken against Pharmville and its associates set vital precedents for future cases. The successful prosecution of these individuals underscored the effectiveness of existing legal frameworks in addressing complex financial crimes and provided a roadmap for handling similar cases in the future.

v Public Awareness: The case brought attention to the sophisticated methods and techniques criminals employ to launder money through international trade. Raising public awareness about TBML can help recognize and report suspicious activities, thereby supporting law enforcement efforts.

To Sum Up the Case

Operation Darkness Falls was a landmark operation that not only disrupted a major darknet fentanyl vendor but also uncovered a sophisticated TBML scheme. The coordinated efforts of various U.S. government agencies, including the DOJ, DEA, and IRS, were instrumental in dismantling the criminal network. The operation showcased the critical role of financial intelligence, international cooperation, and robust regulatory oversight in combating complex financial crimes.

The lessons learned from Operation Darkness Falls underscore the need for collaboration, advanced technology, and public awareness to combat TBML and other financial crimes. Strengthening regulatory frameworks and enhancing scrutiny of international trade and financial transactions are essential steps in evading similar schemes.

Operation Darkness Falls successfully showcased the value of tightly coordinated, multi-agency action in disrupting sophisticated criminal operations and protecting the global financial system.

An Insight: Analyzing the Scope and Characteristics of Global TBML and Its Implications for Development

Understanding TBML: Definition and Overview

TBML is the process of disguising the origins of illicit funds by moving them through trade transactions. This involves techniques such as over- or under-invoicing, false or misdescribed goods or services, and manipulation of customs declarations. Criminals employ TBML to transfer large amounts of money across borders undetected (Global Financial Integrity, 2023).

The Scale of TBML: How Big Is the Problem?

The magnitude of TBML is enormous and growing. Estimates suggest it ranges from $1.4 trillion to $3.5 trillion annually, representing 10% to 30% of all illicit financial flows worldwide (Egmont Group, 2021; FATF, 2020). The FATF highlights that common TBML methods comprise over- or under-invoicing, misrepresenting shipped items, and using informal value transfer systems (FATF, 2020).

Leading Reports on TBML

Several key reports have documented the extent and impact of TBML over the years:

1. FATF's 2006 Report on TBML: This report furnished one of the first comprehensive analyses of TBML, identifying techniques such as multiple invoicing of goods and services, and emphasizing the need for increased regulatory oversight (FATF, 2006).
2. UNODC's 2011 Report: The United Nations Office on Drugs and Crime (UNODC) highlighted the link between TBML and transnational organized crime, noting that TBML supports activities like drug trafficking and human trafficking (UNODC, 2011).
3. Global Financial Integrity Reports: GFI has consistently highlighted the economic impact of TBML. Their 2014 report estimated that developing countries lost $1 trillion annually to illicit financial flows, with TBML being a major contributor (GFI, 2014).
4. OECD's 2018 Report: The Organisation for Economic Co-operation and Development (OECD) focused on the vulnerabilities of the trade finance sector to TBML, calling for improved risk assessment and compliance measures (OECD, 2018).
5. GFI's 2023 Report: This report, "Trade-Based Money Laundering: A Global Challenge," underscores the methods and impacts of TBML on development, security, and innovation, and offers updated figures and case studies (GFI, 2023).

Scope of TBML: Industries and Countries Most Affected

Industries predominantly vulnerable to TBML include textiles, electronics, pharmaceuticals, precious metals and stones, and second-hand goods. These sectors are targeted due to their wide pricing margins and complex supply chains, which provide ample opportunities for manipulation (FATF, 2020). High-risk regions include Asia, Africa, and Latin America. Countries most affected by TBML include the United States, Mexico, Colombia, China, and Hong Kong, which have experienced significant losses in tax and customs revenues (Egmont Group, 2021).

Financial Impact and Challenges

The financial impact of TBML is profound. The global value gap due to TBML was estimated at $8.7 trillion between developing and advanced economies' export and import declarations from 2008 to 2017 (Kellermann, 2021). Financial institutions engaged in trade finance face risks of facilitating money laundering, incurring regulatory penalties, incurring reputational damage, and losing correspondent banking relationships if they fail to implement adequate TBML controls (International Finance Corporation, 2024).

Principal Findings and Impact on Global Trade

Despite comprehensive mapping of TBML cases from 2011 to 2021 revealing only $60 billion in laundered funds, the true scope is likely much larger, reaching hundreds of billions or even trillions annually (Global Financial Integrity, 2023). TBML distorts trade flows, undermines fair competition, and facilitates the financing of illicit activities such as terrorism and drug smuggling. Addressing TBML is crucial for protecting the integrity of the global financial system and ensuring sustainable economic growth (Global Financial Integrity, 2023).

Recommendations for Combating TBML

To effectively combat TBML, the following recommendations are made:

i Raising Awareness: Increasing awareness about TBML and its risk factors.
ii Interagency Collaboration: Encouraging collaboration among various agencies to combat TBML effectively.
iii Beneficial Ownership Registries: Implementing national beneficial ownership registries.
iv Technological Assessment: Utilizing new technologies to evaluate trade transaction pricing.
v Free Trade Zone Supervision: Strengthening supervision over free trade zones.
vi Anti-corruption Strategies: Ensuring national anti-corruption strategies cover international trade and ports.
vii Resource Allocation: Providing customs agencies with adequate financial, human, and technological resources.
viii Curbing Illicit Flows: Reducing illicit financial flows by tackling TBML (FATF, 2020).

TBML poses tremendous challenges for law enforcement, financial intelligence units, and regulatory bodies, undermining global development. A multi-pronged approach is essential to combat the pernicious effects of TBML, which include perpetuating criminal activities, corruption, and tax evasion. Tackling TBML is critical for promoting economic development, good governance, and the rule of law worldwide.

References

Alessa. (2021, April 21). Identifying TBML: 8 trade-based money laundering red flags. https://alessa.com/blog/trade-based-money-laundering-red-flags/

Bussoletti, F. (2018, August 27). Huge US federal joint operation against the drug sellers over the Dark Web. *Difesa e Sicurezza*. Retrieved from https://www.justice.gov/archives/opa/pr/international-law-enforcement-operation-targeting-opioid-traffickers-darknet-results-over-170

Cohen, D. S. (2013). Testimony of David S. Cohen, Under Secretary for Terrorism and Financial Intelligence, United States Department of the Treasury, Before the House Financial Services Committee Subcommittee on Oversight and Investigations.

FATF-Egmont Group. (2020). Trade-based money laundering: Trends and developments. https://www.fatf-gafi.org/content/dam/fatf-gafi/reports/Trade-Based-Money-Laundering-Trends-and-Developments.pdf

Financial Action Task Force. (2006). Trade-based money laundering. Retrieved from https://www.fatf-gafi.org/media/fatf/documents/reports/Trade%20Based%20Money%20Laundering.pdf

Financial Action Task Force. (2020). Trade-based money laundering: Trends and developments. https://www.fatf-gafi.org/media/fatf/documents/reports/Trade-Based-Money-Laundering-Trends-and-Developments.pdf

Global Financial Integrity, Fedesarrollo, Transparency International Kenya, & Advocates Coalition for Development and Environment (2023). Trade-based money laundering: A global challenge. Retrieved from https://gfintegrity.org/report/trade-based-money-laundering-a-global-challenge/

Global Financial Integrity. (2014). Illicit financial flows from developing countries: 2003–2012. https://gfintegrity.org/wp-content/uploads/2014/12/Illicit-Financial-Flows-from-Developing-Countries-2003-2012.pdf

Global Financial Integrity. (2023). Trade-based money laundering: A global challenge. https://gfintegrity.org/report/trade-based-money-laundering-a-global-challenge/

International Finance Corporation. (2024). IFC's initiatives to counter trade-based money laundering. Retrieved from https://www.ifc.org/en/what-we-do/sector-expertise/financial-institutions/global-trade/countering-trade-based-money-laundering

International Finance Corporation. (2024). Countering trade-based money laundering (TBML). https://www.ifc.org/en/what-we-do/sector-expertise/financial-institutions/global-trade/countering-trade-based-money-laundering

Kellermann, M. (2021). Trade-based money laundering: The next frontier in international money laundering enforcement. *Fordham Law Review*, 89(4), 1565–1602. https://ir.lawnet.fordham.edu/flr/vol89/iss4/11

OECD. (2018). Enhancing the role of trade finance in inclusive development. https://www.oecd.org/trade/trade-finance-enhancing-role-inclusive-development.htm

U.S. Attorney's Office, Northern District of Ohio. (2019, February 7). Texas couple sentenced to prison; they were the most prolific dark net fentanyl vendor in the world at the time of their arrest last year. Justice.gov. https://www.justice.gov/usao-ndoh/pr/texas-couple-sentenced-prison-they-were-most-prolific-dark-net-fentanyl-vendor-world

U.S. Department of Justice. (2018). Operation Darkness Falls results in arrest of one of the most prolific dark net fentanyl Vendors in the World. Retrieved from https://www.justice.gov/opa/pr/operation-darkness-falls-results-arrest-one-most-prolific-dark-net-fentanyl-vendors-world

U.S. Department of Justice. (2018). Darknet fentanyl vendor pleads guilty to distributing fentanyl that caused a fatal overdose. Retrieved from https://www.justice.gov/usao-ndca/pr/darknet-fentanyl-vendor-pleads-guilty-distributing-fentanyl-caused-fatal-overdose

United Nations Office on Drugs and Crime. (2011). Estimating illicit financial flows resulting from drug trafficking and other transnational organized crimes. https://www.unodc.org/unodc/en/frontpage/2011/October/illicit-money_-how-much-is-out-there.html

1 Trade-Based Money Laundering

An Overview

Trade-based money laundering (TBML) refers to the method by which dirty money sourced from criminal activities is disguised through the shell of international trade. Dennis Lormel, the former head of the FBI's terrorist financing section, explains that the essence of trade-based money laundering is as old as international commerce itself. However, it has become a persistent regulatory challenge, exacerbated by increased global trade volumes and the facilitation of trade processes, while concurrently posing the challenge of identifying illicit transactions disguised as legitimate ones (FATF, 2019; Lormel, 2025). It is a sophisticated form of money laundering that requires a coordinated and effective response from the global community. Core techniques encompass over- and under-invoicing, misrepresenting goods, and using shell companies to create a legitimate appearance for criminal proceeds (FATF, 2020). This illicit financial activity undermines the integrity of global commerce, facilitates transnational crime and terrorism, and presents a significant detection challenge due to the sheer volume of legitimate trade. (FATF, 2020; Tiwari, Ferrill, & Allan, 2025). These practices facilitate the legitimate movement of funds while disguising the alleged origins of criminal activity and providing comfort and methods for tax evasion. It gives the impression that transnational crime is being financed through legitimate means, disguised as routine commerce.

TBML has a poor global reputation and is widely regarded as unethical. It is not limited to any specific region, location, or country. Its global presence and reach are evident. TBML underscores the necessity for global collaboration to address the significant challenges it poses.

The Scale of the Challenge

TBML is an severe, globally recognized threat. The rising menace has captured the attention of law enforcement authorities, regulators, and banking institutions worldwide. Determined efforts can potentially reduce the proceeds of criminal activities, which are predominantly generated through trade transactions and the facilitation of cross-border illicit financial flows. The global scale of TBML made it a compelling issue. This urgent issue cannot be easily resolved, as it is arduous to detect and prosecute due to the complexity of international trade and the involvement of numerous parties in economic transactions. This complexity necessitates continuous innovation and improvement in our detection methods. We must continually refine our strategies to stay ahead of criminals, emphasizing the importance of remaining proactive and innovative in combating TBML.

Estimating the magnitude of TBML is quite challenging and profound. Due to its covert nature, more data on illegal trade transactions is necessary. However, TBML is irrefutably a significant issue. Estimates suggest that it accounts for a significant portion of global money laundering activity. One study estimated that TBML could account for up to 70% of international

DOI: 10.4324/9781003477631-2

money laundering (FATF, 2015). Another study reports that TBML accounted for 15–20% of global money laundering (Basel Institute on Governance, 2016).

TBML can be perpetrated through various methods, including misinvoicing and false labeling. For instance, misinvoicing could involve intentionally inflating the price of goods on an invoice to facilitate the movement of funds across borders. False labeling could mean misrepresenting the country of origin of goods being traded. Various techniques are employed to camouflage the movement of illegitimate funds.

One way to measure the magnitude of TBML is to use typologies, or patterns and methods commonly employed in its facilitation. The global supervisory body, the Financial Action Task Force (FATF), has identified several typologies widely used in TBML, including false invoicing, under-invoicing, and over-invoicing (FATF, 2015).

False invoicing involves intentionally misstating the value, quantity, or quality of goods or services on invoices to facilitate the movement of illicit funds across borders. Under-invoicing involves deliberately understating the value of goods or services on invoices to evade looming taxes or customs duties. In contrast, over-invoicing involves artificially inflating the value of goods or services on invoices to facilitate the movement of illicit funds through trade transactions.

One practical approach to gauging the extent of TBML is to use trade-based indicators. These indicators, such as disparities in export-import values, abnormal price fluctuations, and discrepancies in the reported and actual use of goods or services, can provide valuable insights into potential TBML activities (Basel Institute on Governance, 2016). By analyzing trade data and identifying these indicators, authorities can pinpoint potential TBML activity and conduct further investigations (Directorate of Revenue Intelligence, 2020).

Although it is tough to determine the exact scope of TBML, the problem's complexity is evident. Assessments place the annual cost in the hundreds of billions of dollars, a figure described as 'staggering' in recent times. This issue is estimated to contribute considerably to the \$2–5% of global GDP laundered annually, or roughly \$3–5 trillion, underscoring the need for comprehensive solutions. This emphasis on the need for comprehensive solutions should convey the seriousness of the issue and instill a sense of urgency for immediate action.

As the United Nations' principal office, the United Nations Office on Drugs and Crime (UNODC) is unwavering in its commitment to combating global challenges affecting drugs, corruption, crime, and terrorism. In its 2020 report on laundering funds and terrorist financing, it characterized TBML as a major global issue. The report spotlights TBML's potential to involve 'substantial sums of money,' with estimates suggesting hundreds of billions of dollars annually. It also underscores that TBML "poses a serious threat to the integrity of the international trade system, as it can facilitate the funding of illicit activities" (UNODC, 2020). The UNODC plays a crucial role in coordinating international efforts to combat TBML, providing guidance, and facilitating cooperation among member states. UNODC's pivotal role in tackling TBML should inspire confidence in its expertise and the significance of its findings.

Common Methods and Illustrative Examples

The primary and most prevalent methods of TBML involve the manipulation of trade documents and values. Table 2.1 summarizes several high-profile cases.

The outcomes of TBML are crucial and have enduring implications. TBML can be employed to fund organized crime, comprising terrorism and the trafficking of weapons. It can also be used to evade taxes and customs duties, resulting in lost government revenue and an unfair advantage

Table 1.1 Illustrative TBML Schemes

Year	*Case*	*Core Method*	*Key Lesson*	*Source*
2017	Odebrecht (Brazil)	Use of false invoices and shell companies within a vast bribery network.	Demonstrates integration of TBML into large-scale corporate corruption.	BBC, 2017
2018	Liu Han (USA/ China)	Misinvoicing through mining/transport companies to launder funds for organized crime.	Highlights the use of legitimate business fronts for cross-border laundering.	U.S. DOJ, 2018
2019	Multinational Tobacco Conglomerate (Africa)	Fictitious invoicing to evade taxes and duties on cigarette imports across multiple countries.	Shows sector-specific vulnerabilities and a severe impact on national revenues.	OCCRP, 2019

for those who engage in TBML. By stifling competition, TBML can also impair legitimate businesses and compromise the integrity of the global trading system.

The FATF is a nongovernmental organization that establishes international guidelines for countering terrorist financing and money laundering. The global body has designated TBML as a top priority and regularly publishes guidance on its detection and prevention. The FATF's role in establishing these standards and providing guidance is crucial to the global fight against TBML. The FATF's recommendations establish the international standards for combating TBML (Government Accountability Office, 2020).

To provide a brief overview, TBML presents a substantial challenge that requires consistent attention and action. Its clandestine nature impedes accurate evaluation of its scale and impact. However, it remains evident that TBML is crucial in facilitating money laundering worldwide and poses grave implications for the global economy and cross-border commerce. Your role in understanding and combating TBML is both significant and crucial. You are not just an observer, but a key player in the fight against TBML. Your contribution can have a significant impact on efforts to combat this illicit activity. Collaborative efforts are essential in this battle, and your contribution is vital. Your actions can have a profound impact.

Trade-Based Money Laundering: Emerging Concerns and Implications

Trade-based money Laundering is not merely a sophisticated and intricate method for obscuring the proceeds of illegal activity through trade transactions. It is a significant and urgent threat that demands our immediate attention. "TBML involves manipulating the value, quantity, or quality of goods or services to conceal the true nature of the funds and make them appear legitimate" (FATF, 2018, p. 6). This insidious practice undermines the integrity of the global trade system and poses a substantial threat to the economy and financial system.

Given TBML's global concern, it is crucial to remain vigilant and adopt a multifaceted approach to combat this illicit activity. Together, we must take this latent risk seriously and protect the credibility and sustainability of the world's financial system. The multifaceted approach is necessary to combat TBML effectively. International collaboration is critical in this battle, and your role is vital. You are not just a bystander but an integral part of the solution. Your actions can have a profound impact.

Economic Concerns of TBML

Regarding economic concerns, TBML results in substantial losses of tax revenue and places legitimate businesses at a competitive disadvantage. It may also cause capital flight, the transfer of wealth offshore in the guise of trade. For instance, in 2010, the United States Department of Justice prosecuted several people arrested in the Venezuelan TBML scheme for exporting goods at excessively overvalued prices to Venezuela and other countries in Latin America. (US DOJ, 2010). The scheme resulted in the loss of millions of dollars in tax revenue for the affected countries.

Social Concerns of TBML

With respect to social concerns, TBML can distort income distribution and pose challenges for financial institutions. For example, a case study by the Basel Institute on Governance found that TBML was used to funnel illicit proceeds from corruption and embezzlement in Angola, enriching a small group of individuals and contributing to income inequality in the country (Basel Institute, 2016; Civil Society Legislative Advocacy Center and Tax Justice Network Africa, 2022).

Security Concerns of TBML

Security concerns related to TBML include the financing of terrorist operations using trade transactions and the blurred lines between criminal and terrorist networks. TBML can also facilitate other illicit activities such as commercial fraud, intellectual property rights infringement, narcotics trafficking, human trafficking, and organized crime. For instance, in 2018, the Australian Federal Police and the Australian Border Force disrupted a TBML scheme involving the export of overpriced goods to the Middle East, with the proceeds used to fund the Islamic State group (Australian Federal Police, 2018).

Case Snapshot:
Primark Supply Chain (BBC, 2019). Primark's supply chain was exploited by third parties who over-invoiced clothing exports to India. While the company was not directly implicated, the case highlighted critical TBML risks within complex global retail supply chains and underscored the necessity of robust third-party due diligence.

Case Snapshot:
China National Tobacco Corporation (2013–2019). An investigation revealed that the state-owned CNTC illegally exported hundreds of millions of cigarettes to Ukraine, thus evading taxes and fueling contraband networks. This case exposed systemic vulnerabilities in the governance of high-value goods and demonstrated how trade systems can launder revenue from illicit products.

A Comprehensive Framework for Combating TBML: Key Elements and Considerations

Emphasizing the significance of a comprehensive framework, it serves as a clear roadmap for preventing and combating TBML. This adaptable, flexible framework must account for various aspects of TBML and provide multiple tools and measures. It acknowledges the dynamic nature of TBML and demands sustained efforts to keep pace with the evolving landscape. This persistence is a critical element in combating TBML, a complex and ever-changing issue that requires continuous attention and adaptation (Table 1.2).

TBML is authoritatively defined as the process of disguising the proceeds of crime by manipulating the value, volume, or type of goods in international trade transactions (FATF, 2020;

Table 1.2 Core Elements of a TBML Compliance Framework

Element	*Description*
1. Clear definitions	Establishing legal definitions of TBML and its standard techniques (e.g., misinvoicing).
2. Legal framework	Implementing and enforcing laws criminalizing TBML, aligned with FATF standards.
3. Risk-based due diligence	Mandating enhanced scrutiny on high-risk customers, jurisdictions, and commodities.
4. Information sharing	Fostering cooperation between domestic agencies (customs, FIUs) and across borders.
5. Training & awareness	Building expertise within banks, customs, and the private sector to recognize red flags.
6. Technology	Utilizing data analytics and AI to monitor trade transactions and identify anomalies.

UNODC, 2018). Its complexity and capacity to move large sums across borders make it a priority for national policymakers, given its implications for revenue and security, as well as for international bodies tasked with coordinating the global regulatory response.

There has been a notable shift in TBML in recent years, with most illicit money transfers now facilitated by e-commerce platforms. These platforms, with their convenience and accessibility, have become a preferred choice for criminal organizations to move goods and services, offering a high level of anonymity. The increasing use of virtual currencies, such as Bitcoin, further complicates the issue, making it more challenging to trace illicit funds.

Other trends observed in TBML include the increasing use of small- and medium-sized enterprises (SMEs) to facilitate and expedite criminal trade activities. Criminal organizations often target SMEs because of their weaker compliance controls and limited resources to properly scrutinize suspicious activity. This may be advantageous for criminal organizations to exploit SMEs as conduits for TBML.

To conclude, TBML is a pressing issue that poses a dual risk profile to the world economy, calling for a coordinated response from governments and other stakeholders to be mobilized, especially financial institutions. These institutions play a crucial role in preventing and detecting TBML, as they are often the first line of defense against money laundering. The potential impact of TBML on the global economy is significant, and it is crucial that we act swiftly. There are indeed mechanisms to regulate and enforce the necessary laws. However, TBML is still a demanding task owing to various international criminal organizations that launder dirty money. For that reason, some measures need to be put in place by the appropriate authorities of a given country, and these include regulatory measures concerning the laws on the adoption of anti-money laundering and counter-terrorism measures, and the use of the Stolen and Lost Travel Documents database to track the different kinds of transactions. Additionally, cooperation and information sharing among the relevant stakeholders will be crucial in combating TBML and other economic crimes.

Chapter Summary

This chapter explores the complex and pervasive TBML issue, emphasizing the crucial role of international cooperation. It begins by providing an overview of TBML and its impact on the global economy. The analysis underscores the various means TBML could employ to camouflage the proceeds of illegal practices or finance terrorism. It also emphasizes the local threats and challenges posed by TBML. The chapter then examines the economic, social, and security concerns associated with TBML and presents a comprehensive framework for addressing the threat. It outlines essential elements and considerations for policymakers and global organizations to address TBML, emphasizing the need for international cooperation.

This chapter offers a comprehensive understanding of the prevalence and implications of money laundering, emphasizing the importance of addressing the issue holistically. It emphasizes the importance of addressing this multifaceted issue and provides a more detailed explanation of its consequences. It underscores the need for a comprehensive framework to address the challenges posed by TBML more efficiently. The context of this chapter will be of great relevance to policy-makers, law enforcement, financial institutions, and scholars studying economic crimes in practice, as it offers the most comprehensive possible picture of TBML and its consequences.

End of Chapter: Discussion Questions

1. What methodologies are employed in gauging the level of trade-based money laundering?
2. What are the implications of TBML for the global economy and society?
3. What are the emerging concerns and implications of TBML?
4. How does TBML impact economic growth and development?
5. What are the social implications of TBML, and how does it affect communities?
6. How does TBML pose a security threat to nations and individuals?
7. What are the key elements and considerations for creating a comprehensive framework for combating TBML?
8. How does the definition of TBML differ from a policymaker's perspective versus a global organization?
9. How does international trade facilitate financial crime and TBML?
10. How can we effectively prevent and detect TBML in the international trade system?

Bibliography

Australian Federal Police. (2018). Counter-terrorism funding team disrupts an illicit trade-based money-laundering scheme. https://www.afp.gov.au/sites/default/files/PDF/annual-report-2017-2018.pdf

Basel Institute on Governance. (2016). Trade-based money laundering: The case of Angola. https://www.baselgovernance.org/trade-based-money-laundering-the-case-of-angola

BBC News. (2017, September 1). Odebrecht case: Politicians worldwide suspected in bribery scandal. https://www.bbc.com/news/world-latin-america-41109132

BBC. (2019, June 19). Primark profits hit by allegations of Indian money laundering. https://www.bbc.com/news/world-latin-america-41109132

Civil Society Legislative Advocacy Centre (CISLAC) & Tax Justice Network Africa (TJNA). (2022). Tobacco industry and illicit financial flows in Africa. https://atca-africa.org/report-exposes-how-multinational-tobacco-companies-aid-illicit-financial-flows-in-nigeria-others/

Directorate of Revenue Intelligence. (2020). Annual report 2019–2020. Government of India. https://dri.nic.in/writereaddata/annualreportebook/files/basic-html/page94.html

Financial Action Task Force. (2006). Trade-based money laundering. FATF/OECD. https://www.fatf-gafi.org/en/publications/Methodsandtrends/Trade-basedmoneylaundering.html

Financial Action Task Force. (2015). Trade-based money laundering. https://www.fatf-gafi.org/topics/trade-based-money-laundering/

Financial Action Task Force. (2018). Trade-based money laundering: Trends and developments. https://www.fatf-gafi.org/media/fatf/documents/reports/Trade-Based-Money-Laundering-Trends-and-Developments.pdf

Financial Action Task Force. (2019). Trade-based money laundering: A global threat. https://www.fatf-gafi.org/publications/fatfrecommendations/documents/trade-based-money-laundering.html

Financial Action Task Force. (2020). Trade-based money laundering: Trends and developments. FATF & Egmont Group. https://www.fatf-gafi.org/content/dam/fatf-gafi/reports/Trade-Based-Money-Laundering-Trends-and-Developments.pdf

Financial Action Task Force & Egmont Group. (2020). Trade-based money laundering: Trends and developments. https://www.fatf-gafi.org/content/dam/fatf-gafi/reports/Trade-Based-Money-Laundering-Trends-and-Developments.pdf

Government Accountability Office. (2020). Trade-based money laundering: The U.S. government has worked with partners to combat the threat, but could strengthen its efforts (Report No. GAO-20–333). https://www.gao.gov/assets/gao-20-333.pdf

Lewis, D. A., & Zdanowicz, J. (2010). Trade-based money laundering: A growing threat to the financial system. *The Journal of Financial Crime*, 17(2), 146–155.

Lormel, D. (2025, February 9). Trade-based money laundering: New impetus for an old threat. *Foreign Policy Association*. https://fpa.org/trade-based-money-laundering-new-impetus-for-an-old-threat

Organized Crime and Corruption Reporting Project. (2019). Vast quantities of Chinese cigarettes were smuggled into Ukraine.

Reuter, P., & Truman, E. M. (2004). *Chasing dirty money: The fight against money laundering*. Washington, DC: Institute for International Economics. Retrieved from https://www.piie.com/bookstore/chasing-dirty-money-fight-against-money-laundering

South China Morning Post. (2015, February 9). China executes mining tycoon Liu Han, who had links to ex-security tsar Zhou Yongkang. https://www.scmp.com/news/china/article/1708082/chinese-mining-tycoon-liu-han-linked-zhou-yongkang-executed

Tiwari, M., Ferrill, J., & Allan, D. M. C. (2025). Trade-based money laundering: A systematic literature review. *Journal of Accounting Literature*, 47(5), 1–26. https://www.emerald.com/jal/article/47/5/1/1267437/Trade-based-money-laundering-a-systematic

United Nations Office on Drugs and Crime. (2019). IND-TBML case study: Overvaluation and shell company networks. https://www.unodc.org/documents/southasia/Presentations/IND-TBML_Case_Study_-UNODC.pdf

United Nations Office on Drugs and Crime. (2020). Global Report on Trafficking in Persons 2020. https://www.unodc.org/documents/data-and-analysis/tip/2021/GLOTiP_2020_15jan_web.pdf

United Nations Office on Drugs and Crime (UNODC). (2020). Organized crime module 4 key issues: Money-laundering. Retrieved from https://www.unodc.org/e4j/en/organized-crime/module-4/key-issues/money-laundering.html

United States Department of Justice. (2010). Individuals are indicted for laundering money and smuggling schemes involving overvalued goods. *Press Release*. Retrieved from https://www.justice.gov/archives/opa/pr/individuals-indicted-participating-money-laundering-and-smuggling-scheme-involving-overvalued

United States Department of Justice. (2018). Press Release on Liu Han Conviction and Trade-Based Money Laundering Enforcement. https://www.justice.gov

World Trade Organization (WTO). (2020). WTO statistics database. Retrieved from https://timeseries.wto.org

Additional Learning Resources

Report

1 "Trade-Based Money Laundering: Overview and Policy Issues" by Rena S. Miller, Liana W. Rosen, and James K. Jackson. Congressional Research Service (2016).
This report provides an overview of TBML, its typologies, and policy issues.

2 "Trade-Based Money Laundering: Risks and Regulatory Responses" by the Australian Institute of Criminology (2012), authored by Clare Linda Sullivan and Evan Smith.
This report examines TBML and its risks, regulatory responses, and case studies.

3 "Trade-Based Money Laundering: Trends and Developments" by the Financial Action Task Force (FATF, 2015).
This report provides an overview of TBML, its typologies, and trends and developments.

4 "John A. Cassara Written Statement for the Hearing On 'Trading with the Enemy: Trade-Based Money Laundering is the Growth Industry'" by John A. Cassara (2016).
This written statement discusses TBML and value transfer, its typologies, and the challenges of detecting and preventing TBML.

Article

5 "Uncovering the Depths of Trade-Based Money Laundering: Evidence from a Seaport in Bangladesh" by Md. Tariq Hassan and Md. Mahfuzur Rahman (2023).
This article presents evidence of TBML in a seaport in Bangladesh and discusses the challenges of detecting and deterring TBML.

Film

6 "The Laundromat" (2019) was directed by Steven Soderbergh with a screenplay by Scott Z. Burns. It is based on the book *Secrecy World: The Panama Papers Scandal* by Jake Bernstein. This film is based on the true story of the Panama Papers scandal and explores the utilization of shell companies and TBML to launder money.

Documentary

8 "The Panama Papers" (2018) directed and written by Alex Winter.
This documentary film explores the Panama Papers scandal, which exposed the use of offshore accounts and shell companies to escape taxes and launder money.

Internet

9 "Trade-Based Money Laundering" by the FATF (2023). https://www.fatf-gafi.org/topics/typologies/Trade-based-money-laundering/
This webpage provides an overview of TBML, its typologies, and the FATF's work on TBML. It also includes resources, such as reports, case studies, and best practices, for detecting and preventing TBML.

2 Trade-Based Money Laundering

A Global Threat

Understanding the Risks and Implications of Trade-Based Money Laundering

Trade-based money laundering (TBML) is a sophisticated tactic used by criminal organizations to move funds and value through seemingly innocent trade transactions. As former Federal Reserve Chair Janet Yellen warned at the 2014 G20 Summit,

> Money laundering poses an international threat that disrupts the stability of the financial system and undermines the integrity of financial markets. The illegal activity enables criminal operations while obstructing law enforcement, with its activities remaining hidden for multiple years. Law enforcement agencies face major difficulties with money laundering operations, which require them to use advanced technology, cross-border cooperation, and to create continuous vigilance systems to identify, investigate, and dismantle such activities.

In simple terms, it involves using trade transactions to disguise the origins of illicit funds. This sophisticated method has become a significant concern for governments, financial institutions, and law enforcement agencies worldwide. This shadowy practice not only allows criminals to conceal the proceeds of their illicit activities but also provides a means to finance the heinous acts of terrorism. "It is a significant concern for governments, financial institutions, and law enforcement agencies around the world, as it can be used to conceal the proceeds of crime and facilitate the financing of terrorism" (Financial Action Task Force, 2019). "TBML is often difficult to detect and can involve multiple jurisdictions and a wide range of trade-related activities, making it a challenging issue to address" (United Nations Office on Drugs and Crime, 2018).

Various forms of TBML exist, each with unique characteristics and challenges. These include false invoicing, misinvoicing, and other trade-related frauds to mask the true nature and origin of funds (Financial Action Task Force, 2020). Understanding these forms is crucial for effective detection and prevention of TBML. TBML can also involve the abuse of free trade zones, customs regimes, and other trade facilitations to evade detection and control measures.

There is an ongoing debate and differing opinions on the most effective ways to combat TBML. Some argue that enhanced regulation and oversight of trade finance and cross-border transactions, as well as increased cooperation and information sharing among relevant authorities, are vital to combating TBML. Others advocate for a risk-based approach that focuses on identifying and addressing high-risk areas and activities rather than imposing blanket measures on the entire trade system.

DOI: 10.4324/9781003477631-3

TBML is a sophisticated method used by criminal organizations to obscure the origins of illicit funds through seemingly legitimate trade transactions. A significant global concern, TBML not only conceals the proceeds of crime but can also facilitate terrorist financing (FATF, 2019). Its methods—such as false invoicing and the abuse of free trade zones—are often difficult to detect, as they involve multiple jurisdictions and complex trade activities (UNODC, 2018). Combating TBML requires a collaborative, risk-based approach involving enhanced regulation, information sharing, and international cooperation.

Objectives of the Study

Active Learning Objectives

Upon completing this chapter, the learner will be able to:

1 Define TBML and identify its standard methods and red flags.
2 Explain the key risks, typologies, and regulatory frameworks associated with TBML.
3 Describe the role of banks and trade settlement processes in TBML detection and mitigation.
4 Articulate the role of international bodies such as the Financial Action Task Force (FATF) in shaping the global response to TBML.
5 Evaluate emerging technologies for TBML detection and prevention.

Relevance of the Problem

This chapter establishes a foundational understanding of TBML by examining:

Mechanics and Identification: The core mechanisms, common typologies, and key red flags of TBML.
Practical Insights: Real-world case examples and lessons from banking sector experience.
Regulatory Response: The roles and tools of key institutions such as the FATF, OFAC, EU, and UN in enforcing compliance and issuing sanctions.
Framework Evaluation: The effectiveness of current international measures in detecting, preventing, and disrupting these schemes.

Case 2.1 The Russian Laundromat (2014)

Core Mechanism: The "Russian Laundromat" was a large-scale money laundering scheme that operated between 2010 and 2014, funneling an estimated $20–70 billion out of Russia. The core method involved obtaining fraudulent Moldovan court rulings to legitimize fictitious debts owed by Russian entities. These court-sanctioned "debts" were then collected through a network of more than 500 shell companies, which moved illicit funds into the global financial system via correspondent accounts at reputable Western banks.

Key Players: The scheme relied on a network of shell companies registered in jurisdictions such as the UK, Cyprus, and New Zealand. It was facilitated by corrupt Moldovan political and judicial elites who authorized the fake rulings and by complicit banks in Moldova and Latvia that processed the transactions. The laundered funds originated from Russian criminals and corrupt officials, with the scheme allegedly orchestrated by Moldovan businessman Veaceslav Platon.

Why It Matters: Key Red Flags and Lessons: This case is a classic instance of systemic TBML vulnerabilities:

Abuse of Legal Systems: It illustrates how fraudulent legal judgments can be weaponized to create a veneer of legitimacy for illicit financial flows.

Shell Company Opacity: The extensive use of layered shell companies concealed beneficial ownership, allowing perpetrators to distance themselves from the crime.

Exploitation of Financial Channels: The scheme leveraged correspondent banking relationships and weak monitoring within certain financial institutions to integrate illicit funds into the mainstream economy.

The Laundromat underscores the critical importance of FATF Recommendation 24 on beneficial ownership transparency. If authorities had timely access to accurate data on who ultimately controlled the shell companies, this scheme could have been detected and disrupted much earlier (FATF, 2012/2023).

Outcome: The scheme was exposed in 2014 by the Organized Crime and Corruption Reporting Project (OCCRP, 2014). While international investigations led to some asset freezes (e.g., the UK's NCA froze £3.6 million) and prompted some regulatory reforms, successful prosecutions of the foremost perpetrators have been limited (NCA, 2019). This outcome starkly demonstrates the challenges of cross-border enforcement and the enduring need for robust international cooperation.

(A detailed flowchart and step-by-step explanation of the scheme are available from the book's product page as an online supplement.)

Organized Crime and Corruption Reporting Project (2014)

Lessons from the Russian Laundromat and the Role of Data Analytics in Combating Financial Crime:

The intricate case of the Russian Laundromat underscores the critical imperative to implement robust measures to identify, detect, and prevent such illicit financial activities. The urgency of international collaboration between authorities and banks is crucial and pressing. As demonstrated by the involvement of various financial institutions, front companies, and cross-border transactions, we all play a vital role in combating money laundering. This urgent need for collaboration underscores the importance of our role in combating financial crimes and the necessity of swift action. International collaboration strengthens detection and disruption of illicit financial networks.

In the fight against money laundering, leveraging cutting-edge technology and powerful insights from data analytics is paramount. The role of sophisticated technology and robust data analytics cannot be overstated. Advanced tools and algorithms enable financial institutions to effectively scrutinize large volumes of data, uncovering suspicious patterns and trends and exposing cases of TBML. The two have done substantial contribution in this regard. Both the EU and the UK recognize the interconnections among financial crime and have made significant strides in collaborating with other jurisdictions to combat it. It is widely believed that collaborating with like-minded partners is one of the most effective strategies to counter these cross-cutting threats. The power of technology should reassure us not only about the effectiveness of our tools in combating economic crimes but also instill confidence in our fight against financial crimes.

The convergence of governmental entities, including the formidable tax and customs authorities, and private enterprises is crucial for sharing critical intelligence and data. By working closely together, they can gain a deeper understanding of the intricate networks and tactics employed by money launderers. This mutually beneficial strategy may lead to more efficient risk assessments, targeted investigations, and the timely implementation of preventive measures.

Technology, a potent weapon in our battle against financial crimes, plays a crucial role in enhancing transaction monitoring and detecting anomalies that may indicate TBML activities. Financial institutions can identify irregular patterns and behaviors by leveraging advanced algorithms, computational power, and machine learning capabilities, thereby enhancing their ability to detect potential money laundering cases. In the digital age, where data privacy is paramount, responsible information exchange and dissemination between the public and private sectors are critical strategies for combating financial crimes. The power of technology should not just reassure us about the effectiveness of our tools in combating economic crimes but also instill confidence in our fight against financial crimes.

The Russian Laundromat is not just a case of financial improprieties but also a deeply rooted issue that extends beyond borders. The collusion between corrupt political and judicial actors and corrupt authorities, the exploitation of regulatory gaps, and the use of shell companies are all systemic vulnerabilities plaguing the global financial ecosystem. We need broader, coordinated efforts to combat these issues effectively across national boundaries. This underscores the urgent need for robust regulatory frameworks, stringent oversight, and, most importantly, international collaboration to dismantle the intricate networks that facilitate money laundering and illicit trade, ensuring the integrity, reliability, and stability of global financial systems. Your role in this international collaboration is significant. As government officials, banking-sector representatives, and regulatory organizations engaged in anti-money laundering efforts, your actions and decisions can significantly affect our collective efforts to combat economic crimes. The importance of your role in this global fight cannot be disregarded.

The Critical Role of Beneficial Ownership Transparency (FATF Recommendation 24):

The Russian Laundromat case exemplifies a fundamental vulnerability in the global financial system: the ability to hide the actual owners of companies and assets. This opacity is directly addressed by the international standard set out in FATF Recommendation 24, which requires transparency regarding the beneficial ownership of legal persons.

What Is Beneficial Ownership?

Beneficial ownership refers to the natural person(s) who ultimately own, control, or benefit from a company or asset, regardless of whose name is on the official documents. To illustrate, consider a lemonade stand run by a group of friends. While all contribute, if one friend, Sarah, provides the capital, makes all key decisions, and takes the profits, she is the beneficial owner. In the context of financial crime, criminals employ layers of shell companies to obscure beneficial ownership, shielding their identities and complicating investigations.

FATF Recommendation 24: The Global Standard

The FATF, the global money laundering and terrorist-financing watchdog, established Recommendation 24 to combat this vulnerability. Its key requirements oblige countries to:

1. Ensure that legal entities obtain and hold accurate, up-to-date beneficial ownership information.
2. Ensure this information is accessible promptly by competent authorities (e.g., financial intelligence units and law enforcement).
3. Implement measures to prevent the misuse of legal entities for illicit finance.

Application in Combating TBML

Beneficial ownership transparency is a pivotal tool against TBML. By piercing the corporate veil, authorities can effectively:

Identify Networks: Trace and track complex trade transactions back to the individuals who ultimately control the involved companies.
Evaluate Risk: Understand the genuine counterparties in a trade deal, moving beyond the shell company to evaluate potential criminal links.
Disrupt Schemes: Target enforcement actions against the beneficial owners who orchestrate laundering, rather than just the front companies they employ.

This principle is being embedded into national laws worldwide. For example, frameworks such as the U.S. Corporate Transparency Act and FinCEN's Beneficial Ownership Information Reporting Rule mandate the disclosure of individuals who hold 25% or more of the equity or exercise significant control, reflecting a global regulatory shift toward greater transparency.

A National Application: The Bangladesh Textile Industry

The significance of beneficial ownership disclosure is evident in its national implementation within high-risk sectors. For instance, Bangladesh has introduced regulations requiring the disclosure of beneficial ownership for companies in its crucial textile export industry. This aims to mitigate TBML risks, such as trade misinvoicing, by increasing transparency into who ultimately owns and controls exporting entities. The effort aligns with FATF standards and demonstrates how a major exporting nation is integrating this tool into its anti-money laundering framework to secure its trade ecosystem.

(Detailed analyses of specific national reports and the comprehensive Bangladesh case study are available in the online supplements.)

Concluding the ongoing discussion on a foremost topic, the introduction of beneficial ownership disclosure regulations in Bangladesh's textile industry demonstrates the country's commitment to combating TBML and enhancing transparency. By promoting adherence to global AML/CFT efforts, Bangladesh aims to enhance the integrity of its financial system. Despite industry challenges and criticism, the disclosure of beneficial ownership remains crucial for promoting accountability, ethical standards, and sustainable growth. Continued enforcement and collaboration among stakeholders will be essential in sustaining the advancements and overcoming current obstacles.

Chapter Summary

TBML is a diverse and constantly evolving method of illicitly transferring funds and value through seemingly legitimate trade transactions. This chapter explores the dark world of TBML. It exposes its blatant implications for the global economy and society, from concealing the proceeds of crime to facilitating the financing of terrorism. Its discussion elucidates how to tackle this threat to the global economy and the societal fabric.

End of Chapter: Discussion Questions

1 What is TBML, and why is it a concern for governments and financial institutions?
2 How does TBML differ from other forms of money laundering?
3 What strategies and technologies are being used to combat TBML?
4 How can cooperation and information sharing between relevant authorities effectively address TBML?

5 How can implementing enhanced regulation and oversight of trade finance and cross-border transactions help prevent TBML?

References

Financial Action Task Force (FATF). (2019). Trade-based money laundering. Retrieved from https://www.fatf-gafi.org/publications/fatfrecommendations/documents/trade-based-money-laundering.html

Financial Action Task Force. (2020). Trade-based money laundering. https://www.fatf-gafi.org/publications/methodsandtrends/documents/trade-based-money-laundering.html

Financial Action Task Force. (2012/2023). International standards on combating money laundering and the financing of terrorism & proliferation: The FATF recommendations. FATF/OECD. https://www.fatf-gafi.org/en/publications/Fatfrecommendations/Fatf-recommendations.html

Organized Crime and Corruption Reporting Project. (2014). The Russian Laundromat exposed. OCCRP. https://www.occrp.org/en/laundromat

National Crime Agency. (2023). Operation Destabilise: NCA disrupts multi-billion Russian money laundering networks. UK Government. Retrieved from https://www.nationalcrimeagency.gov.uk/news/operation-destabilise-nca-disrupts-multi-billion-russian-money-laundering-networks-with-links-to-drugs-ransomware-and-espionage-resulting-in-84-arrests?highlight=WyJ0cmFmZmlja2luZyIsInBvbGljZSJd

United Nations Office on Drugs and Crime (UNODC). (2018). Global Programme against Money Laundering, Proceeds of Crime and the Financing of Terrorism (GPML): Trade-based money laundering. Retrieved from https://www.unodc.org/unodc/en/money-laundering/global-programme-against-money-laundering.html

Additional Learning Resources

To gain a deeper understanding of TBML, the following additional learning resources are recommended:

Book

FV"Trade-Based Money Laundering: The Next Frontier in International Money Laundering Enforcement" by John A. Cassara (2015). This book offers comprehensive insights into TBML, its techniques, and the challenges authorities face in combating the problem.

Documentary

"The Panama Papers" (2018, directed by Alex Winter). This eye-opening documentary explores the global impact of financial crimes, including TBML, and sheds light on the interconnectedness of unlawful financial activities.

Article

"Trade-Based Money Laundering: The Dark Side of International Trade" by John Zdanowicz (2017). This article examines the various forms of TBML, such as false invoicing and misinvoicing, and highlights the need for enhanced regulatory measures to curb this illicit practice.

YouTube Video

"Trade-Based Money Laundering Explained" by The Center for Investigative Reporting (2019). This informative video provides a concise overview of TBML, its implications, and real-life examples, making it an excellent resource for visual learners.

3 Trade-Based Money Laundering

A Global Perspective

An Overview of Common Techniques and Trends in Illicit Trade Transactions

Trade-based money laundering (TBML) represents a complex and insidious form of financial crime that poses mounting threats and ongoing challenges for financial institutions and regulators globally. As Juan Zarate, former Deputy Assistant to the President and Deputy National Security Adviser for Combating Terrorism (2005–2009), notes in his 2013 book *Treasury's War: The Unleashing of a New Era of Financial Warfare*, combating TBML "requires a multidisciplinary approach that draws upon the expertise of those in law enforcement, finance, and trade to detect and disrupt the flow of illicit funds effectively." This chapter provides a global perspective on TBML, offering an overview of common techniques and trends in illicit trade transactions. This overview examines TBML's definitions, typologies, and global trends. Understanding common techniques—such as misinvoicing, the use of shell companies, and document manipulation—is essential. By examining regional TBML vulnerabilities, stakeholders can better contribute to detection and containment efforts.

The Financial Action Task Force (FATF) draws attention to TBML as a complex, sophisticated, and pernicious activity. This entails utilizing trade relations to 'clean up' money gained through illicit and criminal activities. "Trade-based money laundering is a method of disguising the proceeds of crime as legitimate trade transactions" (FATF, 2019). This is a more sophisticated attempt to disguise the illegal proceeds as legitimate business transactions. It poses a tremendous challenge and a profound possibility to improve our detection and prevention efforts. "TBML is the use of trade transactions – including the movement of goods, trade finance, and other trade-related instruments – to launder illicit proceeds" (WCO, 2018). The complexity and cunning nature of TBML make it a formidable challenge to uncover. "This method of disguising illicit funds as legitimate trade transactions is a tremendous danger to the stability of the global trade system" (FATF, 2019). Because the activities that constitute TBML are elaborate and sophisticated, their detection by relevant authorities is challenging, thereby threatening the international trading system. TBML can also be employed to fund other illegal activities, including terrorism, drug trafficking, and organized crime activities, such as arms smuggling or human trafficking.

Several basic techniques are ordinarily used in TBML schemes. These techniques involve manipulating the trade finance system to conceal the illicit origin of funds. They may involve misinvoicing imports and exports, using front businesses, or controlling other trade-related documents.

One common technique is the misinvoicing of imports and exports. This involves deliberately misrepresenting the value, quantity, or type of goods traded to illicitly move funds. For example, a company may under-invoice exports to remit funds abroad or over-invoice imports

DOI: 10.4324/9781003477631-4

to illicitly collect funds from abroad. This technique is difficult to detect because it relies heavily on the manipulation of legitimate trade documents, such as invoices, bills of lading, and customs declarations.

Another common technique is the utilization of shell companies. A shell company is 'an entity known only to exist on paper' and lacks any real commercial substance or activities. These companies facilitate TBML by supporting fake owners who engage in nonexistent business activities, thereby providing them with the resources they need. For example, a shell company can import goods at a low threshold, sell them, and use the proceeds to fund an illegal money-laundering operation. The financial implications of such businesses, coupled with their elusiveness and operations in jurisdictions with lenient or nonexistent disclosure laws, pose a significant challenge to uncovering them.

A third technique commonly used in TBML is the manipulation of trade-related documents. This may include fabricating legal and shipping documents, such as invoices, bills of lading, and insurance certificates, or modifying existing instruments and documents. Document manipulation can conceal the true nature of a trade transaction, making it appear legitimate.

> False shipping, also known as misdeclaration, is a scheming technique in trade-based money laundering, where fake shipping documents or false transport routes are applied to conceal the candid nature of the trade. This deceitful method can seriously threaten the international trade system and make it challenging for authorities to detect illicit activities.
>
> (FATF, 2019)

As the first line of defense against TBML, financial institutions play a crucial and valued role in detecting and averting this threat. Their exclusive role in monitoring and reporting suspicious transactions is integral to the global coordinated effort to combat TBML. By implementing robust anti-money laundering procedures and reporting unusual or suspicious activities, banking institutions make a significant contribution to this mission. In addition to these basic techniques, TBML schemes may involve multiple layers of transactions and the engagement of various parties to conceal the illicit origin of funds further. Such tactics include utilizing fictitious enterprises and moving funds through multiple international banking institutions. As a result, TBML poses a significant threat to the security and stability of both global commerce and the international banking system.

In closing, it is evident that the TBML combating effort requires a comprehensive, multifaceted, and collaborative approach. This approach encompasses enacting harsher and stricter laws, enhancing international cooperation and support, and promoting best practices and guidelines for detecting and stopping TBML. This may involve numerous governmental and nongovernmental actors, underscoring the global and multifaceted nature of this threat and the crucial role of international cooperation in addressing it. It is no exaggeration to say that international cooperation is the linchpin of our unified action against this global menace. The need for such cooperation is paramount to conveying to the audience the importance of their collaborative efforts in combating TBML.

An Insight: The Anti-Money Laundering Act of 2020: A Pivotal Legislation in the Battle against Money Laundering

Money laundering, an enduring global risk to the financial system, is threatened by numerous factors; however, contemporary society has introduced measures to counter these phenomena, such as the Anti-Money Laundering and Countering Financing of Terrorism Act 2020 (AMLA). This act, proposed by the U.S. Congress and plagued by numerous issues, offers some optimism in the struggle against illicit finance (AMLA, 2020). The AMLA is not merely a measure but a significant step toward a more optimistic future in combating money laundering. This comprehensive legislative measure, unlike any before, addresses the problem of illicit finance and will have an impact across the entire financial industry and beyond. Your role in this fight is crucial and empowering.

Key Provisions:
The AMLA incorporates, among other provisions, specific measures to reinforce the deterrent aspects of anti-money laundering statutes. Among other significant amendments, another key requirement is the introduction of new reporting obligations about ownership information. This relates to beneficial ownership. All business entities, such as limited liability companies, registered bodies, and other business organizations, shall comply with and report to the Financial Crimes Enforcement Network (FinCEN) within the U.S. Department of the Treasury. The relevant data would significantly assist law enforcement in enhancing their tracking and scrutiny of criminal activity linked to dirty money, a positive step toward a safer business environment.

AMLA further strengthens FinCEN's power by broadening its regulatory and supervisory reach over virtual currency transactions. The Act incorporates provisions mandating that all virtual currency businesses comply with the anti-money laundering regulations that apply to traditional financial institutions. Moreover, this is a significant measure to address the risks of money laundering and other illicit activities.

The main provisions of the AMLA include:
Beneficial Ownership Disclosure: The AMLA provisions are crucial in combating money laundering, requiring business entities to report their beneficial ownership status and file the forms with FinCEN. This underscores the significant role of FinCEN in combating those who use corporate structures for criminal activities, thereby enhancing the audience's confidence in the law's effectiveness.

Strengthening the AML and CFT Regime: The AMLA strengthened the Anti-Money Laundering (AML) and Countering the Financing of Terrorism (CFT) regime by expanding FinCEN's authority and increasing penalties for AML/CFT violations. The resources of enforcement agencies were increased, and the AMLA and CFT regimes were strengthened.

Virtual Currency: The AMLA's expansion of the definition of 'financial institution' to include entities participating in virtual currency transactions is a significant step in regulating this evolving sector. This provision aims to prevent the misuse of virtual currency in illegal activities, demonstrating the law's adaptability to technological advancements.

Impact and Significance of AMLA:
The AMLA, a substantial update to anti-money laundering regulations in the United States, has had a profound impact on the financial industry. Its comprehensive framework for addressing emerging technologies and evolving financial crime practices attests to its significance. The AMLA's requirement that institutions adopt a risk-based approach to compliance and implement new reporting requirements directly affects their operations, underscoring the requirement's profound impact on the financial industry.

This also has broader implications for other industries, including art dealers, real estate, and precious metals dealers. Under the legislation, businesses in these industries are required to have AML compliance programs. It is essential to report any suspicious activities to the relevant regulator and to maintain records of specific transactions. Your role in closing loopholes and averting illegal activities is crucial and empowering.

The AMLA's impact includes:
Enhanced Transparency: The AMLA's beneficial ownership disclosure provision significantly enhances transparency. This clause makes it more difficult for criminals to use anonymous shell companies to launder money. Thereby, instill confidence in the audience about the law's effectiveness in promoting transparency.

Enhanced Enforcement: With more resources for law enforcement agencies and stricter penalties for violations of AML and CFT. The approach can be more effective for enforcing the AML-CFT regime. We must act now to strengthen our enforcement efforts, sending a clear message to offenders that their illicit business activities will not be tolerated.

At the forefront of the battle against money laundering, the AMLA plays a crucial role in regulating and preventing the use of virtual currency in criminal conduct. This commitment to preventing criminal conduct further demonstrates its capability to bridge the technological gap, providing reassurance about its effectiveness.

Divergence from Previous Legislation:
The AMLA, a significant departure from prior anti-money laundering legislation, introduces key changes that professionals in the finance, law enforcement, and compliance sectors should be aware of. It extends the scope of reporting requirements to include information on the beneficial ownership of entities. The statute establishes a new public registry of these owners and facilitates checks by law enforcement and other domestic parties. However, one of the most significant changes is the application of AML regulations to virtual currency businesses. In the past, this sector has been subject to increasing scrutiny. This move underscores the evolving regulatory landscape. The law requires institutions to adopt risk-based compliance, focusing resources on higher-risk areas rather than adhering to a one-size-fits-all methodology.

Merits and Demerits:
Among the several benefits associated with AMLA is the consolidation of existing anti-money laundering regimes, including those related to virtual currencies, and the curtailment of misuse in the efficient management of the beneficial ownership registry. However, it also has its demerits. Some critics argue that the reporting requirements are overly burdensome and could increase compliance costs. Others contend that the AMLA needs to address issues such as the use of anonymous front enterprises for money laundering.

Some Examples:
The AMLA has made significant strides in the art world. In 2020, the United States introduced new rules requiring art dealers to submit records and documentation of potentially suspicious transactions and to report receiving art valued at more than $5,000. These measures were implemented to address concerns that the art world was becoming a haven for money laundering. The AMLA's impact on this sector, by bringing it under regulatory oversight, sets a precedent for other less-regulated industries. This demonstrates that the AMLA is not merely a financial oversight measure but an anti-money laundering law that covers all sectors, including the art sector, thereby effectively curbing illicit activities.

For instance, enforcement action was taken against the cryptocurrency exchange operator BitMEX. In 2020, the U.S. Department of Justice charged BitMEX with transferring funds in exchange for money laundering and prior breaches, despite minimal AML controls. The exchange was also accused of contravening the Bank Secrecy Act for failing to register as a money service business at FinCEN. Consequently, BitMEX agreed to pay a $100 million fine to settle the charge. This case provides a clear example of the real-life application of the AMLA in the cryptocurrency sector, instilling confidence in the potential for strict compliance with the law.

The 'U.S. District Court for the Southern District of New York,' as announced by the 'Commodity Futures Trading Commission,' issued 'consent orders' against three individuals of BitMEX, Arthur Hayes, Benjamin Delo, and Samuel Reed, who are the co-founders of the cryptocurrency derivative exchange (CFTC, 2022). This underscores the personal consequences of non-compliance with the AMLA, sending a clear message about the law's seriousness and the need for strict adherence.

These examples demonstrate the enhanced scrutiny of regulatory bodies over cryptocurrency exchanges and the need for more robust AML regulations in the digital asset space. Under the AMLA, cryptocurrency exchanges will be subject to the same regulations as traditional financial institutions. This signifies that we should have robust AML programs to conduct customer due diligence and report suspicious activities. However, this legislation is not just about regulation but about transparency. The AMLA essentially expands the definition of a 'financial institution' to include virtual currency businesses. It ensures that these businesses operate under the same regulations and standards as traditional financial institutions, thereby enhancing industry transparency.

There has been some criticism about the AMLA, but it has garnered support from some quarters. Small and medium-sized financial institutions criticize the law, stating that it burdens them and that they may disregard its stipulations. In addition, some were skeptical of the AMLA because it would not prevent excessive overregulation in the financial industry, which could stifle creativity. Common criticisms of such a focus on the AMLA should be considered alongside the regulatory balancing act, which raises concerns about overregulation. However, the industry has yet to reach its most complete stage of development.

However, specific criticisms of the AMLA overlook the broader context; the AMLA represents a significant breakthrough in addressing the scourge of money laundering and financing of terrorism. The law strengthens AML regulations. It increases visibility in the financial industry, making it a potent line of attack with the potential to play an optimistic role.

Case 3.1 Malta-Romania-Turkey Equipment Trade

Core Facts:

- A Maltese company, recently established by a management consultant with no relevant trade experience, purchased specialized construction equipment of worth €6 million from a German supplier on credit.
- The company had no employees, conducted no technical due diligence, and had limited correspondence with the supplier.
- It immediately resold the equipment to a Turkish customer for €6.1 million, also on credit.
- Payments were delayed, and arrangements were altered without justification. The German supplier and Turkish customer shared legal advisors and an address.
- The Maltese company's bank account was in Romania.

Discovery Method:
Uncovered through a combination of approaches such as regulatory oversight, financial intelligence, and Suspicious Transaction Reports filed by the company's bank.

TBML Analysis:

- This scheme exhibits classic TBML red flags: use of a newly formed shell company, lack of commercial logic/ due diligence, complex cross-border payment trails, and misinvoicing (the minimal €0.1 million profit margin on a rapid, high-value resale is a potential marker for value manipulation).
- The structure—a passive intermediary company inserting as a regular party and representing itself in a transaction between two connected parties—effectively laundered funds by disguising them as legitimate trade proceeds (Forvis Mazars, 2021).

Case 3.2 Company X and the $360 Million TBML Fraud, UAE

Core Facts:

- Dubai-based Company X, owned by Mr. Doe, orchestrated a large-scale TBML scheme involving fictitious shipping documents and a network of ghost corporations across multiple countries.
- The scheme utilized numerous bank accounts at 17 different banks to transfer funds, causing an estimated $360 million in losses to the financial system.
- The core activity involved importing high-end electronics using fake invoices and shipping documents, selling them, and repatriating proceeds to Dubai.

Discovery Method:

- Initiated by a bank tip regarding unusual transactional activity linked to Company X.
- A subsequent international investigation coordinated by Dubai Police, the FBI, and Interpol unraveled the network through financial forensics and intelligence sharing.

TBML Analysis:

- This case demonstrates the use of false shipping and document fraud—a primary TBML technique—to create a veneer of legitimate trade.
- The layering of transactions through multiple corporate entities and international banks is a hallmark of sophisticated TBML, designed to obscure the audit trail and the illicit origin of the funds (El Nakib, 2023).

Case 3.3 Australian High-End Electronics TBML Scheme (FATF – Egmont Group, 2020)

Core Facts:

- The Australian Border Force (ABF) investigated a scheme where proceeds from drug sales in North America were laundered through the trade of small, high-value electronics.
- Illicit funds were placed in Southeast Asian banks, then transferred to Australian financial institutions.
- An Organized Criminal Group (OCG) used trade misinvoicing (specifically under-valuation of exports) to inflate the value of funds artificially moved offshore and obscure their source.

Discovery Method:

- ABF employed trade data discrepancy analysis, comparing export declarations from one country with import declarations from another to identify pricing inconsistencies.
- A referral from an international partner agency triggered the investigation, which combined financial intelligence with cooperative work from foreign authorities to map the criminal network.

TBML Analysis:

- This case elucidates the dual exploitation of trade systems:

  1 for value transfer through misinvoicing, and
  2 for layering via multi-jurisdictional bank transfers and shell companies.

- It underscores how TBML directly harms the economy, causing an estimated AUD 500 million in losses through tax evasion and market distortion, while facilitating further criminal activity.

Chapter Summary

From a global perspective, TBML is arguably the most sophisticated and complicated of all the challenges that affect and distort the operations of economic systems. TBML conceals the actual ownership of funds through trade finance and trade more generally, thereby posing a significant financial threat that requires specialized knowledge and skills to counter.

To detect and frustrate TBML activities effectively, monitoring cross-border trade transactions and staying informed about the latest techniques and trends in this evolving threat is crucial. The use of misinvoicing, shell companies, false shipping, and a complex network of dealings and parties are just a few examples of the methods used in TBML schemes. Other tactics include over- and under-invoicing of goods, phantom shipments, and the use of multiple intermediaries to obscure the true origin and destination of the funds.

The challenge of TBML continues to evolve, and we all need to remain cautious and well-informed to protect the stability and security of the global financial system. Effective monitoring and international cooperation are crucial for detecting and preventing TBML activities, and sustained focus on this issue is essential to maintaining the integrity of the economic system. Staying informed about the latest techniques and trends in this evolving threat is crucial to our struggle against TBML. This emphasis on the evolving nature of TBML and the need for continuous vigilance will empower the audience and make them feel integral to the mission.

End of Chapter: Discussion Questions

1 How does TBML differ from traditional money laundering methods?
2 What standard techniques are used in TBML schemes, such as misinvoicing of imports and exports, using shell companies, and manipulating trade-related documents?
3 How does TBML exploit the trade finance system to conceal the illicit origin of funds?
4 What is false shipping, and how does it relate to TBML activities?
5 Why is the effective monitoring of cross-border trade transactions crucial in detecting and preventing TBML activities?

6 What role do multiple transactions and parties play in TBML schemes?
7 How does TBML threaten the stability and integrity of the global financial system?
8 What is the significance of international cooperation in the fight against TBML?
9 Why is it important to stay informed about the latest techniques and trends in TBML to ensure the stability and security of the global financial system?
10 What measures can be taken to mitigate the risk of TBML and improve the resilience of the global financial system? Measures such as strengthening due diligence procedures, implementing robust trade finance regulations, and promoting transparency in trade transactions can help mitigate TBML risk and enhance the resilience of the global financial system.

Bibliography

Commodity Futures Trading Commission. (2022, May 5). A federal court orders BitMEX's three co-founders to pay a total of $30 million for illegally operating a cryptocurrency derivatives trading platform and for anti-money laundering violations (Press Release No. 8522-22). https://www.cftc.gov/PressRoom/PressReleases/8522-22

El Nakib, B. (2023, June 29). Trade-based money laundering – Case Studies. *Compliance Alert*. BBC News. (2017, September 1). Odebrecht case: Politicians worldwide suspected in bribery scandal. https://www.bbc.com/news/world-latin-america-41109132

FATF – Egmont Group. (2020). Trade-based money laundering: Trends and developments. Paris: FATF. Retrieved from www.fatf-gafi.org/publications/methodandtrends/documents/trade-based-money-laundering-trends-anddevelopments.htm.

FATF. (2019). Trade-based money laundering: Trends and developments. Paris: FATF/OECD. Retrieved from https://www.fatf-gafi.org/en/publications/Methodsandtrends/TradeBasedMoneyLaundering.html

Forvis Mazars. (2021). A case study of trade-based money laundering. Retrieved from https://www.forvismazars.com/mt/en/insights/our-articles/an-overview-of-trade-based-money-laundering/a-case-study-of-trade-based-money-laundering

Global Financial Integrity. (2023). Trade-Based Money Laundering: A Global Challenge. https://gfintegrity.org/wp-content/uploads/2023/02/TBML-Policy-Brief-Final.pdf

U.S. Congress. (2021). Anti-money laundering Act of 2020, Division F of the William M. (Mac) Thornberry National Defense Authorization Act for Fiscal Year 2021, Pub. L. No. 116–283. https://www.congress.gov/crs-product/R47255

World Customs Organization (WCO). (2020). Customs Enforcement Guidelines on Countering Money Laundering and Terrorist Financing. Brussels: WCO. Retrieved from https://www.wcoomd.org/en/topics/enforcement-and-compliance/instruments-and-tools/guidelines/money-laundering-and-terrorist-financing

Zarate, J. (2013). *Treasury's war: The unleashing of a new era of financial warfare*. PublicAffairs.

Additional Learning Resources

Book

1 Trade-Based Money Laundering: The Next Frontier in International Money Laundering Enforcement. John A. Cassara. (2015). Wiley.
This book provides an authoritative examination of TBML, including its indicators and patterns, and how analytics can be used to identify it.
2 Money Laundering and Illicit Financial Flows: Following the Money and Value Trails. John A Cassara (2020).
This book explores the various methods used to launder money and move illicit financial flows, including TBML.

Report

3 Trade-based Money Laundering: Trends and Developments. Toronto: Egmont Group of Financial Intelligence Units, (2020).
This report aims to assist the public and private sectors in addressing the challenges of detecting TBML by drawing on numerous case studies.

House Hearing

4 Trade-Based Money Laundering Is the Growth Industry in Terror Finance—United States House of Representatives. (2016).
The Task Force conducted this hearing to investigate Terrorism Financing of the Committee on Financial Services, U.S. House of Representatives, on February 3, 2016. This hearing examines the scope and dimension of TBML and the threat it poses to security.

4 Overview of the Global Regulatory Framework for TBML

The regulatory framework for trade-based money laundering (TBML) is crucial in safeguarding the integrity of the global financial system and combating illicit financial activities. As Christine Lagarde, then managing director of the International Monetary Fund (IMF) from 2011 to 2019, emphasized,

> There is no doubt that money laundering and terrorist financing can threaten a country's economic stability, which is why the IMF has become increasingly active in supporting and promoting the AML/CFT efforts of our member countries, based on the FATF standard.
>
> (Lagarde, 2017)

TBML is a criminal activity that conceals and undermines the core of the economy. In simple terms, TBML refers to a set of highly complex, sophisticated trade transactions designed solely to obscure the identity and movement of dirty money across borders. The TBML international regulatory system is a vital tool that protects the global market from infiltration and misuse, while enabling fair economic activities. However, this is not just an issue of legal or normative provisions. The operational activity aims to contain the spread of TBML and requires all state and international actors to suppress TBML operations.

Functions of the Global Regulatory Framework for TBML

1. The global TBML regulatory regime's primary function is to curtail any trade activity used to launder money and finance organized crime or terrorist activities.
2. The framework's goal is not just a mere aspiration but a concrete commitment to ensure that no trade transactions are conducted in violation of national or international laws, providing a solid foundation for our economic security.
3. The institutional regulatory framework promotes TBML detection by providing financial institutions and other businesses involved in trade with guidelines on recognizing and reporting dubious activity. These entities are crucial in combating TBML, as they are often the first line of defense in identifying and reporting suspicious transactions.

Institutions Involved in the Global Regulatory Framework for TBML

1. The Financial Action Task Force (FATF) is the primary autonomous intergovernmental organization mandated by G7 nations. The organization is dedicated to its crucial role in resolving and allocating resources to the global issues of dirty money and terror financing.

DOI: 10.4324/9781003477631-5

FATF is the most important policymaking organ, holding a unique and influential special consultative status with the United Nations Economic and Social Council (ECOSOC).

2. The World Customs Organization (WCO) is a major player in the global regulatory framework for TBML. It guides the customs agency and serves as a proactive tool for detecting and deterring TBML. The WCO's efforts are a reassuring signal that TBML is not an insurmountable problem despite the challenges encountered in global cooperation and shared responsibility.
3. National governments are responsible for enforcing the global regulatory framework. They enact and enforce laws and regulations framed within their jurisdictions, underscoring the shared global endeavor to combat TBML.
4. Regulators like the Central Bank or financial intelligence units (FIUs) monitor and examine financial transactions. Reporting and alerting on suspicious activities in combating TBML are critical and mandatory.

Global Regulatory Framework: TBML Repercussions and Significance

- Being a regulatory requirement to comply with is not sufficient. It will fulfill the requirements of the global regulatory framework for TBML. However, it is a tangible necessity for financial institutions and other trade-related businesses. There is an obligation to ensure business continuity and stability by protecting against reputational, legal, and financial risks associated with TBML. These laws and regulations could significantly affect businesses and even incur substantial penalties if not complied with. This requires everyone to understand and comply with such restrictions.
- There are valid reasons to justify TBML, which can have adverse outcomes on the quality and equilibrium of the global financial network and tarnish the reputations of countries where it occurs.
- Implementing the framework can help foil criminal and terrorist organizations from using trade transactions to move and launder money, which can have a destabilizing impact on the global economy. This underscores the crucial role of international cooperation in combating TBML, making your collaborative efforts with other stakeholders even more profound and impactful.
- The universal TBML regulatory structure supports and streamlines the international trading system to maintain its security and integrity. On undertaking this step, more secure and transparent global trade environments would be created.

Regulatory Actions and Failures in TBML

The following cases elucidate the critical strengths and vulnerabilities of the global framework for combating TBML.

Chinese Conglomerate and North Korea Sanctions Evasion (2019)

Core Facts: Sanctions by the U.S. Treasury's Office of Foreign Assets Control (OFAC) were placed on a Chinese conglomerate. The specific entity was involved in the falsification of the value of goods in cross-border transactions with North Korea: that is, importing over-invoiced and exporting under-invoiced (U.S. Department of the Treasury, 2019). By following this TBML scheme, the company falsified the values of commodities to create illegal revenue and make it difficult to trace the financial flows that supported the North Korean regime. Hence, it blatantly violated the United Nations and U.S. sanctions.

Regulatory Lesson: This case illustrates the use of financial sanctions as a direct regulatory instrument to disrupt trade networks engaged in illicit activities. It explains how TBML methods are used as a 'weapon' to advance geopolitical objectives. Thus, it became an instrument for compromising the international security systems (Zarate, 2013). The enforcement action underscored the necessity of collaboration between various enforcement agencies in the trade and finance sectors to uncover cases where prices were deliberately manipulated.

Outcome: The organization was cut off from access to the U.S. financial system through targeted U.S. sanctions. For that reason, it served as a deterrent and clarified the integration of financial regulation and foreign policy within the national security framework (Figure 4.1).

Figure 4.1 Sanctions and Surveillance: Regulatory Response to TBML

Halkbank (Turkey) and Iran Sanctions Evasion (2019)

Core Facts: U.S. prosecutors have officially brought a formal indictment against Halkbank. This bank is reckoned as a central Turkish state-run bank. The bank was engineering one of the largest schemes, in the billions of dollars, to avoid Iran sanctions. The indictment alleges that the bank concealed the oil proceeds by misrepresenting them as gold and food, and that it used fraudulent documents and layered transactions through correspondent banks (U.S. Department of Justice, 2019).

Regulatory Failure/Mechanism: This case has been a significant test for the limits of sanctions enforcement against politically connected institutions. The bank was involved in the exploitation of trade finance and correspondent banking by a state-owned entity. It raised the issue that international correspondent banks that process transactions may not conduct sufficient due diligence.

Outcome: The case is of historical significance. It concluded with a $9 billion settlement. In addition, it provided a solid ground for a significant U.S. Supreme Court ruling (2023). The court decision conveyed that the bank could not be granted protection under the sovereign immunity principle set by the court. Thus, it created a vital legal precedent for the accountability of foreign state-owned commercial enterprises. The court decision conveyed that the bank could not be granted protection under the sovereign immunity principle set by the court. Thus, it created a vital legal precedent for the accountability of foreign state-owned commercial enterprises (Supreme Court of the United States, 2023).

HKMA Enforcement vs. Remittance Service (2020)

Core Facts: The Hong Kong Monetary Authority (HKMA) has stopped the operation of a licensed money remittance business that was found to have serious failures in anti-money laundering (AML) controls, among which the most notable was that the company had no system at all for identifying TBML red flags, e.g., misinvoicing (Ernst & Young Global Limited, 2021; Hong Kong Monetary Authority, 2016).

Regulatory Lesson: This is a good example of how a local regulator conducts its risk-based, preventive supervision in a hands-on manner. Aiming at a non-bank financial institution (a remittance service)—a sector generally regarded as at higher risk of money laundering and terrorist financing. The HKMA decided to conduct a deep penetration into the institution's operations. Consequently, it not only required rectifying the program's deficiencies at their source but also limited the issuance of the warning to those illicit transactions in which the entity was directly involved.

Outcome: The public enforcement action sent a loud and clear message to the financial sector. The basic AML controls (customer due diligence, transaction monitoring, and employee training) are essential for any organizational setup. Moreover, Hong Kong has addressed fundamental issues in its domestic operations, is part of the international community, and is fully committed to international norms.

It is evident from this case that proactive AML governance is critical, especially in sectors susceptible to "Terrorist and/or Brokered Money Laundering" (TBML). The great requirements are robust internal controls, real-time transaction monitoring, a compliance culture across financial institutions, and regulatory cooperation to mitigate the detection and occurrence of illicit trade finance schemes.

The fight against TBML remains a pressing issue in our interconnected financial system. The crucial role of the international community in establishing a legal regime to regulate TBML activities cannot be overstated. Your assistance is paramount, as this regime comprises laws and policies that prohibit and combat such crimes.

This framework, designed to prevent the financial system from being used by criminal actors to finance terrorism and other organized crime, is a cornerstone of global financial stability and security. However, we must remain vigilant as the regulatory landscape evolves, with countries and organizations adopting diverse approaches to detecting and deterring TBML operations. It signifies that businesses and financial institutions must stay familiar with the laws and regulations that apply to them and take appropriate measures to ensure prudent compliance.

In sum, the global regulatory framework for TBML is a key weapon against financial crime. A clear, logical, and comprehensive set of rules can prohibit the magnitude and spread of TBML enterprises and protect the integrity of the global economic system.

Key Global Actors in the TBML Regulatory Framework

A network comprising international organizations and national bodies leads the fight against TBML. Each entity plays a specific yet complementary role in standard-setting, facilitating cooperation, and enforcing standards. In the following section, we present a concise summary of the key actors in the global TBML framework.

Financial Action Task Force

Core Mandate: The FATF 40 Recommendations were developed to establish global standards that provide a basis for implementation. It ensures that legal, regulatory, and operational m easures are put in place to comprehensively eradicate money laundering, terrorist financing, and other activities that could undermine the integrity of the international financial system.

Significant TBML Relevance: The FATF is the most important policymaking body for TBML. It describes the offense and issues, typologies, red-flag indicators, and best practices, all intended solely for the detection of trade-based schemes. Its mutual evaluation programs are used tool assess countries' AML/CFT regimes, including the surveillance of trade finance.

Impact Mechanism: By means of its prohibitive regime, the "Gray List" and "Blacklist," the FATF imposes closer monitoring and possible economic countermeasures against non-compliant jurisdictions, which in turn amplify the regulatory reforms and convergence in the world.

The Egmont Group of Financial Intelligence Units

Core Mandate: To be the most secure platform for national FIUs to exchange information and cooperate with them.

Key TBML Relevance: The Egmont Group, through its cross-border sharing of financial intelligence and Suspicious Transaction Reports (STRs). These enable FIUs to 'connect the dots' on complex, multi-jurisdictional TBML schemes that are difficult to discern in isolation within individual countries.

Impact Mechanism: The network's security features support and enable operational collaboration. This has been crucial during TBML investigations of high-profile cases. It even helped trace illicit funds concealed as cross-border trade payments.

United Nations Office on Drugs and Crime

Core Mandate: Urge for hot pursuit against illegal drugs, crime, corruption, and terrorism in the respective Member States.

Key TBML Relevance: The United Nations Office on Drugs and Crime (UNODC) provides essential capacity-building and technical assistance to nations, particularly developing countries, to support compliance with FATF standards. The measures include strengthening legal frameworks, training financial investigators, and developing the analytical capacity of FIUs to combat TBML.

Impact Mechanism: The UNODC, through field projects and global programs, supports the creation of institutions and the development of a national pool of experts. Professionals must effectively detect and investigate TBML.

OECD Working Group on Bribery

Core Mandate: To keep track of and encourage the complete adoption of the OECD Anti-Bribery Convention, which prohibits bribing someone in another jurisdiction.

Key TBML Relevance: The unlawful bribery of public officials in foreign markets essentially underpins money laundering through trade-based methods, such as over-invoicing for goods or services. If bribery is controlled, the TBML's funding source will be directly disrupted.

Impact Mechanism: The Working Group's rigorous peer-review process holds countries accountable for prosecuting foreign bribery cases. Thus, the flow of corrupt funds into the financial system and trade is reduced.

European Union

Core Mandate: The development of a legal and regulatory infrastructure across its jurisdictions.

Key TBML Relevance: The EU's Anti-Money Laundering Directives are regional regulations grounded in the FATF standards. The most important measures relevant to TBML are that banks are required to conduct enhanced due diligence on cross-border correspondent relationships and on beneficial ownership registries, and that customs authorities have specific obligations to detect the smuggling of cash and goods.

Impact Mechanism: The EU's single market requires a unified AML approach. The directives of the EU, which are carried out by the European Banking Authority and national regulators, provide a regulatory perimeter that is uniform and makes it more difficult for criminals to take advantage of the differences between member states for TBML.

World Bank Stolen Asset Recovery Initiative

Core Mandate: A partnership between the World Bank and the UNODC to facilitate the recovery of assets stolen through corruption and hidden in foreign jurisdictions.

Key TBML Relevance: TBML is a widely used technique for moving corruptly obtained funds from one place to another; it is a standard method of laundering funds. The Stolen Asset Recovery (StAR) Initiative provides countries with a range of practical tools and assistance to trace, seize, and repatriate assets stashed in foreign jurisdictions.

Impact Mechanism: By supporting asset recovery cases, StAR deprives criminals of their illicit gains. It demonstrates that the international trade system cannot be employed with impunity to obscure the proceeds of grand corruption.

OECD Working Group on Bribery

Core Mandate: To watch the OECD Anti-Bribery Convention with full implementation and compliance. It advocates such compliance, thereby making bribery and corruption punishable.

Key TBML Relevance: Most foreign bribery generates illicit funds that are laundered through trade-based techniques, such as overpricing goods or services. The war on the major crime of bribery is, therefore, a war against the TBML source of funds.

Impact Mechanism: The rigorous peer-review process holds nations accountable for prosecuting foreign bribery. Thus, the flow of corrupt money into the financial and trade systems is reduced.

United Nations Commission on International Trade Law

Core Mandate: The modernization and harmonization of international trade law processes are United Nations Commission on International Trade Law (UNCITRAL)'s core business.

Key TBML Relevance: The legal recognition of electronically transferable records (such as e-bills of lading) enables the digitalization of trade. Thus, one of the main avenues through which UNCITRAL affects TBML. Trade documentation is becoming more transparent, thereby reducing opportunities for document fraud in TBML schemes.

Impact Mechanism: By providing a legal framework for digital trade, UNCITRAL facilitates the transition from opaque, paper-based systems to more transparent, auditable digital processes.

Financial Crimes Enforcement Network

Core Mandate: The FIU of the U.S. Department of the Treasury. The agency oversees and administers the Bank Secrecy Act (BSA).

Key TBML Relevance: Financial Crimes Enforcement Network (FinCEN) is the mainstay for U.S. financial institutions. It offers collection and analysis of Suspicious Activity Reports (SARs) and Currency Transaction Reports (CTRs). Moreover, it will identify areas of concern in TBML through advisory statements and, by issuing geographic targeting orders (GTOs), require the application of temporary enhanced due diligence measures to specific trade sectors or regions.

Impact Mechanism: FinCEN's examination transforms unrefined financial data into practical intelligence for U.S. law enforcement. Hence, it supports the principal TBML investigations. Moreover, its regulatory actions could indirectly facilitate the identification and mitigation of systemic weaknesses in trade finance.

National Financial Intelligence Units

Core Mandate: National centers are responsible for receiving, assessing, and disseminating financial intelligence related to suspected money laundering or terrorist financing.

Key TBML Relevance: FIUs, as the domestic nexus of the AML/CFT framework, are the primary sources of STRs related to TBML. This provides banks, customs, and other institutions with reliable reporting. They monitor transaction flows to identify irregularities in trade and liaise with foreign FIUs through the Egmont Group to share information.

Impact Mechanism: The role of active FIUs is the operational linchpin of TBML detection. Their analytical output initiates local investigations and provides leverage for international collaboration. Thus, they are indispensable to the conversion of information into law enforcement actions.

An Insight: Understanding FATCA's Role in Detecting Financial Crimes through Reporting Requirements

The U.S. Foreign Account Tax Compliance Act (FATCA), enacted in 2010, is U.S. legislation designed to prevent U.S. citizens and U.S. residents from concealing their wealth in foreign financial institutions (FFIs). It achieves this by requiring information reporting on certain accounts (as detailed in Schedule 1) owned by U.S. taxpayers or foreign persons (including foreign companies) where a U.S. person has substantial control of that company. FATCA's primary objective is to promote awareness of international financial transactions, thereby curbing activities related to money laundering and terrorism.

What is FATCA, and why was it enacted?

Recognizing the escalating tax revenues being funneled into offshore tax avoidance schemes, the U.S. government became increasingly apprehensive and took proactive action. The Internal Revenue Service estimated that annual fiscal losses to the U.S. economy totaled $100 billion, prompting the development of FATCA. This legislation was not a reactive measure but a proactive and pragmatic one designed to combat tax evasion. It also provides a robust mechanism for prevention and control.

Financial institutions play an indispensable role in combating tax evasion. They are the ones who establish the information connections that demonstrate that certain entities own at least 25% of specific foreign financial assets or foreign entities that the U.S. IRC does not cover. This information is vital for identifying U.S. taxpayers with foreign accounts. Moreover, these institutions enforce FFI reporting requirements, which withhold 30% of certain payments from non-compliant account holders. These provisions motivate FFIs to comply with applicable laws and help the IRS identify tax evaders, underscoring the crucial role of FFIs in this strenuous effort.

IGAs, or agreements between the United States and other countries, are integral to FATCA. They are essential in streamlining the reporting process, particularly for FFIs in certain countries. Under FATCA, these FFIs must only comply with IGAs and report information to their local tax offices, which then transmit the data to the IRS. This arrangement significantly reduces the reporting burden on FFIs and enhances reporting efficiency, providing reassurance about the system's effectiveness.

How Does FATCA Work?

Under FATCA, FFIs are required to identify and report on the following types of accounts:

- Depository accounts, such as checking and savings accounts
- Custodial accounts, such as accounts holding securities
- Investment accounts, such as mutual funds and other investment vehicles

FFIs must report the account holder's name, address, taxpayer identification number (TIN), account balance, and any income earned on the account. They must also report any income earned on accounts held by U.S. taxpayers that are not subject to the automatic information exchange under a relevant Intergovernmental Agreement (IGA).

Two primary approaches apply to the provisions of foreign financial institutions in meeting the requirements of the FATCA. They may register directly with the Internal Revenue Service or elect to comply with the IGA, a legally binding agreement between the United States and the country in which they operate. The IGAs can further be split into two categories:

Model 1 IGAs: In this approach, FFIs provide the necessary information to their tax authority, which then exchanges it with the IRS.

Model 2 IGAs: Under this scheme, FFIs pay the IRS directly for all information, bypassing local tax authorities.

Considering the diverse regulatory frameworks across several nations, the underlying mechanism effectively reduces the complexities associated with the FATCA.

Impact of FATCA on AML Efforts

FATCA's Impact on AML Efforts: By mandating that FFIs report on accounts held by U.S. taxpayers, FATCA has considerably raised the bar for criminals seeking to conceal their illicit gains in offshore accounts.

FATCA and Zuercher Kantonalbank (ZKB) Settlement (2018)

Core Facts: The Swiss bank ZKB was fined $98.5 million for its role in a scheme that facilitated U.S. clients' tax evasion through asset concealment in unreported accounts and the use of sham companies to obscure ownership (SwissInfo, 2018; U.S. Department of Justice, 2018).

Regulatory Lesson: The U.S. FATCA was a key driver of AML measures. The legislation not only required foreign banks to disclose U.S. depositors but also to provide a data trail that revealed tax evasion and associated money laundering. It was a clear demonstration that tax transparency entails financial transparency.

Outcome: FATCA settlements exemplify how U.S. financial regulations are globally enforced. They also increase compliance costs and associated risk for foreign banks that serve U.S. clients covertly. Thus, it effectively closes off a major route for the placement of undeclared assets. By requiring foreign banks to report on U.S. account holders, it created a data trail that exposed not just tax evasion but also the underlying concealment mechanisms employed for money laundering. It exhibited how tax transparency drives financial transparency.

The 1MDB Scandal (2015)

Core Facts: The 1MDB sovereign wealth fund in Malaysia became the target of a large-scale embezzlement and money laundering scheme. The widescale scam was committed with the active participation and complicity of numerous countries. The primary method used was TBML, which used fictitious investment contracts and shell corporations to portray the flow of money as trade and investment. The primary method used was TBML, which used fictitious investment contracts and shell corporations to portray the flow of money as trade and investment (Ellis-Petersen, 2020; U.S. Department of Justice, 2021).

Regulatory Failure/Mechanism: The scandal revealed catastrophic failures in the integrity of gatekeepers. Major global financial institutions facilitated flows despite obvious red flags, while legal and accounting professionals helped design the opaque structures. It demonstrated how TBML can scale to obscure the proceeds of grand corruption when enabled by private-sector complicity.

Outcome: In an extraordinary display of international collaboration, the recovery and repatriation of assets totaling more than $1 billion were accomplished (U.S. Department of Justice, 2021). The convictions of top government officials and bankers made the case quite visible and highlighted negligence and personal liability (Helmore, 2022; Ratcliffe, 2022). The entire episode heightened the level of scrutiny of politically exposed persons and complex cross-border investment schemes.

Operation Casablanca (1998)

Core Facts: A massive undercover operation by the United States and Mexico took the lid off a vast dark money laundering network, where drug lords were the customers, and TBML methods—like fake trade bills and the use of front companies—were the main techniques of moving their money through Mexican banks (U.S. Department of the Treasury, 1998).

Regulatory Lesson: The operation was the clear winner in cross-border financial intelligence sharing and joint investigation, demonstrating its utmost value. It was illuminating how TBML schemes exploit jurisdictional boundaries, where police and FIUs must cooperate and, at times, their connection must be in real time to map the entire network.

Outcome: At least 100 suspects were arrested, and major asset seizures were made. The operation was a real blessing in terms of police close cooperation, as it laid the groundwork for future joint task forces and, more importantly, highlighted the critical role of SARs at alert banks in triggering such complex investigations.

Chapter Summary

Key international organizations spearhead the global effort to combat money laundering and terror financing. Each plays a distinct role and wields considerable impact. The FATF sets international standards to combat money laundering and the funding of terrorism. It seeks to avert the criminal exploitation of the financial system. Thus, it makes a significant contribution to the global fight against economic crime. The Egmont Group enhances the operations of FIUs to combat money laundering and support terrorist activities. Through its determined efforts, the group improves the effectiveness of international financial crime detection and prevention. The UNODC assists countries in combating and eradicating criminal enterprises. The UNODC provides services across several areas, including technical support, capacity building, and policy guidance, to help nations strengthen their legal and institutional frameworks to combat TBML. The Stolen Asset Recovery Initiative (StAR) is a component of the World Bank's robust enterprise that aims to recover misappropriated funds through anti-corruption measures, thereby significantly advancing the fight against financial crime. Much like the OECD Working Group on Bribery, targeting the problem of bribing foreign officials primarily aims to reduce and control a menace while also contributing to the creation of a global culture of integrity. Combating terrorist financing in Europe is primarily the responsibility of the European Union, given the complexity of anti-money laundering policies across member states. This cohesive regulatory framework supports the broader effort to maintain financial stability and security. The primary mission of UNCITRAL is to address disparities and modernize trade laws worldwide. In addition, it is part of modern information and communication technologies, as it actively promotes and builds technological capacity in poorer countries that receive legal assistance. These organizations collectively form a robust global framework to combat TBML and enhance financial stability and security. Their combined efforts demonstrate the value of international cooperation in combating financial crime.

The FIUs play a crucial role in receiving, analyzing, and disseminating financial intelligence. They provide invaluable support to law enforcement agencies, regulators, and other relevant authorities in combating TBML, empowering everyone who can benefit from their operational contributions. Their crucial role is essential to reinforcing the system's ability to detect and counter TBML, providing a sense of security and confidence in their effectiveness.

End of Chapter: Discussion Questions

1 What is the role of the global regulatory framework for TBML in combating financial crime?
2 How does the Financial Action Task Force (FATF) establish and promote international standards for anti-money laundering and counter-terrorist financing, and in what ways do member jurisdictions implement these policies to strengthen global efforts against financial crime?
3 What is the purpose of the Egmont Group in combating money laundering and terrorist financing?

4 What specific activities does the United Nations Office on Drugs and Crime (UNODC) undertake to support countries in combating money laundering and terrorist financing, and how do these efforts contribute to strengthening the global framework against financial crime?
5 What is the role of the World Bank's Stolen Asset Recovery Initiative (StAR) in combating corruption and recovering stolen assets?
6 What is the focus of the OECD Working Group on Bribery, and how does it help combat foreign bribery?
7 How does coordination among international organizations fighting money laundering and terrorist financing enhance the effectiveness of global TBML countermeasures, and why is understanding these collaborative dynamics essential for stakeholders engaged in financial crime prevention?
8 Why must businesses and financial institutions stay informed of the laws and regulations related to TBML?
9 What challenges do international organizations encounter in combating money laundering and terrorist financing, and how does recognizing these obstacles enable stakeholders to prioritize actions and contribute more effectively to the global fight against financial crime?
10 How can businesses and financial institutions actively contribute to preventing TBML activities, and in what ways does understanding this responsibility empower them to uphold the integrity and stability of the global economic system?
11 How does the UNCITRAL promote the harmonization of international trade law?
12 How has the UNCITRAL helped developing countries in international trade law?
13 What are the challenges and limitations of the UNCITRAL in regulating digital trade?
14 What recommendations do you have for UNCITRAL's future role in promoting digital trade?
15 What is an FIU, and how does it assist in detecting and preventing money laundering and terrorist financing?
16 How do FIUs cooperate internationally to combat cross-border money laundering schemes, especially those involving TBML?
17 What are the challenges faced by FIUs in sharing information and collaborating with other agencies and jurisdictions, and how can these be addressed to enhance the effectiveness of the AML/CFT regime?
18 What is the role of FinCEN in combating financial crimes in the United States?
19 How does FinCEN collect, analyze, and disseminate financial intelligence to law enforcement and regulatory agencies?
20 How does FinCEN implement the recent regulatory developments to strengthen the AML framework in the United States?

Bibliography

Adam. (2022, August 24). How Malaysia's 1MDB scandal shook the financial world. *The Washington Post*. https://www.washingtonpost.com/business/how-malaysias-1mdb-scandal-shook-the-financial-world/2022/08/24/a7b2b5d4-2377-11ed-a72f-1e7149072fbc_story.html

Brown, M. (2021, November 29).The rising standards of AML/CFT compliance in Hong Kong. Mondaq. Retrieved from https://www.mondaq.com/hongkong/money-laundering/1136220/the-rising-standards-of-amlcft-compliance-in-hong-kong

Ellis-Petersen, H. (2020, July 28). 1MDB scandal explained: A tale of Malaysia's missing billions. *The Guardian*. https://www.theguardian.com/world/2018/oct/25/1mdb-scandal-explained-a-tale-of-malaysias-missing-billions

FATF. (2020a). Japan: Virtual assets and virtual asset service providers. Retrieved from https://www.fatf-gafi.org/media/fatf/content/images/Japan-3rd-MUTUAL-EVALUATION-REPORT.pdf

FATF. (2020b). Japan: Follow-up report on mutual evaluation. Retrieved from https://www.fatf-gafi.org/media/fatf/documents/reports/Follow-Up-Report-Japan-2020.pdf

Federation of American Scientists. (1998, May 26). Anti-drug efforts: Operation Casablanca—What were U.S. motives? https://irp.fas.org/news/1998/05/wwwhm526.html

Financial Action Task Force. (2006). Trade-based money laundering. https://www.fatf-gafi.org

Financial Action Task Force. (2018, August 21). U.S. Department of the Treasury. https://home.treasury.gov/policy-issues/terrorism-and-illicit-finance/financial-action-task-force

Financial Action Task Force. (2021). Best practices on trade-based money laundering. https://www.fatf-gafi.org/publications

Financial Action Task Force (FATF) & Egmont Group of Financial Intelligence Units. (2020). Trade-based money laundering: Trends and developments. Paris: FATF/OECD. Retrieved from https://www.fatf-gafi.org/content/dam/fatf-gafi/reports/Trade-Based-Money-Laundering-Trends-and-Developments.pdf

FTI Consulting. (2025). The new "Operation Casablanca"? Challenges and opportunities in the designation of Mexican cartels as FTOs. https://www.fticonsulting.com/insights/articles/new-operation-casablanca-challenges-opportunities-designation-mexican-cartels-ftos

Helmore, E. (2022, April 8). Ex-Goldman banker Roger Ng was found guilty in a billion-dollar 1MDB scandal. *The Guardian*. https://www.theguardian.com/world/2022/apr/08/roger-ng-1mdb-scandal-fraud-found-guilty

Hong Kong Monetary Authority. (2016). Guidance paper on combating trade-based money laundering. Retrieved from https://www.hkma.gov.hk/media/eng/doc/key-functions/banking-stability/aml-cft/Guidance_Paper_on_Combating_Trade-based_Money_Laundering.pdf

Lagarde, C. (2017, June 22). Working together to fight money laundering & terrorist financing. Speech at the FATF Plenary Meeting, Valencia, Spain. *International Monetary Fund*. Retrieved from https://www.imf.org/en/News/Articles/2017/06/22/sp062217-working-together-to-fight-money-laundering-and-terrorist-financing.

Money Laundering Watch. (2024, October 25). Halkbank faces prosecution: U.S. Court of Appeals denies sovereign immunity. Ballard Spahr LLP https://www.moneylaunderingwatchblog.com/2024/10/halkbank-faces-prosecution-u-s-court-of-appeals-denies-sovereign-immunity/

NPR. (2008, December 16). Siemens fined $1.6 billion in bribery case. https://www.npr.org/2008/12/16/98317332/siemens-hit-with-1-6-billion-fine-in-bribery-case

OECD. (2014). Alstom settlement. Retrieved from https://www.oecd.org/corruption/oecdworkinggrouponbriberyininternationalbusinesstransactionsalstomsettlement.htm

OECD. (2019). Resolving foreign bribery cases with non-trial resolutions: Settlements and non-trial agreements by parties to the Anti-Bribery Convention. https://www.oecd.org/corruption/Resolving-Foreign-Bribery-Cases-with-Non-Trial-Resolutions.htm

OECD. (2021). Working group on bribery. Retrieved from https://www.oecd.org/corruption/oecd-anti-bribery-working-group.htm

Private Banker International. (2018, August 17). Zuercher Kantonalbank to pay $98.5m to settle US tax evasion probe. https://www.privatebankerinternational.com/news/zuercher-kantonalbank-pay-98-5m-settle-us-tax-evasion-charges

Ratcliffe, R. (2022, August 23). Malaysia's former Prime Minister Najib was sent to prison after losing the final appeal in the 1MDB case. *The Guardian*. https://www.theguardian.com/world/2022/aug/23/malaysia-ex-pm-najib-razak-loses-1mdb-appeal

RFE/ RL. (2017, April 29). Ukraine begins confiscating $1.5 billion allegedly stolen by Yanukovych. RadioFreeEurope/RadioLiberty. https://www.rferl.org/a/ukraine-confiscates-money-yanukovych-allegedly-stole/28458549.html

Stolen Asset Recovery Initiative. (2013). *Tunisia's cash-back*. World Bank. https://star.worldbank.org/blog/tunisias-cash-back

Stolen Asset Recovery Initiative. (2014). *Ukraine forum on asset recovery*. World Bank. https://star.worldbank.org/events/ukraine-forum-asset-recovery

Supreme Court of the United States. (2023, April 19). Turkiye Halk Bankasi A.S. v. United States. https://www.supremecourt.gov/opinions/22pdf/21-1450_5468.pdf

SwissInfo. (2018, August 14). Zurich Bank settles tax-evasion probe with the U.S. https://www.swissinfo.ch/eng/business/legal-settlement_zurich-bank-settles-tax-evasion-probe-with-us/44320444

New Lines Magazine. (2021, May 7). The Tunisia heist. New Lines Magazine. Retrieved from https://newlinesmag.com/reportage/the-tunisia-heist/

Timothy Loh LLP. (2021). Money service operators & the Anti-Money Laundering Ordinance in Hong Kong. Retrieved from https://www.timothyloh.com/insights/guides/money-service-operator

U.S. Department of Justice. (2019, October 15). Turkish Bank charged in Manhattan Federal Court for its participation in a multibillion-dollar Iranian sanctions evasion scheme. https://www.justice.gov/opa/pr/turkish-bank-charged-manhattan-federal-court-its-participation-multibillion-dollar-iranian

U.S. Department of Justice. (2021, August 5). Over $1 billion in misappropriated 1MDB funds now repatriated to Malaysia [Press release]. https://www.justice.gov/opa/pr/over-1-billion-misappropriated-1mdb-funds-now-repatriated-malaysia.

U.S. Department of the Treasury. (1998, May 18). U.S. Customs Service takes down major drug traffickers, corrupt banks, and bankers in the largest drug money laundering case ever. https://home.treasury.gov/news/press-releases/rr2452

U.S. Department of the Treasury. (2019). The Treasury Department sanctions a Chinese entity supporting North Korea's illicit financial activities. https://home.treasury.gov

UNODC Regional Office for Southeast Asia and the Pacific. (2019). With UNODC support, the Philippines adopts a National Strategy against money laundering and terrorist financing. United Nations. https://www.unodc.org/roseap/en/2019/01/money-laundering-terrorist-financing/story.html

United Nations. (1966). United Nations Commission on International Trade Law (UNCITRAL). Retrieved from https://www.uncitral.org/

United Nations Commission on International Trade Law (UNCITRAL). (2005). UNCITRAL model law on electronic commerce with guide to enactment 1996, with additional article 5 bis as adopted in 1998. United Nations. Retrieved from https://uncitral.un.org/en/texts/ecommerce/modellaw/electronic_commerce

United Nations Office on Drugs and Crime. (2020). The global threat of transnational organized crime. https://www.unodc.org

Wikipedia Contributors. (2023, July 8). Financial action task force. Wikipedia. https://en.wikipedia.org/wiki/Financial_Action_Task_Force

Wisconsin Project. (2019). Central Turkish banks were prosecuted in an unprecedented case involving the evasion of Iran sanctions. Retrieved from https://www.wisconsinproject.org/major-turkish-bank-prosecuted-in-unprecedented-iran-sanctions-evasion-case/

World Bank. (2019). Blockchain and development: Hype vs reality. Retrieved from https://www.worldbank.org/en/topic/digital-finance/brief/blockchain-and-development-hype-vs-reality

Zarate, J. C. (2013). *Treasury's war: The unleashing of a new era of financial warfare*. PublicAffairs.

Zürcher Kantonalbank reaches an agreement with the US Department of Justice. (2018). Retrieved from https://www.zkb.ch/en/home/media/media-releases/zuercher-kantonalbank-reaches-agreement-with-us-department-of-ju.html

Additional Learning Resources

Books

1 "Combating money laundering and terrorist financing: A model of best practice for the financial sector, the professions, and other designated businesses" by Commonwealth Secretariat (2006). cir.nii.ac.jp
This book provides an overview of current anti-money laundering and counter-terrorist financing efforts and offers a model of best practices for the financial sector.

2 "Transnational Crime and Global Security" [1 ed.] edited by Philip Reichel and Ryan Randa. (2018). This book examines transnational crime, including money laundering, and its impact on global security. It provides insights into the methods and trends of transnational criminal activities.

3 "Handbook of Anti-Money Laundering" by Dennis Cox (2014). John Wiley & Sons.
This handbook provides an in-depth examination of anti-money laundering laws and regulations and offers practical guidance on implementing effective anti-money laundering programs.
4 StAR Initiative. (2011). "Asset Recovery Handbook: A Guide for Practitioners." World Bank and UNODC. https://star.worldbank.org/sites/star/files/asset_recovery_handbook_0.pdf
5 A Guide for Practitioners offers a how-to guide for recovering stolen assets and draws on the experience of a wide range of experts in the field. The handbook covers topics such as the legal framework for asset recovery, the role of financial intelligence, and the use of mutual legal assistance. Downloadable at: https://star.worldbank.org/sites/star/files/asset_recovery_handbook_0.pdf

Films

6 "The Laundromat" (2019), directed by Steven Soderbergh
This film is based on the real story of the Panama Papers scandal, which exposed a global network of money laundering and tax evasion.
7 "The Accountant" (2016), directed by Gavin O'Connor and written by Bill Dubuque.
This film is an American action thriller. The movie follows a forensic accountant who uncovers a massive money-laundering scheme.

Documentaries

8 "The Kleptocrats" (2018), produced by Mike Lerner and directed by Sam Hobkinson and Havana Marking.
This documentary explores the 1MDB scandal, in which billions of dollars were stolen from a Malaysian sovereign wealth fund and laundered through a complex web of shell companies.
9 "The Panama Papers" (2018), directed and written by Alex Winter
This documentary tells the story of the journalists who broke the Panama Papers story and the global impact of the revelations.

Articles

10 Corruption and the global economy, Mark Pieth (1997). Institute for International Economics, http://www.iie.com
This article provides an overview of the current state of anti-money laundering efforts and discusses the challenges and opportunities for improving global cooperation in this area.
11 "TBML Suspicious Activity Reports – A Financial Intelligence Unit Perspective" by Mohammed Naheem Ahmad (2018). Journal of Financial Crime.
This article presents the perspective of an FIU on TBML. It examines the challenges and opportunities for detecting and preventing TBML using suspicious activity reports.
12 "In Search of Transnational Financial Intelligence: Questioning Cooperation between Financial Intelligence Units" by Antoine Amicelle and Killian Chaudieu (2018). The Palgrave handbook of criminal and terrorism financing law.
This article examines the challenges and opportunities for cooperation between FIUs in combating money laundering and terrorist financing.

Online Resources

13 "Anti-Money Laundering: A Comparative and Critical Analysis of the UK and UAE's Financial Intelligence Units" by Dr. Waleed Alhosani (2016). Available at: books.google.com: https://tinyurl.com/Alhosa
This online resource provides a comparative analysis of FIUs in the UK and the UAE and offers insights into best practices for combating money laundering and terrorist financing.

Online Resource

14 Convention on Combating Bribery of OECD Legal Instruments Foreign Public Officials in International Business Transactions (2022). Available at: https://legalinstruments.oecd.org/public/doc/205/205.en.pdf
The Convention on Combating Bribery of Foreign Public Officials in International Business Transactions is a legally binding agreement established by the Organisation for Economic Co-operation and Development (OECD) to criminalize bribery of foreign public officials in international business transactions. The Convention applies to governments, businesses, and other stakeholders committed to combating corruption and promoting ethical business practices. The Convention provides a framework for cooperation and coordination among countries to avert and prosecute bribery of foreign public officials. It establishes standards for transparency, accountability, and good governance in international business transactions.

Open Knowledge Repository Beta

15 StAR Initiative - Books in the Stolen Asset Recovery Series are available for free at https://openknowledge.worldbank.org/handle/10986/2172

5 Underground Financial Systems in the Global Economy

An Overview

Underground financial systems—the networks operating outside regulated, institutional channels—represent a parallel architecture within the global economy. While often conflated with illegality, these systems are, in fact, positioned along a continuum ranging from community-based informality to the most criminal enterprises. Hidden beneath the surface of their continuance are the significant shortcomings of formal financial inclusion, the strength of non-state trust networks, and the relentless circumvention of state controls. This chapter analyzes four prominent systems—the black market, the peso exchange, hawala, and Fei-Chien—to elucidate their operational logics and their dual role in providing essential services while posing systemic risks.

The Black Market: The Umbrella of Informality

The black market constitutes the largest form of underground economic activity, encompassing not only the trade in prohibited goods but also the unregulated provision of services (BoyceWire, 2023; Invezz, 2024). It is primarily found in contexts in which the state has limited capacity or access, or is not recognized as legitimate (BoyceWire, 2023; Invezz, 2024). Although it is associated with crime and corruption, it remains a means of adaptation for people living in areas of shortage, heavy regulation, or hyperinflation, as it provides access to necessities that are otherwise unavailable (BoyceWire, 2023; Wikipedia, 2023). This duality makes it a barometer of systemic economic dysfunction.

The Peso Exchange: Arbitraging State Control

The peso exchange is a specific foreign currency black market, most notably in Argentina. It emerges directly from state-imposed capital controls and from divergent official and market exchange rates. This system operates through informal brokers who connect buyers and sellers, thereby creating a liquidity pool for U.S. dollars outside banking channels (BlueDollar.net, 2025; Brooke Beyond, 2024). It is less a criminal enterprise than a market-driven correction to state policy, demonstrating how financial activity migrates to the shadows when formal channels are artificially constrained.

Hawala: Trust-Based Global Transfer

Hawala is a centuries-old system that facilitates value transfers based solely on trust, without requiring the physical movement of currency. The client hands over funds to the hawaladar at one location, and the hawaladar transmits instructions to the counterpart at the other location to

DOI: 10.4324/9781003477631-6

transfer the equivalent amount to the designated recipient. This facilitation mechanism, whose origins date back to 8th-century South Asia, is still widely used in regions today where banking services are either nonexistent or difficult to access (The Hawala System, 2023; Team, 2020). Because it is inexpensive and highly efficient, the method has become crucial for migrant workers, who remit their salaries via hawala. Simultaneously, it provides anonymity, which poses a risk of financial crime.

Fei-Chien ("Flying Money"): Evading Capital Barriers

Similar in function to hawala but distinct in context, Fei-Chien is a Chinese underground banking system designed explicitly to evade stringent national capital controls. It facilitates the cross-border movement of wealth through complex, unrecorded asset and obligation swaps. Its scale can be monumental, as evidenced by a single uncovered network moving over $64 billion from China (Xinhua, 2009). Fei-Chien illustrates the high-stakes battle between the world's free flow of capital, which seeks to go everywhere, and the nation's right to control its financial borders.

The Regulatory Paradox

All these systems point to a central paradox: they are, simultaneously, both the cause of market failures and the source of communities' requirements. They operate like formal systems, providing financial inclusion, currency stability, and remittance channels where the latter are absent or the systems are oppressive or prohibitively costly for people. However, their opacity risks usually facilitate money laundering, terrorist financing, and tax evasion. Hence, the issue of governance cannot be resolved through suppressive strategies only. It must include understanding the demand drivers—financial exclusion, unreasonable controls, and the lack of accessible products—and addressing them through targeted transparency, smarter regulation, and the development of inclusive formal alternatives.

Exploring the Black Market: An Overview of Underground Financial Systems

The "Black Market," also known as the Underground Economy or Shadow Market, signifies unregulated or illegal economic activities conducted outside formal financial systems (Minnaar, 2017). These actions can cover the sale of unlawful goods and services, such as drugs, firearms, and stolen property. The market denotes the exchange of currency or other assets through channels that bypass conventional financial institutions, relying instead on informal or anonymous payment methods (Frank & Mikhaylov, 2020). The black market is frequently linked with organized crime and corruption. Still, it can also be a means for individuals to access goods and services that are otherwise unavailable or heavily regulated. This duality complicates enforcement and policy responses (Minnaar, 2017).

One of the most well-known examples of the black market is the drug trade, which generates billions of dollars in revenue every year. The illegal or prohibited drug trade is a global challenge that impacts countries across the world considerably. It is frequently controlled by organized criminal networks that exploit digital anonymity and decentralized payment systems to evade detection (Frank & Mikhaylov, 2020). This underscores the urgency of addressing this issue. However, there is hope in the form of international cooperation, which can significantly curb the influence of the black market. The need for such cooperation in combating such activities is crucial. In addition to drugs, the black market is also employed to sell other illegal goods, such as stolen art and antiques, weapons, and counterfeit goods. Transactions on the black market often occur using cash or alternative currencies, such as Bitcoin. Cryptocurrency offers anonymity and decentralization. For example, an online black marketplace known as the Silk Road operated on the dark web until its shutdown by the Federal Bureau of Investigation (FBI) in 2013. The Silk Road functioned to buy and sell illegal drugs, fake IDs, and other illegal goods and services, and it had over 100,000 clients and $1.2 billion in annual sales (Bilefsky, 2014).

The black market, which is not limited to illegal goods, also serves as a means of exchange for legal goods and services that are heavily taxed or regulated by the government. This practical aspect of the black market can offer a viable mechanism for individuals to access items and services without relying on traditional financial institutions (Sanchez et al., 2023). However, the black market is not limited to illegal or unregulated activities. It may include legal transactions deliberately concealed from the authorities to avoid taxation (McLaren, 1996). The 'gray market,' not necessarily illegal but often associated with tax evasion, can adversely affect governments and society by minimizing the revenue available for public services and infrastructure (McLaren, 1996). Moreover, the economic effects of the black market, intricately linked to corruption and organized crime, are of growing concern (Sanchez et al., 2023). The black market, often controlled by criminal organizations, serves as a tool for money laundering, evading law enforcement, exploiting regulatory gaps, and maintaining anonymity within financial systems (Sanchez et al., 2023). These enterprises employ the black market to sell unlawful products and services and engage in activities that are most likely human trafficking and illicit arms dealing, often operating beyond the reach of conventional oversight (McLaren, 1996). Corrupt individuals, such as politicians, business leaders, and corporate elites, may also use black-market mechanisms to conceal their wealth and evade taxation, thereby further eroding institutional trust (Sanchez et al., 2023). Despite its negative connotations, the black market remains a substantial component of the global economy and is not likely to disappear anytime soon. This underscores the significance of understanding and addressing its implications. As individuals and organizations, we have the power to make informed decisions and contribute to a more transparent and fair financial system, thereby gaining a deeper understanding of the global economic landscape. Estimates indicate the underground economy represents a significant portion of global GDP and may continue to grow as more actors seek to circumvent market regulations and tax burdens (McLaren, 1996). The black market can provide access to goods and services that would otherwise be inaccessible; however, due to its collusion with corruption and crime, the complexity and opacity of the underground economy, and its role in the global economic landscape, it is problematic. This duality underscores the complexity of the issue.

Peso Exchange: An Overview of Underground Financial Systems

The peso exchange, an underground or informal financial system, is a global phenomenon that encompasses the transfer of money and other assets outside formal financial institutions, such as banks, credit cards, and other regulated lending schemes (Passas, 2003). These systems are prevalent worldwide, particularly in countries with limited access to formal financial institutions or where people and businesses must avoid taxation or legal constraints (Wilson, 2005).

One prominent example is the Hawala money transfer system, which is popular in the Middle East and South Asia (El Qorchi, 2002). The Hawala system relies on a trust-based, personal-relationship model in which agents in different geographic locations can exchange funds for clients without requiring a physical transfer. This trust-based mechanism is highly effective for rapid, low-cost remittances and has served migrant communities and informal economies for centuries (Wikipedia, 2023). The Hawala network is often used to transfer money to and from the system, which relies heavily on trust among agents in different locations who settle balances based on mutual obligations rather than on the physical movement of funds (Moin, 2024). Hawala is often employed to move funds across borders in contexts where formal banking is inaccessible or where regulatory avoidance is desired (El Qorchi, 2002).

Peso exchange systems, especially the Black-Market Peso Exchange (BMPE), represent another variant of informal currency transfer. These systems are often part of larger black-market economies, dealing in the illegal sales of goods such as drugs, weapons, and stolen property, and also unregulated currency exchanges (Passas, 2003). These markets are often controlled by organized crime and serve as conduits for disguising the proceeds of illegal activities and evading law enforcement scrutiny (Wilson, 2005).

Informal financial systems, such as hawala, peso exchange, and black markets, do not work in isolation from the formal economy. They have significant implications for tax revenue and compliance. These systems are predominantly cash-based and lack institutional regulation, which often leads to blatant underreporting of tax and tax evasion (Moin, 2024). The gray market, while not illegal, likely has the same impact on public finance by intentionally or inadvertently shifting economic activity outside formal transactions, reducing allocations to infrastructure and public services (Wilson, 2005). We must address the dual nature of informal financial systems, which facilitate access to finance while simultaneously creating opportunities for illegal activity, through a balanced regulatory response.

The peso exchange and other underground financial systems can have both positive and negative impacts on individuals and societies. The more traditional networks, such as hawala, play crucial roles in providing access to financial services that people and businesses might otherwise rely on through traditional institutions. They also facilitate the trade of goods and services without sanctions and the use of taxes and regulations. Moreover, the use of peso exchange houses or other underground financial systems by law enforcement can facilitate money laundering and the avoidance of law enforcement oversight. They can facilitate criminal activities, such as the sale of illegal goods and services, and evade taxes and regulations. For instance, in Argentina, the peso exchange rate, or "blue dollar," has existed for decades to circumvent stringent currency controls and chronic inflation (Brooke Beyond, 2024). The blue dollar is typically higher than the official exchange rate, reflecting widespread distrust. It is helpful for many transactions involving the movement of goods for import or export, the payment of professional services, and the purchase of real estate. Thus, it can be concluded that the peso exchange and other informal financial systems entrenched in the global economy are extensive and, to some extent, will remain permanent due to structural and socio-economic factors (García-Figal et al., 2024). While it is imperative to examine the adverse aspects of those systems, especially in relation to criminal finance and money laundering, we also want to highlight their positive aspects in providing financial access for individuals excluded from formal banking infrastructure (Wilson, 2005).

A well-balanced policy and regulatory response is required that acknowledges risks while also recognizing the socio-economic value of informal financial systems and fosters a more comprehensive understanding of their global footprint.

The involvement of the peso exchange in the scheme of shadowy financial systems is demonstrated by these few examples:

1 U.S. v. Iranian Shadow Banking Network: Sanctions Evasion and Money Laundering via Front Companies (United States, 2018):

   In 2018, the U.S. Department of Justice and the Department of the Treasury exposed an elaborate money-laundering operation linked to the Iranian government through shadow-banking structures (U.S. Department of Justice, 2018). The scheme involved the laundering of billions of dollars in Iranian oil and petrochemical revenues. (ii) The Iranian money launderers used Iranian exchange houses, foreign front companies, and fictitious invoices. (iii) They laundered the profits through jurisdictions with low levels of regulatory oversight (the UAE, Hong Kong, etc.).

i And systematically masked their transactions as humanitarian trade (e.g., food, medicine), seeking to exempt themselves from sanctions.

The network was linked to the Zarringhalam brothers, who allegedly owned and/or operated dozens of entities used to move money covertly. Their actions were illegal and/or violated several laws of the United States, including but not limited to: Executive Order 13902 (targeting Iran's financial and petrochemical sectors); (ii) Executive Order 13846 (re-imposing sanctions on Iran); (iii) wire fraud and conspiracy statutes. OFAC designated more than 30 individuals and entities for their roles in the scheme. FinCEN issued advisories to enhance banks' capacity to recognize red flags associated with Iranian illicit finance. The case exacerbated tensions between the United States and Iran, and enhanced the "maximum pressure" campaign. It has heightened recognition of the requirement for beneficial ownership transparency, enhanced cross-border anti-money laundering (AML) cooperation, and trade verification processes. This case demonstrates how state-sponsored financial networks use global trade and banking practices to circumvent sanctions and fund destabilizing activities (U.S. Department of State, 2025). The case underscores the need to reinforce real-time financial intelligence sharing, conduct more diligent examination and verification of trade documentation, and enhance international cooperation to dismantle shadow banking infrastructure.

2 Black-Market Peso Exchange and Regulatory Intervention in Colombia (Colombia, 2015):

In 2015, Colombian authorities intensified efforts to investigate the widespread use of the BMPE, a sophisticated informal financial mechanism for converting Colombian pesos into U.S. dollars outside formal banking channels. This investigation was prompted by growing concerns over the BMPE's role in facilitating TBML, tax evasion, and the repatriation of illicit drug proceeds, particularly those linked to transnational criminal organizations operating across Latin America and the United States (U.S. Department of State, 2015; Financial Crimes Enforcement Network, 2015).

The BMPE allows Colombian importers to buy products abroad with the drug dollars traffickers have in the United States, and effectively allows the importers to contravene financial regulations, currency controls, and customs laws. The goods are brought back into Colombia via smuggling or invoiced at less than their full value; in both cases, the parties launder their money without being flagged as engaged in any form of illicit activity. The 2015 investigation initiated a multi-agency, regional, and international effort to expose the networks, which were highly credible due to the financial intelligence units and cross-border shared connections. The policy priority was to disrupt networks that exploited environments characterized by limited oversight, regulatory failure, and the willful negligence of the private sector.

This case highlights the need for regulatory and law-enforcement oversight across all jurisdictions, while maintaining sufficient financial transparency to better understand the impunity with which underground financial systems operate. It is critical to the success of any case involving BMPE programs, as criminal networks for BMPE typically operate across multiple jurisdictions, enabling actors to exploit oversight deficits in one jurisdiction while remaining permitted to continue the business of illegal smuggling and money laundering across a variety of foreign markets. From a policy perspective, the initiative's achievements in Colombia offer a model for how AML frameworks can be complemented by trade facilitation and forensic financial analysis.

3 Cracking the Vault: China's 2013 Crackdown on Underground Banking Networks (Hsu, 2014) (China, 2013):

In 2013, the Chinese government initiated a comprehensive clampdown on underground banking as part of its broader anti-corruption agenda and financial regulatory reforms. These unofficial financial operations had become agencies of laundering funds, evading taxes, and issuing mortgages without authorization. Underground banks were undermining established banks and inflating housing prices through capital flight.

The campaign was directly aligned with President Xi Jinping's anti-corruption campaign and targeted not only actors but also particular institutions. Underground banks, as discussed with government officials and documented in research on underground banking operations, were often located in private homes and used multiple registered accounts to circumvent foreign exchange limits and facilitate illegal remittances and overseas property purchases. Underground banking operations emerged in Beijing and Zhejiang province.

Underground banks often used multiple personal accounts to remit funds overseas, thereby exceeding the $50,000 annual per-person limit on personal accounts. The underground banks also facilitated illegal mortgage lending and property speculation, thereby distorting the housing market.

This case has significant regulatory implications because, in a single operation, law enforcement arrested 59 suspects and froze 264 bank accounts. The operation reaffirmed the role of formal banking institutions and tightened foreign exchange controls. The case advanced regulatory changes during China's deleveraging campaign (2013–2021), specifically targeting shadow banking and systemic risk (Wright, 2023). Media exposés and official government position statements stated the illegality of such operations and urged citizens to comply with financial regulations.

Hawala Networks: A History of Informal Money Transfer Systems

Hawala networks, or hawaladars, are informal money transfer networks that operate outside the banking system, relying on personal trust and the movement of funds between agents in different locations on behalf of their clients (El Qorchi, Maimbo, & Wilson, 2003). By design, these systems respect and employ an honor-based model in which 'agents' are located at each location and move funds on behalf of 'clients' without the physical movement of money (Corporate Finance Institute, 2023). Hawala networks are relatively more common in the Middle East and South Asia but have also been observed in Africa, Europe, and North America, demonstrating their flexibility and robustness across regions (Wikipedia, 2023).

Multiple historians argue that the origins of Hawala networks coincide with those of human civilization. Hawala networks originated in ancient trade routes, such as the Silk Road, where messengers and agents facilitated the transfer of money and goods before the advent of modern banking (Corporate Finance Institute, 2023). The term 'hawala' is derived from the Arabic term that means 'transfer' or 'trust.' 'Hawala' has been used to classify informal money transfer systems for centuries (Wikipedia, 2023).

Hawala networks in their modern form emerged during the late 19th and early 20th centuries, particularly in regions undergoing rapid economic and social transformation, such as the Middle East and South Asia (El Qorchi, Maimbo, & Wilson, 2003). Increased international travel and trade necessitated more efficient systems for transferring money over distances, leading to the development of hawala as a fast and convenient service uniquely based on trust and operating outside formal financial institutions (Corporate Finance Institute, 2023).

Given their long history, Hawala networks have played many crucial functions; however, most significantly, they enabled trade and commerce, particularly in the Middle East and South Asia, in the 20th century. In addition to facilitating trade, hawala played an important role in the global economy by enabling merchants and traders to move money across borders without using banks or other regulated financial institutions (El Qorchi, Maimbo, & Wilson, 2003). Migrants and expatriates also relied on hawalas to send money to their families in their countries of origin, particularly in regions without banks or a functional formal banking system (Corporate Finance Institute, 2023).

However, the increasingly radical Hawala networks, with deep roots in disaster relief and development initiatives, face immense challenges. They have a unique position to provide fast and reliable money transfers from A to B in regions lacking established financial services, thereby representing regional efficacy. This is certainly promising for combating underground financial systems (FATF, 2013). They also provide a fundamental role in delivering humanitarian assistance to developing countries, and access to healthcare clearly supports their function (El Qorchi, Maimbo, & Wilson, 2003).

While Hawala networks are significantly utilized and indispensable to the global economy, they have malicious relationships in the realm of money laundering and financing terrorism (KYC Hub, 2023). There are instances in which these networks transferred funds to criminal counterparts or to circumvent regulatory oversight through tax avoidance (FATF, 2013). Therefore, Hawala networks have come under enhanced scrutiny from regulatory authorities and law enforcement agencies in recent years (KYC Hub, 2023). The directive explains the alarming instances of Hawala networks being used to channel funds for terrorist financing and other illegal acts. It also extensively covers the use of Hawala operations to facilitate prohibited financial undertakings. The U.S. Treasury Department's Financial Crimes Enforcement Network implicated these activities in its 2018 report, highlighting the need for vigilance and concern. This reiteration of the need for attentiveness and serious concerns underscores the urgency. Hawala networks commonly serve as conduits for restricted financial activity (FinCEN, 2018). The advisory quoted several cases and provided concrete examples of Hawala networks that have been engaged in transferring funds to facilitate terrorist financing and bolster terrorism, drug trafficking, and other unscrupulous activities.

FinCEN cited a case involving a group of individuals and businesses accused of using the Hawala network to launder money for the Iranian government (US Department of Justice, 2018). The individuals and businesses involved in the case were accused of infringing U.S. sanctions against Iran and conspiring to defraud the U.S. financial system.

FinCEN has brought to light a case where a group was charged with using the Hawala network, a significant aspect, to launder money for a terrorist organization in Pakistan (US Department of Justice, 2015). The charges against these individuals include conspiracies to launder money and conspiracies that materially and financially support a foreign terrorist organization.

These cases demonstrate the potential for Hawala networks to facilitate illicit financial activity. Hawala networks have a long, volatile history and have also been associated with deceitful operations such as money laundering and the financing of terrorism.

Hawala networks, or hawaladars, are informal systems for transferring money without formal financial institutions. Instead, they serve as essential intermediaries for agents stationed in various locations, disbursing funds to their clients. Hawala networks have existed since antiquity and persist to the present. Initially intended for trade and commerce, they have recently helped facilitate money transfers by migrants and expatriates, enabling them to send urgent emergency funds to their families through remittance channels.

Hawala and Remittance Flows in Afghanistan: An Exploration of the Informal Money Transfer System

Globalization, driven by economic opportunities, political instability, and climate change, has increased internal and cross-border migration rates. This demand for remittance services has increased exponentially, and millions of people are sending remittances to their families and loved ones in their home countries. Many developing countries may require greater access to, or more adequate, services provided by traditional financial institutions. In this context, informal money transfer systems, such as hawala, play a crucial role. This case study investigates the Hawala system in Afghanistan as a mechanism for remittance flows.

Hawala: A Brief Overview

Hawala, or hundi, is more than a means of transferring informal funds outside the traditional banking system. Originating in the Middle East and South Asia, it is commonly practiced in Afghanistan, India, Pakistan, and Somalia. Its use provides insight into what it has become today. With nothing lost through its continuous tradition for hundreds of years, the Hawala system of trust and reliability facilitates the transfer of funds from one person's possession to another, potentially crossing international borders.

The Operation of Hawala in Afghanistan

In Afghanistan, the Hawala system is a well-established and widely used method for transferring funds. Approximately 90% of the country's remittances are sent through the Hawala system, underscoring its importance to the Afghan economy. The Hawala system works through a network of trusted agents who send and receive funds on behalf of their clients. Clients provide the funds to their local Hawala agent, along with the recipient's details; the Hawala agent then contacts another agent in the recipient's location to deliver the funds, deducting a fee for the service.

Hawala and Remittances in Afghanistan

Afghan migrant workers are among the major expatriate communities that use Hawala to send money home. As of 2016, Afghanistan heavily depended on remittances as a share of its GDP. According to the World Bank, remittances at that time accounted for about 25% of the GDP and were sent mostly through Hawala, representing around 90% of the volume of the flows (Ratha, Mohapatra, & Plaza, 2017, p. 4).

In this case, migrant workers in a foreign country may use a hawala broker to send money to their families in Afghanistan. The broker in the foreign country will receive the funds from the migrant worker and then arrange for a corresponding payment to the family in Afghanistan through the Hawala network. This enables the rapid and efficient transfer of funds without the need for a formal financial institution or cash.

Advantages of Hawala in Afghanistan

One of the main advantages of the Hawala system in Afghanistan is its accessibility. Traditional financial institutions, such as banks, are often not widely available in rural areas, and many people need access to formal banking services. This makes Hawala a crucial alternative for many people, enabling them to send and receive funds without relying on traditional financial institutions. Another advantage of the Hawala system is its speed and efficiency. Transactions can be completed within hours, whereas traditional remittance services can take days or weeks. Finally, the Hawala system is often more cost-effective than traditional remittance services because fees are lower and more transparent.

Challenges of Hawala in Afghanistan

Despite the numerous benefits of Hawala, it has its problems. These challenges make regulations, policies, and transparency paramount in financial systems. The most obvious issue is the lack of regulatory and supervisory control, which creates spaces and vast opportunities for money laundering, illegal activities, and even terrorism. The informal and unrecorded nature of transactions also raises concerns about transparency, fairness, and accountability. Moreover, the susceptibility of Hawala operators to theft, corruption, and fraud makes it challenging to provide protection and ensure the safety of clients' funds. Hawala is often perceived as a parallel economy that undermines the stability of the officially sanctioned economy and the government's control over monetary policy.

Fei-Chien: A History and Analysis of Underground Banking in China

Fei-Chien, or 'flying money,' is an underground banking system that originated in mainland China (Office of Justice Programs, 1990). It involves moving funds between individuals or businesses using informal networks of brokers and agents. According to a report by the China Banking Regulatory Commission (CBRC),

> Fei-Chien networks are utilized to evade strict state capital controls and move illegal capital out of the national territories. These networks recruit individuals, known as 'mules,' to physically transport cash across borders or use false trade invoices (invoices that falsely document a trade transaction) to justify the movement of funds.
>
> (CBRC, 2018)

Fei-Chien, with deep roots in China's historical context, provides evidence of the adaptability of financial systems (AML Intelligence, 2022). Some sources even date it as far back as the Qing dynasty (1644–1912). One reason the Fei-Chien system was established was the need for a formal banking system in China. In the Qing dynasty, the Chinese government issued paper money as an authoritative tool and exerted a monopoly, while private banks were not permitted to issue other paper money. This created a space for the emergence of the Fei-Chien as a convenient vehicle for transferring funds between individuals or businesses.

Fei-Chien operates through a network of brokers and agents, facilitating fund transfers between individuals or businesses. The process typically involves the transfer of a promissory note or I Owe You (IOU), which is settled on a subsequent date by the transfer of an equivalent amount of money or goods (RegTech Times, 2023).

Fei-Chien, despite its association with illegal activities, has also facilitated legitimate transactions. It has been used for various purposes, including transferring funds for trade and business transactions, moving money to avoid government restrictions or taxes, and transferring dissipated funds between individuals or families.

Despite its widespread use, Fei-Chien has also been associated with criminal activity and targeted by the Chinese government in its crackdown on illegal activities. In recent years, the Chinese government has tried to formalize and regulate the Fei-Chien system, including establishing a licensing system for Fei-Chien brokers.

An example illustrating how Fei-Chien pertains to Chinese business is meant to circumvent governmental restrictions on capital movement. According to the International Monetary Fund study, "Some firms have sought to circumvent controls on cross-border capital flows and exchange rate policies" (Yao & Chen, 2017, p. 15).

In this case, businesses may employ Fei-Chien to move funds across borders or to exchange currencies at rates that differ from the official exchange rate set by the government. This allows companies to circumvent government restrictions and access capital or exchange rates that are not readily available through formal channels.

Case 5.1 *People's Republic of China v. Xu Lai & Fei Chien*: China's Underground Banking Crackdown (China and Southeast Asia, 2019)

Underground banking, or Fei-Chien, refers to an informal financial system operating outside the regulated banking sector. Amid this widespread occurrence, certain criminal activities stand out, including tax evasion, money laundering, and the financing of terrorism. The Xu Lai Fei-Chien network, a vast underground financial operation in China, is the focal point of this case study. The Chinese authorities uncovered this network in 2019 and found it operating on a massive scale, laundering billions of yuan through a network of offshore accounts and sham firms.

The Xu Lai Fei-Chien Network

The Xu Lai Fei-Chien network was not just an underground banking operation but an elaborate and sophisticated one. It meticulously planned its operations, using shell companies and offshore accounts to launder money. Led by Xu Lai, a prominent businessman and member of the Chinese Communist Party, and his associate, Fei Chien, the network operated primarily in Guangdong province and was intricately connected to other underground banking operations in Southeast Asia and the Pacific region.

Authorities pointed out that this network was discreetly engaged in a range of punishable crimes, including money laundering, tax evasion, and the sponsoring and funding of terrorism. The network's use of shell entities and offshore accounts was a deceptive tactic that made it nearly impossible for authorities to trace the illicit movement of billions of Yuan. The network's use of false invoices and receipts was another deceptive move. They would issue fraudulent invoices and receipts to make it appear that the funds were being spent on legitimate business interests, thereby creating a false image and further complicating the investigation. This situation underscores the urgent need for immediate and stricter financial regulations.

The Arrest and Trial of Xu Lai and Fei Chien

Chinese authorities arrested Xu Lai and Fei Chien, along with other network members, in 2019 as part of a broader crackdown on underground banking and money laundering. This crackdown, which involved extensive investigations and coordinated efforts among various law enforcement agencies, was a significant step in combating financial crime in China. The charges against Xu Lai and Fei Chien included illegal banking, money laundering, and tax evasion.

The media widely covered the trial of Xu Lai and Fei Chien. The Chinese government has been making strenuous efforts to eradicate certain forms of underground banking and money laundering, which have been described as a major victory. During the trial, corroborating evidence revealed the scale of the network's operations and the criminal activities in which it was deeply involved. The two suspects were found guilty and sentenced to hefty prison terms.

Impact of the Xu Lai Fei-Chien Network on the Chinese Economy

The Xu Lai Fei-Chien network was not just one of China's most noteworthy underground banking operations; its activities significantly impacted the Chinese economy. According to authorities, the network laundered billions of yuan, damaging the country's tax revenue and contributing to the growth of the shadow economy. The shadow economy, or informal or underground economy, refers to economic activities that are neither recorded in official GDP nor taxed by the government. This underscores the urgent need for stricter financial regulations and more effective enforcement measures. The substantial loss of tax revenue and the growth of the shadow economy attributable to the network's activities have profoundly affected the Chinese economy, undermining its financial health and stability.

Moreover, this network's activities have adversely discredited the Chinese financial system. Such unlawful actions were perpetrated by a top businessman who is a member of the Communist Party, causing immense embarrassment to the government and raising doubts over its regulatory and enforcement measures. The network's activities have not only led to financial losses but also tarnished the reputation of the Chinese financial system, highlighting the broader consequences of underground financial systems.

In 2017, the network was uncovered by Chinese authorities as part of investigations into its operations. Authorities have uncovered a substantial network of shell companies and offshore accounts that, over several months, facilitated the laundering and illicit transfer of funds. It encompasses illegal money transfers, falsified invoices, and other illicit methods, as established by Fei-Chien and Xu Lai at the center of this network, to facilitate the transfer of billions across borders.

The scale of such a discreetly established operation was staggering. It was described as a network associated with China's most prominent underground banking operation, with an annual turnover of illicit funds exceeding $100 million. This continuous flow of funds underscores the operation's ongoing impact. Hence, financing was provided through a range of criminal activities, including human smuggling, drugs, and organized crime.

Despite the Chinese government's determined attempts to bring the network to justice, Xu Lai and Fei-Chien remained elusive. They escaped the country shortly after the investigation began and were believed to be sheltering in Southeast Asia. However, the authorities continued to pursue them with unwavering determination, and eventually, in 2019, the two were arrested in a joint operation between the Chinese and Thai authorities. They were extradited to China and later sentenced to long prison terms for their involvement in the network.

It underscores the monumental scale of the task that the Chinese government must still undertake to reverse the flow, apprehend perpetrators, and investigate underground banks and money-laundering operations. Despite their relentless attacks on these activities and their desperate attempts to understand their intricacies, the sheer scale and complexity of the task make it seem insurmountable. However, the Chinese government remains committed to combating these activities, and the arrest and sentencing of Xu Lai and Fei-Chien sends an impeccable message to those involved that they will not be spared or tolerated.

The case of the Xu Lai Fei-Chien network underscores the pivotal role of international collaboration in combating organized crime and money laundering. The successful joint operation by Chinese and Thai authorities that led to the arrest of Xu Lai and Fei Chien serves as a model for other nations, underscoring the importance of coordinated operations and cooperation in bringing perpetrators of such activities to justice.

The implications of the Xu Lai Fei-Chien Network on the Chinese Economy are significant, as they highlight the broader impact of such criminal activities on the country's financial health and stability.

However, one of the major implications of this crackdown is heightened scrutiny of the banking sector. Following the crackdown, banks and financial institutions are expected to face increased supervisory scrutiny regarding AML compliance and operational transparency. This may lead to high costs for banks and financial institutions, as they must invest in new systems, processes, and structures to comply with the latest regulations. The increased regulatory pressure and the need for substantial investments in compliance measures may significantly impact the operations and profitability of the banking sector in China.

In addition, these efforts may help improve the overall state of the economy by curbing activities such as corruption, tax evasion, and money laundering. By tightening regulations governing these activities, the government has made it easier for businesses and individuals to compete on a level playing field, thereby promoting greater economic growth and stability. However, the untiring struggle against underground banks and money laundering could cause unintended tensions in the Chinese economy. For instance, a crackdown on virtual currencies could reduce illicit activity and, in turn, economic activity, particularly in sectors that rely heavily on anonymous transactions. This could impede the development of SMEs, which are fundamental to China's economy, and could slow economic growth.

Attempting to demonetize cash inflows from underground banking or money laundering within the Chinese context is crucial to restoring the country's financial health and disincentivizing capital flight. While this move is expected to make the banking sector much more straightforward, it may also constrain the growth space for SMEs. Therefore, the government must strike a much-needed balance by weighing the pros and cons of the disincentive. This balanced approach, which considers both the potential benefits and risks of virtual currencies, will ensure that policies effectively deter illicit activities without unduly constraining economic activity, thereby reassuring all stakeholders.

To summarize, the Xu Lai Fei-Chien network episode is a prime example of China's complex and sophisticated underground banking and money-laundering operations. Despite the Chinese government's strenuous efforts to combat covert activities, they remain a persistent challenge. In this case, the Chinese government played a crucial role in investigating and dismantling the network. However, the Xu Lai Fei-Chien network is an illustrative example of the progress made in combating these activities and the significance of international collaboration in bringing those involved to justice. This underscores the importance of global cooperation in combating illicit activities and prohibiting their shocking spread, which requires urgent attention and concerted efforts from all stakeholders. The need for such cooperation is not just a matter of law enforcement but a global imperative for the integrity of financial systems and the safety of all.

Chapter Summary

Underground financial systems, also known as black markets, are parallel economies that operate outside the reach of traditional economic systems and regulatory bodies. A need for privacy, tax evasion, and circumvention of government restrictions drives these systems. These systems can take various forms, including informal money transfer systems such as Hawala, underground banking networks such as Fei-Chien, and illegal currency exchanges such as the Peso Exchange. Hawala is a trust-based system in which money transfers are made without the movement of physical cash. Instead, the sender transfers funds to a Hawala operator, who then instructs another Hawala operator in the recipient's location to release them to the recipient. This system has been used for centuries and is especially prevalent in regions with political instability or economic sanctions, such as Afghanistan. Fei-Chien is an underground banking system operating in China that specializes in facilitating large-scale money transfers. These are money-laundering arrangements widely known for facilitating the movement of funds out of China despite strict restrictions and capital controls. A case study on underground banking and money laundering within China is the Xu Lai Fei-Chien network. It was discovered and dismantled by Chinese authorities in 2018, and then its operators were arrested and charged with money laundering and other illegal activities. The Xu Lai Fei-Chien network may serve as a warning sign, indicating the scope and limitations of underground financial systems across China. It reflects the government's ongoing efforts to eradicate such activities. Ultimately, underground financial systems have had considerable influence on the global economy because they provide services to individuals seeking privacy and tax evasion, and to governments seeking to circumvent restrictions. However, such systems also harbored illegal activities, sometimes perverting a country's financial stability and security.

End of Chapter: Discussion Questions

1. What significant role do underground financial systems play in shaping the global economy?
2. How do the intricate workings of underground financial systems set them apart from the more transparent and regulated formal financial systems?
3. What role do Hawala networks play in the remittance sector in Afghanistan?
4. What is Fei-Chien, and how does it differ from other underground financial systems?
5. What is the Xu Lai Fei-Chien network, and how does its dismantling serve as a cautionary tale about the potential risks and consequences of underground financial systems?
6. How do Hawala networks affect remittance flows in regions like Afghanistan?
7. What makes the Hawala system popular in regions with political instability or economic sanctions?
8. What are the potential risks associated with underground financial systems?
9. What efforts are governments making to crack down on underground financial systems?
10. What is the future of underground financial systems in the global economy?

Bibliography

AML Intelligence. (2022, October 25). Inside China's underground banking network and assessing exposure to money laundering risk. https://www.amlintelligence.com

Bilefsky, D. (2014, October 2). Feds shut down Silk Road online black market. *The New York Times*. https://www.nytimes.com/2014/10/03/world/feds-shut-down-silk-road-online-black-market.html

BlueDollar.net. (2025, September 5). Blue dollar rates: Informal, formal, and bank rates. https://bluedollar.net/

BoyceWire. (2023, May 31). Black market: Definition, effects & examples. https://boycewire.com/black-market

Brooke Beyond. (2024, January 15). Argentina's blue dollar: Buying pesos on the black market. https://brookebeyond.com/argentinas-blue-dollar

Corporate Finance Institute. (2023). Hawala - What it is, history, and why it is preferred. https://corporatefinanceinstitute.com/resources/wealth-management/hawala/

El Qorchi, M. (2002). Hawala: How does this informal fund transfer system work, and should it be regulated? *IMF Finance & Development*, 39(4), 31–33. https://www.imf.org/external/pubs/ft/fandd/2002/12/qorchi.htm

El Qorchi, M., Maimbo, S. M., & Wilson, J. F. (2003). Informal funds transfer systems: An analysis of the informal hawala system (IMF Occasional Paper No. 222). International Monetary Fund. https://www.imf.org/external/pubs/nft/op/222/

Financial Action Task Force. (2013). The role of hawala and other similar service providers in money laundering and terrorist financing. https://www.fatf-gafi.org/en/publications/Methodsandtrends/Role-hawalas-in-ml-tf.html

Financial Crimes Enforcement Network (FinCEN). (2015). BSA Reporting Initiates Case Involving Major Black Market Peso Exchange Scheme. Retrieved from fincen.gov.

Financial Action Task Force. (2019). Anti-money laundering and counter-terrorist financing measures: People's Republic of China mutual evaluation report. FATF. https://www.fatf-gafi.org/content/dam/fatf-gafi/mer/MER-China-2019.pdf

FinCEN.gov. (2026). FinCEN.Gov. https://www.fincen.gov/illicit-wire-activity-destined-sanctioned-country

Frank, R., & Mikhaylov, A. (2020). Beyond the 'Silk Road': Assessing illicit drug marketplaces on the public web. In R. Frank (Ed.), *Open-source intelligence and cybercrime* (pp. 89–111). Springer. https://link.springer.com/chapter/10.1007/978-3-030-41251-7_4

García-Figal, A., Lage-Castellanos, A., Amaro, D. A., & Mulet, R. (2024). On the efficiency of the informal currency markets: The case of the Cuban peso. *Computational Economics*, 65, 2317–2350. https://link.springer.com/article/10.1007/s10614-024-10638-w

Hsu, S. (2014, November 22). China's underground banks busted. *The Diplomat*. https://thediplomat.com/2014/11/chinas-underground-banks-busted/

Invezz. (2024, May 31). What is the black market? Definition & examples. https://invezz.com/definitions/black-market/

KYC Hub. (2023). Hawala money: A complete guide to Hawala money laundering. https://www.kychub.com/blog/hawala-money-laundering/

McLaren, J. (1996). Corruption, black markets, and the fiscal problem in LDCs: Some recent findings. *Eastern Economic Journal*, 22(4), 491–502. https://www.jstor.org/stable/40325746

Minnaar, A. (2017). Online 'underground' marketplaces for illicit drugs: The prototype case of the dark web website' Silk Road'. *Acta Criminologica: Southern African Journal of Criminology*, 30(1), Special Edition, 23–47. https://www.researchgate.net/publication/333646270

Moin, B. (2024). Taming the untamable: Rethinking, regulating, and revamping Hawala. *Journal of Academics Stand against Poverty*, 5, 20–43. https://journalasap.org/index.php/asap/article/download/40/42

Office of Justice Programs. (1990). Fei-Chien, or flying money: A study of Chinese underground banking. *NCJRS Virtual Library*. https://www.ojp.gov/ncjrs/virtual-library/abstracts/fei-chien-or-flying-money-study-chinese-underground-banking

Passas, N. (2003). Hawala and other informal value-transfer systems: How should they be regulated? *Risk Management*, 5(2), 49–59. https://www.academia.edu/108183439/Hawala_and_Other_Informal_Value_Transfer_Systems_How_to_Regulate_Them

Ratha, D., Mohapatra, S., & Plaza, S. (2017). *Migration and remittances: Recent developments and outlook*. World Bank Group.

RegTech Times. (2023, August 14). Exclusive guide to Chinese underground banking. https://regtechtimes.com/exclusive-guide-to-chinese-underground-banking

Reuters. (2009, August 10). China breaks up a large underground bank ring. China Digital Times. https://chinadigitaltimes.net/2009/08/china-breaks-up-large-underground-bank-ring/

Sanchez, C., Schwaerzler, C., Parravicini, S., Aouad, W., & Onal, I. (2023). Unveiling the shadow economy. *Boston Consulting Group*. https://www.bcg.com/publications/2023/unveiling-the-shadow-economy

Team, C. (2020, December 10). Hawala. Corporate Finance Institute. https://corporatefinanceinstitute.com/resources/wealth-management/hawala/

The Hawala System: A risky alternative to traditional banking. (2023, March 10). ACAMS Today. https://www.acamstoday.org/the-hawala-system-a-risky-alternative-to-traditional-banking/

United States Department of the Treasury Financial Crimes Enforcement Network Informal Value Transfer Systems. (n.d.). https://www.fincen.gov/system/files/advisory/advis33.pdf

U.S. Department of Justice. (2015). Two men were charged with conspiring to provide material support to Islamic state. Retrieved from https://www.justice.gov/usao-ma/pr/two-men-charged-conspiracy-provide-material-support-islamic-state

U.S. Department of Justice. (2016, March 21). Turkish national arrested for conspiring to evade U.S. sanctions against Iran, money laundering, and bank fraud [Press release]. Office of Public Affairs. Retrieved from https://www.justice.gov/opa/pr/turkish-national-arrested-conspiring-evade-us-sanctions-against-iran-money-laundering-and

U.S. Department of Justice. (2020, May 18). Founder and CEO of Iranian financial services firm extradited on money laundering, wire fraud, and conspiracy charges [Press release]. Office of Public Affairs. Retrieved from https://www.justice.gov/archives/opa/pr/founder-and-ceo-iranian-financial-services-firm-extradited-money-laundering-wire-fraud-and

U.S. Department of State. (2015). International Narcotics control strategy report Volume II: Money laundering and financial crimes – Colombia. *Bureau of International Narcotics and Law Enforcement Affairs*. Retrieved from state.gov.

U.S. Department of State. (2025, June 6). Sanctioning Iran's "Shadow Banking" Network of money launderers and illicit oil traders. https://www.state.gov/releases/office-of-the-spokesperson/2025/06/sanctioning-irans-shadow-banking-network-of-money-launderers-and-illicit-oil-traders.

U.S. Department of the Treasury. (2025, June 6). Treasury sanctions Iranian network laundering billions for the Regime through a shadow-banking scheme. https://home.treasury.gov/news/press-releases/sb0159.

Wikipedia contributors. (2023). Black market. Wikipedia. https://en.wikipedia.org/wiki/Black_market

Wikipedia contributors. (2023). Hawala. Wikipedia. https://en.wikipedia.org/wiki/Hawala

Wilson, J. F. (2005). CHAPTER 30 Hawala and other informal payment systems: An economic perspective. IMF eLibrary. https://doi.org/10.5089/9781589063341.072.ch030. Retrieved from https://www.elibrary.imf.org/display/book/9781589063341/ch030.xml?rskey=QwQu2m&result=1

Wright, L. (2023, May 31). Timeline of China's deleveraging campaign. *Center for Strategic and International Studies*. https://features.csis.org/timeline-of-chinas-deleveraging-campaign/

Xinhua. (2009, March 11). Money laundering rampant with more underground banks. China.org.cn. http://www.china.org.cn/english/China/193395.html

Yao, Y., & Chen, Y. (2017). *Capital flow management in China: Experience and challenges*. International Monetary Fund.

Additional Learning Resources

Books

1 Rogue Money and the Underground Economy. An Encyclopedia of Alternative and Cryptocurrencies. (2020). John C. Edmunds (Anthology Editor). Bloomsbury Publishing
https://www.bloomsbury.com/us/rogue-money-and-the-underground-economy-9781440864551/.
This book examines the impact of rogue money systems on global financial stability and their role in facilitating illicit financial activities.

2 The shadow economy: An international survey. (2013). Friedrich Schneider und Dominik H. Enste. Cambridge University Press, UK.
This volume provides a comprehensive survey of the shadow economy and underground financial systems worldwide.

Films

3 "The Laundromat" (2019, Director: Steven Soderbergh).
This film explores the Panama Papers scandal, exposing how offshore financial systems are exploited by the wealthy and powerful.

4 "The Godfather" (1972, Director: Francis Ford Coppola).
A classic crime film that showcases the involvement of underground financial systems in organized crime and money laundering.)

Documentaries

5 “Dirty Money” (2018–present).
A documentary series on Netflix that delves into various financial crimes, including money laundering and the use of underground systems.

6 “The Bitcoin Gospel” VPRO documentary. (2015). https://tinyurl.com/bitgospel
This documentary examines the role of cryptocurrencies, such as Bitcoin, in facilitating illicit financial transactions and their potential impact on the global economy.

Articles

7 “Shadow banking: Reasons of emergence and directions of development.” Vladimir Aleksandrovich Slepov, et al. (2019) International Journal of Civil Engineering and Technology 10.2: 1747–1754.
This article provides an insightful study on the emergence and development of shadow banking, the reasons behind its rise, and offers valuable directions for its future trajectory.

8 The blood bankers: Tales from the global underground economy. James S. Henry. (2014). Basic Books.
This is a thought-provoking book; it offers a compelling glimpse into the clandestine realm of the global underground economy, providing captivating stories that illuminate its inner workings.

YouTube Stuff

9 “Hawala Money Transfer Explained” (2021, kingacademy.com). https://rb.gy/auhz5
This educational video provides a concise explanation of the Hawala system and its operation as an alternative remittance system.

10 “Bitcoin: Beyond the Bubble” (2018, 100thMonkeyChannel). https://tinyurl.com/Beyondbub
A documentary-style video that examines the rise of Bitcoin and its potential impact on the traditional financial system and underground economies.

6 Exploring the World of Virtual Currency

Bitcoin and Its Role in Illicit Activities

Introduction: The Dual Promise of Virtual Currency

In traditional finance, cryptocurrencies such as Bitcoin are often framed as having enormous potential alongside substantial risks. Christine Lagarde, former Managing Director of the International Monetary Fund (IMF), aptly captured this by stating that such assets "can change the very nature of how we carry out financial transactions [by offering] a decentralized and highly secure way of moving value that does not require relying on traditional intermediaries." She also, however, cautioned that "their volatility and regulatory challenges require careful consideration" (Lagarde, 2018). The contradiction at the center between the two extremes of the efficient and inclusive financial paradigm and the perils of instability and criminal misuse constitute the core of their complex and ambivalent role. This chapter argues that cryptocurrencies have features that are both their greatest strengths and the reason they are a classic dual-use technology. To understand the regulation of virtual currency and its criminal misuse. It is necessary to know that one should examine the legalization of harm and the industry's setbacks. One must pay attention to the history of the Silk Road and the regulatory landscape changes that have resulted from such scenarios.

Core Mechanism: Anonymity, Decentralization, and Illicit Finance

The encryption and decryption of monetary transactions, along with the pseudonymous wallets and international liquidity, which are the main architectural strengths of cryptocurrencies, make them especially susceptible to illicit activities. The rise and fall of the Silk Road. It was the first central darknet marketplace and demonstrated this dramatically and catastrophically. Between 2011 and 2013, Silk Road was a massive online marketplace for all types of illegal drugs, weapons, and other contraband items. All payments and associated transactions were made exclusively in Bitcoin. Ross Ulbricht, the site's creator, was inspired by libertarian principles to establish a platform "beyond government control" (U.S. Attorney's Office, 2015). This is where people could exchange goods and services freely. The case provided conclusive evidence that large-scale criminal organizations could exploit the characteristics of virtual currency. It also made clear one of the main regulatory problems: how to inhibit illegal transactions while allowing the technology to innovate. The following sections of this chapter examine the regulatory changes resulting from such incidents.

The closure of Silk Road and Ulbricht's life sentence following convictions for money laundering, computer hacking, and conspiracy to traffic narcotics marked a watershed (U.S. Attorney's Office, 2015). The case provided definitive proof of concept that large-scale criminal enterprises could weaponize virtual currency features. It crystallized the primary regulatory dilemma: how to suppress illicit activity without stifling the underlying technological innovation. The subsequent sections of this chapter analyze the regulatory evolution prompted by such exploits.

DOI: 10.4324/9781003477631-7

The Regulatory Frontier: From Chaos to Clarity

Closing down the Silk Road was a mere tactical victory, as it did not resolve the problem of a strategic regulatory void. Indeed, the virtual currency ecosystem continues to develop, posing new challenges: on the one hand, the extreme volatility of assets such as Bitcoin, which are not backed by any central authority. On the other hand, some stablecoins claim, however, do not always—to provide stability. Finally, increasingly complex decentralized finance (DeFi) protocols have emerged. The regulatory efforts, which have evolved from skepticism to the establishment of structured frameworks, aim to bring this new domain under control by addressing three critical issues: payment stability, market integrity, and legal accountability.

The first major piece of legislation was the Guiding and Establishing National Innovation for U.S. Stablecoins (GENIUS) Act of 2025. The main point of this Act was to address the payment system risks. This was brought to light by the collapse of algorithmic stablecoins such as TerraUSD. This act directly targeted the payment system risks highlighted by the collapse of algorithmic stablecoins like TerraUSD. By mandating 100% reserve backing of any dollar-pegged stablecoin with high-quality liquid assets, the GENIUS Act sought to transform stablecoins from speculative instruments into reliable digital cash for payments and remittances (Congressional Research Service, 2025). Its provisions on real-time attestations and clear consumer redemption rights were designed to prevent bank runs and to protect users, thereby directly addressing the volatility and fraud that plagued the early market.

However, defining what constituted a "stablecoin" required a broader classification of the entire digital asset ecosystem. This was the purpose of the complementary Digital Asset Market Clarity (CLARITY) Act of 2025. The CLARITY Act resolved the debilitating jurisdictional conflict between the SEC and CFTC by creating a functional taxonomy. It distinguished among digital commodities (e.g., Bitcoin, regulated by the CFTC), investment contract assets (treated as securities under the SEC), and the newly defined category of permitted payment stablecoins under the GENIUS Act (U.S. House Financial Services Committee, 2025). This tripartite framework was designed to end "regulation by enforcement" and provide the legal certainty necessary for institutional adoption, channeling innovation into regulated pathways.

Legislation alone cannot define a market. Enforcement is crucial to determine its limits. The Avraham Eisenberg and MNGO Markets exploit case of 2023 is a major milestone, elucidating that new DeFi methods cannot serve as a loophole to provide legal immunity. Eisenberg carried out a complex "oracle manipulation" attack, creating a false collateral value on the MNGO Markets protocol to borrow and later drain $110 million. He argued that he was permitted to do so because the protocol's open-source code constituted his permission. However, the court rejected this argument.

Commodity Markets Manipulation: The CFTC charged him with the allegation (CFTC, 2023), and the SEC also initiated a parallel action, alleging that MNGO tokens were unregistered (SEC, 2023). This multi-agency move made it clear as a bright day: the fundamental laws of traditional finance, i.e., no deception and no market manipulation, remain applicable to the digital assets sector. The Eisenberg case operationalized the principles behind the CLARITY Act. It demonstrated that code is not law and that statutory law governs code (Table 6.1).

This development, from a crackdown on a massive criminal organization (Silk Road) to the establishment of legal frameworks (GENIUS, CLARITY) to implementation/technical intervention (MNGO Markets), is indicative of a regulatory approach that is becoming more sophisticated. The emphasis is now more on designing the structures of the marketplace that can take care of the risks Lagarde identified, while still making room for the technological innovations she commended, rather than on simply prosecuting criminals.

Table 6.1 The Evolving U.S. Regulatory Framework for Digital Assets

Regulatory Challenge	*Legislative/Policy Response*	*Key Mechanism*	*Enforcement Precedent*
Payment/stability risk	GENIUS Act (2025)	100% reserve requirement for stablecoins; consumer protections.	Implied response to pre-Act collapses (e.g., TerraUSD).
Market structure/classification	CLARITY Act (2025)	Functional taxonomy dividing assets between CFTC and SEC jurisdiction.	Provides a framework for cases such as SEC v. Ripple concerning the status of securities.
On-chain fraud & manipulation	Application of existing commodities & securities laws.	CFTC & SEC parallel enforcement actions based on economic reality.	CFTC/SEC v. Eisenberg (MNGO Markets, 2023).

Case 6.1 The Silk Road and Ross Ulbricht

This case is a classic example of a darknet marketplace, quite literally indicating how cryptographic technology (such as Bitcoin and the TOR network) can form the basis of a pseudo-anonymous, worldwide platform for drug and weapons trafficking. Its operational model has become a pattern for other darknet markets and has posed a profound challenge to both traditional financial systems and law enforcement.

Case Snapshot

Topic of Discussion: The Silk Road was a darknet market. Its creator/operator was Ross Ulbricht.

Operating Timeline: The period encompasses February 2011–October 2013.

Core Idea: Essentially, a web marketplace for the sale of illegal drugs and other criminal traffic. Bitcoin is invariably used as a mode of payment.

Outcome: Ulbricht's case ended with a guilty verdict on counts including conspiracy to commit drug trafficking and money laundering, resulting in a life sentence without parole after U.S. federal law enforcement decommissioned the website and ceased operations (United States Department of Justice, 2015).

Core Points

Ross Ulbricht was a university student with extremely liberal beliefs. He was the founder, operator, and primary motivator of the Silk Road. His identity was denoted as "Dread Pirate Roberts." Ulbricht explained that he aimed to create a libertarian free market devoid of government regulation (Ulbricht, 2013, cited by Barratt, 2012). It was a secret site on the TOR network that offered complete anonymity to its users. The trading was conducted through an escrow service. It was Bitcoin as the sole currency; more than 1.5 million transactions, totaling over 9.5 million Bitcoins (approximately $1.2 billion at the time of seizure) (FBI, 2013).

Identification Method

The FBI assumed the lead in the inquiry. Other agencies have provided support. One significant discovery was that the Silk Road server was located due to a configuration error. Thus, it exposed the IP address. Additionally, the detectives conducted standard detective work, for example, by acting as buyers and sellers. They meticulously analyzed the Bitcoin public blockchain to trace the movement of funds. The figure associated with the online account was identified through a correlation between his online conduct and his offline actions. For instance, authorities intercepted the delivery of fraudulent identity documents to him, and, through his early forum posts about the site, they could link it to him (*U.S. v. Ulbricht*, 2014). His capture occurred at a public library in San Francisco, and at that time, he was logged in as an administrator to the site's backend.

Trade-Based Money Laundering Analysis

The Silk Road introduced a form of digital trade-based money laundering (TBML). Instead of misrepresenting the price, quantity, or quality of physical goods, it was used to launder money through a digital drug trade. Method: Bitcoin was the core medium. Buyers would first purchase Bitcoin on exchanges. Thereafter, transfer it to Silk Road wallets and use it to buy illicit goods. Vendors would get Bitcoin as a payment that they could "cash out" through various mixing services or exchanges. In this way, they would be able to integrate their illicit earnings into the legitimate financial system effectively. Value Transfer & Layering: The operation itself was the primary mechanism of layering. The process of converting fiat money into Bitcoin, conducting a semi-anonymous transaction over the TOR network, and then converting the money back to fiat currency constituted a complex digital layering process intended to obscure the origin of the funds (FATF, 2014).

Impact: This case demonstrated how digital currencies can be misused to facilitate TBML globally, posing a challenge for regulators in developing new frameworks to supervise decentralized, non-fiat financial flows.

Insight: The Use of Blockchain-based Digital Currencies as an Alternative Remittance System

Remittances, the transfer of money by foreign workers to their home countries, offer immense potential for income for many families and communities worldwide. The World Bank reported that global remittances reached $689 billion in 2019, with developing nations receiving the lion's share of these flows. However, conventional remittance systems can be relatively costly, slow, and unreliable. In recent years, new technologies and alternative remittance systems have emerged to tackle these challenges. One such alternative is to use blockchain-based digital currencies for remittances.

What Is a Blockchain-Based Digital Currency?

A blockchain is a digital ledger hosted on several machines and distributed among them. This ledger books transactions across a network of computers and, as a result, systems. All transactions are grouped into blocks, linked chronologically in a chain, forming a 'blockchain' or 'chain.' Each block contains a record of multiple transactions, and once a block is appended to the blockchain, the information it contains becomes immutable, permanent, and secure.

The currency is typically in digital form. It relies entirely on blockchain technology and a digital currency (virtual currency). The first decentralized virtual currency, Bitcoin, was introduced in 2009. Since then, it has paved the way for many other cryptocurrencies (Nakamoto, 2008). Digital currencies on the blockchain facilitate direct peer-to-peer transactions, eliminating the necessity for intermediaries such as banks (Investopedia, 2025).

How Does a Blockchain-Based Digital Currency Remittance System Work?

Using blockchain technology, you can establish a secure and transparent remittance process in which digital currency is sent and received across borders without intermediaries. As the transaction's sender, you make this possible by moving the digital currency to the recipient's wallet address. Once the transaction is validated, the recipient can withdraw the funds directly, without intermediaries, as soon as it is included in the network.

An example of the potential of remittance capability is a blockchain-based system that uses Bitcoin for international remittances. To begin with, the sender must purchase Bitcoin on a virtual currency exchange and then transfer it to the recipient's wallet. The recipient could then access and sell the funds for their local currency.

Advantages of Blockchain-Based Digital Currency Remittance Systems

Lower costs: Remittance systems based on blockchain digital currencies are likely to impose lower transaction fees than conventional systems. To elaborate, traditional money transfer companies can charge up to 10% or more for overseas transactions.

Experience the efficiency: A typical blockchain-based digital currency transaction can be processed in a few minutes. It is a noticeable difference from traditional bank transfers, which can take days or sometimes weeks. Moreover, this is a significant relief, as it guarantees that your transactions are completed swiftly and conveniently.

Ensuring inclusivity: Blockchain-powered digital remittances can be a promising solution for increasing access to cost-effective, inclusive financial services among underbanked and unbanked communities. The potential of financial inclusivity ensures that no one is left behind in the digital economy.

Increased transparency: Blockchain provides a foundation for transparency by recording all transactions on a publicly accessible ledger. For instance, Ripple is utilized as a new and secure remittance system.

Ripple is a blockchain-based digital currency and a real-time gross settlement system that aims to provide fast and low-cost international money transfers. Ripple's network, known as RippleNet, connects banks, payment providers, and digital asset exchanges to facilitate near-instant cross-border transactions.

One apparent example of Ripple's use as a remittance system is its partnership with Santander. Santander's One Pay FX utilizes RippleNet to provide near-instant, low-cost international money transfers for customers in the UK, Spain, Brazil, and Poland. This allows customers to make international transfers in minutes, with end-to-end transparency on fees and exchange rates.

Alternative remittance systems have a key role in the global economy. It provides financial services to underserved or unbanked populations. The unconventional system enables users to transfer money across borders quickly, efficiently, and securely. The swift movement of funds occurs without solely relying on established banking and financial institutions. These techniques have been routinely employed for decades, but technological advances have enabled the development of modern, innovative remittance methods, such as blockchain-based digital currencies. Despite the numerous benefits of alternative remittance methods, there are serious reservations about their ability to support money laundering and other illegal financial crimes. Regulators must strike a delicate balance between promoting innovation and protecting against criminal activity. Developing robust AML/CFT legislation, along with effective enforcement, will ensure that alternative remittance mechanisms can be employed safely and securely.

It is also worth mentioning that alternative remittances are being adopted by many countries, organizations, and individuals worldwide. Numerous examples of the use of digital currencies, mobile money, and AI-based remittance services exist. The emergence of contemporary technologies and innovations will continue to adapt the appearance of remittances and offer exciting new opportunities for those looking to move money across borders. In the future, it is crucial to maintain a constant, vigilant oversight of the ever-evolving alternative remittance system and its various applications, so that the key takeaways from this case study can be effectively harnessed.

Insight: The GENIUS Act and Stablecoins: Economic Implications and Regulatory Framework

The Officially recognized Guiding and Establishing National Innovation for U.S. Stablecoins (GENIUS) Act, was enacted in July 2025 (Congressional Research Service, 2025). The legislation represents a milestone in U.S. financial regulation. The act establishes a strengthened federal regulatory framework for stablecoins. It seeks to promote innovation while safeguarding consumers and maintaining macroeconomic stability. This article examines the act's provisions and their potential economic implications.

Key Provisions and Economic Implications

1. Reserve Requirements and Support for the Dollar as the Dominant Reserve Currency: The GENIUS Act prescribes 100% reserve backing for stablecoins using liquid assets, either U.S. dollars or short-term treasuries. This requirement will place significant upward pressure on U.S. Treasury instruments, potentially reducing long-term interest rates and strengthening the dollar's status as a global reserve currency. Some observers anticipate that the supply of stablecoins could grow to between $500 billion and $3.7 trillion by 2030, of which 90% would be denominated in U.S. dollars.
2. Consumer Protection and Market Stability: The act prioritizes consumer claims in the case of insolvency for stablecoin backed by reserves and prohibits misleading claims of federal insurance. It requires monthly public disclosures of reserve compositions, thereby increasing transparency and reducing the risk of runs (as seen with certain algorithm-based stablecoins such as TerraLUNA).
3. Anti-money Laundering (AML) Enforcement: The Bank Secrecy Act applies to stablecoin issuers, which fundamentally requires issuers to have robust AML and sanctions compliance programs. The act fits within a broader strategy to block certain illicit financial activities while still allowing the inclusion of digital assets in the regulated financial system.

Contrast with CBDCs and Tokenized Deposits

The United States has explicitly opposed central bank digital currencies (CBDCs) due to concerns about privacy, bank disintermediation, and operational risks. Instead, the GENIUS Act encourages the use of stablecoins in the private sector and evaluates tokenized deposits—digital representations of commercial bank liabilities—as an alternative. The Agorá and Regulated Settlement Network (RSN) projects are piloting tokenized deposits for cross-border payments, which could provide added efficiency without destabilizing the banking system (Bank for International Settlements, 2024; SIFMA, 2024).

In closing, the GENIUS Act positions the United States to drive innovation in digital assets while mitigating systemic risks. Its effectiveness will largely depend on whether it can maintain adequate regulatory safeguards while enabling growth in the digital economy.

Notes:

- GENIUS Act Provisions: Details on reserve requirements, consumer protections, and AML mandates are derived from the White House Fact Sheet (2025).
- Economic Impact: Data on stablecoin growth and Treasury demand projections are sourced from Visa Corporate's analysis (2025).
- CBDC Contrast: The U.S. opposition to CBDCs is documented in State Street's regulatory preview and the Atlantic Council's CBDC Tracker (2025).
- Tokenized Deposits: Examples of projects like Agorá and RSN are from Visa Corporate (2025).

Insight: Regulating Digital Assets—the CLARITY Act and Future Implications

The Digital Asset Market Clarity (CLARITY) Act was introduced in 2025 to resolve a long-standing jurisdictional issue between the Securities and Exchange Commission (SEC) and the Commodity Futures Trading Commission (CFTC) by defining digital assets into two separate, distinct classes. This case study analyzes its framework and potential market impacts (U.S. House Financial Services Committee, 2025).

Classification and Regulatory Clarity

1 Asset Categorization: The CLARITY Act divides digital assets into three categories:

   - Digital Commodities: Assets such as Bitcoin derive value from the functional characteristics of blockchains.
   - Investment Contract Assets, including tokens sold for capital raising purposes (e.g., initial coin offerings), are temporarily classified as, or treated as, securities.
   - Permitted Payment Stablecoins: Regulated under the GENIUS Act.

2 Jurisdictional Clarity: The CFTC gains exclusive authority over digital commodities markets, while the SEC oversees investment contract assets. This aims to end "regulation by enforcement" and provide legal certainty for innovators.

3 Intermediary Regulation: The legislation requires simplified registration for crypto exchanges and brokers, allowing for their operation under coordinated regulatory systems from the SEC and CFTC. The legislation also advances technological neutrality in record-keeping and allows blockchain-based records.

Broader Regulatory Initiatives

The CLARITY Act complements other federal efforts.

- Repeal of SAB 121: The SEC's elimination of this accounting bulletin enables traditional banks to custody digital assets without onerous capital requirements, encouraging institutional participation.
- Project Crypto: A program designed by the SEC to refresh the regulation of custody of crypto assets, trading, and classification of crypto assets to facilitate the "onshoring" of digital asset businesses.

Challenges and Future Implications

The enactment of the CLARITY Act is likely to determine whether the United States remains competitive with other jurisdictions, such as the EU. The EU is already one step ahead in the race, as it passed the Markets in Crypto-Assets (MiCA) regulation in 2023.

In short, the CLARITY Act is a significant step toward creating a more coherent and consistent regulatory framework for new digital assets. By defining the rights of different jurisdictions and thereby providing a fundamental framework within its innovation agenda, the act is likely to have a significant impact on the future of digital finance in the United States.

Notes

- CLARITY Act Framework: Classification details and jurisdictional rules are from Arnold & Porter's legal advisory (2025).
- Regulatory Initiatives: The repeal of SAB 121 and Project Crypto are covered in DLA Piper's Blockchain News and State Street's regulatory preview.
- Banking Opposition: Concerns from banking associations are reported in DLA Piper (2025).
- Global Context: Comparisons with MiCA are drawn from State Street (2025) and Visa Corporate (2025).

The MNGO Markets Case: How a $110M DeFi Exploit Went Criminal (USA, 2023).

Avraham Eisenberg thought he was smarter than the system. Eisenberg exploited MNGO Markets, a decentralized exchange (DEX) on the Solana blockchain. He stole $110 million in October 2022 by manipulating the platform's price oracle. This case marks a watershed moment for DeFi law, undermining the notion that "code is law" and suggesting that manipulative conduct in the digital asset space will also be subject to traditional financial regulations, with the potential for criminal liability.

How the Exploit Worked

MNGO Markets is a DeFi protocol that facilitates margin trading and lending via smart contracts and algorithmic price oracles. Eisenberg, a self-described "applied game theorist," exploited vulnerabilities in MNGO's oracle system by artificially inflating the price of its native token, MNGO (by 3,700%), by initiating a huge leveraged trade in a thin market. He was borrowing far more than the protocol would permit due to the artificial price spike detected by the oracle. He drained liquidity and then attempted to justify his theft by proposing a governance vote to return some funds, contingent on users agreeing not to pursue any legal action.

Mechanism of Exploit

Eisenberg traded MNGO tokens on exchanges while using multiple accounts, creating data for MNGO's price oracle. In 30 minutes, MNGO's price surged 13 times. The inflated value was then used as collateral to withdraw $110 million in USDC, SOL, and other assets. Eisenberg suggested returning $67 million if MNGO's DAO agreed not to initiate any legal action against him—a dubious usage of decentralized governance.

Litigation and Regulatory Response

The CFTC charged Eisenberg with commodities fraud and market manipulation under the Commodity Exchange Act, marking its first enforcement action related to oracle manipulation on a

Table 6.2 Comparative Regulatory Analysis

Jurisdiction	*DeFi Legal Framework*	*Oracle Manipulation Treated as*	*Governance Token Status*
United States	Commodity Exchange Act, SEC rules	Commodities fraud, securities fraud	Potentially securities (SEC)
European Union	MiCA (Markets in Crypto-Assets)	Market abuse under financial law	Subject to classification tests
Singapore	Payment Services Act	AML and fraud under the digital payment law	Case-by-case basis

decentralized platform (CFTC, 2023). Simultaneously, the SEC filed a parallel civil complaint, alleging that the MNGO tokens were unregistered securities and that Eisenberg engaged in securities fraud (SEC, 2023). Federal prosecutors did not adopt the defense that smart contract logic created a defense to criminal liability. Eisenberg was arrested in Puerto Rico and charged with wire fraud and market manipulation (Cointelegraph, 2025).

Why This Case Matters

The DOJ did not accept the defense of "it is just smart contract logic." Eisenberg was charged with commodities fraud and market manipulation under the Commodity Exchange Act. To make matters worse, the SEC intervened and declared the MNGO tokens to be unregistered securities. Above all, courts ruled that it is a criminal act to use a technical loophole to commit fraud, regardless of what the code permits (Table 6.2).

Main Takeaways

- DeFi is not beyond the legal constraints of traditional finance. If you engage in an illegal activity in conventional finance, it is unlawful on-chain.
- Oracles are weak points. Bad price feeds can be easily manipulated—and invite regulatory scrutiny.
- Governance tokens are risky. The SEC's involvement indicates that many of them may be classified as securities.

Case 6.2 Reconciling GDPR and Blockchain: The German-Swiss Supply Chain Dispute of 2023

Background

A multinational supply chain involving parties from Germany and Switzerland had a smart contract in place to automate payments to each member contingent upon verification of the shipment of goods. The terms of the contract were executed on a blockchain, leveraging its transparency and immutability. A dispute arose when a compliance issue was identified under the European Union's General Data Protection Regulation (GDPR) concerning personal data stored on the distributed ledger (BeyondOTC, 2025).

Legal Issues

The core challenge was a direct conflict between foundational principles of blockchain technology and EU law. The immutability of blockchain (the capacity to ensure that data is written and not rewritten) directly violates the GDPR's "right to be forgotten" (Article 17), which allows individuals to have their personal data erased under certain circumstances (BeyondOTC, 2025; Mik, 2017). This created a serious jurisdictional and regulatory impasse between the parties, as the Germans were under significant regulatory scrutiny with the GDPR. At the same time, the Swiss organization was exempt from such constraints.

Resolution Process

Initial attempts to resolve the dispute in traditional German courts stalled due to the novel nature of the conflict and jurisdictional complexities. The German court reportedly questioned the validity of the smart contract due to concerns about GDPR compliance (BeyondOTC, 2025). Accordingly, the parties decided to utilize specialized blockchain arbitration. The arbitration panel comprised both legal scholars and blockchain technologists, utilizing a hybrid legal-technical solution. Initially, they implemented appropriate privacy-enhancing technologies, specifically zero-knowledge proofs, to validate transactions without disclosing sensitive personal data, while enabling off-chain data storage solutions (BeyondOTC, 2025).

Outcome and Significance

The arbitration ruling necessitated modifications to the smart contract's implementation to ensure GDPR compliance while preserving the blockchain's transactional integrity. The panel established that "blockchain technology can be adapted to meet regulatory requirements through appropriate technical implementations without compromising the core benefits of smart contracts" (BeyondOTC, 2025). This case is of paramount significance because it reveals that the conflict between the immutability of blockchain execution and the flexibility of the law is potentially resolvable. Moreover, it elucidates the benefits of specialized arbitration that combines legal and technical expertise. It also offers a practical model for reconciling tech innovation with regulatory limitations, such as the GDPR.

Chapter Summary

Virtual currency, a digital asset transforming finance, has attracted extensive attention. Cryptocurrencies such as Bitcoin and Ethereum have become a standard part of commercial parlance. The currencies have dominated the scene with trailblazing headlines. Hence, it is crucial to understand how they function and their effects on the viability of financial markets. These currencies are widely traded on decentralized platforms, with Bitcoin being the most widely used and recognized digital asset. Like traditional money, their value shifts with supply and demand. However, virtual currency is undeniably not without its underlying problems. Its anonymity and lack of oversight make it a killing combination for illegal activities. In 2013, the U.S. Department of Justice identified virtual currency as a potential threat to global financial stability and security. There are certainly some clear benefits. Transactions are faster, cheaper, and offer more privacy. Users can benefit by completely circumventing traditional banking systems. However, the market is inherently volatile, and hacking is a persistent threat, rendering these assets hazardous investments. Major trading hubs are spread across Asia and North America. However, their exact locations are mutable, and determining them precisely is challenging given the decentralized and unregulated nature of the virtual currency.

End of Chapter: Discussion Questions

1. What is a virtual currency, and how does it differ from traditional currency?
2. What has Bitcoin been used for in illicit activities such as money laundering and drug trafficking?
3. How is virtual currency traded, and how has this evolved?
4. What are the benefits and drawbacks of using virtual currencies for trade and commerce?
5. How are virtual currencies regulated, if at all, and what are the implications of this lack of regulation?
6. What impact has the growth of virtual currencies had on traditional financial markets, such as stocks and commodities?
7. How are governments and law enforcement agencies responding to the rise of virtual currencies and their use in illegal activities?
8. How do virtual currencies, such as Bitcoin, compare with traditional currencies in terms of security and stability?
9. How does the use of virtual currencies impact financial markets on a global scale?
10. What is the future of virtual currencies, and what is their impact on financial markets?

References

Arnold & Porter. (2025). Clarifying the CLARITY Act: What to know about the House crypto market structure bill. Retrieved from https://www.arnoldporter.com/en/perspectives/advisories/2025/08/clarifying-the-clarity-act

Atlantic Council. (2025). Central Bank digital currency tracker. Retrieved from https://www.atlanticcouncil.org/cbdctracker/

Bank for International Settlements. (2024, April 3). Project Agorá: Central banks and the banking sector undertake a major initiative to explore the tokenization of cross-border payments. https://www.bis.org/press/p240403.htm

Barratt, M. J. (2012). Silk Road: eBay for drugs. *Addiction*, 107(3), 683–683. [Relevant for ideological context].

Beyond OTC. (2025, March 28). Cross-border smart contracts: Legal challenges. BeyondOTC. https://beyondotc.com/blog/cross-border-smart-contracts-legal-challenges/

CoinMarketCap. (2022). Virtual currency market overview. CoinMarketCap. https://coinmarketcap.com/

Cointelegraph. (2025, May 24). Judge overturns fraud convictions in Mango Markets exploit case. https://cointelegraph.com/news/judge-overturns-avraham-eisenberg-fraud-convictions-mango-markets

Commodity Futures Trading Commission. (2023, January 9). CFTC charges Avraham Eisenberg with a manipulative and deceptive scheme to misappropriate over $110 million from Mango Markets [Press release]. https://www.cftc.gov/PressRoom/PressReleases/8647-23

Congressional Research Service. (2025, July 11). Stablecoin legislation: An overview of S. 1582, GENIUS Act of 2025 (CRS Insight IN12553). https://crsreports.congress.gov/product/pdf/IN/IN12553.

Digital Asset Market Clarity Act, H.R. 3633, 118th Cong. (2025). https://www.congress.gov/bill/118th-congress/house-bill/3633/text

DLA Piper. (2025). Blockchain and digital assets news and trends – August 2025. Retrieved from https://www.dlapiper.com/en/insights/publications/blockchain-and-digital-assets-news-and-trends/2025/blockchain-and-digital-assets-news-and-trends-august-2025

Federal Bureau of Investigation (FBI). (2013, October 25). Silk Road operator Ross Ulbricht sentenced to life in prison [Press release].

Financial Action Task Force (FATF). (2014). Virtual currencies: Key definitions and potential AML/CFT risks. [Relevant for TBML analysis framework].

Guiding and Establishing National Innovation for U.S. Stablecoins Act, S. 1582, 118th Cong. (2025). https://www.congress.gov/bill/118th-congress/senate-bill/1582/text

Investopedia. (2025). Blockchain. Retrieved from https://www.investopedia.com/terms/b/blockchain.asp

Lagarde, C. (2018, November 14). Winds of change: The case for new digital currency. Speech at the Singapore FinTech Festival. *International Monetary Fund.* https://www.imf.org/en/news/articles/2018/11/13/sp111418-winds-of-change-the-case-for-new-digital-currency

Mik, E. (2017). Smart contracts: Terminology, technical limitations, and real-world complexity. *Law, Innovation and Technology*, 9(2), 269–300. https://doi.org/10.1080/17579961.2017.1378468

Nakamoto, S. (2008). Bitcoin: A peer-to-peer electronic cash system. Retrieved from https://bitcoin.org/bitcoin.pdf

Regulation (EU) 2016/679 of the European Parliament and of the Council of 27 April 2016 on the protection of natural persons concerning the processing of personal data and on the free movement of such data, and repealing Directive 95/46/EC (General Data Protection Regulation), OJ L 119/1, art. 17

Reuters. (2013, October 2). Silk Road mastermind Ross Ulbricht jailed for life over online drugs bazaar. *Reuters*. https://www.reuters.com/business/silk-road-mastermind-ross-ulbricht-jailed-life-over-online-drugs-bazaar-2013-10-02/

Securities and Exchange Commission. (2023, January 20). SEC Charges Avraham Eisenberg with Manipulating Mango Markets' Governance Token to Steal $116 Million of Crypto Assets [Press Release]. https://www.sec.gov/news/press-releases/2023-13

Securities Industry and Financial Markets Association. (2024). Regulated settlement network proof-of-concept. SIFMA. Retrieved from https://www.sifma.org/research/white-papers/regulated-settlement-network-proof-of-concept

State Street. (2025). 2025 regulatory preview: Understanding the new US administration's approach to digital assets and AI. Retrieved from https://www.statestreet.com/in/en/insights/digital-digest-march-2025-digital-assets-ai-regulation

United States Department of Justice. (2015, May 29). Ross Ulbricht, the creator and owner of the Silk Road website, was sentenced to life in prison [Press release].

U.S. Attorney's Office, Southern District of New York. (2015, Feb 5). Ross Ulbricht, the creator and owner of the "Silk Road" website, was sentenced in Manhattan federal court to life in prison [Press release]. U.S. Department of Justice. https://www.justice.gov/usao-sdny/pr/ross-ulbricht-creator-and-owner-silk-road-website-found-guilty-manhattan-federal-court

U.S. House of Representatives, Committee on Financial Services. (2025, May 29). Digital Asset Market Clarity (CLARITY) Act of 2025 (H.R. 3633). 119th Congress, 1st Session. Retrieved from https://www.congress.gov/bill/119th-congress/house-bill/3633/text

U.S. v. Ulbricht, 31 F. Supp. 3d 540 (S.D.N.Y. 2014). [Primary court documents].

Visa Corporate. (2025). Update on key digital asset technologies. Retrieved from https://corporate.visa.com/en/sites/visa-economic-empowerment-institute/update-on-key-digital-asset-technologies.html

White House. (2025). Fact Sheet: President Donald J. Trump Signs GENIUS Act into law. Retrieved from https://www.whitehouse.gov/fact-sheets/2025/07/fact-sheet-president-donald-j-trump-signs-genius-act-into-law/

World Bank. (2019). Migration and remittances: Recent developments and outlook. Retrieved from https://www.worldbank.org/en/topic/migrationremittancesdiasporaissues/brief/migration-remittances-data

Additional Learning Resources

Book

1 "Digital Gold: Bitcoin and the Inside Story of the Misfits and Millionaires Trying to Reinvent Money" by Nathaniel Popper (2015).
This book provides an engaging narrative that examines the early days of Bitcoin, its rise in popularity, and its association with illicit activities.

Film

2 "The Rise and Rise of Bitcoin" was directed by Nicholas Mross (2014).
This documentary film examines the history of Bitcoin, its impact on the financial system, and its association with both legal and illicit transactions.

Article

3 "The dark side of Bitcoin." Kate Allman. (2018). Published in LSJ: Law Society Journal, (42), 28–29.
This article examines the use of Bitcoin in illicit activities and the challenges it poses for law enforcement agencies.

YouTube Video

4 "Bitcoin: The End of Money as We Know It" was written by Torsten Hoffmann and directed by Torsten Hoffmann and Michael Watchulonis (2015). http://rb.gy/49744
This documentary-style video provides an in-depth analysis of Bitcoin's origins, its potential impact on traditional financial systems, and its involvement in illegal transactions.

7 International Gold Trade and Illicit Proceeds

A Closer Look

The Illicit Gold Trade: A Conduit for Financial Crime and Systemic Risk

Gold has a host of attributes and has long been a valuable store of value because of its unique properties—extremely high value per unit mass, anonymity in exchange, and worldwide acceptance. However, it not only renders it a symbol of wealth. Incidentally, it is also a primary vehicle for financial crime. As the United Nations Office on Drugs and Crime (UNODC) has affirmed, "Gold is one of the most attractive commodities for money launderers due to its universal value, high liquidity and ease of transport" (UNODC, 2015, p. 2). The illegal gold trade is a tremendous vulnerability in the global economic system. Gold is widely used for money laundering, fuels conflict, and distorts perfectly legal markets. The section discusses the mechanisms of gold laundering, the volume and structure of the global market that enable it, and stresses the necessity of strengthened international regulatory collaboration.

Gold as a Mechanism for Laundering Illicit Proceeds

The process of integrating illicit funds into the legal economy through gold—known as trade-based money laundering—exploits the metal's intrinsic characteristics. Criminals can purchase gold with cash proceeds from crimes such as drug trafficking or corruption in one jurisdiction and move it to another. The proceeds of crime are transported across borders with minimal detection due to their high value-to-weight ratio. It is also sold into the legitimate market elsewhere. Thus, with a piecemeal process, it is "cleaning" the money. This method relies on the anonymity of cash transactions at the point of purchase and on the often-fragmented oversight of the gold supply chain, from artisanal mines to refiners to retailers.

The Scale and Vulnerabilities of the Global Gold Market

The sheer size and specific features of the gold market's legal structure make it an attractive environment and breeding ground for illegal activities. In 2022, the global annual gold demand was 4,748 tons, equivalent to more than $270 billion (World Gold Council, 2023). A small proportion of illegal gold could infiltrate to generate billions of dollars in illicit financial flows.

Public demand for gold has lately exceeded the volume of gold being extracted. In 2022, gold mines only produced around 3,612 tons (World Gold Council, 2023). The continual structural imbalance between demand and supply from primary sources is the system's major weakness. The gold market indicates that demand regularly exceeds supply. The demand for gold and the volume of gold mined are two key determinants that affect the gold market.

DOI: 10.4324/9781003477631-8

This continuous vacuum is filled by recycled gold and, significantly, illegal gold entering the formal chain.

The key weaknesses are evident across market segments, including the Artisanal and Small-Scale Gold Mining (ASGM) sector. This segment accounts for approximately 20% of global gold production. It is often characterized as an informal and poorly regulated sector (UNEP, 2018). Thus, it makes it susceptible to exploitation by criminal networks and becomes a significant source of the illegal gold supply.

Complex Supply Chains: Gold passes through many hands—miners, local traders, consolidators, international refiners, and bullion banks—before reaching consumers. Weak regulatory enforcement at any node, particularly in jurisdictions with high corruption, allows illicit gold to be "washed" into the legal stream through falsification of documentation (INTERPOL, 2021).

High-Value, Portable Wealth: Unlike bulk cash, gold enables the discreet cross-border transfer of enormous value, complicating detection efforts by customs and law enforcement (Global Financial Integrity, 2020).

Market fluctuations, such as the demand dip during the COVID-19 pandemic, do not diminish this vulnerability but can alter criminal incentives. Economic uncertainty often increases gold's attractiveness as a stable, anonymous store of value for illicit actors. As the World Gold Council has noted, "Criminal activities potentially influenced a prominent portion of this demand" (World Gold Council, 2020, p. 5), highlighting that illicit gold seamlessly integrates into and exploits the legitimate market's cycles.

Laundering Methodologies: Exploiting Inherent Market Characteristics

Criminals exploit standard industry processes to obscure the origin of illicit gold by melting diverse sources into anonymous bars (Teichmann & Falker, 2024). Thereby, launder it through the appearance of legitimate commerce.

1 Obfuscation through Refining and Smelting: These processes can obscure the provenance of the gold. These very processes that purify gold are also good ways to make it anonymous. When gold from different sources, such as stolen jewelry or nuggets from conflict zones, is melted into a single bar, it squanders its physical history. This "recycling" step is standard industry practice, but provides perfect cover for integrating illicit material with legitimate scrap.
2 Exploitation of the Bullion Trade: The high-value, low-volume nature of gold bullion makes it ideal for cross-border value transfer. Criminals purchase bullion with cash in one jurisdiction, exploit weak customs documentation requirements to transport it, and sell it into the legitimate market in another country. The bullion is indistinguishable from other bullion, rendering its criminal origin untraceable and converting "dirty" cash into clean, bankable funds (INTERPOL, 2021).

Hiding in Plain Sight: The Use of Gold as a Cover-up

Disguising or concealing illicit proceeds is a standard method of laundering them through the gold industry (UNODC, 2015). This involves using illegal proceeds to purchase gold. It is then exchanged for legal tender. Thus, it converts illegal funds into legitimate funds and complicates authorities' efforts to trace their origins (Teichmann & Falker, 2024).

Collateral for Corruption: Using Gold as Loan Security

Another standard method of laundering illicit proceeds through the gold trade is to use gold as collateral for loans (INTERPOL, 2021). The gold secures loans that are then used to acquire tangible assets, allowing money launderers to obtain legal funds without immediately offloading the gold (Global Financial Integrity, 2020).

Tax Evasion and Capital Controls: The Use of Gold for Profit

Gold can be used skillfully to circumvent taxation and capital controls (UNODC, 2015). Illicit funds are used to purchase gold. It is then sent to a country with lower taxes or fewer restrictions on gold trading. The sale proceeds can thereafter be deposited into a bank account or reinvested in legal investments. This process, therefore, enables the accumulation of profits free from tax or transfer regulations (Teichmann & Falker, 2024).

The Cost of Illicit Activities: The Impact on International Financial Markets

The use of gold to clean dirty money severely tarnishes the reputation of the gold industry. It also invariably undermines the global financial systems (INTERPOL, 2021).

Combating the Ripple Effects of Illicit Activities

The Role of Financial Regulators and Law Enforcement Agencies. Illegal actions, such as smuggling, increase the exposure and unpredictability of financial markets, harming investors and the economy. Financial regulators and law enforcement agencies are crucial to combating these issues through the implementation and enforcement of regulations, the conduct of investigations, and the prosecution of offenders. Their role is pivotal in maintaining the integrity of financial markets and protecting the economy.

The Role of International Gold Trade in Illicit Activities: A Gateway for Money Laundering

The international gold trade is a major conduit for laundering illicit proceeds. Law enforcement struggles to trace the source of the metal when criminals procure gold in one nation and resell it in another destination. Data from the World Gold Council indicate that China, the United States, Japan, India, and the UK ranked among the top five major gold-importing countries in 2019. These nations experienced substantial demand for gold during that period, as they served as hubs for international gold trade. Consequently, their prominence in the industry renders them vulnerable to the misuse of gold for illicit purposes, posing a serious threat to the integrity of financial systems.

Various Kinds and Markets for Gold

"Gold is traded in numerous different markets, including the London Bullion Market Association (LBMA), the Intercontinental Exchange (ICE), and the Shanghai Gold Exchange (SGE)" (World Gold Council (2021).

> Each of these markets has its advantages and disadvantages, and they cater to various types of buyers and sellers. For example, the LBMA is the largest and most well-established gold market, while the SGE focuses more on the Chinese market.
>
> (World Gold Council, 2021)

The Merits and Demerits of the Gold Market

Although the gold market has numerous advantages, such as stability and the capacity to hedge against inflation and currency devaluation, this market also has key drawbacks; for instance, the lack of restrictions across various gold markets facilitates money laundering. Moreover, trading gold is frequently associated with criminal activities, including smuggling, thereby threatening global financial markets.

Major Gold Markets and Susceptibility to Illicit Activities

Because of the large number of buyers and sellers, key gold markets in major financial centers such as London, New York, and Shanghai are predominantly vulnerable to criminal activity. This vulnerability enables individuals to blend in rapidly and covertly through approved transactions, posing an enormous threat to market integrity. For example, the LBMA operates the most dominant trading floor. The LBMA is recognized as one of the most notable and well-established gold markets, with a daily turnover of over $20 billion. However, the LBMA's colossal trading volume renders it more vulnerable to money laundering operations. It unwittingly offers opportunities to crooks. Criminals may conveniently obfuscate their illicit proceeds through legitimate transactions. Recognizing these vulnerabilities is crucial to implementing effective security measures and maintaining regulatory compliance in these marketplaces.

In recent years, the LBMA has demonstrated its commitment to implementing various initiatives to address money laundering in the gold industry. Multiple initiatives include enhancing due diligence procedures, advocating for more transparent gold transactions, and collaborating with law enforcement agencies. The LBMA sought to identify criminal enterprises to prevent unlawful activities. These efforts demonstrate the industry's commitment to concentrating on the issue and should reassure the audience of its resolution. Despite these solid endeavors, the LBMA remains a prime target for money launderers due to its sheer size and massive influence in the global gold market.

The New York Commodity Exchange (COMEX) occupies a prominent position within the global gold market. It provides a robust platform for trading in the highly liquid, internationally interconnected sector of this market. However, like several major financial markets, it is not immune to the risks posed by unlawful practices. The inherent characteristics of the gold trade—its vast and sprawling global reach, high liquidity, and sheer scale of transactions—make it an attractive target for individuals or entities. The market seeks to exploit systemic exposures for unlawful intent and purposes. As the world's largest futures exchange, with daily overwhelming trading volumes exceeding 1 million contracts, COMEX has a predominant role in shaping market dynamics. Although it plays a dominant role and has high trading volume, the exchange remains susceptible to exploitation and misuse, particularly for money laundering and other illicit activities. Criminal actors may exploit their extensive operations to conceal the origins of unlawful funds, discreetly integrating them into the financial system undetected. This underscores the critical need for robust regulatory oversight, continuous monitoring, and stringent compliance frameworks to address and mitigate these ongoing exposures effectively.

The Shanghai Gold Exchange (SGE), another leading physical gold market, has experienced an unprecedented increase in gold transaction activity in recent years. With its fabulous potential and average daily trading volume of over 400 tons, the SGE is a fascinating target for money launderers. This market has become a large and growing source of illegal proceeds. Despite the Chinese government's rigorous efforts to tighten regulations and curb unlawful operations, the SGE remains vulnerable to money laundering and other illicit activities.

Case 7.1 TBML in the Gold Sector

Several cases have come to light where illicit proceeds were laundered through the gold trade. To provide a more comprehensive understanding, let us consider a few more examples:

Case 7.1.1 The Golden Trail: Uncovering the Shady Side of the Precious Metal Industry (USA, 2018)

In finance, gold is often referred to as an "unfreezable asset." Its long-standing value and consistent reliability make it a popular choice for those seeking to obscure their wealth from authorities. Unfortunately, the rising and sustained reputation has also made the precious metals industry a prime target for those engaged in illegal practices, such as money laundering and the trade in illicit funds. This was more apparent in the case of a gold merchant from Colombia who was sentenced to a decade in prison in 2018 for deliberately participating in a large-scale money laundering operation. According to a report by the U.S. Department of Justice (DOJ), a trader allegedly utilized drug money to purchase gold and subsequently exported the gold to the United States, where it was sold for clean cash. This daring operation successfully laundered $19 million in drug proceeds through the gold trade (US Department of Justice, 2018).

The Tarnished Crown: How Gold Became the King of Illicit Funds

The genuine tale of Colombian gold traders is imaginable, as it involves severe abuse and exploitation in the mining industry. The law enforcement resources dedicated to resolving the issue contribute to an enhanced understanding of the circumstances. This case demonstrates that any person may be morally corrupt and that wealth can be a source of embarrassment.

The lawsuit focused on how gold might be used for illicit purposes, such as money laundering and the concealment of unlawful funds. Cases involving gold have become more commonplace in recent years, with traffickers and smugglers exploiting its relative secrecy, convenience, and portability to move large sums of money across borders.

This discussion highlights that the issue of unfreezable assets is complex and evolving, necessitating a multifaceted approach. This encompasses ongoing endeavors to detect and prevent illicit practices, as well as initiatives to promote transparency and accountability in the gold market. By doing so, we can ensure that gold remains a precious asset for legitimate trade and financial operations while protecting against its use to obfuscate illicit funds transfers.

Case 7.1.2 The Great Heist: A Tale of Money Laundering and Its Ties to Illicit Funds (United States, 2015)

The complex discipline of finance is frequently rife with fraud and corruption, as evidenced by a 2015 money laundering investigation by the DOJ. The DOJ seized over $1 billion in assets, including gold, making it one of the most remarkable and celebrated anti-money laundering operations in history. According to the United Nations Office on Drugs and Crime (UNODC), gold is now the most coveted commodity for money laundering and other illicit activities because it is not only low-profile but also difficult to trace and locate (UNODC, 2017). The Malaysian sovereign wealth fund was the focal point of the investigation, which stemmed from the misappropriation of illicit funds initially intended for the purchase of luxury real estate and other gold assets.

Money Laundering and Its Ties to Illicit Funds

Money laundering is the act of turning illegally gotten gains (often from drug trafficking, terrorist funding, financing, and/or corruption) into lawful money. It is an enormous and cross-border phenomenon; the blame is primarily on economies and is a substantial cause of social decay. The United States, for example, took legal action against criminals by seizing $1 billion in 2015. The statement indicates that the annual total of laundered funds that pass through the global financial system exceeds several billion dollars.

The Malaysian Sovereign Wealth Fund Scandal

The Malaysian sovereign wealth fund at the center of the investigation was found to have used its resources to purchase luxury real estate and other assets, including gold, in the United States. The DOJ's probe revealed an extensive alliance of money launderers and corrupt individuals within the then-regime, who used the fund as a cover for their unlawful practices. The scale of the operations was so enormous that the DOJ was compelled to take decisive legal action, resulting in the seizure of more than $1 billion in assets.

The Impact of the Seizure

The seizure of more than $1 billion in property significantly affected the global capital system, alerting those engaged in money laundering and other illegal activities. In addition, it demonstrated the effectiveness of anti-money laundering measures and the DOJ's commitment to combating financial crimes through its efforts. The seizure also sent the unmistakable message that the United States had zero tolerance for the abuse of its monetary system.

Historical Lessons and the Future of Anti-money Laundering Efforts

The DOJ's 2015 money laundering investigation serves as a lesson for future generations, underscoring the importance of ongoing efforts to combat money laundering. Governments and financial institutions must continue to invest in anti-money laundering measures to impede the abuse of the financial system for illegal purposes. Ensuring the integrity of the global economic system is an ongoing endeavor, and combating money laundering requires a collaborative approach by all stakeholders (US Department of Justice, 2018). This joint effort is crucial to uphold the flow and protect the authenticity of global financial transactions.

The 2015 DOJ investigation into money laundering exemplified the scale of this activity and its potential implications for the global financial sector. The confiscation of more than $1 billion in assets essentially revealed the DOJ's commitment to reducing financial fraud and protecting the robustness of the economic system. Expertise in AML/CFT is also central to discussions of the need for continued investment in anti-money laundering measures to ensure system security and the success of banks and governments collaborating to counter the global problem.

Case 7.1.3 Operation Porto Victoria: Dismantling a Transnational Laundering Network in Brazil (BBC News, 2015)

In June 2015, the Brazilian authorities achieved a significant milestone in the fight against financial crime by dismantling an extensive network that had evaded foreign currency tariffs and laundered more than $800 million (Customs Today, 2015). Eleven people were arrested in operations conducted in three states, including Allan Simoes Toledo, a former vice president of the government-owned Bank of Brazil (Vermelho, 2015).

The Difficulty of Tracking Financial Crime in Brazil

In Brazil, despite the strenuous efforts of law enforcement, financial crimes, encompassing drug trafficking, arms smuggling, and software issues, remain a serious and widespread problem. The U.S. State Department report noted that the country lacks accurate records on convictions and arrests, which is a substantial obstacle to understanding the full extent of money laundering trends and other associated criminal patterns.

The Tactics of the Criminal Network

The criminal network at the heart of the probe employed various tactics to launder its illegal proceeds. One illicit strategy for withdrawing hard currency from Venezuela involved the use of counterfeit import orders from Brazilian companies. By artificially inflating product prices by up to 5,000%, this scheme enabled the movement of funds to circumvent Venezuela's stringent currency controls.

The Operation Spanning the Globe

The criminal organization has been active and intensely involved for at least three years. These enterprises were primarily focused on circumventing currency regulations and laundering money, operating across multiple countries. The investigation, which began in 2014 at the request of U.S. Immigration and Customs Enforcement, resulted in intensive searches in several cities. The searches took place in São Paulo, Curitiba (the capital of Paraná State), and Resende (in Rio de Janeiro State). The funds were sent to Hong Kong via fraudulent loans or import orders and were subsequently distributed internationally.

The Consequences for the Perpetrators

The individuals responsible for this criminal network will face severe repercussions for their actions. The individuals accountable for this criminal network faced severe repercussions for their actions. Last month, Nestor Cervero, a former executive at Petrobras, was sentenced to five years in prison for money laundering. Another former executive, Paulo Roberto Costa, was sentenced to 7.5 years in prison last April. More than 100 people have been indicted, and at least 50 politicians are reportedly under investigation for having received bribes.

The Takeaway

This successful operation underscores the continued importance of proactive measures in combating financial crime and money laundering. The swift dismantling of this elaborate network by Brazilian officials demonstrates that illegal activities will be met with immediate and harsh repercussions.

The Dark Side of the Gold Trade

The above scenarios re-emphasize the need for greater transparency and oversight in the gold sector. The sector is frequently misused as a conduit for illicit activities and money laundering, posing a threat to the stability of the global financial system. A FATF report found that the gold trade is particularly vulnerable to abuse due to insufficient regulation and the inherent difficulty of tracing the metal's provenance (FATF, 2018).

Case 7.1.4* Rihan v. Ernst & Young Global Ltd: *EY's Cover-Up of Organized Crime's Smuggling, Gold, & Drug Money (UK, 2020) (The New York Times, 2023)

A global accounting firm, EY (earlier Ernst & Young), was caught up in a severe and profound scandal that revealed its involvement in covering up evidence of smuggling by an organized crime gang. The gang was involved in laundering British drug proceeds. The stunning BBC Panorama inquiry revealed that EY amended a compliance report to conceal the crime after failing to disclose suspicious activity at one of the world's largest gold refineries and its so-called best client.

Background:
EY, one of the world's most extensive auditing and consulting firms, was recently implicated in a cover-up involving a significant smuggling operation run by an organized crime gang. According to media reports, EY was retained by a client to investigate a matter involving suspicious activity. However, instead of informing the client of the alleged discoveries, EY altered, falsified evidence, and sent a tainted report to its client, apparently to protect the organized crime syndicate from carrying out illegal operations, encompassing laundering millions of dollars in proceeds from drug trafficking and other criminal activities.

The Investigation Unfolds

BBC Panorama (BBC, 2020) exposed that the gang laundered money by selling 3.6 tons of gold to the Kaloti refinery in Dubai. Despite the ingenious efforts of the money laundering gang, they were eventually caught, and 27 members were incarcerated in France in 2017. The gang had collected cash from drug dealers in the UK and other European countries, and they then laundered the dirty money by buying and selling black market gold (Verity & Robinson, 2019).

The Role of EY

In 2013, EY was asked to review Kaloti's compliance with rules designed to prevent gold from illicit sources from entering the global supply chain. The auditors discovered that Kaloti had paid $5.2 billion (£4 billion) in cash in 2012, but EY failed to report the suspicious activity to the money-laundering authorities (Slingo, 2019).

Amjad Rihan, the lead auditor for EY in Dubai in 2013, stated that he intended to report the suspicious activity at the time. However, his supervisors diluted the reports and told him not to inform the authorities. Rihan stated, "If you identify a suspicious transaction, you should report it to the authorities, and what we identified was way beyond suspicion. Instead of reporting and exposing the crimes I told them about, my bosses covered them up" (Martello Risk, 2019).

The Cover-up

The panorama saw several drafts of a compliance report to a Dubai regulator. In the initial report, Kaloti appeared to acknowledge purchasing gold-coated bars, stating, "We acknowledge an incident… with the bars coated with silver." However, EY rewrote the report to say, "We acknowledge transactions… in which there were certain documentary irregularities." EY turned the crime into a "documentary irregularity." EY declined to comment on the revision of the report but stated that it was confident that all legal and reporting obligations had been met, and that it had submitted its findings to the relevant regulator in Dubai (BBC News, 2020).

Legal Duty to Report

Under the Proceeds of Crime Act, accountants are legally required to report suspicious activity to the police. In its legal dispute with Rihan, EY admitted that the disguised gold "provided reasonable grounds for knowing or suspecting… money laundering." However, the accountancy firm claimed it did not have to report this to the police because its auditors were not doing accountancy work at Kaloti.

Kaloti's Statement

Kaloti denied any misconduct and claimed it had completed all required anti-money laundering verifications. The company stated,

> Kaloti would not knowingly enter into a trading relationship with any party in the knowledge that such party had been engaged in financial impropriety or criminal activity. It is categorically denied that Kaloti purchased gold coated in silver from Renade or anyone else.

Kaloti added that cash payments were made daily in Dubai, but it no longer accepts cash for gold (Global Witness, 2014).

The Implications of EY's Involvement

A significant financial institution's involvement in covering such a widespread issue raises concerns about the effectiveness of anti-money laundering measures in the financial sector. Regulators and financial institutions should use this situation as a prompt to critically scrutinize their practices and procedures to ensure they do everything possible to detect and stop illicit economic activity.

The Failure of Anti-money Laundering Measures

EY's case demonstrates the ineffectiveness of anti-money laundering measures in detecting and deterring illicit funds flows. Despite the many anti-money laundering regulations, frameworks, and systems in place, organized crime gangs and other criminal organizations continue to find ways to launder their funds through the financial sector. The absence of effective enforcement and oversight has enabled these criminal organizations to operate with relative impunity (UNODC, 2022).

The Need for Better Regulation and Oversight

To remedy these weaknesses, authorities and financial institutions must seek to improve their practices and procedures. This entails implementing effective anti-money laundering measures and strengthening oversight and enforcement (World Bank, 2021). It also requires further training and education for financial sector employees to enable them to recognize suspicious practices and to follow through with appropriate reporting and documentation.

The case involves EY's suspected concealment of evidence related to smuggling committed by an organized crime gang. The case manifests a compelling incident that underscores the significance of accountability and transparency within the financial sector. EY's failure to disclose suspicious activity, coupled with the modification of the investigation report, underscores the need for sturdy regulatory oversight in the industry (Reading Chronicle, 2019).

The implications of this case reach well beyond the immediate repercussions for EY and the affected clients. It raised substantial concerns and disapproval about the efficacy of anti-money laundering measures in the global financial system. The incident prompted critical scrutiny of existing safeguards and called for sustained efforts to ensure the integrity and effectiveness of anti-money laundering frameworks.

The international gold trade remains a substantial focus for money launderers and criminals. The World Gold Council has reported that money launderers and criminals frequently employ gold to move and store the proceeds of crime. The movement of gold is facilitated by its high liquidity and the ease with which it can be converted into cash. The major gold markets, such as London, New York, and Shanghai, are highly susceptible to illegal practices. The vulnerability stems from their massive trading volumes, and criminals can readily blend in with legitimate transactions. Law enforcement agencies, governments, and market actors collaborate in concerted measures. This alliance promotes transparency, strengthens regulations, and enhances due diligence processes. Concurrently, extensive efforts are underway to regulate the gold trade and prevent money laundering. It remains an arduous job for law enforcement officials as they struggle to discover and dismantle culpable enterprises.

An Insight: Navigating the UAE's Role in the Gold Industry

An Overview of the UAE's Gold Industry

Dubai, with its long, splendid history, has emerged as a leading country in the gold market. Dubai, also one of the world's leading gold trading centers, accounts for 80% of the country's gold trade. The United Arab Emirates, whose gold trade is around $75 billion annually, is the biggest competitor in the global gold market.

1 UAE: The Rising Star of the Middle East's Gold Market in 2022

The World Gold Council (WGC) claimed that Dubai and the UAE were the Middle East's top gold markets. Consumer demand reached 46.9 tons of gold jewelry, marking a whopping 38% soar compared to last year. The demand for gold in the Middle East is unprecedented, and the UAE is in the lead.

Jewelry remained a popular choice among consumers in the UAE, with overall Middle Eastern demand rising by 15% to 190.4 tons, outpacing demand in other regions, including the Americas and Europe. Despite a 3% decline in global consumption, gold demand worldwide increased by 18% to 4,741 tons in 2022, driven by a 10% increase in investment demand.

Central banks also acquired a sizeable amount of gold, amounting to 1,126 tons. This status was the highest level in 55 years. In early 2022, gold surged to $2,000 per ounce before declining due to U.S. Federal Reserve monetary policy and a strong dollar. However, prices have been mounting since October 31, 2022, hitting more than $1,924 per ounce by the end of January 2023 (WGC, 2020).

2 The Growth of the UAE's Gold Industry

The UAE's gold industry has experienced significant growth in recent years. This has inevitably reinforced the country's status in the global gold market. According to the World Gold Council, the UAE's gold trade was valued at approximately $70 billion in 2019, elevating its status to the fourth-largest gold market globally, behind China, India, and the USA. This rising pattern bodes well for the future of the UAE's gold industry.

2.1 Factors Driving the Growth of the UAE's Gold Industry

Favorable Tax System: The UAE's tax-friendly regime has made it an attractive destination for gold trading companies. Strategic Location: The UAE is the entry point to the enormous Gold Markets of Asia and Europe

Reputation as a Safe and Secure Place to Trade: The UAE has an excellent reputation as a secure and reliable location for trading gold, which attracts global investors and traders.

Government Investment: The UAE government has invested copiously in essential facilities. This helps the gold industry flourish and incentivizes businesses to operate successfully in Dubai and other parts of the UAE.

3 The Laundering of Illicit Proceeds Through the UAE's Gold Industry

The growth of the UAE's gold industry has not come without its apparent challenges. One of the major concerns is the use of the gold trade for money laundering. According to the United Nations Office on Drugs and Crime (2019), billions of dollars of illegal proceeds are laundered through the gold trade each year.

3.1 The Risks of Money Laundering in the UAE's Gold Industry

Despite the UAE's gold trade industry having grown dramatically in its standing, it also presents a substantial risk of money laundering. There are various reasons for the gold trade, including limited transparency, anonymity, and ease of transport. These characteristics of gold trading create apparent opportunities for illicit-fund laundering.

A study by the FATF identified the potential for money laundering in the gold trade, particularly in countries with a thriving gold sector, such as the UAE. The report explains that the gold industry is highly susceptible to money laundering due to its frequent use of cash transactions, which complicate tracking and monitoring.

3.2 The Impact of Money Laundering on the UAE's Gold Industry

Money laundering jeopardizes the integrity of the gold trade. It also undermines the industry's reputation and poses a serious risk to the UAE's identity and its central role in the gold trade. This unlawful financial activity boosts the scope of drug and human trafficking, which are substantial risks to the stability and security of the nation. Money laundering is a persistent threat to the gold market, destabilizing markets, eroding confidence, and undermining the industry's credibility. In addition, money laundering through gold can drive a surge in demand for the metal, thereby inflating gold prices. This may cause a ripple effect on the global gold market and invariably impact honest traders and legitimate customers worldwide.

Methods of Laundering Illicit Funds through the Gold Trade

Various methods are employed to launder illicit funds through the gold trade, including the use of front companies, gold smuggling, and gold counterfeiting. Front companies, also known as shell companies, are used to conceal the valid owner of the gold and obscure the source of the laundered funds. Gold smuggling involves moving gold, commonly in the form of imports and exports, illegally across borders, while gold counterfeiting is the act of producing fake gold bars and coins.

The Need for Regulatory Measures to Combat Money Laundering in the UAE's Gold Industry

To combat money laundering in the UAE's gold trade, the government and regulatory bodies must urgently implement stringent measures to enhance transparency and more effectively monitor the gold trade. This involves mandatory reporting of large gold transactions, the establishment of a central database to track such transactions, and the enforcement of stringent anti-money laundering measures by financial institutions and gold traders.

To summarize the discussion, the UAE leads the Middle East gold market, with continued consumer demand for gold jewelry, having reached a record high in 2022 and maintaining robust growth through 2026. The gold trade boom in the UAE is attributable to several factors: an attractive tax regime, geographic advantages, and a reputation as a safe and secure gold trading destination. However, the rapid growth of the UAE's gold industry has attracted the attention of money launderers, who use the gold trade to conceal the proceeds of their illicit activities. The laundering of criminal funds through the gold trade has a significant impact on the sector and a debilitating influence on global financial markets. It is equally a source of concern for government regulators, financial institutions, and law enforcement officials.

Nugget of Advice: The Unfreezable Asset: Exploring the Intersection of Gold, Sanctions, and Russia Economic sanctions, a formidable foreign policy tool, have tremendously impacted global politics. These methods compel certain countries or individuals to alter their conduct. However, amidst these efforts, one asset remained resilient and often stood the test of time—gold. In this exploration, we examine the intricate relationship between gold, sanctions, and Russia, highlighting how this precious metal plays a decisive and dominant role in mitigating the effects of economic sanctions.

Gold as a Safe Haven in Times of Uncertainty

Gold has long been recognized as a safe haven. It manifests as a reliable store of value during economic and political turmoil. During periods of financial uncertainty, currency devaluation, trade conflicts, or global crises, investors frequently seek wealth protection, and gold provides a hedge against exposed risks. The global financial crisis of 2008 and the COVID-19 pandemic have underscored gold's status as a safe-haven investment.

The Sanctions Era

Since 2014, Western nations have gained momentum in imposing a myriad of strict economic sanctions against Russia owing to its conflict with Ukraine. These harsh sanctions have had a significant impact on the Russian economy, particularly on its lending and international investments. Russia's gold reserves, however, have allowed the country to mitigate the effects of the economic sanctions, as these reserves can be used to back the currency abroad and bolster the economy. The World Gold Council reports that Russian gold reserves have continued to rise, from approximately 25% between 2014 and 2019 to 2,285 tons in 2019, representing a substantial increase relative to 1,836 tons in 2014 (World Gold Council, 2020).

The Impact of Sanctions on Russia

Russia has recently been the target of a spate of economic sanctions. Such restrictive measures have considerably limited access to international financial markets, making it pretty tough for Russian companies to raise capital and even conduct transactions internationally (IMF, 2020).

Gold to the Rescue

Despite the formidable barriers of sanctions, Russia has demonstrated remarkable resilience by leveraging gold to mitigate the impact of these restrictions. It is notable when a country uses gold strategically and continues to accumulate it in its reserves as a medium of exchange in international transactions. In 2019, the Central Bank of Russia reported that gold accounted for 18.2% of its reserves, up from 10.9% in 2014 (World Gold Council, 2019).

The Connection between Gold and Money Laundering

However, the use of gold to circumvent sanctions has also raised concerns about its potential link to illicit activities, such as money laundering. The appeal of using gold for those seeking to launder money or circumvent financial restrictions lies in its capacity to remain anonymous and be easily transported.

Lessons from the Past

The current situation in Russia echoes historical precedent from the Cold War, when the United States imposed sanctions on the Soviet Union, prompting it to pursue a gold option to evade the restrictions. During the late 1970s and early 1980s, the Soviet Union embarked on a massive gold-buying spree, which expanded its gold reserves by more than 500% (Central Intelligence Agency, 1983). Throughout this period, gold served as a means of circumventing sanctions, economic restrictions, and heightened scrutiny. While sanctions may be potent instruments for inducing behavior in nation-states, they can readily be blamed for additional economic instability and suffering. Gold serves as a channel to protect from high-stakes uncertainties, offering stability to nations concerned as a store of value that remains relatively unaffected by political and economic fluctuations. This is a lesson that other countries may learn when considering how best to respond to threats and address the challenges posed by financial sanctions.

Ultimately, gold's reputation as a safe haven and its ability to withstand economic sanctions have benefited nations such as Russia, which will face financial constraints. Despite concerns about its potential link to criminal activities such as sanctions evasion and money laundering, countries have traditionally turned to gold during economic instability, underscoring its enduring reputation as a store of value for preserving wealth.

Chapter Summary

We examined the international gold trade to assess how it facilitates the laundering of illicit proceeds. Discover the techniques to mask dirty money, from blending in with legitimate sources to leveraging gold for loan collateral. Examine the impact of illegal activities on global financial markets and the role of gold in tax evasion and capital controls. Assess the merits and drawbacks of the gold market and identify which major gold markets are most vulnerable to illicit activities. This detailed examination reveals a complex and often overlooked aspect of financial crime.

End of Chapter: Discussion Questions

1. What makes the gold trade particularly susceptible to illicit activities such as money laundering?
2. How is using gold as a cover-up hiding in plain sight in money laundering activities?
3. What are some of the methods used to launder illicit funds through the gold trade?
4. How does using gold as loan security facilitate corruption and money laundering?
5. How do tax evasion and capital controls play a role in using gold for illicit profits?
6. How does the cost of illicit activities impact international financial markets and the gold trade?
7. What is the role of the international gold trade in illicit activities and money laundering?
8. What are the merits and demerits of the gold market regarding its susceptibility to illicit activities?
9. Name some major gold markets and their susceptibility to illicit activities.
10. What measures can be taken to combat the laundering of illicit proceeds through the international gold trade?

References

BBC News. (2015, June 12). A $800 million money laundering network in Brazil has been dismantled. *BBC*. https://www.bbc.com/news/business-33107933

BBC News. (2019, October 27). EY: Gold, drug money, and a major auditor's "cover-up". https://www.bbc.com/news/uk-50194681

BBC News. (2020, April 17). Ex-EY whistleblower wins $10.8m in damages. https://www.bbc.co.uk/news/business-52331443

Customs Today. (2015). Brazilian authorities dismantled an $800 million money-laundering network. https://customstoday.media/brazilian-customs-breaks-800m-money-laundering-network/

Ferwerda, J., & Reuter, P. (2022). National assessments of money laundering risks: Learning from eight advanced countries' NRAs. World Bank Group. https://documents1.worldbank.org/curated/en/099302204122255265/pdf/IDU02386c9b80f623045e70bf8a09a30b6162595.pdf

Financial Action Task Force. (2018). Report on the trade in gold. https://www.fatf-gafi.org/publications/fatfreports/documents/report-on-the-trade-in-gold.html

Global Financial Integrity & Association of Certified Financial Crime Specialists. (2020, July). Inside the illicit gold trade: Using financial tools and public policy to fight money laundering [Webinar]. Global Financial Integrity. Retrieved from https://gfintegrity.org/acfcs-gfi-webinar-inside-the-illicit-gold-trade/

Global Witness. (2014, February 25). Ernst & Young: Why Dubai's first conflict gold audit was silenced. https://taxjustice.net/2014/02/26/dubais-first-conflict-gold-audit-via-ernst-young-silenced/

INTERPOL. (2021). Illegal gold mining in Central Africa. https://www.interpol.int/content/download/16493/file/2021%2007%2027%20ENGLISH%20PUBLIC%20VERSION_FINAL_Illegal%20gold%20mining.pdf

Martello Risk. (2019, October 29). EY: Gold, drug money, and a major auditor's 'cover-up'. https://martellorisk.com/gold_drug_money

Reports - Metals Focus. (2022). Metals Focus. World Gold Council. https://www.metalsfocus.com/reports/

Slingo, J. (2019, October 28). EY helped smuggle drug money, BBC claims. Law Gazette. https://www.lawgazette.co.uk/news/ey-helped-smuggle-drug-money-bbc-claims/5101965.article

Teichmann, F. M. J., & Falker, M.-C. (2024). Money laundering through raw diamonds. *Journal of Money Laundering Control*, 27(1), 1–4. https://doi.org/10.1108/JMLC-07-2019-0057

The New York Times. (2023, January 1). EY implicated in cover-up of major smuggling operation.

United Nations Environment Programme. (2018). Global mercury assessment 2018: Sources, emissions, releases and environmental transport. https://wedocs.unep.org/bitstream/handle/20.500.11822/26448/GMA_2018.pdf

United Nations News. (2025, May 19). Organized crime groups are increasingly embedded in gold supply chains. https://news.un.org/en/story/2025/05/1163456

United Nations Office on Drugs and Crime (UNODC). (2015). World drug report 2015: Special section on illicit financial flows and gold trafficking. United Nations. Retrieved from https://www.unodc.org/unodc/en/data-and-analysis/WDR-2015.html

United Nations Office on Drugs and Crime. (2015). UNODC's crime classification: A key tool against criminal activities worldwide. https://www.unodc.org/unodc/en/frontpage/2015/August/unodcs-crime-classification_-a-key-tool-against-crime-worldwide.html

United Nations Office on Drugs and Crime (UNODC). (2017). Guidance manual for Member States on terrorist financing risk assessments. United Nations Office on Drugs and Crime. Retrieved from https://www.unodc.org/documents/terrorism/Publications/CFT%20Manual/Guidance_Manual_TF_Risk_Assessments.pdf

United Nations Office on Drugs and Crime. (2019). Money Laundering through the Physical Trade of Gold. https://www.unodc.org/documents/money-laundering-and-terrorist-financing/Reports/Money_Laundering_through_the_Physical_Trade_of_Gold.pdf

United Nations Office on Drugs and Crime. (2022, December 22). Money laundering in the financial sector: A growing concern.

U.S. Department of Justice. (2016, July 20). The United States seeks to recover more than $1 billion that was obtained through corruption involving the Malaysian sovereign wealth fund. Office of Public Affairs. Retrieved from https://www.justice.gov/opa/pr/united-states-seeks-recover-more-1-billion-obtained-corruption-involving-malaysian-sovereign

US Department of Justice. (2018, March 29). Colombian gold trader sentenced to 10 years in prison for role in $19 million drug money laundering scheme. Press Release. Retrieved from DOJ archives: https://www.justice.gov/archives/opa/press-releases

Vermelho. (2015, June 11). Allan Toledo, ex-vice-presidente do BB, é preso em São Paulo. https://vermelho.org.br/2015/06/11/allan-toledo-ex-vice-presidente-do-bb-e-preso-em-sao-paulo/

Verity, A., & Robinson, T. (2019, October 28). EY: Gold, drug money, and a major auditor's 'cover-up'. BBC Panorama. https://www.bbc.com/news/uk-50194681

World Bank. (2021). Annual report 2021: From crisis to green, resilient, and inclusive recovery. World Bank Group. https://www.worldbank.org/en/about/annual-report-2021

World Gold Council. (2019). Gold demand trends: Full year 2019. Retrieved from https://www.gold.org/goldhub/research/gold-demand-trends/gold-demand-trends-full-year-2019

World Gold Council. (2019). Russia's Central Bank gold reserves. World Gold Council.

World Gold Council. (2020). Gold demand trends for Q4 and full-year 2019. https://www.gold.org/goldhub/research/gold-demand-trends/gold-demand-trends-full-year-2019

World Gold Council. (2020, January 30). Gold demand trends: Full year and Q4 2019. World Gold Council. Retrieved from https://www.gold.org/goldhub/research/gold-demand-trends/gold-demand-trends-full-year-2019

World Gold Council. (2020). Gold demand trends: Full year 2020. https://www.gold.org/goldhub/research/gold-demand-trends/gold-demand-trends-full-year-2020

World Gold Council. (2021). Gold market structure and flows. https://www.gold.org/about-gold/market-structure-and-flows

World Gold Council. (2022). Gold demand trends. Retrieved from https://www.gold.org/research/gold-demand-trends

World Gold Council. (2023). Gold demand trends: Full year 2022. https://www.gold.org/goldhub/research/gold-demand-trends/gold-demand-trends-full-year-2022

World Gold Council. (2026). Central Banks' gold reserves by country. Retrieved from https://www.gold.org/goldhub/data/gold-reserves-by-country

Additional Learning Resources

Article

1 The global gold market and the international monetary system. Catherine R Schenk. (2013). In The Global Gold Market and the International Monetary System from the Late 19th Century to the Present: Actors, Networks, Power (pp. 17–38). London: Palgrave Macmillan UK.
This scholarly article examines the role of the global gold market in the international monetary system and its potential vulnerabilities to illicit activities.

Book

2 "Gold Warriors: America's Secret Recovery of Yamashita's Gold" by Sterling Seagrave and Peggy Seagrave (2003).
This book explores the hidden history of gold looted by the Japanese during World War II and its subsequent involvement in global financial networks.

Documentary

3 "Dirty Gold War: The Gold Industry's Dark Side" is a documentary film released in 2015.
It was written and directed by Emmanuel Grasset and produced by ENDEVR Documentary. Available at: https://rb.gy/4fm8p
The documentary explores the dark side of the gold industry, examining the environmental and social impacts of gold mining, including its connection to illicit activities.

Film

4 "Galamsey - For a Fistful of Gold," the film was released in 2017. It was directed by Johannes Preuss and produced by EyeSteelFilm. Available at: https://rb.gy/ey457
The film investigates the illegal gold-mining trade in Ghana and the human and environmental costs associated with this activity. It exposes its links to money laundering, ecological destruction, and human rights abuses.

YouTube

5 "The True Cost of Gold" by National Geographic (2009). Available at: https://rb.gy/4fooe
This investigative video by National Geographic examines the environmental and social consequences of gold mining, including its links to illegal activities and human rights violations.

8 Sundry Topics, Such as Barter Trade and Misuse of Free Trade Zone

The Art of Bartering: Pros, Cons, and Regulatory Challenges

Barter trade is also known as countertrade or direct exchange. Barter—the direct exchange of goods and services without currency—remains prevalent in those environments where money is scarce or when trade is subject to strict regulations and control. In such cases, it can account for up to 20% of total economic activity in some developing nations (GAO, 2010). This has been a theme in the analysis of the overall trade policy. The United Nations Conference on Trade and Development (UNCTAD, 2016), in its countertrade paper, mentions that such arrangements "may offer a reasonable solution to developing countries having a problem of foreign exchange; thus, they also bring about issues of valuation, transparency, and the possibility of misuse in evading trade controls" (p. 45). When people misuse them for their own advantage, such as through smuggling, tax evasion, or sanctions circumvention. It requires a robust control mechanism. The barter trade is so adaptable that it creates considerable problems for the regulators.

At any rate, a person in a developing economy, through barter, could come out quite well: a farmer could exchange produce. For example, a farmer may trade crops for a set of tools rather than cash, thereby facilitating essential transactions and effectively opening new markets (GAO, 2010). However, this very attribute of barter makes it quite open to manipulation. The same traits that enable legitimate traders to carry out legitimate business can be turned into the means of evading restrictions, thus becoming the mode of illicit trade by letting in, e.g., weapons and embargoed commodities, and through that, inflicting adverse economic effects and undermining the principles of fair trade (GAO, 2010).

The Dark Side of Barter Trade

Ultimately, a barter arrangement is a promising and vital opportunity, especially when resources are limited. Still, its abuse underscores an urgent need for the entire environment to be subject to increased and ongoing international monitoring. It requires establishing effective deterrence/control mechanisms. It is crucial to harness its positive aspects. Combat the opposing forces and prevent unscrupulous practices that contribute to the spread of global insecurity.

Case 8.1 Sanctions Evasion via Barter Trade (United States, 2019)

Case Snapshot: Two Chinese nationals were charged by the U.S. Department of Justice in 2019 with conspiring to violate the U.S. sanctions on Iran. The accused have employed a barter-like system and a network of front companies to carry out the illicit export of goods (U.S. Department of Justice, 2019).

DOI: 10.4324/9781003477631-9

Core Facts: The accused are said to have conducted an elaborate scheme to supply Iran with dual-use items illegally. It also includes other goods with a total value of several million dollars, evading the U.S. sanctions. Their tactics included establishing shell companies and creating fraudulent invoices to obscure the proper destination and type of transactions. The culprits have employed financial structures that made it difficult to trace the funds. The scheme did not involve a direct, simple goods-for-goods swap. However, it was instead a coordinated evasion of economic and trade controls through the disguising of transactions (U.S. Department of Justice, 2019).

Discovery Method: The discovery was probably a joint effort of traditional financial intelligence and law enforcement collaborating closely. When a company repeatedly conducts transactions with countries that pose a high risk of money laundering, it is considered a red flag. There are inconsistencies in shipping documents, and the company is using vehicles whose ownership is difficult to trace. Other types of transactions lead to investigations. The entity was engaged with sanctioned parties (Iran). That was a signal to trigger transaction-monitoring alerts across the global banking system. Subsequently, it drew heightened scrutiny from the U.S. Treasury's Office of Foreign Assets Control and prompted a criminal investigation by the DOJ.

TBML Analysis: This case exemplifies a TBML technique intertwined with sanctions evasion, specifically over- and under-invoicing of goods. By issuing fraudulent invoices, the perpetrators could justify illicit financial flows by disguising them as trade payments. The "barter" element here is not a classic exchange but rather the use of trade as a deceptive facade to enable prohibited financial activity and the transfer of value. The case underscores how TBML methods are central to sanctions-busting schemes, as they create a veneer of legitimate commerce to conceal the movement of value to a prohibited counterparty (FATF, 2006). The exploitation of the corporate veil and trade documentation highlights acute vulnerabilities in trade finance and customs oversight.

The Dark Side of Free Trade: Uncovering the Misuse of Free Trade Zones

Free trade zones (FTZs) are often portrayed as facilitators of trade and economic growth. However, as with many things, there is usually a dark side. The unrestricted access to international markets offered by FTZs may entice those seeking to violate the law, leading to widespread misuse and exploitation.

"Designated areas within a country where goods can be imported, exported, and re-exported without being subject to tariffs or other trade barriers" (UN, 1990). FTZs are intended to cater to a conducive business environment by attracting foreign investment and promoting economic development. However, the very same freedoms that make FTZs appealing can also be utilized to exploit the global trade system. Companies seeking to avoid tariffs or other trade barriers can import goods into an FTZ and re-export them to a third country, thereby evading the tariffs they would otherwise incur. This results in a loss of revenue for the countries imposing the tariffs, as they cannot collect the levies to which they are ordinarily entitled.

FTZs can be used as a cover for illegal practices, such as money laundering and the trade in illegal goods. The economic liberalization that typically accompanies FTZs often results in market depression, inadequate oversight, and a high propensity for misuse by criminal organizations to facilitate the clandestine transfer of funds and other goods. It increases the likelihood of the shadow economy's proliferation, thereby creating instability and driving insecurity.

Monitoring FTZs: Protecting the Global Trade System and the Fight Against Illicit Funds

The Crucial Role of Monitoring FTZs: Safeguarding the Integrity of the Global Trade System

This involves implementing effective measures to monitor the flow of goods and funds into and out of FTZs. This approach allows us to defend the global trade system efficiently and ensure that the purpose of FTZs, which is to promote economic growth and development responsibly and sustainably, is fulfilled.

Misuse of FTZs

Free trade zones often promote trade and economic development by attracting foreign investment and providing a more favorable business environment. However, FTZs can also be misused in numerous ways. This abuse is more widespread and involves the use of FTZs to circumvent tariffs or other import restrictions. To illustrate, the company imports products to the FTZ and exports them to a third country without paying any applicable tariffs on their import to that country. This could result in losses for countries imposing tariffs, as they cannot collect the expected revenue.

As an advanced method of exploiting FTZs, the establishment of shell companies may involve the use of other corporate structures to evade taxes or regulations. For instance, a firm may establish a subsidiary in an FTZ to obtain tax waivers and regulatory benefits while continuing to operate in other countries that impose taxes and regulations. Consequently, this can result in economic losses for countries in which the company avoids paying taxes, since they would not be able to collect the revenues to which they would otherwise be entitled.

We provide a few instructive examples of barter trade and FTZ abuse:

i In the 1990s, the United Nations imposed sanctions to put excessive pressure on the Iraqi government to comply with international demands. However, Iraq has circumvented these restrictions by using barter to acquire restricted goods entering and leaving the country through the "oil-for-food" program, under which Iraq has committed a large quantity of oil to trade for essential food and other humanitarian supplies, including medicines. Although aimed at assisting the Iraqi people, it encountered a barrage of criticisms due to its misuse in securing forbidden products for Iraq and enriching government officials and elites.

ii In 2010, the U.S. Government Accountability Office (U.S. GAO). A report has been issued that evaluates the abuse of FTZs in the United States. The report revealed that several companies have exploited FTZs to evade tariffs on imported goods and other trade barriers, resulting in substantial losses to the U.S. government. The report also found that these companies failed to meet all requirements of the FTZ program. The GAO report observed that the exploitation of FTZs is also a complicated issue. The lack of transparency in the FTZ program and the challenges of enforcing and complying with the rules are among the factors contributing to the problem.

iii The World Trade Organization (WTO) in 2014 ruled against Russia for violating trade sanctions against Ukraine through barter trade. WTO found out that Russia was utilizing barter trade with Ukraine and re-exporting goods from there to other countries in circumvention of trade sanctions imposed against Ukraine. Subsequently, it re-exported the goods to circumvent trade restrictions imposed by the EU and the U.S., resulting in substantial losses, as Ukraine became effectively crippled and could not sell directly in EU and U.S. markets.

This clearly indicates the urgent need to address the misuse of the UAE FTZ. Free traders attract gold smuggling because these zones operate under lax regulations and tax incentives, allowing smugglers to evade substantial customs duties and taxes when importing gold. Once gold is smuggled into a designated zone, it would be easy to export it and sell it at a higher price in the open market.

Globally, this problem has caused staggering losses amounting to billions for other countries. For example, European Union (EU) studies have estimated that smuggling of gold from the

UAE has resulted in more than €1 billion in lost customs duties. Billions of dollars in customs duties have also been lost due to gold smuggling from the UAE into the United States.

Estimating the damage caused by the misuse of exchanges through barter and FTZs is challenging because it depends on numerous variables, including the nature of goods and services traded, the nations involved, and the trade barriers circumvented. This exploitation will harm the countries involved at a high cost, thereby incurring losses of immense economic magnitude.

For instance, the oil-for-food program in Iraq is estimated to have cost the United States and other countries with sanctions against Iraq many billions of dollars. Likewise, the abuse of the FTZs in the United States and the EU is expected to have caused hefty losses for the countries.

Case 8.2 TBML via a Toy Wholesaler (USA, 2012)

Case Snapshot: In 2012, a U.S.-based company, Woody Toys, and its owners were charged with laundering drug proceeds of around $2 million for Colombian and Mexican drug cartels. The company employed a Black-Market Peso Exchange (BMPE)-type scheme and imported toys from China to disguise the operation (U.S. Department of Justice, 2012).

Core Facts: The company was receiving cash in bulk from drug trafficking organizations (DTOs). The money was used to purchase toys from China, which were then shipped to and sold in the U.S. market. The sales of toys generated "clean" U.S. dollars, which were then transferred to DTO agents, thereby finishing the laundering cycle. The defendants confessed to money laundering, conspiracy, and failure to report cash transactions on IRS Form 8300 (U.S. Department of Justice, 2012; and U.S. Immigration and Customs Enforcement, 2012).

Discovery Method: This multi-agency investigation was mainly conducted by the FBI. Other agencies included the Drug Enforcement Administration, the Internal Revenue Service–Criminal Investigation, and Homeland Security Investigations. Potential red flags may have included structuring cash deposits to avoid compulsory reporting. The company's reported business volume does not align with its actual financial flows, and unusual trading patterns (e.g., import values or volumes inconsistent with the domestic market). The sources of cash and the trade transactions could have been identified through traditional law enforcement financial investigation methods.

TBML Analysis: This is a perfect example of the BMPE, the most common method of TBML. The plan involves using the international trade system to launder and legitimize illicit funds. The main TBML techniques employed were over- and under-invoicing (altering the toys' value for customs declarations) and misrepresenting the goods (using toys as an uncontroversial commodity while at the same time hiding the drug proceeds). This case is a significant illustration of how money-laundering purposes can lead to the use of legitimate trade sectors without committing the predicate crime, e.g., by exploiting loopholes in cash-reporting requirements and trade-documentation verification (FATF, 2006). This is a reminder that various agencies must collaborate, and financial institutions should exercise particular care in trade finance.

Chapter Summary

The discussion centers on barter, describing its key elements and the merits and drawbacks of this mode of exchange. Barter is the exchange of goods or services without the use of money. This trade has existed for centuries, with associated advantages and disadvantages. For example, barter allows individuals to exchange goods and services without the constraints imposed by traditional financial systems. This entails the absence of currency requirements and transaction charges. On the downside, barter trade can be misused, leading to adverse effects such as circumventing sanctions and concealing illegal activities.

Uncovering the misuse of FTZs exposes how such free trade areas can be applied to circumvent barriers and commit illegal activities. FTZs are designated areas within a country where goods may be imported, exported, and re-exported. Goods entering these areas are exempt from tariffs and taxes, with no time limit. This system can also be manipulated to evade tariffs or other trade barriers, resulting in losses for the countries that levy them.

Protecting the global trade system and the fight against illicit funds is a critical engagement that underscores the imperative of international cooperation to recognize FTZs and prevent their use for illegal activities. Governments and agencies must take serious action to ensure that FTZs are not used to launder money or to engage in any unlawful activity that could have significant global economic consequences.

End of Chapter: Discussion Questions

1 How does barter trade impact the traditional financial system?
2 How can barter trade be misused and lead to negative consequences?
3 What is the importance of monitoring FTZs?
4 How can illegal activities in FTZs, such as money laundering, harm the global economy? The potential for significant economic damage underscores the importance of preventing the misuse of FTZs.
5 What steps should governments and agencies take to prevent the misuse of FTZs?

References

"Barter trade." Investopedia, www.investopedia.com/terms/b/barter.asp

Financial Action Task Force. (2006). Trade-based money laundering. Paris: FATF/OECD. Retrieved from https://www.fatf-gafi.org/media/fatf/documents/reports/Trade-Based-Money-Laundering.pdf

Investopedia. (n.d.). Barter trade. Retrieved from https://www.investopedia.com/terms/b/barter.asp

U.S. Government Accountability Office. (2010). Barter trade: Issues and implications. U.S. Government Accountability Office. https://www.gao.gov/assets/gao-10-399

U.S. Government Accountability Office. (2010, March). Foreign trade zones: CBP should enhance its capacity to assess and address compliance risks throughout the program (GAO-10-399). Washington, DC: Author. Retrieved from https://www.gao.gov/products/gao-10-399

U.S. Immigration and Customs Enforcement. (2012, January 31). LA toy company owners sentenced in international money laundering scheme [Press release]. Washington, DC: ICE Newsroom. Retrieved from https://www.ice.gov/news/releases/la-toy-company-owners-sentenced-international-money-laundering-scheme

U.S. Department of Justice. (2012, August 1). Mexican toy dealer pleads guilty in drug money laundering case. https://www.dea.gov/press-releases/2012/08/01/mexican-toy-dealer-pleads-guilty-drug-money-laundering-case

U.S. Department of Justice. (2015, December 17). Chinese national charged with criminal conspiracy to export U.S. power amplifiers to China [Press release]. Washington, DC: DOJ Office of Public Affairs. Retrieved from https://www.justice.gov/archives/opa/pr/chinese-national-charged-criminal-conspiracy-export-us-power-amplifiers-china

U.S. Department of Justice. (2021, January 29). Chinese national charged with criminal conspiracy to export U.S. power amplifiers to China; Avnet Asia admits criminal liability and agrees to pay more than $3.2 million [Press release]. Washington, DC: DOJ Office of Public Affairs. Retrieved from https://www.justice.gov/opa/pr/chinese-national-charged-criminal-conspiracy-export-us-power-amplifiers-china

United Nations. (1990). Free trade zones. United Nations Department of Economic and Social Affairs.

United Nations Conference on Trade and Development. (2016). Trade and development report 2016: Structural transformation for inclusive and sustained growth (UNCTAD/TDR/2016). Geneva: United Nations. Retrieved from https://unctad.org/system/files/official-document/tdr2016_en.pdf

Additional Learning Resources

Articles

1 The Myth of the Barter Economy. Strauss, I. E. (2016, February 26). The Atlantic.
In this article, Ilana E. Strauss challenges the belief that barter systems preceded currency-based economies. She argues that there is no evidence supporting this claim and suggests that various forms of exchange, such as gift economies, were more common in non-monetary societies.

2 Trade in counterfeit goods and free trade zones: Evidence from recent trends. OECD. (2018) Paris: OECD.
The report examines the potential for free trade zones (FTZs) to be misused for trade in counterfeit and pirated goods. The report finds a clear link between FTZs and trade in counterfeit goods, and that FTZs can confer several advantages on counterfeiters. The report concludes by recommending some measures to combat counterfeiting in FTZs.

Books

3 Bad Samaritans: The myth of free trade and the secret history of capitalism. Ha-Joon Chang (2008). Bloomsbury Publishing USA.
The writer challenges the conventional wisdom about free trade and globalization. Chang argues that developed countries have used their economic power to force developing countries to open their markets, even when this has not been in their best interests. He also argues that free trade has not always been the engine of economic growth, it is often portrayed to be.

4 Free trade under fire (4th ed.). Douglas A. Irwin (2020). Princeton University Press. books.google.com
The book examines the economic arguments for and against free trade. The book has been updated four times since its first publication in 2002, with the most recent edition being published in 2020. It explores the economic evidence of the impact of trade, both on countries as a whole and on individual workers. The book further discusses the role of trade agreements in the global economy.

Films

5 Fernando Meirelles directed "The Constant Gardener" (2005).
This film tells the story of a British diplomat who investigates the misuse of a free trade zone in Kenya.

6 "The International" was directed by Tom Tykwer (2009).
This thriller film examines the corrupt practices of a powerful bank, highlighting the potential for misuse and manipulation within the global financial system.
Documentaries:

7 Adam Wishart directed Barter Kings (2006).
This documentary follows a group of people who use barter trade to buy and sell goods and services.

8 "The True Cost" is a thought-provoking documentary film directed by Andrew Morgan and released in 2015. Available at: https://tinyurl.com/Truecost1
The film examines the impact of the fashion industry on people and the planet, shedding light on the hidden costs behind the garments we wear. Although it focuses on the fashion industry, this documentary examines the impact of globalization and free trade on workers and the environment, offering insights into the potential pitfalls of unregulated trade practices.

YouTube Videos

9 "The Hidden Costs of Free Trade" by Vox (2019).
In this video, Vox explores the unintended consequences of free trade, including the potential for exploitation and inequality, and offers a concise overview of the topic.

9 The Shadow Economy

Uncovering the Menace of Illicit Financial Flows

The expression "illicit financial flows" (IFFs) was coined in 2021 by the Tax Justice Network. It describes the illegal movement of money across borders, which has long posed massive challenges to the global financial system. IFFs constitute financial crimes that weaken economies, diminish the tax base, and sustain organized crime and terrorism. This discussion will elaborate on the gravity of IFFs, explore their various types, explain reasons for preventing such flows, and discuss methods for blocking illegally acquired money.

IFFs constitute financial crimes that weaken economies, diminish the tax base, and sustain organized crime and terrorism. This discussion will elaborate on the gravity of IFFs, explore their various types, explain reasons for preventing such flows, and discuss methods for blocking illegally acquired money. Representing the consensus among multilateral institutions, the managing director of the International Monetary Fund recently pointed out that "the shadow economy and illicit financial flows are major obstacles to global economic development and social progress." He added that such flows "harm legitimate markets, reduce tax revenue, and increase inequality," thus, in her view, these issues need coordinated actions from "governments, international organizations, and civil society" (Georgieva, 2023, para. 4).

What Are Illicit Financial Flows?

IFFs are the transnational movement of money. Proceeds of crime are obtained through illegal or unlawful means. It encompasses various unlawful schemes ranging from corruption and tax evasion to money laundering and illegal trading. The United Nations Office on Drugs and Crime (UNODC) estimates that money laundering accounts for a proportionate share of global GDP, ranging from 2% to 5% (UNODC, 2025). IFFs impede economic prospects, frustrate development agendas, and, even more significantly, entrench social disparities.

Types of Illicit Financial Flows

These IFFs comprise tax evasion, corruption, money laundering, and trade mispricing. Tax evasion refers to the deliberate failure to pay taxes to the government's exchequer. Corruption implies the abuse of public office for private gain. Money laundering merely obfuscates the proceeds of illegal or criminal activity as legitimate income. There is an expansive definition of "trade mispricing," which refers to the artificial inflation or deflation of the prices of goods or services in cross-border transactions to facilitate the illicit movement of funds.

DOI: 10.4324/9781003477631-10

Why Should Illicit Financial Flows be Deterred?

IFFs have several damaging implications for the global financial system. First, they erode the tax base and significantly impede the government's ability to finance essential public services. Second, they help fund organized crime and terrorism and pose a major threat to national security. Third, these flows destabilize economies and also significantly contribute to income disparity.

Recognizing Illicit Financial Flows

Identifying illegal financial flows becomes challenging because they are often camouflaged within various financial structures and can be transferred quickly across national borders. However, certain red flags may indicate the likelihood of illegal flows. These comprise transactions that appear suspicious, including unusual activity, large sums moving into and out of accounts, and the use of shell companies and offshore accounts to conceal asset ownership.

The Cost of Illicit Financial Flows

Although the cost of IFFs is nearly impossible to quantify accurately, an estimate suggests that several trillion dollars may be the appropriate value. Global Financial Integrity (GFI), an organization that closely monitors IFFs, estimates that $1.3 trillion in IFFs left developing nations in 2018 (Global Financial Integrity, 2019), underscoring the gravity of the issue. This implies that funds could have been allocated to provide all required social services, such as education and health care.

The Fight against Illicit Financial Flows

It is a global collaborative effort by all concerned parties, including financial institutions, governments, and international organizations, to combat IFFs. A critical step in progress is to implement international standards, including the Common Reporting Standard (CRS) established by the Organization for Economic Co-operation and Development (OECD), which became operative in 2017. This obliges the automatic exchange of information on financial accounts between institutions and the tax authorities of the other contracting party (Cobham et al., 2017).

The Link between Illicit Financial Flows and Money Laundering

IFFs resulting from money laundering are loosely stated, yet closely related. Money laundering typically conceals the proceeds of illicit activities, including corruption, tax evasion, and the sale of illegal goods or services. The United Nations Office on Drugs and Crime asserts that organized crime and corruption are worth about $1.6 trillion every year. Most of this "dirty" money gets cleaned up in the closet of the global financial system.

Deterring and Stopping Illicit Financial Flows

It requires the meticulous addressing of several issues, including increased transparency, tighter regulation, and international collaboration, as well as the public disclosure of beneficial ownership registers and the implementation of country-by-country reporting. It is difficult for individuals and organizations to conceal their assets and the proceeds of crime. Institutions that fail to comply with laws and regulations, which are not freely set but are subject to contractual obligations, face penalties. For instance, the Common Reporting Standard also requires financial institutions to report suspicious activities to the relevant authorities. Various jurisdictions, such as tax information exchange, enable authorities to track cross-border financial flows, ultimately leading to the apprehension of criminals.

Estimating the Global Loss from Illicit Financial Flows

Determining the best estimate of the global loss from IFFs and quantifying the illegal financial operations that are intentionally hidden or shrouded is immeasurably challenging. The GFI published a stunning analysis in 2014. The analysis made a loud claim that illicit financial outflows cost developing countries more than US$1 trillion in tax income each year (Global Financial Integrity, 2014). Such staggering losses of income will have a profoundly devastating impact on public services, including education and healthcare, thereby perpetuating poverty.

Historical Lessons

The struggle against IFFs has been ongoing for some time. In the 1970s and 1980s, the international community responded to money laundering by advocating anti-money laundering measures, including mandatory suspicious transaction reporting and the establishment of anti-money laundering departments within financial institutions. However, the threat of illicit financial practices remains unabated, necessitating an adaptive international response.

IFFs remain a significant concern for the global economy, undermining the reliability of financial systems in developing nations and eroding their tax bases. While it is difficult to estimate the exact magnitude of these flows, current approximations suggest that trillions of dollars are squandered annually. The repercussions of this trend have far-reaching impacts on economic stability and social justice.

IFFs, often associated with other crimes such as money laundering, tax evasion, and corruption, require the concerted efforts of the international community to address them. The first and foremost step in addressing this issue is to enhance transparency and strengthen accountability within the global financial system. With aspirations of advancing that system, tax transparency measures, including automatic multilateral exchanges of tax information, transparency in beneficial ownership, and country-by-country reporting, are positive developments in this direction. Although imperfect, these measures would be prerequisites for gaining a better understanding of the extent and characteristics of illegal financial transactions and of the contribution of multinational corporations in facilitating them.

From the foregoing, one clear lesson concerning the global fight against IFFs is that no country or institution can resolve the problem solely. This calls for a unified global effort involving collaboration among developed and developing countries, international financial institutions, and civil society organizations. As the global economy continues to accelerate its globalization, countering IFFs requires joint action more than ever. It is essential to recognize that IFFs, deterrence, and stoppage constitute a complex and persistent set of challenges. On the other hand, they are equally critical to sustaining stability and growth in the global economy. Hence, every little step toward creating a more just, stable, and equitable global community. It must, at a minimum, reinforce transparency, foster cooperation, and ensure that individuals who engage in illegal financial transactions are held accountable, thereby significantly contributing to our objective.

IFFs threaten the integrity of the global economic system; hence, combating them is essential. Moving forward, collaborative efforts toward transparency should help deter and stop these flows for the common good of all nations, thereby stabilizing and guaranteeing an equitable global economy.

The Shadowy World of Illicit Financial Flows: Uncovering the Methods and Impacts

In this section, we will examine the various schemes employed to facilitate IFFs, the implications of these illicit actions, and the measures necessary to combat them effectively.

Trade Misinvoicing: The Deliberate Manipulation of Trade Transactions

One of the primary approaches for facilitating IFFs is trade misinvoicing. This contains the deliberate falsification of the value, volume, or composition of trade transactions to transfer funds across borders or escape taxes, customs duties, or other regulations (UNCTAD, 2018). The result is the theft of government revenue that could otherwise be exercised for public goods and services.

Shell Companies: A Tool for Money Laundering and Tax Evasion

Another standard scheme employed to facilitate IFFs is the operation of shell companies. These companies, registered in offshore havens or onshore, can be exploited to launder money and evade taxes (ICIJ, 2016). The anonymity of the ownership makes it arduous for authorities to track and regulate these operations.

Underground Banking Systems: A Way to Transfer Funds Anonymously

Underground banking systems, such as Hawala and Fei-Chien, provide an alternative means of facilitating illegal money transfers. These systems operate outside the formal financial system, enabling anonymous transfers without the need for traditional financial institutions (UNODC, 2010; CBRC, 2018). These networks hinder the government's ability to monitor and regulate the illicit money flow, posing significant challenges.

The Impacts of Illicit Financial Flows: Depriving Governments of Revenue and Undermining the Integrity of the Financial System

The harmful impacts of IFFs are substantial and wide-ranging. They deprive governments of much-needed revenue and undermine the credibility of the financial system. IFFs can also facilitate the financing of criminal and terrorist operations, as well as contribute to income inequality and economic instability. A study by GFI found that IFFs through the international trade system have become a growing concern. GFI estimates that, on average, approximately 20% of developing countries' overall trade with advanced economies is attributable to trade-related IFFs (GFI, 2021). These illicit flows encompass both inflows and outflows and have a profound impact on the global economy.

The study conducted by GFI analyzed trade-related IFFs across 134 developing countries from 2009 to 2018 (GFI, 2021). The report offers valuable insights into the scale and impact of these IFFs.

In addition, a previous report by GFI indicates that between 2006 and 2015, IFFs accounted for more than 20% of developing-country trade (GFI, 2019). These flows were almost evenly split between outflows and inflows. This study examines the persistence of IFFs and their impact on the global financial system.

IFFs substantially threaten the stability and integrity of the global economic system. Robust measures are required to deter and eliminate illegal financial flows. Governments and international organizations must take appropriate action to promote transparency and accountability in the financial system. The use of trade misinvoicing, shell corporations, and underground banking systems facilitates IFFs and must be duly regulated. Only by working collaboratively can we prevent these unlawful actions and maintain the stability and integrity of the global financial system.

Major Money Laundering Centers: Notorious Hubs of Illicit Financial Flows

As stated in the 2020 report of the United Nations Office on Drugs and Crime (UNODC), money laundering is a universal and recurring problem characterized by the movement of illicit funds through the financial system, intending to obscure their illegal source.

Major Money Laundering Centers

Some of the significant money laundering centers in the world include:

i The United States: The country enjoys the most extensive financial system and the laxest state laws, which eventually provide opportunities to criminals as a haven for money laundering operations.
ii Switzerland: The country's stringent bank secrecy laws make it one of the best hiding spots for criminals to keep their wealth secret.
iii Hong Kong: The country is a major money laundering center. Being a financial hub in Asia, it provides access to the rest of the world.
iv The United Arab Emirates: The combination of a lax regulatory environment with a strategically located country has made it a much-favored money laundering hotspot.

Notorious Activities in These Centers

These money laundering centers are a breeding ground and are notorious for facilitating and promoting a plethora of illegal activities: drug trafficking, arms smuggling, human trafficking, and even corrupt practices.

Impact on the Global Economy

Money laundering has an unparalleled impact on the global economy, surpassing that of any other factor. It distorts the market structure, breeds a lack of confidence in financial institutions, and depletes government tax revenues. It also encourages terrorism and other illegal operations.

Challenges in Enforcing Laws against Money Laundering

Enforcing laws against money laundering is challenging due to several factors, including:

i The complexity of financial transactions: Money launderers have intricate ways of distracting authorities from tracking, capturing, and charging them.

ii Lack of international support: There is an international support deficit. Money laundering has become a global issue that necessitates a collaborative effort among countries. Many countries, however, are reluctant to share and reveal information because of their implicit interests.

 i Political influence: Some nations and individuals with political influence will exploit their advantage to obstruct investigations and prosecutions.

Money laundering significantly hinders the global economy, with key hubs worldwide enabling and facilitating illicit activities. Despite ongoing efforts to address the issue, the challenges of enforcing anti-money laundering laws remain overwhelming.

An Insight: The Dark Side of Life Insurance Policies and Money Transfer Services

Money laundering has become a global issue, undeniably affecting the stability of the financial system. This unlawful act directly endangers the viability of the economic system by facilitating the laundering and legitimation of criminals' illicit gains and their subsequent use in further criminal ventures. The array of channels that may facilitate money laundering includes life insurance policies and the misuse of money and value transfer services.

Life Insurance Policies

Life insurance policies can be a vulnerable channel for money laundering, as they provide a mechanism for criminals to conceal their illicit proceeds and legitimize them as insurance payouts. The potential for abuse arises from the lack of transparency in the sale and management of life insurance policies, which can obscure the policy's actual ownership and the source of funds used to purchase it (UNODC, 2021).

According to a report by the Financial Action Task Force (FATF, 2021), Life insurance policies can be employed for money laundering through the following methods:

a Premium laundering: Acquiring a life insurance policy employing proceeds from illegal practices and claiming the policy proceeds as a legitimate source of income.
b Premium diversion: The diverting of premium payments from an insurance company to another bank account, thereby facilitating the movement of illegal proceeds.
c Layering: The process of creating multiple layers of transactions to disguise the valid owner of the policy and mask the source of funds used to purchase the deal.

Abuse of Money and Value Transfer Services

Money and value transfer services, in addition to hawala and informal remittance systems, are equally susceptible to misuse for money laundering. Individuals often use these services to transfer money from one location to another without requiring intervention from a conventional bank. Their lack of oversight and monitoring makes them a preferred method for money laundering.

According to a report by the United Nations Office on Drugs and Crime (UNODC, 2021), money and value transfer services are employed for money laundering in the following ways:

a Smurfing: The practice of dividing substantial quantities of money into smaller amounts to escape discovery by authorities.

b Concealment: The concealing of illegal proceeds within legitimate transactions by employing false invoices or misstating the purpose of the transaction.
c Structuring: Manipulating transaction amount and timing to circumvent reporting requirements.

To summarize, life insurance policies, money, and value transfer services are vulnerable to money laundering; as a result, tightening regulation and oversight is urgent. Collaboration and coordination among international institutions that are actively combating money laundering are essential. The problem has catastrophic repercussions for the financial system and must continue to be addressed, with a focus on bodies such as the FATF and UNODC.

Case 9.1 Odebrecht S.A.: Bribes Across Latin America to Secure Public Contracts and Influence Political Power (Latin America, 2014–2016)

Background

Odebrecht S.A. was established in 1944 and is a Brazilian conglomerate headquartered in its tax home in Salvador, Bahia. The company's portfolio of activities comprises engineering and construction, chemicals, and petrochemicals. Norberto Odebrecht Construtora, the parent company of Odebrecht S.A., is the largest engineering and contracting company in Latin America. Transparency International (2018) has called the Odebrecht Scandal the "Largest Corruption Scheme in Latin American History." However, the name Odebrecht became notorious and contributed to its downfall through a major bribery scandal that spanned from 2001 to 2016.

The Scandal

Odebrecht, the Brazilian construction giant, disbursed more than $788 million in bribes across more than 15 years in Latin America, primarily to secure government contracts. The organization has, moreover, been in the public eye for a case related to Operation Car Wash, wherein Marcelo Odebrecht, the former CEO, was arrested in 2015 and later sentenced to 19 years and 4 months in prison for bribing executives of the Brazilian oil giant Petrobras in exchange for contracts.

The company has also been fined $2.6 billion by the U.S. Department of Justice, making this case the largest ever prosecuted under the U.S. Foreign Corrupt Practices Act. According to BBC News (2016), Odebrecht was penalized "$2.6bn in settlement by the United States."

Widespread Implications

The extensive network of politicians and individuals involved in the bribery scheme orchestrated by Odebrecht spanned multiple countries, such as Panama, Peru, and Venezuela. Forty-three people were accused of involvement in the Panama scandal. Odebrecht was the country's leading government contractor, with contracts valued at more than $500 million, including the construction of Panama City's subway system.

According to reports, Odebrecht has shaken Peru's political system. Former presidents Alejandro Toledo, Ollanta Humala, and Pedro Pablo Kuczynski, and ex-First Lady Nadine Heredia have faced allegations of bribery involving Odebrecht and high-ranking officials in the country's ruling elite. Keiko Fujimori is the daughter of former President Alberto Fujimori. She was also apprehended, possibly due to her dubious involvement in the campaign finance scandal. An inquiry into bribery was launched against former president Alan Garcia, which ultimately proved fatal. Alan committed suicide in April 2019.

The Odebrecht Scandal immensely impacted Venezuelans, as President Nicolás Maduro and opposition candidate Henrique Capriles were the victims.

The Paradise Papers, published in November 2017, revealed that 17 offshore companies run by Odebrecht were employed to pay bribes in Operation Car Wash. Marcelo Odebrecht, his father Emílio Odebrecht, and his brother Maurício Odebrecht were among those named as being outrageously involved in the operation.

The Aftermath

Brazilian and international authorities, including the Federal Police of Brazil, the Public Prosecutor's Office, and the Court of Auditors of Brazil, were required to undertake concerted efforts to uncover the Odebrecht corruption scheme. This extensive examination commenced with a tip-off from a former Odebrecht executive and led to an inquiry that encompassed a network of companies and individuals.

The bribery scheme had severe effects. The company and its executives were required to pay substantial fines to authorities in the United States and Switzerland, totaling $2.6 billion. The Brazilian people and economy were severely impacted, with far-reaching consequences in several Latin American and Caribbean nations, including Argentina, Colombia, Ecuador, Peru, and Venezuela.

Odebrecht and its top executives were subjected to legal actions that have resulted in the arrest and imprisonment of quite many people, including former CEO Marcelo Odebrecht. The company is also a signatory to several leniency agreements with several countries under which it has agreed to pay a fine and to cooperate with investigations in exchange for reduced penalties. In addition to criminal proceedings, there are civil suits against Odebrecht and its executives, in which individuals harmed by the bribery scheme seek damages for their injuries.

Following the unprecedented bribery scandal, Odebrecht was required to undertake a major overhaul and restructuring of its corporate framework. In 2016, under a leniency agreement with the Brazilian authorities, the company was required to pay $3.5 billion (£2.8 billion) penalty. The agreement also requires the company to cooperate with investigators and accept reduced penalties. The corporation, however, had to adopt anti-corruption measures and strengthen governance, risk management, and compliance processes (DOJ, 2016).

According to a report by the Brazilian Institute of Corporate Governance (2017), Odebrecht has made considerable strides in upgrading its governance and compliance systems. However, the company continues to face substantial challenges in rebuilding its reputation and restoring public trust. The report focuses on the need to sustain efforts to reinforce the company's compliance culture and to stabilize its internal controls.

In sum, the Odebrecht corruption scandal may well be the most consequential event in corporate corruption in history. It brought far-reaching consequences for the corporate house, executives, and the countries implicated in the bribery scheme. While Odebrecht and the authorities were already undertaking efforts to address the problem, the company continued to confront significant challenges in regaining public confidence and rebuilding its reputation.

Case 9.2 Wirecard AG and the €1.9 Billion Fraud: The Truth Behind the Accounting Fraud and Money Laundering Scandal (Germany, 2020)

Wirecard AG was once a darling of the stock market, achieving a market capitalization of over €24 billion in 2018 as the preferred German payment processor. However, in June 2020, *The Financial Times* published a series of articles that began raising questions about the company's accounting and business practices (McCrum, 2019). These suggested that the company was engaging in round-tripping revenues, an elaborate mechanism for inflating revenues through fictitious transactions. Thus ensued the spate of different investigations. In June 2020, the company announced that it could not locate the €1.9 billion that it had previously stated had been placed in escrow with a third party in the Philippines. That led the company to insolvency.

Red Flags

The articles published in the Financial Times raised several red flags that the company's auditor overlooked. For example, the articles questioned the existence of third-party partnerships that were supposed to generate substantial revenue for Wirecard. They also raised concerns about the need for greater transparency regarding Wirecard's business activities in certain countries and the substantial amounts of money flowing through the company's accounts. Moreover, Wirecard's use of "special purpose vehicles" and "related-party transactions" also should have raised suspicions among auditors and regulators. Besides, the company's management has been under probe by the Financial Supervisory Authority (BaFin) since 2019. According to BaFin's annual report, the regulator has been investigating reports of potential market manipulation. This should have been considered a red flag and investigated further.

The Financial Times journalist Dan McCrum published a barrage of articles in 2019 regarding an investigation into Wirecard's questionable accounting practices. He reported that Wirecard had overstated its sales and profits over several years, casting doubt on the authenticity of the company's positive financial representations. Following publication, the company's share price declined sharply.

The Financial Times had by now become convinced of Wirecard's fraud, having published a series of investigative articles on the detection of the company's fraudulent financial practices. Wirecard had inflated its sales and profits for several years, creating a complex web of shell companies and false invoicing to conceal the fraud. Other tricks included the round-tripping of funds between companies, usually related parties, to give the appearance of increased business activity. The company and its stakeholders sustained significant damage, prompting widespread speculation. The share price fell sharply upon the realization that Wirecard was not transparent, resulting in many investors losing substantial sums. The company subsequently filed for insolvency in June 2020.

The Red Flags That Were Present in This Case Include

Large amounts of money were stashed in bank accounts in countries where the company had little or no business activities.

Wirecard's financial statements revealed substantial assets and substantial bank debt, which should have raised questions about the authenticity and reliability of the assets.

The company's auditor failed to request the outstanding balance owed by Wirecard and did not perform a crucial audit to verify its existence. Several industry experts observed that the auditor's failure to conduct proper due diligence was a notable red flag that should have been identified sooner. Marcel Pheijffer, in the NRC, said, "Why opt to earmark such a large amount in an account far from Germany in a country where you have relatively few activities?" (Pheijffer, 2019). Moreover, according to the head of AMCL in the Philippines, the amount that should have been held was only 5% of the €1.9 billion in foreign currency. Even a brief review of the financial statements and financing structure should have prompted questions from the auditor or other interested parties. Additionally, internal documents and spreadsheets published by *The Financial Times* in 2019 revealed that Wirecard was actively considering preventing auditors from conducting a thorough examination of its financial statements. This involved preventing auditors from conducting impairment tests and ensuring that large customers did not raise any red flags. These examples suggest that specific details were deliberately kept out of the auditor's reach and that special care was taken to prevent them from asking more probing questions.

The ultimate result of all these red flags and missed opportunities was a devastating loss for Wirecard and its stakeholders. Wirecard's market capitalization collapsed, wiping billions of euros of shareholder value. Customers, employees, and investors suffered significant losses. The company's management and board of directors have been disparaged for their lack of oversight and transparency.

Hence, this fraud is unlikely to recur. It becomes imperative that auditors, regulators, and stakeholders be more vigilant in scrutinizing financial statements and take seriously any reports that reflect fraud or market manipulation. These audits must be rigorous, unbiased, and thorough, regardless of any steps management takes to downplay a given suspicion. Regulators should implement stringent regulations and impose harsher penalties on companies engaged in market manipulation and fraud. Stakeholders, including investors, must conduct due diligence before investing in a company and remain vigilant for warning signs of potential fraud.

The implications of this case are significant. Wirecard succumbed to fraud for a combination of reasons: auditors failed to conduct due diligence, regulators did not enforce the rules against Wirecard rigorously, and, lastly, the company's management and board failed to conduct thorough due diligence and to maintain transparency. The eventual outcome has dealt a devastating blow to Wirecard and its numerous stakeholders, thereby underscoring the urgent need for financial oversight and transparency.

Chapter Summary

IFFs refer to illegal cross-border movements and serve as catalysts for other crimes, including tax evasion, money laundering, and corruption. Preventing IFFs is indispensable because they reduce tax revenue, undermine economic activity, and contribute to global poverty. IFFs are often challenging to detect because complex financial structures obscure their transactions, but they are invaluable in combating them. Estimates suggest that the high cost of IFFs translates to trillions of dollars in annual losses worldwide. There is a close relationship between IFFs and "money laundering," which complicates fighting IFFs. As a result, all countries must cooperate to implement complementary measures among governments, financial institutions, and law enforcement agencies to address IFFs.

End of Chapter: Discussion Questions

1 Can you provide examples of illicit financial flows?
2 Why is deterring IFFs important for the global economy?
3 How can we recognize IFFs?
4 Can you estimate the cost of IFFs?
5 How does the link between IFFs and money laundering complicate the fight against IFFs?
6 How can IFFs be deterred and stopped?
7 What role do governments, financial institutions, and law enforcement agencies play in the fight against IFFs?
8 How are estimates of the global loss from IFFs calculated?

Bibliography

Bundesanstalt für Finanzdienstleistungsaufsicht (BaFin). (2020). Annual report 2019. BaFin. https://www.bafin.de/DE/die-bafin/publikationen-daten/jahresbericht/jahresbericht-2025/jahresbericht-2025_node.html

Brazilian Institute of Corporate Governance. (2017). Odebrecht: A case study in corporate corruption. www.ibgc.org.br/en/publications/odebrecht-a-case-study-in-corporate-corruption

CBRC. (2018). Underground banking systems. *China Banking Regulatory Commission.*

Cobham, A., Gray, C., & Murphy, R. (2017). *The political economy of the country-by-country reporting by multinational enterprises.* Tax Justice Network.

Europol. (2016). Odebrecht bribed across Latin America. https://www.dw.com/en/odebrecht-bribed-across-latin-america/a-36887600

Federal Ministry of Finance (Germany). (2020, July 16). Responses to parliamentary questions on Wirecard. Retrieved from https://www.bundesfinanzministerium.de

Financial Action Task Force. (2006). Trade-based money laundering. Paris: FATF/OECD. Retrieved from https://www.fatf-gafi.org/publications/methodsandtrends/documents/trade-based-money-laundering.html

Financial Action Task Force (FATF). (2021). Life insurance and annuities. https://www.fatf-gafi.org/topics/life-insurance-and-annuities/

Financial Action Task Force. (2025, Oct). The FATF recommendations. Paris: FATF/OECD. Retrieved from https://www.fatf-gafi.org/en/publications/Fatfrecommendations/Fatf-recommendations.html

Fischbacher-Smith, D. (2020, November 23). Wirecard scandal: When all lines of defense against corporate fraud fail. Oxford Business Law Blog. https://blogs.law.ox.ac.uk/business-law-blog/blog/2020/11/wirecard-scandal-when-all-lines-defense-against-corporate-fraud-fail

Georgieva, K. I. (2023, March 14). Tackling the shadow economy and illicit financial flows: A global imperative. *International Monetary Fund.* https://www.imf.org/en/News/Articles/2023/03/14/sp031423-tackling-the-shadow-economy-and-illicit-financial-flows

Global Financial Integrity. (2014). *Illicit financial flows from developing countries: 2003–2012.* https://gfintegrity.org/report/2014-global-report-illicit-financial-flows-from-developing-countries-2003-2012/

Global Financial Integrity. (2019). Illicit financial flows to and from 148 developing countries: 2006–2015. https://www.gfintegrity.org/wp-content/uploads/2019/01/GFI-2019-IFF-Update-Report-1.29.18.pdf

Global Financial Integrity. (2021). Trade-related illicit financial flows in 134 developing countries, 2009–2018. Washington, DC: GFI. Retrieved from https://gfintegrity.org/research

Global Financial Integrity. (2023). Trade-related illicit financial flows in the middle east and north Africa (2013–2022). Washington, DC: GFI. Retrieved from https://gfintegrity.org/research

ICIJ. (2016). The shell game: How offshore shell companies are used to hide assets and evade taxes. *International Consortium of Investigative Journalists.*

McCrum, D. (2019, October 15). Wirecard shares slump as FT publishes accounting fraud investigation. *Financial Times.* https://www.ft.com/content/10d8f0a6-efdb-11e9-9743-db5a370481bc

Pheijffer, M. (2019, October 16). Wirecard: fraude of een grote blunder? NRC. https://www.nrc.nl/nieuws/2019/10/16/wirecard-fraude-of-een-grote-blunder-a3987404

Reuters. (2016, December 20). Brazilian firms to pay record $3.5 billion penalty in corruption case. https://jp.reuters.com/article/business/brazilian-firms-to-pay-record-35-billion-penalty-in-corruption-case-idUSKBN14A1Z1/

Seidenstuecker, H. (2019, April 16). German regulator suspects manipulation of Wirecard stock, informs prosecutors. Reuters. https://investing.com/news/stock-market-news/german-regulator-suspects-manipulation-of-wirecard-stock-informs-prosecutors-1837501

Tax Justice Network. (2021). Illicit financial flows. *Tax Justice Network.*

Transparency International. (2020, April 7). *Transparency International Brazil and JOTA present previously unreleased data on Odebrecht cases.* https://www.transparency.org/en/press/transparency-international-brazil-and-jota-present-previously-unreleased-da

U.S. Department of Justice. (2016, December 21). Odebrecht and Braskem have pleaded guilty and agreed to pay at least $3.5 billion in global penalties. https://www.justice.gov/archives/opa/pr/odebrecht-and-braskem-plead-guilty-and-agree-pay-least-35-billion-global-penalties-resolve

UNCTAD. (2018). *Trade misinvoicing.* United Nations Conference on Trade and Development.

UNODC. (2010). *Money laundering and the financial system*. United Nations Office on Drugs and Crime.

United Nations Office on Drugs and Crime. (2020). World drug report 2020. https://wdr.unodc.org/wdr2020/

United Nations Office on Drugs and Crime. (2021). *Money laundering and terrorist financing through the abuse of the life insurance sector*. United Nations.

United Nations Office on Drugs and Crime (UNODC). (2021). *Money laundering, proceeds of crime and the financing of terrorism: Financial sector perspectives*. United Nations Office on Drugs and Crime. Retrieved from https://www.unodc.org/unodc/en/money-laundering/index.html

United Nations: Office on Drugs and Crime. (2025). World Drug Report 2025. Vienna: UNODC. Retrieved from https://www.unodc.org/unodc/en/data-and-analysis/world-drug-report-2025.html

Additional Learning Resources

Article:

1 "The shadow economy." Matthew H. Fleming, John Roman, and Graham Farrell. (2000). Journal of international affairs, 387–409.
The authors explore the concept, causes, and implications of the underground economy. They examine the motivations for its existence, the methods used to measure its size, and its potential impact on government revenue and social welfare programs.

2 "The shadow economy and work in the shadow: What do we (not) know?", Friedrich Schneider (2012). IZA Discussion Papers, No. 6423, Institute for the Study of Labor (IZA), Bonn, https://nbn-resolving.de/urn:nbn:de:101:1-201207125564
The writer examines the shadow economy, focusing on the extent of our knowledge of its characteristics, causes, and consequences. Through a comprehensive analysis, Schneider aims to illuminate the gaps in our understanding of this hidden sector and its implications for policymaking and economic development.

Book

3 "The shadow economy: An international survey." Friedrich Schneider und Dominik H. Enste. (2013). Cambridge University Press. Available at: books.google.com
This book provides an overview of the shadow economy, including illicit financial flows, and discusses the causes, consequences, and measurement of this phenomenon.

4 "The Blood Bankers: Tales from the Global Underground Economy" by James S. Henry (2005).
This book explores illicit financial flows, including money laundering, tax evasion, and corruption, and provides insights into the global underground economy.

Documentary

5 "The Price We Pay" (2014) - Directed by Harold Crooks. The video can be streamed at: https://tinyurl.com/shadoweco
This documentary examines tax avoidance and its societal impact, highlighting the mechanisms used by corporations and individuals to conceal their wealth.

YouTube Video

6 "Understanding Illicit Financial Flows" by AfDBGroup. Available at: https://tinyurl.com/Illicitflow
Viewers gain valuable insights into the complex issue of illicit financial flows. The video aims to raise awareness of the causes and consequences of these flows. It is presented by the African Development Bank Group (AfDBGroup) to educate and inform the audience on this critical topic.

10 Money Laundering

Stages and Importance in Combating Criminal Activity

We shall examine how these illicit financial flows are integrated into the formal financial system. Laundering of funds is the process by which criminals conceal the actual ownership or control of money obtained illegally by making it appear that it came from a legitimate source. It is a means for criminals to launder money earned from unlawful activities without attracting attention to themselves or to the underlying activity. According to FinCEN, money laundering occurs in three stages: placement, layering, and integration (FinCEN, 2022). This could create difficulties for law enforcement in finding and confiscating illicit proceeds of crime.

Money laundering is the process by which criminals conceal the origin of funds obtained from illegal activities. That appears to come from legal sources. Criminals often conceal their illegal activities while using the proceeds from these operations. FinCEN has classified the money laundering scheme into three stages: placement, layering, and integration (FinCEN, 2022). That makes it hard enough for enforcement agencies to detect and confiscate the proceeds of crime. Pointing toward the necessity of proper policies, the European Union Agency for Law Enforcement Cooperation (Europol, 2023) has remarked that "money laundering is the lifeblood of criminal networks; it gives them the means to use illegally acquired money as if it were legal and to conceal their crimes," thus "governments, financial institutions, and law-enforcement agencies must work together and set up strong measures to prevent and detect money laundering; by cutting off the supply of illegal money to criminals, we would be inflicting a serious blow to crime" (para. 3).

i Placement Stage: In the placement stage of money laundering, criminals introduce illegal funds into the money laundering cycle by physically placing them within the financial system. Smurfing is a common practice in placement, in which large amounts are broken into smaller transactions to evade detection by financial institutions (U.S. Department of the Treasury, 2020). This stage is specifically significant, as it transitions physical cash into electronic or institutional assets that are opaque to regulators.

An interesting case of institutional control failure occurred in 2025 at Barclays Bank, which was fined £42 million by the UK Financial Conduct Authority (FCA) due to serious deficiencies in anti-money laundering controls. In this example, Barclays allowed the movement of funds associated with criminal enterprises through poor onboarding and inadequate monitoring of its high-risk clients, including WealthTek and Stunt & Co. These failures made Barclays susceptible to placement-stage laundering and exposed significant systemic weaknesses in its compliance environment (Financial Conduct Authority, 2025; VinciWorks, 2025).

We proceed with another example. According to Reuters 2012, Standard Chartered was fined $667 million for infringing U.S. sanctions and facilitating money laundering, including placing laundered funds into the U.S. financial system (Freifeld, 2023).

DOI: 10.4324/9781003477631-11

ii Layering Stage: In the layering stage, criminals engage in financial transactions to distance illicit funds from their illicit source. One technique to accomplish this is to use shell companies and offshore accounts, which makes it harder to trace the money. According to a 2019 report, Danske Bank was found to have laundered $234 billion through its Estonian branch by employing a network of shell companies to move funds (BBC, 2019).

iii Integration Stage: In the integration stage, criminals reintroduce the laundered funds back into the economy, making it appear as though they are legitimate. An example of this is the use of real estate to invest laundered funds, as property can be bought and sold anonymously, making it difficult to trace the funds' illicit origin. The U.S. government seized numerous assets and recovered funds from the 1Malaysia Development Berhad (1MDB) state fund. According to Bloomberg, of the $8 billion amassed by 1MDB through bond sales, the United States alleged that more than half was systematically siphoned off. The U.S. Department of Justice has been at the forefront of the investigation, focusing on theft, bribery, and money laundering. As part of the investigation, the United States reached a settlement with Jho Low, a central figure in the scandal, to recover nearly $700 million in assets, including high-end real estate in the U.S. In addition, Malaysia dismissed all criminal charges against Goldman Sachs in exchange for a $2.5 billion cash payment and the return of at least $1.4 billion from seized 1MDB assets (Adam & Ho, 2022).

The Commonwealth Bank of Australia (CBA) was found to have breached anti-money laundering and counter-terrorism financing laws on more than 50,000 occasions in 2018 (ABC News, 2018). This breach resulted in the imposition of a substantial $700 million fine, reflecting the bank's role in the integration stage of the money-laundering process.

Understanding Stages of Money Laundering and the Role of the FATF

At this crucial juncture, it is imperative to delve into the stages of money laundering and the FATF's active and practicing role in containing the threat:

i Placement is the first stage of money laundering, where the money launderer integrates illegal funds into the legitimate financial system. This is achieved by breaking up large financial transactions into smaller units to avoid detection by regulators and law enforcement (United Nations Office on Drugs and Crime, 2021). For example, rather than making a single large deposit, a drug trafficker could opt to split the money into multiple smaller deposits at various banks to avoid drawing suspicion (FATF, 2012).

ii Layering separates illegal proceeds from their source by applying multiple financial transactions. This is implemented to distance the funds from their source and make them more challenging to trace. Money launderers may employ various methods, such as trading stocks or currencies across numerous markets or wiring funds through a series of bank accounts worldwide (FATF, 2012–2023). These transactions may be camouflaged as payments for goods or services to give them a legitimate appearance.

iii Integration marks the final point in the money-lending process, where the laundered money is pooled and brought into a legitimate commercial setting. The point, therefore, arises when it becomes nearly impossible to distinguish whether the money is legal or illegal. For example, a money launderer may use the funds to purchase real estate or other assets that can be resold at a profit, and the proceeds are then reintegrated into the legitimate economy.

The fight against money laundering is not merely a regulatory problem. Still, it has also become a substantial focus aimed at disrupting criminal operations and maintaining the integrity of the financial system. As an international watchdog, the FATF sets the benchmark for combating money laundering. It has regularly laid down stringent anti-money laundering and counter-terrorist financing directives. Governments and financial institutions that adopt FATF recommendations create stronger frameworks for preventing, detecting, and prosecuting such unlawful practices. Efforts are geared toward maintaining the integrity of financial channels, thereby safeguarding the global economic system.

One successful anti-money laundering operation, Operation Car Wash (Operação Lava Jato), originated as an investigation into black-market money dealers. Instead, it expanded to form a massive network of bribery, bid rigging, and embezzlement surrounding Petrobras, Brazil's state oil company. This massive operation revealed a substantial money-laundering network involving politicians, business magnates, and financial institutions. The figures are staggering: more than $2 billion was laundered through this scheme, and indictments were issued to more than 100 individuals (BBC, 2017). Another aspect of this operation revolutionized money laundering by revealing the significance of global cooperation and intelligence in combating it. Of course, it has also been demonstrated that even the best-coordinated efforts would eventually undermine the most substantial and entrenched criminal networks.

To conclude, the discussion suggests that the adverse effects of money laundering are most blatant, pervasive, and far-reaching. Thus, governmental authorities and financial institutions must be at the forefront of efforts to reduce these illegal activities and curb unlawful operations. Concrete steps must be taken to thwart these operations at their roots. Success in such endeavors often stems from severing ties to illegal conduct and conveying clear concerns about criminal acts—impunity is not an option. As such, criminal networks can quickly undermine and compromise the financial system's integrity.

Case 10.1 HSBC and the $1.9 Billion Settlement: A Global Bank's Failure to Prevent Criminal Financial Flows (United States, 2012)

It is 2010, and HSBC, one of the world's major banks, is now facing the repercussions of all its decisions. HSBC failed to establish adequate mechanisms to prevent money laundering, thereby exposing the bank to the risk of facilitating the movement of hundreds of millions of dollars from drug sales through its internal systems. The fine for this blatant violation of the law was an astounding $1.9 billion, irreparably damaging the bank's reputation (U.S. Department of Justice, 2012).

Relationship with Other Illicit Funds

Money laundering is a sophisticated phenomenon; in most cases, it is coupled with other very sordid financial crimes. For instance, HSBC was embroiled in money laundering and facilitated funds for drug cartels and terrorist operations. Such unlawful actions infringe upon the rule of law and threaten national security and societal stability. The far-reaching ramifications necessitate urgent and immediate measures to address these financial misdeeds.

The Cost of Negligence

"In 2010, the U.S. Department of Justice fined HSBC a record $1.9 billion for its lack of anti-money laundering controls" (U.S. Department of Justice, 2012). HSBC's record-breaking penalty was the largest ever imposed recompense upon a financial institution. The declaration clearly stated the severe consequences of neglecting anti-money laundering controls. The fine was not the end of HSBC's troubles; they were also required to implement comprehensive changes to their anti-money laundering program and submit to ongoing government oversight.

Criminal Proceedings

The HSBC scandal resulted in significant financial and legal losses. The bank was prosecuted for facilitating the movement of illegal funds and was compelled to acknowledge its shortcomings and accept responsibility for its actions. The criminal proceedings served as a wake-up call for the financial industry, demonstrating the consequences of neglecting anti-money laundering controls.

The Importance of Anti-Money Laundering Measures

The HSBC scandal underscores the critical importance of anti-money laundering measures in the financial industry. Financial institutions are responsible for establishing anti-money laundering controls and for reporting suspicious activity to the relevant authorities. Failing to do so puts the institution's reputation at inordinate risk, with ramifications for the economy and societal norms.

Historical Lessons

The HSBC scandal of 2012 exemplifies the dire consequences that can arise from a financial institution's lack of enforceable anti-money laundering measures. Money laundering is the practice of concealing the proceeds of crime as legitimate income. This concealment approach undermines the global financial system. Money laundering destroys the economic fabric of society and creates many other incidents, such as terror financing, drug trafficking, and tax evasion. This HSBC fiasco exposes the weaknesses inherent in the design of our financial institutions. Suppose regulators and financial entities internalize the lessons from this episode. In that case, they will work together to strengthen anti-money laundering frameworks, thereby ensuring the stability and security of the global economy.

As a quick recap, as is evident from the HSBC scandal, the possible outcomes that may befall a financial institution if it does not make effective anti-money laundering policies are that such institutions must have in place and always be on guard in detecting and preventing money laundering, and thus tightly collaborate with law enforcement to combat such a serious crime. The repercussions of neglecting such measures are catastrophic and may span several years or even resonate for years to come.

Case 10.2 The Deutsche Bank Scandal: A Global Financial Giant Entangled in Russian Money Laundering, Oversight Failures, and Regulatory Backlash (Germany and Russia, 2011–2014)

In 2020, Deutsche Bank, a major institution in the global financial landscape, suffered a significant setback when regulators in the United States and the UK jointly imposed a $150 million fine. This punitive sanction resulted from the bank's collusion with a major money-laundering scheme that siphoned more than $10 billion in illicit funds through its channels (DOJ, 2020). The Department of Justice reported that Deutsche Bank failed to adequately monitor its clients and transactions, thereby enabling extensive money laundering without adequate controls. This was a significant blow to Deutsche Bank's image and underscored the prevalence of a growing, deep-seated money-laundering problem, along with the complex, interconnected issues associated with other criminal undertakings.

The Russian Money Laundering Scheme

The Russian money-laundering scheme occurred between 2011 and 2014, during which Deutsche Bank served as a conduit for the transfer of substantial sums from Russia to the West, without disclosing the sources of the illicit funds. It is understood that Deutsche Bank channeled more than $10 billion in illegal money during this period. The Financial Conduct Authority revealed that the bank has been unsuccessful in monitoring customers and transactions, thereby enabling the integration phase of money laundering (Financial Conduct Authority, 2020).

Deutsche Bank's Neglect

Deutsche Bank, in default of its anti-money laundering obligations, had found itself embroiled in a massive financial scandal. The bank's failure to establish robust controls for detecting and deterring suspicious transactions, combined with inadequate due diligence on its clients, facilitated the integration of funds of questionable origin into the financial system. Hence, the negligence permitted the mixing of dirty money with clean, legitimate assets, thereby denying access to the money for tracing. The scandal was a sheer illustration of the bank's malfunctioning monitoring and governance systems, foreshadowing grave challenges in combating money laundering.

The Consequences

Following the fallout of Deutsche Bank, the ramifications were serious. Regulators from the United States and the United Kingdom fined the bank $150 million. They even suggested that significant changes be made to the bank's AML processes and controls to prevent such breaches in the future. The scandal further damaged Deutsche Bank's reputation, which several prior financial scandals had already tarnished. The lessons learned from the penalties and subsequent reforms must be deeply ingrained in the consciences of all banking institutions; rigorous AML compliance is essential, and the implications of noncompliance are grave.

The Relationship between Money Laundering and Other Illicit Funds

Money laundering is the most serious financial crime and a gateway to various other crimes. Specifically, the integration phase enables criminals to launder dirty money with clean funds, thereby erasing its trail and making it untraceable. These aspects highlight the profound significance of AML regulations. Such regulations are not merely bureaucratic hurdles; instead, they serve as defenses to protect financial institutions against being lured into facilitating the laundering of criminal funds and broader criminal activities.

Historical Lessons

This financial scandal sets alarm bells ringing for financial institutions regarding the critical importance of AML compliance. It underscores the realization that money laundering is a pervasive concern, constantly evolving and eluding the awareness of financial authorities, thereby encouraging them to remain vigilant in recognizing and preventing such blatantly illegal acts. The other aspect of this scandal serves as an invaluable lesson in the need for scrupulous due diligence, continuous monitoring, and a holistic view of customers and transactions. Failure to fulfill these responsibilities can have dire consequences, as evidenced by the fallout from this case. It is a wake-up call across the entire financial marketplace to fortify its defenses against the persistent threat of this scourge, money laundering.

To summarize these discussions, the Deutsche Bank scandal serves as a prime example of the potential consequences of neglecting AML obligations and the integration stage of money laundering. As a salient caveat, financial institutions that prioritize their AML obligations and implement all safeguards against money laundering operations face the risk of substantial fines; the scandal imposed a $150 million fine on the bank, thereby damaging its reputation. The act underscores the extent to which AML regulations protect financial institutions from being used for money laundering and other unlawful activities. It seems to lend some credence to the other nuggets of wisdom: establishing and maintaining proper, diligent monitoring and reasonable due diligence are essential. The case is thus a wake-up call on the implications of dismal failure in these spaces and bounds, both financially and reputationally.

To briefly review, the 2020 Deutsche Bank case underscores the critical importance of vigilant monitoring and due diligence in the financial sector. This case aims to barricade the integration stage of money laundering and the flow of criminal funds. Moreover, conveyed a powerful message, offering an indispensable lesson to financial institutions: prioritize anti-money laundering measures and continuously review and update processes to ensure regulatory compliance.

An Insight: Prohibiting Money Laundering in Jordan: A Study of Commercial Banks' Measures to Mitigate Risks during the Placement Stage

Money laundering poses a significant threat to the integrity of the international financial system. This practice, whereby the proceeds of unlawful acts are concealed as legitimate funds to impede law enforcement authorities' ability to trace their origin, is highly pernicious. The placement stage of money laundering is the initial step, during which illegal funds are introduced into the financial system. Hence, financial institutions should closely monitor this critical juncture to prevent the laundering of these funds.

In this context, a recent study by Suleiman J. Mohammad et al. (2022) examined the measures taken by Jordanian commercial banks to deter money laundering during the placement stage. The study, published in the *International Journal of Public Law and Policy* (Vol. 8, No. 1), examined the policies and procedures of these banks and assessed their effectiveness in combating money laundering.

The Placement Stage in Money Laundering

Money laundering unfolds in three stages: placement, layering, and integration. The initial act, recognized as placement, is where illegal gains first encounter the financial system. At this critical juncture, the launderer strives to transform dirty money into a form that can be readily integrated into the economic landscape. During this phase, the launderer is most susceptible to detection, as the veil of secrecy is the thinnest.

Jordanian Commercial Banks and Money Laundering

Jordan is the financial heartbeat of the Middle East, with commercial banks being a linchpin of the national economy. The Central Bank of Jordan (CBJ) governs and supervises commercial banks. The CBJ has proactively established stringent regulations and guidelines to prevent money laundering. The changing dynamics of the Jordanian financial landscape are rooted in a broader narrative of awareness and regulatory oversight.

Preventing Money Laundering in the Placement Stage

The study focuses on the measures that Jordanian commercial banks have implemented to counter money laundering at the point of entry into the system or during the placement stage. The research employed a qualitative approach, and data were collected through interviews with senior managers of commercial banks in Jordan. The study revealed that Jordanian commercial banks have adopted numerous measures to hinder money laundering during the placement stage, covering the following:

Customer Due Diligence

Jordanian commercial banks have implemented robust customer due diligence processes, including identification and risk assessment. These measures include collecting client identity information, verifying credentials, and obtaining information about a business's operations or sources of funds.

Suspicious Activity Reporting

The CBJ is the prime custodial institution that receives reports of suspicious operations filed by commercial banks. Commercial banks adhere to standards, procedures, and processes established for such institutions. These activities concern the detection and reporting of money-laundering operations.

Training and Awareness

Commercial banks in Jordan have introduced training and awareness programs for their employees to assess and prevent money laundering. Such programs educate staff on the laws and regulations governing anti-money laundering activities, helping them identify suspicious behavioral scenarios.

Technology and Systems

Commercial banks in Jordan have made substantial investments in technology and systems to detect and prevent money laundering. This involves applying advanced software systems to monitor transactions and detect unusual behavioral patterns.

The study highlights some robust measures adopted by Jordanian commercial banks to thwart money laundering at the placement stage. The results offer valuable insights into the dynamic nature of these financial institutions in combating illicit financial operations. Measures include rigorous customer due diligence, thorough reporting of suspicious matters, practical training and awareness programs, and investment in state-of-the-art technology and systems. The study offers valuable insights into the efforts of other financial institutions and regulators in combating money laundering.

The research by Mohammad et al. (2022) provides an in-depth understanding of the obstacles Jordanian commercial banks confront in combating money laundering during the placement stage. The study emphasizes that the effective implementation of anti-money laundering practices is paramount and that financial institutions and regulatory agencies must work together in a concerted effort.

Money Laundering: An Example of the Placement, Layering, and Integration Stages

Money laundering poses a serious threat to the global financial system and the entire economy (FATF, 2022). Money laundering is the concealment of the proceeds of crime as legitimate funds. The processes by which criminals launder their money are designed to render cash forms "less visible" and to infiltrate the legitimate economy. Highly sophisticated criminal activity ultimately becomes imperceptible to even the most advanced detection systems. Money laundering occurs in several stages, and the best way to understand it is to consider the layers of placement, layering, and integration.

Placement Stage: In this hypothetical scenario, a cohort of criminals in Country A opens multiple fraudulent accounts across multiple banks nationwide. Subsequently, they gradually deposit small amounts of cash into these accounts to evade detection. This phase is termed placement, and its primary goal is to integrate illicit funds into the banking system, akin to introducing toxins into a healthy organism.

Layering Stage: Subsequently, these criminals use fraudulent accounts to initiate initial remittances under the guise of service imports to various service providers. This phase is characterized by layering, intended to obfuscate authority and conceal the traceable funding source. The remittances are transferred to a specific account in a tax haven, obfuscating the funds' trail.

Integration Stage

Integration Stage: Ultimately, the illicit funds return to Country A, the remittance origin, disguised as foreign direct investment (FDI). This phase is referred to as integration, during which illicit funds are seamlessly incorporated into lawful financial transactions, making it practically impossible to trace their origin.

This example illustrates how money launderers use numerous transactions and shell accounts to obscure the funds' legitimate sources and reintegrate them into the lawful economy. Governments and financial institutions must rigorously oversee, detect, and evade money laundering. The measures disrupt illegal operations and protect the economy from the shocks of potential hazards.

Mystifying the World of Money Laundering: Discovering Phases

The objective of money laundering is to obscure the origins of illicit funds and convert them into legally permissible funds. It focuses on three phases of money laundering: placement, layering, and integration. This process evaluates how they function globally by applying a lens to one of contemporary history's most devastating and disruptive financial catastrophes: the Panama Papers.

Placement: The First Step in the Money Laundering Process

The first phase of money laundering involves injecting illegally derived proceeds into the financial system. This process is recognized as the placement stage. Criminals employ various methods to launder money, including making small deposits across multiple accounts and using shell companies to facilitate transfers.

Layering: Concealing the Source of Funds

Once the funds are integrated into the mainstream financial system, the next step is to obscure their origin. This is termed the layering stage. Criminal transactions are often facilitated by wire transfers, which are part of a complex network of financial transactions that enable criminals to move funds from one account to another and from one jurisdiction to another, making it difficult to determine the point of origin of the funds.

Integration: Bringing Illicit Funds Back into the Legitimate Economy

Integration is the final stage of money laundering, in which illicit funds are reintroduced into the conventional economy. This stage frequently entails investing the laundered funds into real estate, stocks, or other assets to legitimize them.

The Panama Papers: A Real-World Example of Money Laundering

The Panama Papers, a significant leak of financial documents from the Panamanian law firm Mossack Fonseca, provided an unambiguous depiction of the money-laundering process (ICIJ, 2016). The released records revealed a web of offshore businesses, shell corporations, and covert bank accounts misused to launder money and evade taxes.

The Panama Papers exposed how affluent individuals and corporations employed offshore organizations to channel funds into the financial system, layer transactions through an elaborate network of shell companies, and incorporate the laundered funds into the traditional economy. This incident exposed flaws in the global financial system that enabled money launderers to operate with impunity (OCCRP, 2016).

To summarize the main point, Money laundering is a persistent threat that undermines the credibility of financial institutions and potent economies. The Panama Papers have demonstrated the need for collaboration among law enforcement agencies and governments worldwide to identify criminal activities and to prevent circumvention of enforceable laws. This issue also highlights a long history of relationships linking money laundering to other forms of illicit financial activity, including tax evasion, bribery, and organized crime.

Chapter Summary

The final stage of money laundering is typically integration, in which the laundered funds are reintegrated into the economy and appear as legitimate assets. The Financial Action Task Force—a genuinely international watchdog—examines the establishment of robust standards to deter the financial crimes of money laundering, terrorism financing, and proliferation. Such stakes are overwhelming. A lapse in such detection and prohibition would result in serious criminal proceedings and costly damages for financial institutions and governments. Anti-money laundering measures are not mere external formalities for compliance; they are the trenches in the ongoing war against crime that endangers the seamless functioning of the global economy.

End of Chapter: Discussion Questions

1 What are the three stages of money laundering?
2 What role does the FATF play in combating money laundering?
3 What are some examples of criminal activities that result in the need for money laundering?
4 How can financial institutions and governments prevent money laundering?

5 Why is it essential to have anti-money laundering measures in place?
6 What are the consequences of not detecting and preventing money laundering?
7 What is the impact of money laundering on the economy?
8 What are some challenges in detecting and preventing money laundering?
9 How does money laundering relate to other illegal activities, such as terrorism financing and drug trafficking?
10 What can be done to improve international cooperation in combating money laundering and other illicit activities?

Bibliography

ABC News. (2018, June 4). *Commonwealth Bank to pay $700m fine for anti-money laundering, terror financing law breaches*. ABC News. Retrieved from https://www.abc.net.au/news/commonwealth-bank-pay-700-million-fine-money-laundering-breach/9831064

Adam, S., & Ho, Y. (2022, August 24). How Malaysia's 1MDB scandal shook the financial world. *Bloomberg*. Retrieved from [bloomberg.com]

Council on Foreign Relations. (2021, April 18). *Lava Jato: See how far Brazil's corruption probe reached.* https://www.cfr.org/articles/lava-jato-see-how-far-brazils-corruption-probe-reached

Europol. (2023, September 11). *The other side of the coin: An analysis of financial and economic crime in the EU.* https://www.europol.europa.eu/publications-events/publications/other-side-of-coin-analysis-of-financial-and-economic-crime

Europol. (2023, September 14). *Money laundering: The lifeblood of organized crime.* https://www.europol.europa.eu/publications-events/publications/other-side-of-coin-analysis-of-financial-and-economic-crime

Financial Action Task Force (FATF). (2012, February). The FATF recommendations: International standards on combating money laundering and the financing of terrorism & proliferation. Paris: FATF/OECD. Retrieved from https://www.fatf-gafi.org/en/publications/Fatfrecommendations/Fatf-recommendations.html

Financial Action Task Force (FATF). (2022, February 14). Money laundering. Retrieved from www.fatf-gafi.org/topics/money-laundering/

Financial Action Task Force. (2023, October). The FATF recommendations. Paris: FATF/OECD. Retrieved from https://www.fatf-gafi.org/en/publications/Fatfrecommendations/Fatf-recommendations.html

Financial Conduct Authority. (2017, January 29). *FCA fines Deutsche Bank £163 million for serious failings in anti-money laundering controls*. https://www.fca.org.uk/news/press-releases/fca-fines-deutsche-bank-163-million-anti-money-laundering-controls-failure

Financial Conduct Authority. (2025, July 16). The FCA fines Barclays £42 million for failing to adequately manage financial crime risks. Press Release. https://www.fca.org.uk/news/press-releases/fca-fines-barclays-42-million-poor-handling-financial-crime-risks

Financial Crimes Enforcement Network (FinCEN). (2022). *What is money laundering?* Washington, DC: U.S. Department of the Treasury. Retrieved from https://www.fincen.gov/what-money-laundering

Freifeld, K. (2023). Exclusive: Standard chartered expected to pay just over $1 billion to resolve U.S., U.K. probes. *Reuters*. Retrieved from https://www.reuters.com/article/us-stanchart-sanctions-settlement-exclus/exclusive-standard-chartered-expected-to-pay-just-over-1-billion-to-resolve-u-s-u-k-probes-idUSKCN1RK26F

Global Programme against Money Laundering. (2021). United nations office on drugs and crime. https://www.unodc.org/unodc/en/money-laundering/global-programme-against-money-laundering/.html

International Consortium of Investigative Journalists. (2016, April 3). The panama papers: Exposing the rogue offshore finance industry. Washington, DC: ICIJ. Retrieved from https://panamapapers.icij.org/

Mohammed, S. J., Tahtamouni, A., Aldaas, A. A., & Sumadi, M. A. (2022). Preventing money laundering during the placement stage: The case of Jordanian commercial banks. *International Journal of Public Law and Policy*, 8(1), 37–51.

Organized Crime and Corruption Reporting Project. (2016). The Panama Papers: Exposing the rogue offshore finance industry. OCCRP. Retrieved from https://www.occrp.org/en/panamapapers/

Reuters. (2022, November 8). *Danske Bank ex-CEO cleared in $322 mln investor lawsuit.* https://www.reuters.com/business/finance/danske-bank-ex-ceo-cleared-liability-investor-lawsuit-2022-11-08/

Santos, H. F., & Bronzato, A. (2021). Car Wash Operation and Odebrecht: A case that will end? *Revista Científica Multidisciplinar Núcleo do Conhecimento*, 10(2), 61–75. https://www.researchgate.net/publication/351724604

United Nations Office on Drugs and Crime. (2021). Money laundering, proceeds of crime and the financing of terrorism. Vienna: UNODC. Retrieved from https://www.unodc.org/unodc/en/money-laundering/index.html

U.S. Department of Justice. (2012). HSBC Holdings Plc. and HSBC Bank USA N.A. admit to anti-money laundering and sanctions violations, forfeit $1.256 billion in deferred prosecution agreement. Washington, DC: DOJ Office of Public Affairs. Retrieved from https://www.justice.gov/opa/pr/hsbc-holdings-plc-and-hsbc-bank-usa-na-admit-anti-money-laundering-and-sanctions-violations

U.S. Department of Justice. (2020, July 7). *Deutsche Bank agrees to pay a nearly $150 million penalty for significant compliance failures*. U.S. Department of Justice. https://www.justice.gov/usao-sdny/pr/deutsche-bank-agrees-pay-nearly-150-million-penalty-significant-compliance-failures

U.S. Department of the Treasury. (2020). *National strategy for combating terrorist and other illicit financing.* https://home.treasury.gov/system/files/136/National-Strategy-to-Counter-Illicit-Financev2.pdf

U.S. Department of Justice. (2021, January 7). *Deutsche Bank agrees to pay over $130 million to resolve Foreign Corrupt Practices Act and fraud case.* https://www.justice.gov/usao-edny/pr/deutsche-bank-agrees-pay-over-130-million-resolve-foreign-corrupt-practices-act-and

VinciWorks. (2025, July 21). Inside Barclays' AML breakdown: Lessons from the FCA's £42m fine. https://vinciworks.com/blog/inside-barclays-aml-breakdown-lessons-from-the-fcas-42m-fine/

Additional Learning Resources

Books

1 The Money Laundering Handbook: A Guide to Understanding and Detecting Money Laundering by Jack Blum (2009).
This book provides a comprehensive overview of money laundering, from the basics of how it works to the latest techniques used by criminals. It also discusses the role of the FATF and other international organizations in combating money laundering.

2 Money Laundering: A Guide for Criminal Investigators by Christopher J. Bruce (2017)
This book is a practical guide for law enforcement officers who are investigating money laundering cases. It covers the basics of money laundering and the investigative techniques used to identify and prosecute money launderers.

Films

3 The Laundromat (2019)
This film is a comedy-drama that depicts the Panama Papers scandal. It stars Meryl Streep as a widow who discovers that her late husband's offshore accounts were used to launder money.

4 The Wolf of Wall Street (2013). www.imdb.com
This film is a biographical crime drama that tells the story of Jordan Belfort, a stockbroker who was convicted of money laundering and securities fraud. It stars Leonardo DiCaprio as Belfort.

Documentaries

5 Dirty Money (2018-present). www.imdb.com
This documentary series investigates the world of financial crime. Each episode focuses on a different case of money laundering, corruption, or fraud.

6 The Panama Papers (2016). www.imdb.com

This documentary recounts the Panama Papers scandal, which exposed the offshore financial dealings of the world's wealthy and powerful.

Articles

7 "Understanding the Stages of Money Laundering" by the Financial Crimes Enforcement Network (FinCEN). www.investopedia.com
This article provides a detailed overview of the three stages of money laundering: placement, layering, and integration.
8 "The Role of the FATF in Combating Money Laundering" by the Financial Action Task Force (FATF). www.fatf-gafi.org
This article discusses the role of the FATF in setting international standards for combating money laundering.

YouTube Videos

9 "What is Money Laundering?" YouTube video by Khan Academy. www.dawn.com
This video provides a brief overview of money laundering and its operation.
10 "The FATF and Money Laundering" by the Financial Action Task Force (FATF) www.fatf-gafi.org
This video discusses the role of the FATF in combating money laundering.

11 Anti-money Laundering Measures

A Brief Overview

Money laundering is the process by which criminals conceal the actual ownership and control of the proceeds of their illegal activities by making them appear to originate from a legitimate source. To combat such unlawful conduct, governments and financial institutions worldwide have implemented anti-money-laundering policies and procedures. These policies establish the framework for the identification, warning, and prosecution of persons and acts involved in money laundering. Reflecting the widespread consensus among regulators, former Federal Reserve Chair Janet Yellen (2016) remarked that "anti-money-laundering measures are not only a matter of law but a moral imperative," asserting that "when we prevent the flow of illegal money, we safeguard the integrity of our financial system and hence, the stability and security of our society" (para. 2).

Criminal organizations and terrorist financiers employ three primary methodologies to move money and disguise its source: the financial system, the physical movement of bulk cash, and variations in value (through goods and services).

The Financial Action Task Force (FATF) was established in July 1989 (FATF, 2023) and seeks to address organized crime and other prohibited activities and their numerous manifestations, such as money laundering, fictitious operations, and terrorist financing. The FATF is primarily an intergovernmental body that develops guidelines, enforces regulations, and recommends legislation to combat money laundering and terrorist financing. Moreover, the FATF has issued a series of recommendations recognized as the gold standards for anti-money laundering (AML) and the combating of the funding of terrorism (AML/CFT). These recommendations have been modified and updated on numerous occasions, most recently in 2012, to address evolving patterns and tactics used in money laundering (FATF, 2023).

One specific area of concern is trade-based money laundering (TBML). This methodology addresses the abuse of trade transactions and financial systems for money laundering. TBML has become increasingly popular in recent years, as AML controls have tightened, making it more difficult to launder money through the banking system and to move the most vulnerable cash. FATF recognized TBML as one of the three primary methods of money laundering in a study conducted in 2006 (FATF, 2006). However, the definition of TBML was expanded in 2008 to encompass the movement of licit funds for illicit activities, including terrorism financing and sanctions evasion. TBML can be challenging to detect and disrupt because it involves using legitimate trade transactions to conceal illicit proceeds. It often involves complex cross-border transactions with multiple intermediaries, illustrating the challenges of tracing funds in trade flows.

DOI: 10.4324/9781003477631-12

Brief History of Anti-money Laundering Measures

Over the years, AML strategies and policy measures have been extensively used and reinforced. Some significant developments and milestones in the fight against money laundering and financial crimes include:

1 The Bank Secrecy Act (BSA) of 1970 is a key piece of legislation widely acknowledged as the Currency and Foreign Transactions Reporting Act. Signed into law by the U.S. Congress, this act requires financial institutions to report significant cash transactions to the U.S. Department of the Treasury; the disclosure pertains to guidance on suspicious activities reported under FinCEN (2021). One of the law's main prerequisites is that the institution reports transactions exceeding US$10,000. The law also requires the routine retention of records that may be called for in criminal, tax, or regulatory proceedings.
2 The FATF, established in 1989 by the G7, is an intergovernmental organization tasked with "developing policies and robust guidelines to combat illicit money laundering and terrorist financing" (FATF, 2023). This body has further issued recommendations to countries on how to design and implement criminal economic systems with effective AML measures.
3 The USA PATRIOT Act in 2001: The extensively acknowledged legislation, "Uniting and Strengthening America by Providing Appropriate Tools Required to Intercept and Obstruct Terrorism Act," or the USA PATRIOT Act has significantly strengthened the BSA and expanded its scope. The law has bestowed upon financial regulators much greater authority. The legislation thus strengthens the powers to combat money laundering and terrorist financing. This law requires financial institutions to implement customer identification and due diligence procedures (US Congress, 2001).

   i The adoption of this breakthrough convention, entitled "International Convention for the Suppression of the Financing of Terrorism," took place in 1999 at the United Nations. It made it compulsory for states to define terrorism, cooperate fully in investigations, and freeze accounts linked to terrorist assets (United Nations, 1999).
   ii The Third EU Money Laundering Directive in 2005: The European Union brought in that directive, which set minimum standards on AML measures for EU member states and required financial institutions to carry out customer due diligence.
   iii Under "FATF Recommendations," the FATF updated and revised its AML and counter-terrorism financing standards in 2012. These standards are widely applied and accepted by countries worldwide.
   iv The Fourth EU Money Laundering Directive in 2015: This directive strengthened AML measures across the EU, covered entities in scope, introduced a risk assessment requirement, and mandated more risk-based policies and procedures.
   v The Financial Stability Oversight Council (FSOC). In a 2016 report, the FATF assessed the illicit finance risks posed by virtual currencies and recommended that it reassess these risks in its updated guidance.
   vi In 2018, the Fifth EU Money Laundering Directive was rolled out to boost the Union's fight against money laundering. At its core, the measure aimed to enhance transparency and encourage EU member states to collaborate to prevent the misuse of the financial system for money laundering or terrorist financing. Instead of following a neat list, the directive (Directive (EU) 2018/843) prompted member states to establish easily accessible registers for beneficial ownership, enhance information sharing with their financial supervisors, and tighten controls on transactions involving high-risk third countries. It

also urged them to curb anonymous use of prepaid cards and extend AML rules to cover new sectors and groups. In most cases, these steps—though sometimes inconsistent—were implemented to strengthen the AML framework and more effectively combat financial crime (Directive (EU) 2018/843).

vii 6AMLD is the Sixth Directive of the Anti-Money Laundering Regulation of the European Union. This directive was ratified on 23 October 2018. All member states must incorporate it into national legislation by 3 December 2020. The directive sets out provisions for financial institutions to implement internal procedures to detect, evaluate, and mitigate risks of money laundering and terrorist financing (European Union, 2018). This directive builds on prior AML regulations and introduces additional measures to enhance the effectiveness of AML frameworks in the EU. It also requires countries to establish central registers of beneficial ownership information for trusts.

viii The FATF updated its guidance on the risk-based approach to AML and counter-terrorist financing in 2021 (FATF, 2021). The updated guidance provides nations with more detailed instructions for conducting spot evaluations and mitigating risks of money laundering and terrorist financing. It also underscores the importance of mutual coordination among countries in combating financial crime.

ix The Corporate Transparency Act (CTA) was passed and enacted in the United States in 2020 under the aegis of the National Defense Authorization Act for Fiscal Year 2021 (FinCEN, 2021). The statute has unequivocally compelled certain specified corporate entities to report and be accountable for beneficial ownership to the Financial Crimes Enforcement Network (FinCEN). This agency reports to the U.S. Department of the Treasury. The same sentiment applies to being "corruption-free," as CTA seeks to enhance the U.S. financial system's transparency further, thereby making it harder for criminals to operate.

x In 2021, the FATF updated its standards on digital assets (FATF, 2021) to direct countries to regulate and supervise digital asset activities to thwart their use for money laundering and terrorist financing.

Trade-Based Money Laundering: Concealing the Proceeds of Illegal Conduct through Trade Transactions

International trade can be susceptible to a variety of threats and vulnerabilities that can be exploited by criminal groups, professional launderers, and terrorist organizations to launder the proceeds of illegal activities and finance terrorism under the guise of legitimate trade. The massive volume of trade flows and the complexity of multiple foreign exchange transactions and trade financing arrangements create significant risks that can be exploited for this intent.

According to the FATF, TBML refers to methods used by criminals to conceal the actual ownership and control of illicit funds through trade transactions, thereby obscuring the funds' sources and creating an appearance of legality. TBML refers to the illegal shifting of money through trade transactions, including fraudulent invoicing, expeditious classification of goods to evade controls, and numerous customs and tax violations. Unlike trade-related predicate offenses, which focus on the goods moved, TBML's primary concern is the money moved.

TBML can be challenging to detect in international trade, as it involves multiple parties across various jurisdictions. Typically, TBML refers to the vertical activities of importing and exporting goods through trade finance channels used for money laundering. This is mainly confined to a few areas, including high-value, low-volume items, such as precious metals, and low-value, high-volume items, such as second-hand textiles. Such products indicate several sectors at risk of TBML exploitation; among them are goods with wider price margins, longer trade cycles involving shipping across multiple jurisdictions, and items that are difficult for customs authorities to inspect. For example, criminal entities may initially engage in a legitimate shipment of cosmetic goods and create sufficient valid documentation. They may then carry out subsequent phantom shipments by misusing these documents. Sometimes, a transaction may remain completely legitimate without any TBML procedures being used. However, the shipped goods may have no value, be unsaleable, and be discarded upon arrival (e.g., second-hand textiles).

The misuse of trade can also involve capital flight or the transfer of wealth offshore, which can severely harm weak economies. While many governments have laws governing citizens' overseas investments, individuals and businesses may seek to evade these controls by channeling value through trade goods and payments.

Example: 1 Trade-Based Money Laundering in the Diamond Industry

A widely recognized instance of TBML concerns the diamond sector. Diamonds are high-value, low-volume, and easily transportable goods that may be used for large-scale money laundering. For instance, a criminal organization may obtain diamonds with illicit funds and sell them to a legitimate diamond dealer at a low price, who will then sell them at the full market price, thereby legitimizing the funds. The process would be immensely problematic to detect since diamonds may pass through informal sales channels and lack a substantiated paper trail. Moreover, diamonds may be exported from the country of origin in rough form and shipped to various countries for cutting and polishing, thereby making it arduous, if not impossible, to establish the actual country of origin.

Example: 2 Trade-Based Money Laundering in the Textile Industry

The textile industry has recently emerged as a lucrative sector for money launderers seeking to illegally transfer funds out of the country. According to the FATF report, TBML in the textile sector is on the rise (FATF, 2017). Concealed shipment cuts involve vast sums of money being smuggled out of a country by criminals who inflate the value of textile shipments with fake invoices and other false documents under the guise of legitimate trade transactions.

One example of this type of activity occurred in 2017, when a network of individuals and companies based in India and Dubai was found to exploit the textile trade to launder money for a range of criminal organizations. According to an FATF report, the group established a sophisticated network of shell companies and fraudulent invoices to move millions of dollars out of India, often through the United Arab Emirates.

The case underscores the challenges of detecting and addressing TBML in the textile industry, which has substantial international trade and often involves complex supply chains. It also highlights the need for enhanced regulatory oversight and improved information sharing among law enforcement agencies to combat this financial crime effectively.

To summarize, TBML poses a significant threat to the integrity of international trade and the global financial system. It involves exploiting trade transactions to conceal the proceeds of illegal conduct. Detecting and averting TBML is as complex as international trade, and it involves multiple parties operating across various jurisdictions. High-value, low-volume, low-value, and high-volume goods are among the sectors vulnerable to TBML. Governments, financial institutions, and businesses should be alert to the substantial underlying risks and implement reasonable controls to prevent, detect, and report TBML cases. Duties such as customer and counterparty due diligence, suspicious transaction monitoring, and robust internal controls to detect and prevent illicit activity must be incorporated into these controls.

Other sectors, including financial institutions, may be vulnerable to TBML. For example, high-value, low-volume products, such as luxury goods, may attract money launderers because they can be readily transferred and sold at a premium. Low-value, high-volume products, such as bulk commodities, may also be susceptible to TBML because they are difficult to trace and can be used to launder large amounts of money.

Governments, financial systems, and entities must exercise caution and implement proactive measures to mitigate the risks of TBML. To that end, mitigating controls must be in place to prevent, detect, and report such illegal activities. Those practices include conducting due diligence on customers and counterparties, closely monitoring transactions to detect suspicious activity, and implementing robust internal controls to deter and detect wrongdoing.

All governments and regulatory bodies are instrumental in addressing TBML through the establishment of legal and regulatory frameworks. This means establishing clear rules and standards for financial institutions and other regulated entities, empowering law enforcement agencies to investigate and prosecute TBML cases effectively.

All stakeholders must recognize that TBML is a complex and ever-evolving issue that requires sustained attention and adaptation. Governments, financial institutions, and the corporate world can proactively unite in combating TBML to help protect the integrity of the global economic system from being exploited by criminals and terrorists.

Case 11.1 United States v. Bernard L. Madoff (Federal Bureau of Investigation, 2009): FBI's "Shadow" Operation, Uncovering A Massive Money Laundering Scheme (USA, 2008–2009)

In 2008, the FBI's undertaking of an enormous operation named "Shadow" was to investigate a lengthy and extensive money-laundering scam (Federal Bureau of Investigation, 2008). This operation stemmed from a two-year investigation aimed at dismantling the criminal organization behind the scheme and punishing its members.

The Scheme: How It Worked

The scheme involved a complex network of individuals and companies that facilitated the laundering of vast sums through transactions. Proceeds from illegal activities such as drug trafficking, fraud, and embezzlement enable criminals to purchase luxury goods at higher prices from honest buyers, including jewelry, expensive cars, and real estate. This would cleanse the money of all traces of its illegal origin, making it appear as if the funds were obtained legally and without blemish.

The Loss Estimate

According to FBI estimates, the scheme laundered well over $250 million in illicit proceeds, which were then used to purchase luxury items that could be readily resold for profit, further increasing its profitability. The proceeds also financed other unlawful activities, including drug trafficking and terrorism. In its strongest terms, the FBI has declared that this is likely one of the largest money-laundering schemes the agency has ever encountered, posing a greater threat to the economy and national security.

The Fate of the Perpetrators

The FBI worked around the clock to bring justice to the individuals and companies behind the operational scheme (Southern District of New York, 2019). Over a few hundred arrests were made, mostly of individuals charged with offenses including money laundering, conspiracy, and racketeering. The FBI seizure was also used as evidence at trial, involving assets valued at more than $100 million U.S. Department of Justice (2024).

The trial, which spanned several years, resulted in verdicts against several individuals alleged to be part of the scheme. This led to their spending considerable time in prison and incurring substantial fines. This operation, as noted, marked a historic achievement for the FBI, demonstrating its commitment to combating financial crimes and protecting the economy.

Case 11.2 The Pink Panthers: A Global Syndicate Stole Over €330 Million in Valuables Using Military Precision and Sophisticated Tactics. 2000 (first known heist); formally identified by Europol in 2008

Crime takes many forms and is constantly evolving and operating with a flamboyant style. The Great Temptation, the Pink Panthers, a globally renowned criminal network (Jeweller Magazine 2019), a transnational criminal network believed to consist of ex-soldiers from the Balkans, predominantly Serbia, Montenegro, and Bosnia, who repurposed military skills for organized crime. The gang is recognized for reconnaissance missions and excellent planning. They used disguises, ram-raid vehicles, and ambush tactics. The Pink Panthers have been involved in more than 340 robberies throughout Europe, the Middle East, Asia, and the United States, taking an estimated value of €330 million ($374 million) in jewelry and other valuables (Europol, 2018). The group is highly dexterous in employing sophisticated techniques; this high-end network is linked to several money-laundering ventures. In this space, we examine the Pink Panthers, their discovery, the scheme they employed, the estimated loss, and the fate of the perpetrators. In this space, we examine the Pink Panthers, including their discovery, the operation of their scheme, the estimated losses, and the fate of the perpetrators.

The Discovery of the Pink Panthers

In the early 2000s, the first law enforcement agencies began to address the Pink Panther issue. According to Europol (2018), the first reported robbery attributed to the Pink Panthers occurred in 2000 in London. The robbers stole jewelry valued at €1 million. Since then, law enforcement agencies have observed a pattern in high-value jewelry thefts reported worldwide and have begun to track criminal networks (ITV News, 2018). In 2008, Europol officially designated the group the "Pink Panthers" and initiated an investigation into the group's covert operations.

How the Scheme Worked

The Pink Panthers have been recognized for their sophisticated methods and well-planned operations. According to Europol (2018), the Pink Panthers often conducted reconnaissance missions to gather information about their targets. The next step would be to use the information to plan how to carry out the theft, which is generally shrouded in secrecy among two or three robbers. The robbers often employed violence or intimidation to break in or assault to get what they wanted. Still, they were also called disguised robbers because they preferred to remain quiet, so that the noise they usually made would not draw attention to them at the crime scene.

The Loss Estimate and the Fate of the Perpetrators

The estimated loss due to the Pink Panthers' clandestine activities is staggering. According to Europol (2018), the Pink Panthers have completely stolen jewelry and valuables worth at least €330 million ($374 million) in total (Europol, 2018). Law enforcement agencies have made considerable efforts to arrest this group, but they have evaded the dragnet for an extended period. However, in recent times, several group members have expressed apprehension due to the severity of the law enforcement crackdown. According to Europol (2018), more than 120 Pink Panthers have been detained, and over 2,000 stolen items have been recovered.

Loss to the Economy

Jewels and other valuables lost during the Pink Panthers' underground activities result in significant economic losses. Not only of financial value, but also often of cultural and historical significance, stolen items and their loss can have a profound impact on a nation's cultural heritage and cause substantial financial losses to the jewelry and antiques sector. Insurance claims have cost the insurance industry due to the Pink Panthers, resulting in payouts of millions.

As a quick recap, the name Pink Panthers has become almost a synonym for sophisticated high-level jewelry theft followed by money laundering, and, across the globe, it is infamous as being the worst in this line of crime. Notably, despite numerous attempts by law enforcement, the Pink Panthers have stolen jewelry and other valuables worth approximately €330 million ($374 million) (Europol, 2018). The loss of such valuables implies financial, cultural, and historical implications. Their future hangs in the balance as the forces of law join hands strongly to bring the group's members to justice.

Chapter Summary

AML measures aim to prevent illicit funds from entering the financial system and to combat crimes such as money laundering, terrorist financing, and terrorist crimes. To that end, FATF was established in 1990 and, since then, has laid out international standards for AML measures. The FATF has issued various recommendations, and the standards have been revised to keep pace with the evolving trends and strategies employed by criminal organizations. Several measures to combat money laundering were enacted, including the Bank Secrecy Act of 1970, the USA PATRIOT Act of 2001, and the EU Money Laundering Directives. Moreover, the FATF has updated its risk-based approach guidance and standards on digital assets to keep pace with the dynamic financial landscape.

End of Chapter: Discussion Questions

1. What is the role of the FATF in combating money laundering and terrorism financing?
2. What is TBML, and what are some standard methods used?
3. What is the history of AML measures?
4. What was the purpose of the Bank Secrecy Act of 1970, and how did it impact AML measures?
5. How did the USA PATRIOT Act of 2001 contribute to AML efforts?
6. What is the purpose of the EU Money Laundering Directives, and what changes have been made to them over time?
7. How has the FATF updated its risk-based approach guidance and standards to keep pace with evolving financial trends?
8. What was the impact of the FSOC report on virtual currencies and illicit finance risks?
9. How has the CTA in the United States impacted AML measures?
10. What steps does the FATF take to address the use of digital assets in money laundering activities?
11. What are the consequences for financial institutions and individuals who do not comply with AML measures?

12 How do AML measures affect the financial system's stability?
13 What is the importance of international cooperation in the fight against money laundering and terrorism financing?
14 What challenges exist in implementing AML measures, and what measures are being taken to overcome them?

Bibliography

Congressional Research Service. (2025). Guiding and establishing national innovation for U.S. Stablecoins (GENIUS) Act. CRS Report IN12553. Retrieved from https://crsreports.congress.gov/product/pdf/IN/IN12553

Directive (EU) 2018/843 of the European Parliament and of the Council of 30 May 2018 amending Directive (EU) 2015/849 on the prevention of the use of the financial system for money laundering or terrorist financing, and amending Directives 2009/138/EC and 2013/36/EU, *Official Journal of the European Union*, L 156, 19.6.2018, pp. 43–74. https://eur-lex.europa.eu/eli/dir/2018/843/oj.

European Union. (2018). Directive (EU) 2018/843 of the European Parliament and of the Council of 30 May 2018 amending Directive (EU) 2015/849 on the prevention of the use of the financial system for money laundering or terrorist financing, and amending Directives 2009/138/EC and 2013/36/EU. Official Journal of the European Union, L 156/43.

FATF. (2006). Trade-based money laundering. Financial Action Task Force. Paris: FATF/OECD. Retrieved from https://www.fatf-gafi.org/publications/methodsandtrends/documents/trade-based-money-laundering.html

FATF. (2017). Trade-based money laundering in the textile industry. Paris: FATF/OECD. Retrieved from https://www.fatf-gafi.org/en/publications/Methodsandtrends/Trade-based-money-laundering-in-the-textile-industry.html

FATF. (2021). Guidance on the risk-based approach to AML and CTF. Paris: FATF/OECD. Retrieved from https://www.fatf-gafi.org/en/publications/Fatfrecommendations/RBA-guidance.html

FATF. (2021). Updated guidance for a risk-based approach to virtual assets and virtual asset service providers. Paris: FATF/OECD. Retrieved from https://www.fatf-gafi.org/en/publications/Fatfrecommendations/RBA-virtual-assets-VASP.html

FATF. (2023). About the FATF. Paris: FATF/OECD. Retrieved from https://www.fatf-gafi.org/en/about.html

FATF. (2023). The FATF recommendations. Paris: FATF/OECD. Retrieved from https://www.fatf-gafi.org/en/publications/Fatfrecommendations/Fatf-recommendations.html

Federal Bureau of Investigation. (2008). Operation Shadow: Uncovering a massive money laundering scheme [Press release]. Washington, DC: FBI. Retrieved from https://www.fbi.gov/news/stories/operation-shadow-uncovering-a-massive-money-laundering-scheme

Federal Bureau of Investigation. (2009, March 10). Bernard L. Madoff was charged in an 11-count criminal information. FBI Archives. https://archives.fbi.gov/archives/newyork/press-releases/2009/nyfo031009.htm

FinCEN.gov. (2021). FinCEN.gov. https://www.fincen.gov/resources/statutes-and-regulations/bank-secrecy-act

Financial Action Task Force. (2012). International standards on combating money laundering, the financing of terrorism, and proliferation. https://www.fatf-gafi.org/media/fatf/documents/recommendations/pdfs/FATF_Recommendations.pdf

Financial Crimes Enforcement Network. (2021). Bank Secrecy Act. https://www.fincen.gov/resources/statutes-and-regulations/bank-secrecy-act

Financial Crimes Enforcement Network. (2021). Corporate Transparency Act – Beneficial ownership information reporting. Washington, DC: U.S. Department of the Treasury. Retrieved from https://www.fincen.gov/boi

Financial Crimes Enforcement Network. (2022). What is money laundering? Washington, DC: U.S. Department of the Treasury. Retrieved from https://www.fincen.gov/what-money-laundering

Financial Stability Oversight Council. (2016). Illicit finance risks posed by virtual currency. https://www.treasury.gov/press-center/press-releases/Documents/Illicit%20Finance%20Risks%20Posed%20by%20Virtual%20Currency.pdf

ITV News. (2018, November 29). The Pink Panther gang stole €200,000 worth of jewellery in less than a minute. https://www.itv.com/news/2018-11-29/pink-panther-gang-steal-200-000-worth-of-jewellery-in-less-than-a-minute

Jeweller Magazine. (2019, August 16). Pink Panthers: Europe's mysterious gang of jewellery thieves. https://www.jewellermagazine.com/Article/8486/Pink-Panthers-Europes-mysterious-gang-of-jewellery-thieves

Southern District of New York. (2009, March 10). Criminal information filed against Bernard L. Madoff. U.S. Department of Justice. https://www.justice.gov/usao-sdny/pr/manhattan-us-attorney-and-fbi-assistant-director-charge-announce-filing-criminal

Spapens, T. (2014). Macro and micro analyses of organized predatory crime and human trafficking. *Trilateral Research Reports*, 13–15.

United Nations. (1999). International convention for the suppression of the financing of terrorism. https://treaties.un.org/doc/db/Terrorism/english-18-11.pdf

US Congress. (2001). Uniting and strengthening America by providing the appropriate tools required to intercept and obstruct terrorism (USA PATRIOT ACT) Act of 2001. https://www.congress.gov/107/plaws/publ56/PLAW-107publ56.pdf

U.S. Department of Justice. (2024, December 30). *The Justice Department's tenth distribution provides over $4 billion in nearly full recoveries to over 40,000 victims of the Madoff Ponzi scheme*. U.S. Attorney's Office, Southern District of New York. Retrieved from https://www.justice.gov/usao-sdny/pr/justice-department-s-tenth-distribution-provides-over-4-billion-in-nearly-full-recovery

Additional Learning Resources

Book

1 "Money Laundering Law and Regulation: A Practical Guide". Robin Booth, Simon Farrell QC, Guy Bastable, and Nicholas Yeo. (2011). Oxford University Press.
This comprehensive guide provides practical insights into anti-money laundering measures, including risk assessment, compliance, and detection techniques.

2 "Dirty Dealing: The Untold Truth about Global Money Laundering and International Crime," by Peter Lilley. (2003). Kogan Page Publishers.
This book uncovers the dark world of money laundering, exposing the tactics employed by criminals and the challenges faced by law enforcement agencies.

3 Money laundering: A guide for criminal investigators. John Madinger. (2011). CRC Press.
This book is a practical guide for law enforcement officers who are investigating money laundering cases. It covers the basics of money laundering and the investigative techniques used to identify and prosecute money launderers.

Article

4 "Global Anti-Money Laundering and Combating Terrorism Financing Regulatory Framework: A Critique" by William Gaviyau and Athenia Bongani Sibindi. It was published in the Journal of Risk and Financial Management in 2023.
The article aims to provide an overview of global AML/CFT regulations, their application, and how they should evolve in a dynamic environment.

5 Money laundering is a global threat-IMF. Nassali Fatiah. (2017, October 19). Nile Post. https://nilepost.co.ug/2017/10/19/money-laundering-a-global-threat-imf/
The article discusses the International Monetary Fund (IMF)'s perspective on money laundering and examines the potential consequences and challenges of combating these activities worldwide.

Film

6 "The Laundromat" (2019), directed by Steven Soderbergh.
Inspired by real events, this film explores the Panama Papers scandal, shedding light on the intricate web of money laundering and offshore accounts.

Documentary

7 "The Kleptocrats" (2018), directed by Sam Hobkinson & Havana Marking.
This documentary delves into the 1MDB scandal, revealing how billions of dollars were laundered through international financial systems.

8 "The Panama Papers" (2018), directed by Alex Winter.
This documentary examines the most significant financial data leak in history, revealing the extent of global money laundering and tax evasion.

YouTube Video

9 "Understanding Money Laundering in 5 Minutes" (2019) by Investopedia.
This concise video provides a brief overview of money laundering, its stages, and the methods used to conceal illicit funds.

12 Understanding Mode, Methods, and Techniques of Settlement and Financing in International Trade

An Overview

Global trade and financial systems drive economic growth. However, they remain at constant risk from those who exploit regulatory weaknesses and transparency gaps. The exposure of the trade system is a significant issue that international organizations have addressed. It basically means that if the integrity of the system is maintained, it will be challenging to use the system for "laundering" the illicit funds (World Trade Organization [WTO], 2020; and FATF, 2020). Trade financing is the cornerstone of international business. It enables firms to secure the capital necessary to purchase goods and services from foreign suppliers. One of the most significant aspects of trade financing is the settlement method, the procedure by which payments are exchanged between the buyer and the seller. There are different modes of settlement, each having its own features and risks, which the buyer and the seller must comprehend and agree upon.

The International Chamber of Commerce (ICC), established in Paris in 1919, plays a pivotal role in setting standards and providing dispute resolution services for trade finance. One of the ICC's notable contributions is the development of widely adopted trade finance instruments, including the Uniform Customs and Practice for Documentary Credits (UCP). The UCP specifies a standardized set of rules for letter-of-credit transactions (International Chamber of Commerce, n.d.).

Banks and financial institutions play a crucial role in facilitating trade finance by providing essential funding for international trade transactions between buyers and suppliers. Banks must conduct thorough due diligence on their clients to mitigate the risk of incriminating trade-based money laundering. Regrettably, several high-profile cases reveal failures in due diligence. The Danske Bank scandal is a readily observable example in which the bank was found to have facilitated the movement of illicit funds amounting to billions of dollars (FATF, 2020).

There are various methods of settlement of trade transactions, including:

i Open account: This method involves the buyer purchasing goods from the seller and consenting to pay at a subsequent date, typically 30–60 days after delivery. This payment method is risky for the seller, as there is no guarantee the buyer will make the required payment.

ii Letter of credit: In this method, the buyer's bank issues a letter of credit in the seller's favor, assuring the seller will receive payment if the required documents are presented to the bank. This method reduces the seller's risk because the bank guarantees payment.

iii Documentary collections: In this method, the seller entrusts the payment collection to a bank, which acts as an intermediary between the buyer and seller. The bank releases the documents to the buyer upon receipt of payment.

iv Cash in advance: In this method, the buyer pays the total amount to the seller before the goods are shipped. This is the least risky method for the seller, as payment is received before the goods are delivered.

DOI: 10.4324/9781003477631-13

The mode of payment in trade finance can be either in cash or through a financial instrument, such as a letter of credit or documentary collections. The procedure for financing in trade finance typically entails the following steps:

i The buyer and seller mutually concur with the terms of the sale, including the price and delivery terms.
ii The buyer applies for financing from a financial institution, such as a bank.
iii The financial institution carefully reviews the application and determines whether to grant the financing.
iv If the financing is approved, the financial institution issues a letter of credit or facilitates the documentary collection process.
v The seller ships the goods and presents the required documents to the financial institution.
vi The financial institution releases the payment to the seller and effectively concludes the transaction at the appropriate time.

An open account is a trade financing arrangement in which the buyer procures goods directly from the seller, with a promise to pay the purchase price at a later date. Some characteristics of an open account transaction include:

Credit risk: The risk of the buyer's default looms large, as the seller is not assured of payment until the agreed-upon date.

Lack of documentary evidence: An open account transaction lacks physical documentation, such as letters of credit, that would guarantee payment.

Payment terms: Ordinarily, an open account transaction requires payment within 30–60 days after delivery of the underlying goods.

Banks should conduct due diligence and thoroughly examine all aspects. It should prove that the transaction is, per se, real and not fictitious, and that the funds are genuinely for their intended purpose. Due diligence involves an in-depth examination of the document's authenticity to protect the integrity of the properties introduced and to ensure that there are no red flags in the transaction.

A significant weakness comes from the failure of banks and financial institutions to perform proper due diligence. The Danske Bank case was an obvious disaster. Its internal controls at its Estonian branch were so lax that up to $234 billion in suspicious transactions occurred (BBC News, 2018). Thereby highlighting the risk to the entire system posed by weak monitoring.

Agricultural Bank of China was a leading figure in the 2012 loan scandal, owing to inadequate oversight that facilitated widespread fraud.

Common Vulnerabilities across Primary Settlement Methods

Trade-based money laundering is a highly sophisticated process. It involves concealing criminal proceeds through regular commercial transactions, specifically designed to subvert financial controls and facilitate illegal transfers of value (Table 12.1). This practice, one of the most perilous methods of money laundering, is compatible with operations that could go undetected and disrupted. The TBML exchange will either manipulate the transaction value, volume, or composition, or employ shell or front companies, while exploiting loopholes in trade-financing instruments.

TBML can employ various methods of trade settlement and intermediaries. These consist of open account transactions, documentary collections, letters of credit, and structured financing products.

Table 12.1 Common Vulnerabilities in Trade Settlement Instruments

Vulnerability	*How It Manifests*	*Most Exposed Instruments*
False or fictitious invoicing	Inflating/deflating prices or quantities on invoices to move value or deceive financiers.	Open accounts, documentary collections, letters of credit
Misrepresentation of Goods	Shipping inferior, different, or phantom goods versus documentation.	Letters of credit, documentary collections
Use of shell/front companies	Obscuring actual beneficial ownership to break audit trails and facilitate illicit flows.	Open accounts, all structured finance products
Document fraud	Forging or manipulating key documents (Bills of Lading, Certificates of Origin).	Letters of credit, documentary collections
Over-/under-shipment	Physically shipping more or fewer goods than declared to alter the value.	All methods, especially with loose inspection.

While each settlement method has unique operational features, they share common vulnerabilities that fraudsters and money launderers exploit. These core risks are summarized in the table below, with the specific instrument's characteristics shaping the manifestation of each risk.

In the following sections, we will examine each technique's characteristics and how money launderers can exploit the related vulnerabilities:

Open Account Transactions

According to the U.S. Government Accountability Office (GAO), in December 2020, open accounts were the most prevalent method of trade settlement, accounting for approximately 80% of international trade processed through banks and other financial institutions.

Open account transactions are a widely practiced method of trade settlement in which an exporter ships its goods to an importer, and payment is made later, typically after a significant delay or upon completion of a performance-related milestone. Open account transactions can benefit both the exporter and the importer: the former does not require prior payment, and the latter does not have to transfer documents through intermediaries. These, however, are the most uncertain types of arrangements because they depend heavily on the importer's creditworthiness and trustworthiness in making payments.

This method is preferred in low-exposure markets with strong relationships and trust between the parties. However, it carries significant uncertainty for the seller, as the buyer may default on payment after shipment. Financial institutions have a limited role in open account transactions and may lack access to complete information about the underlying commercial transactions or the parties involved. This can make it formidable for them to detect TBML or other illicit practices.

Documentary Collections

Documentary collections refer to the processing and transmission of documents for a commercial transaction conducted at arm's length between the buyer and the seller. Typically, this process involves a bank or another financial institution. Therefore, it is essential to recognize that the bank plays a withdrawable role in a documentary collection; it does not verify the documents or guarantee payment, but is primarily responsible for managing the exchange of documents for delivery and for collecting payment. The ICC's Uniform Rules for Collection (URC) 522 applies to documentary collections (International Chamber of Commerce, n.d.).

To mitigate the unrelenting exposure of TBML through documentary collections, financial institutions should implement robust due diligence measures and review trade documentation judiciously. This includes verifying document accuracy and confirming that they are standardized, conducting risk assessments, and applying extended due diligence as necessary. It is also fundamental for banks to clearly understand their customers' business activities and trade patterns, and to monitor for any red flags or unusual activity.

In closing, it is evident that documentary collections are a standard method of trade settlement and are vulnerable to TBML using false or fictitious invoicing. Financial institutions and regulators should implement appropriate measures to guard against and detect such activities, thereby preserving the integrity of the international trade system.

To conclude, letter of credit (L/C) fraud is a primary problem in international trade, resulting in substantial financial losses for buyers and banks. Thus, all parties to L/C transactions must remain vigilant and proactive in addressing the situation. Thereafter, by recognizing the risks posed and strengthening measures, including enhanced due diligence and comprehensive risk management frameworks, the parties concerned will actively deter fraudulent practices or mitigate their impacts. The global trade community can establish a more secure and reliable trading environment through collective efforts and a steadfast commitment to combating Letter of Credit (L/C) fraud.

Trade-Based Money Laundering: An Overview of Structured Financing Products

Structured finance products, such as pre-shipment and post-shipment finance, factoring, and buyer's credit, facilitate the exchange of goods and services in international trade. Such instruments alleviate financial pressure on business participants across various stages of the trading process and mitigate exposure for buyers and sellers. However, the financial instruments in question can also facilitate money laundering in international trade.

Pre-shipment financing is financing arranged before goods are shipped from the seller to the buyer. It generally covers costs associated with exposure to raw materials, labor, and other production expenses. Pre-shipment financing can be available through a loan, a letter of credit, or a guarantee.

Although suitable for sellers who require financing to finalize their orders, this financing option is highly susceptible to TBML. For example, the seller may employ pre-shipment financing to produce goods that do not exist or are of lower quality than those agreed upon by both parties. This type of fraud can result in substantial losses for the financier and harm the industry's reputation overall.

Post-shipment finance is a seller-centric financing arrangement that benefits the seller after goods are shipped to the buyer. Under this arrangement, the seller uses the funds to finance shipping and insurance costs incurred during transit. Post-shipment finance, like pre-shipment finance, may also be provided through loans, letters of credit, or guarantees. Post-shipment finance can help sellers secure financing to fulfill deliveries; however, this financing is subject to TBML risks. The Punjab National Bank (PNB) fraud in 2018 is a prime example. Nirav Modi and Mehul Choksi devised a $1.09 billion scheme. This used forged letters and invoices to secure financing before shipment. The scam revealed significant gaps in the bank's operational controls and governance.

Punjab National Bank v. Nirav Modi & Mehul Choksi (India, 2018): This is the flagship example of pre-shipment fraud. Pre-shipment financing is a mechanism in which a lender extends a loan to a borrower to support the production of goods, typically before shipment. In many cases, fraudsters provide false information about the shipped goods, misrepresenting their type, quantity, or quality, to obtain a larger loan from the financing institution. The peer review, which certifies it, categorizes it as due diligence in trade finance, providing a clear path of informed choices against the exposures associated with this activity. This was the year when Mehul Choksi and Nirav Modi systematically defrauded PNB (Wikipedia contributors, 2025) by approximately 70.8 billion Indian rupees, equivalent to roughly $1.09 billion, by submitting fraudulent invoices and documents in 2018. This is the most significant known case of bank fraud in India involving pre-shipment finance. The fraud had duped banks without cash (Krishna, 2018; Staff, 2020). The fraud was detected when PNB filed a complaint with law enforcement, which revealed fraudulent and unauthorized transactions (Mahender, 2022). The Gitanjali Group of Companies, controlled by Mehul Choksi, and companies controlled by Nirav Modi were alleged to have defrauded the bank of an additional 3.22 billion rupees and to have misappropriated the funds for purposes other than those for which the loans were granted. Therefore, fraud in India's financial sector prompted the government and central bank to implement a crackdown, which, in turn, prompted lenders to take appropriate action. The Securities and Exchange Board of India (SEBI) fined Gitanjali Gems Ltd. and its managing director 50 million rupees ($695,700) for withholding information about a $2 billion bank fraud (Krishna, 2018; Staff, 2020).

Several Incidents Revealed How Easily Post-shipment Finance Can Be Defrauded

Reebok India (2012). Among the dishonest practices employed by executives to launder money and artificially boost sales. The employees were using fake invoices and shell companies, coupled with post-shipment finance and factoring.

The case of *Rasmala v. Trafigura* (UK, 2017–18) illustrates the risk of documentary fraud in the commodity trade. The traders have obtained $21.6 million by using forged shipping documents.

UAE Factoring Fraud (2019). In this incident, a $10 million fraud was perpetrated in the UAE by submitting false invoices to a factoring company, thereby exploiting the trust embedded in the system.

Buyer's Credit Fraud (2023). A buyer diverted a $20 million credit facility intended for the procurement of goods to purchase gold. As a result, the bank incurred defaults and losses.

Factoring is the sale of a company's receivables at a discount. Businesses that would adopt it require cash and immediate cash flow to meet obligations. Unlike a bank loan, factoring is popular among small businesses because it provides immediate access to cash without requiring collateral. It, however, also unlocks avenues for TBML. A company can factor in fictitious or overvalued receivables to a financial institution, thereby incurring substantial losses for the financier.

Buyer's credit is financing provided by a financial institution to a buyer. A buyer's credit is primarily extended to finance large purchases or investments that the buyer lacks the cash to pay for. Buyer's credit can be extended through loans, letters of credit, and guarantees. This type of financing is suitable for buyers needing a financial leg up in their purchases; however, it can also be vulnerable to TBML. For instance, a buyer may use a buyer's credit to purchase goods that do not exist or are of inferior quality relative to the contract specifications. Such fraud could cause terminal losses for financiers and tarnish the reputation of the financial industry. The capacity for such losses warrants prompt remediation to address TBML in trade finance.

This type of fraud comprises two primary methods: submitting false invoices and manipulating the factoring process. The fraudster created fraudulent invoices supported by fabricated documentation, using software and graphic design tools to make them appear legitimate. In addition, the fraudster exploited an established relationship with the factoring company to introduce fraudulent invoices, relying on the factoring company's trust and thereby bypassing the usual verification and background checks.

1 Buyer's credit fraud is an illegal act committed by a buyer who is approved for credit by a bank or financial institution to purchase goods or services from a seller, thereby misusing the credit granted for another purpose or failing to repay the loan. In a relevant case study, a buyer in India obtains credit from a bank to purchase goods from a seller in China, then uses that credit to procure gold and other commodities from a third party. The buyer defaulted, resulting in a $20 million loss for the bank due to fraud. To the fraud, the buyer's statements suggested that he obtained credit from the bank by fraudulent means and thereafter misutilized the funds for personal gain. The fraud occurred in India and China, involving both the buyer and seller. The loss was approximately $20 million, borne by the bank that extended credit to the buyer (Magazine, 2023).

To prevent and detect TBML through trade financing instruments, the 'know your customer' (KYC) and 'know your customer's customer' (KYCC) principles are coupled with suspicious transaction reporting, as required by regulators and financial institutions. In contrast, the business and the client would have to live by KYC and KYCC practices to guard against TBML. Therefore, sound KYC and KYCC would help design a safe and secure trade finance environment, and such vigilance is necessary in combating trade finance fraud.

An Overview of Post-shipment Finance: Types, Uses, and Characteristics

Post-shipment financing, also known as export finance, refers to loans (local or foreign) provided to an exporter after the shipment of goods. When goods are shipped, they are exported then. It essentially provides financing to exporters, bridging the period between shipment and the buyer's receipt of payment. Post-shipment finance is primarily used to provide exporters with working capital, enabling them to cover costs incurred during production, shipment, and other expenses before receiving payment from the importer. It is a critical form of finance for small and medium exporters, providing immediately available funds to manage cash flows effectively and, therefore, avoid severe financial repercussions from buyer delays.

There are various types of post-shipment finance, including bill discounting, factoring, and factoring with forfeiture. Each works slightly differently and has unique characteristics. Each is compared in detail later in this chapter.

Its key characteristics are: (i) financing is provided after shipment but before buyer payment, creating a critical gap; and (ii) it is typically short-term (90–180 days), relying on the authenticity of the presented shipment documents as primary collateral.

Under post-shipment finance, the exporter presents the bill of exchange or invoice to the bank or financial institution. After receiving these documents, the financial institution makes a partial payment of 80–90% of the invoice amount. The exporter can then use this amount to meet his working capital requirements. Upon the importer's payment of the bill, the remaining balance is remitted to the financial institution, along with a nominal financing fee.

Fraud in post-shipment finance can occur in various forms. One example is when the exporter submits fraudulent documents to a financial institution to obtain financing. Another example is when the exporter ships substandard or defective goods not specified in the invoice. This can result in a loss for both the financial institution and the importer.

One specific instance of fraud in post-shipment financing was the case of Nirav Modi in India. Since 2018, it has been revealed that Nirav Modi and some of his employees have fraudulently obtained post-shipment funding from several banks in India by submitting false and/or forged documents. Banks incurred losses exceeding US$2 billion.

Understanding Export Factoring Mechanism

Export Factoring Mechanism and Risk Profile

Export factoring provides exporters with a mechanism to manage accounts receivable. Companies selling goods on credit use this service to secure immediate working capital. The exporter transfers ownership of the invoice to a financial intermediary. The intermediary assumes collection duties and advances funds. Fraud risk stems from receivable quality. Criminal networks submit fictitious or inflated invoices to secure unauthorized financing.

Fraud in Export Factoring

Despite the benefits of export factoring, fraud remains prevalent. One example of fraud in export factoring is when the exporter submits fake invoices to the factor to receive advances on non-existent sales. Another instance is when the buyer conspires with the exporter to mount fake invoices to disburse cash from the factory.

Eksport Kredit Fonden (EKF) is a government-owned institution that provides financial support. Its name is derived from Danish; it is state-owned and addresses issues related to monetary assistance for Danish companies engaged in international transactions. It primarily provides guarantees, loans, and insurance to enable such activity without undue risk. The 2011 fraud involved only Eksport Kredit Fonden, Denmark's export credit agency. This fraud was perpetrated by a Danish company that had obtained loans from EKF to finance the export of wind turbines to another company in Sri Lanka. The Danish company then transferred the loan funds to a Singapore bank account controlled by a Sri Lankan company not involved in the wind turbine project. The Sri Lankan company then used the funds for other purposes, and the wind turbine project was never completed. Fraud was discovered in 2012, and EKF reported it to the police. As a result of this fraud, EKF incurred a loss of DKK 100 million (approximately USD 16.5 million), underscoring the need for due diligence in export credit financing and the importance of robust risk management systems within export credit agencies to counter fraudulent practices (Just Finance International, 2021).

The primary rationale for conducting due diligence on clients before extending finance is to mitigate the ever-increasing risk of fraud. They may also require the exporter to provide financial statements, invoices, shipping documents, and other necessary documentation to verify the transaction's authenticity. Export factoring entails hidden risks that should be recognized and mitigated through robust measures.

Understanding Export Forfeiting, Its Characteristics, and Mechanisms

Export forfeiting is a specialized financial instrument in international trade. It facilitates transactions by mitigating payment risk for exporters. In essence, it involves the outright sale of an exporter's medium- to long-term receivables. Usually, it is evidenced by negotiable instruments such as bills of exchange or promissory notes and transferred to a specialized financier known as a forfeiter. This sale is executed on a non-recourse basis, a critical feature under which the forfeiter irrevocably assumes the full risk of non-payment, including commercial, political, and transfer risks, from the moment the agreement is concluded.

The principal utility of this mechanism lies in its capacity to provide exporters with immediate liquidity and comprehensive risk transfer. By converting future payment obligations into present cash, exporters can offer attractive credit terms to foreign buyers without impairing their working capital or balance sheet. This is specifically advantageous for financing high-value capital goods or contracts in emerging markets. In traditional credit lines, it may be constrained or perceived as prohibitively risky. Consequently, the exporter is freed from the burdens of collection and credit management, thereby enhancing financial predictability.

However, the forfeiting model concentrates significant risk upon the financier, necessitating rigorous due diligence as a fundamental safeguard. The forfeiter's security is predicated entirely on the authenticity of the underlying trade transaction, the creditworthiness of the obligor (and any guarantor bank), and the flawless integrity of all documentation. High-profile fraud cases illustrate the potential vulnerabilities. In those cases where misrepresented shipment details or fabricated buyer credentials have led to substantial losses. The value of forfeiture as a financial tool hinges on careful verification and ongoing transaction monitoring. Financiers must thoroughly investigate the creditworthiness of foreign buyers and ensure that all information provided by the exporters is accurate and unblemished. Readers can find more information on forfeiture structures, contract details, and relevant legal cases in the online supplements.

Understanding the Key Differences between Factoring and Forfeiting

Factoring and forfeiting are forms of trade financing that provide exporters and importers with working capital. Although both factoring and forfeiting involve finance receivables, they differ fundamentally in terms of length, recourse options, and required documentation. A comparison of these differences is available in the online supplement.

Vulnerabilities in Factoring and Forfeiting

There are fraud and other risks associated with both factoring and forfeiting. In factoring, the principal risk is that the accounts receivable being disposed of to the factor may not constitute bona fide transactions or may be overstated to the extent that they would result in a loss for the factor. Furthermore, if the factor fails to perform due diligence, it may inadvertently purchase accounts receivable from a company experiencing financial stress and insufficient cash flow.

The default risk is that an exporter may lack proper title to the goods or ship goods that differ from those specified in the sale contract, resulting in total losses for the forfeiter. Additionally, suppose the forfeiter fails to conduct proper due diligence. In that case, he can give money to a company engaged in illegal money laundering or, worse, in violating sanctions.

Key Takeaways from the Discussion

Proper due diligence is essential in factoring and forfeiting. It helps determine whether accounts receivable or the financed items are legitimate. It also involves assessing the customer's creditworthiness and verifying the seller's provided details. Moreover, it is essential to understand the distinguishing features of factoring and forfeiting, as these determine the type of funding available, the associated risks, and the required level of due diligence.

Companies must implement internal controls to mitigate fraud and other risks, such as proper invoicing, shipment documentation, and credit checks of foreign buyers. In addition, the company should be aware of other red flags, such as a buyer's request for payment outside established terms or a sudden change in the buyer's creditworthiness that may indicate fraud.

One key difference between factoring and forfeiting is that factoring is a financing option that improves the company's cash position. In contrast, forfeiting is a financing mechanism used to mitigate exposure to non-payment by foreign buyers. In factoring, the company sells its accounts receivable to a financing company at a discount, which is converted into cash immediately. In a foreclosure, the company transfers title to such receivables to a bank or financial institution in exchange for cash. However, the bank now has full access to the risk of non-payment.

Both factoring and forfeiting have vulnerabilities that must be considered. Factoring is susceptible to fraud if the invoices for the transaction being financed are illegitimate or inflated. Forfeiting can be vulnerable to fraud if the buyer is not creditworthy or if the goods financed are not shipped as mutually agreed.

Critical takeaways for corporate bodies involved in international trade: Southern firms must assess the credibility of their foreign buyers by verifying the accuracy of their credentials. Moreover, a robust invoicing and shipping documentation system should be implemented to prevent fraud. In addition, companies must monitor red flags that may indicate fraud, such as a buyer requesting payment outside standard terms or exhibiting sudden changes in creditworthiness.

Such exposure typically arises when the company incurs a financial loss due to a fraudulent scheme involving false export documentation. It warns companies engaged in international trade to exercise due care in assessing the creditworthiness of foreign buyers and the accuracy and authenticity of the information provided.

In brief, one may conclude that factoring and forfeiting are distinct financial instruments in international trade transactions. However, unlike the foregoing, one must consider the exposure of these two methods. Understanding and implementing sound internal controls will enable companies to mitigate fraud and other financial losses.

Understanding Buyer's Credit: Vulnerabilities and Protections

What is Buyer's Credit, and how does it work:

Buyer's credit, or export credit as it is sometimes called, is a financing scheme in which an exporting company sells and delivers goods or provides services to a foreign buyer on credit, with payment expected at a future date. Typically, the buyer obtains funds from a financial institution (usually a bank) to pay the exporter for goods or services rendered. Generally, buyer's credit is used when foreign buyers lack the funds to pay in advance for goods or services, or when exporters seek to minimize the risks associated with nonpayment by the foreign buyer.

It can be short-term, medium-term, or long-term and is often used for capital goods or projects. The lender's security is primarily the buyer's creditworthiness and the underlying trade documents.

Vulnerabilities and Risks of Buyer's Credit

There are essentially threats to the borrower's creditworthiness. A few of those threats are listed below:

- Default risk: The main risk here is that the foreign buyer may be unable to repay the borrowed amount.

- Political risk: The foreign buyer's loan repayment exposure is affected. For example, the government of the foreign buyer's country may amend its laws or regulations to adversely affect the buyer's ability to repay the loan.
- Currency risk: The risk is that the loan may be evaluated or the fallback for repayment may be enormously affected by the fluctuation in the exchange rate.
- Fraud: The foreign buyer provides the lending institution with bogus or misleading information to obtain a loan.

Fraud in Buyer's Credit

Fraud in a buyer's credit can take several forms, including:

- Misrepresentation of the goods or services bought: In this type of fraud, the foreign buyer provides inaccurate information to the financial institution to secure a foreign buyer loan. For example, the buyer may provide fictitious financial statements or misrepresent his assets or liabilities.
- Misrepresentation of the goods or services bought: In this type of fraud, the foreign buyer misrepresents the kind of goods or services in the documentation to justify a more considerable amount as a loan than is otherwise warranted.
- Diversion of funds: In this type of fraud, a foreign buyer might use the credit funds the buyer received for purposes not intended by the buyer, like speculation or transfers to other accounts under the buyer's control.

Companies must thoroughly assess the creditworthiness of foreign buyers, verify the accuracy and trustworthiness of the information they provide, maintain proper documentation, and implement internal controls. In addition, banks that extend buyers' credit should have robust policies and processes for managing risk and for quickly detecting and thwarting fraud.

Public development was associated with buyer credit fraud by Daewoo Logistics in the early 2000s. This Korean entity borrowed buyer credit from international banks and other financial institutions for a big infrastructure project. However, it diverted that funding toward a speculative venture and subsequently defaulted on the loans, resulting in substantial economic losses to the financiers. This example is a stark reminder of the serious risks associated with buyers' credit and the need for an effective risk management process.

In closing, buyers' credit can be an effective tool for facilitating international trade. It also poses risks, especially in fraud cases. To mitigate these exposures, companies and financial institutions should implement robust due diligence and risk management processes to assess the foreign buyer's creditworthiness and the integrity of the underlying transaction.

TBML: Misinvoicing, Short Shipping, Multiple Invoicing, and Other Methods:

One critical aspect all stakeholders must understand is how trade-based money laundering works. Mis-invoicing, over-invoicing, and under-invoicing are risks, not just techniques; they must be recognized and mitigated. Awareness of methodologies can help maintain an informed position and protect against further risks and ignorance in transactions.

TBML is often described as the illicit movement of funds within international trade transactions by concealing the proceeds of legitimate activity. Mispricing the trade transaction constitutes a substantial means of perpetrating TBML. Misinvoicing involves manipulating the price, quantity, or quality of goods or services on invoices to facilitate the movement of funds across borders (Figure 12.1).

Figure 12.1 How Trade Misinvoicing Works

Source: Kar a Spanjers (2014)

The countries involved in misinvoicing include South Africa as the importer, the British Virgin Islands as the intermediary, and Japan as the exporter. Suppose a South African importer purchases $2 million worth of electronics from a Japanese exporter. In that case, the process begins when the South African importer sends the transaction through a shell company in the British Virgin Islands, where the goods are "re-invoiced" at $2.8 million. This shell company then remits the $2 million to the Japanese exporter. Notably, the shell company retains the $800,000 in excess funds, which are diverted to an offshore account controlled by the South African importer, thereby laundering funds out of South Africa under the cover of legitimate trade (Kar & Spanjers, 2014).

Numerous different techniques can be employed in mis-invoicing, including:
Over-invoicing (or short shipping): Inflating the invoice value of goods to justify moving excess funds out of the boundaries of a country.

Under-invoicing (or over-shipping): Giving the declaration of goods as being less in value than the market price to pay fewer customs duties and get the residual value transferred abroad.

Multiple Invoicing/Financing: Issuing multiple invoices for the same shipment. This is done to obtain duplicate financing or to exaggerate trade volumes.

Other common methods include:
Mis-declaration of Goods: This involves fraudulently declaring that misrepresents the nature, type, quality, or quantity of goods shipped.

Carousel Fraud: Taking advantage of the VAT refund system through the use of fake circular trades within and across borders.

Fake Trade Finance Instruments: Forged use of bills of lading, letters of credit, or insurance certificates.

Fraudulent Alteration of Documents: Secretly changing crucial shipment or financial documents after they have been issued.

Financial institutions and businesses play a crucial role in preventing trade-based money laundering. Comprehensive KYC and anti-money laundering checks are crucial, but the lack of credible, representative data on illicit transactions undermines them. These checks help identify red flags, such as high trade volumes with high-risk jurisdictions, trades without an economic rationale, and payments to overseas parties without proper verification and justification. They can effectively combat money laundering by remaining diligent and conducting these checks.

Case 12.1 Trails of Deceit: Cross-Border Misinvoicing Schemes (USA, Hong Kong, China, 2013)

In 2013, two individuals were charged in the United States for laundering drug proceeds through international trade, along with shell companies and misinvoicing (Global Financial Integrity, n.d.). The defendants utilized shell companies incorporated in Hong Kong and China to acquire goods from suppliers at inflated prices. They would resell to another set of shell companies, also incorporated in Hong Kong and China, at lower prices. The difference between the inflated purchase prices and the lower resale prices was diverted to bank accounts controlled by the defendant. Laundered funds were then used to purchase real estate and luxury goods in the United States, thereby channeling illicit proceeds into the legal economy (US Department of Justice, 2013). Ultimately, the prosecution has taken place. Indictments result in asset forfeiture and prosecution under U.S. anti-money laundering laws. Real estate and other assets that were purchased with illegal funds were forfeited. The case prompted renewed calls for beneficial ownership transparency and enhanced regulation of trade transactions. The case has been widely referenced in AML training and forensic accounting courses as a textbook model of TBML.

Case: An Example of Misinvoicing: Layers of Illusion: How Shell Firms and Export Fraud Were Used to Launder Criminal Wealth via the Meat Trade (Brazil & USA, 2019): In 2019, Brazilian law enforcement arrested a businessman who coordinated a large-scale export misinvoicing scheme for meat product transactions. The case was part of a broader effort to address illicit financial flows and tax avoidance in Brazil's agribusiness. The UNODC reported that the businessman inflated the value of meat exports by up to 800%, used shell companies to obscure transactions, and then laundered the proceeds by purchasing property in the United States and Europe. The case also represents an institutional weakness in Brazil's oversight of export certification and customs inspection with respect to compliance in high-volume markets, such as meat and poultry. It underscores the role of offshore jurisdictions in facilitating TBML schemes. The business's meat products were declared with values exceeding the market price by 800%. Offshore entities were established to facilitate the transaction and obscure the ownership trail. By submitting inflated invoices, the businessman obtained higher export incentives and evaded domestic taxation. Ultimately, the businessman was arrested. He was indicted on charges of customs fraud, money laundering, and tax evasion. Authorities seized properties and bank accounts related to the scheme. The case raised new questions about Brazil's oversight of export and shed new light on the potential use of shell company structures in trade finance. The case also highlighted that cooperation on cross-border TBML and the verification of beneficial ownership is lacking.

Short Shipping and Tax Evasion in the U.S. Tobacco Trade: A Case of Cross-State Smuggling and Financial Laundering (United States, 2015):

In 2015, several individuals in the United States were indicted for short-shipping cigarettes to evade taxes. It was orchestrated by purchasing cigarettes in low-tax states and then shipping them to a warehouse in New York to repackage and increase the selling price. The individuals underreported the number of cigarettes sold, thereby evading taxes and laundering the proceeds (FATF, 2020).

Key Elements of the Scheme: (i) cigarettes were purchased legally in low-tax jurisdictions (Tax Foundation, 2015), (ii) shipment to New York was ultimately for resale. However, cigarettes will not be reported as sold to authorities, (iii) proceeds were laundered and would never be disclosed to taxing authorities, and (iv) false documents and miscounting of shipments were employed to conceal the number of cigarettes ultimately traded. At the time of the event, New York had the highest cigarette tax rate in the United States; therefore, it lost substantial revenue. Individuals implicated in the operation were charged with tax evasion, conspiracy to commit fraud, and money laundering. This criminal case heightened scrutiny of outbound tobacco shipments and underscored the ongoing need to improve tax policy standards and real-time tracking systems. According to the Tax Foundation, New York had an estimated inbound smuggling rate of 56.8% and was the country's highest net importer of illicit cigarettes in 2015. This case demonstrates how short shipping, when combined with tax arbitrage, can become a lucrative criminal enterprise. It underscores the need for: (i) Stronger inter-state coordination, (ii) Digital tracking of tobacco shipments, (iii) Enhanced enforcement of excise tax compliance, and (iv) Cross-agency collaboration to detect and dismantle TBML schemes.

Malabu Oil Scandal: (Faull, 2017) TBML via Multiple Invoicing (Nigeria, 2017): Back in 2017, a Nigerian businessman was arrested for using multiple invoicing to launder money from a $180 million oil deal by creating numerous invoices for the same shipment of oil, each with a different value, to acquire financing and transfer the proceeds to foreign accounts (OECD, 2017). The scheme allowed the perpetrator to: (i) Obtain more money than required from banks and trading partners. (ii) Deposit the illegal money into foreign bank accounts, making it look like it came from normal business operations. (iii) Avoid being spotted by taking advantage of loopholes in customs and financial oversight.

This situation appears to be linked to the Malabu Oil and Gas scandal, specifically the alleged pollution of the OPL 245 oil block deal, which has been under investigation in Nigeria, Italy, and the UK for some time (Wikipedia contributors, 2024). The transaction allegedly involved senior public officials and multinationals in bribery, corruption, and money laundering across multiple levels. Nigeria is reported to have lost over $1 billion (US) due to scams and mismanagement of funds. This case was brought to the attention of international oversight institutions, including the OECD, Transparency International, and Global Witness, which pointed to issues in international trade finance.

Case 12.2 Transfer Pricing Manipulation, Shell Entity Abuse, and Regulatory Loopholes: Dutch Trading Company Case (Netherlands, 2017)

In 2017, a Dutch trading corporation was charged with manipulating transfer pricing to evade taxes and facilitate money laundering. The corporation allegedly employed deceptive practices, including abuse of shell companies and price manipulation, to artificially transfer profits to low-tax jurisdictions (OECD, 2017).

It strengthens the framing of transfer pricing as a fault line against financial misdeclaration. The intention was to minimize tax liability and, through the process, disperse the true nature of the transaction by exploiting loopholes in the international tax system.

According to the OECD, transfer pricing manipulation refers to the mispricing of goods, services, or intangible assets in a transaction between two multinational enterprises for tax purposes (OECD, 2017). In this case, a Dutch trading company was manipulating transfer prices to artificially minimize tax revenue, thereby constituting tax evasion and potentially facilitating money laundering.

Shell companies enable criminal activity to operate within a company. Such entities conceal their absolute ownership and control over funds, maintain little to no meaningful operations or

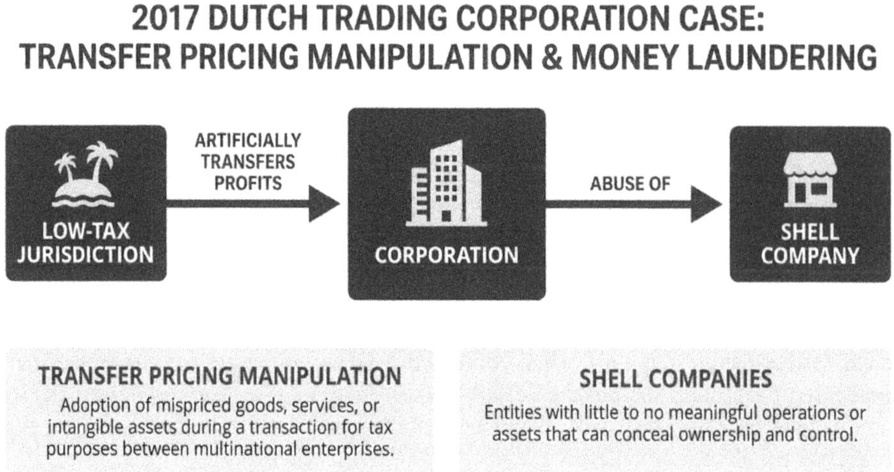

Figure 12.2 Transfer Pricing Manipulation & Shell Entity Abuse: The 2017 Dutch Trading Company Case

assets, and make it extremely difficult for authorities to trace the flow of funds and identify the ultimate beneficiaries.

From the standpoint of tax evasion and money laundering, these practices compromised transparency and accountability (Cazacu, 2017).

The case, while some judicial outcomes remain secret or are understated, contributed to:

- More accountability to the arm's length principle and documentation (OECD, 2017).
- More scrutiny into outbound transactions and increased disclosure requirements.
- Heightened the role of forensic accounting approaches to detect financial misrepresentations from transfer pricing and also account for deterrents.

The following infographic captures the entire saga. The diagram outlines the key entities, deceptive mechanisms, and the directional flow of actions that lead to tax evasion and money laundering (Figure 12.2).

Case 12.3 *Kenya vs. AVIC International Beijing (EA) Ltd*: (Academy of Tax Law, 2025) Transfer Pricing Irregularities (Kenya, 2024)

AVIC International Beijing (EA) Ltd. is a subsidiary of a Chinese multinational company, established in Kenya in 2015 to import and assemble automotive components. An audit of the company conducted by the Kenya Revenue Authority (KRA) from 2016 to 2021 identified underdeclared income, transfer pricing documentation, and tax compliance issues. The audit aimed to determine whether AVIC had manipulated intercompany pricing to transfer profits to its foreign entities while minimizing the tax it would pay in Kenya. AVIC's pricing practices effectively raised concerns about the arm's-length nature of its pricing for transactions with related foreign entities.

One way the company leveraged its strategic modus operandi was to use different pricing for similar goods and services offered to related entities, thereby shifting profits. AVIC employs the Resale Price Method (RPM), which more accurately reflects its revenue-generating mechanism.

KRA was adamant about using the Transactional Net Margin Method (TNMM) and concluded that AVIC would require improved benchmarking and functional analysis. Using GRANT, he moved funds to other foreign entities at a reduced taxable margin. With reportable foreign income, the Kenyan tax. AVIC's reports did not have adequate comparable information and supporting rationale to [support the point-of-departure for its pricing and related return.]

Due to various malpractices, initial assessments were estimated at KShs. 530,528,802, which was later reduced to KShs. 514,154,336 following objections. The tribunal ruled that TNMM is the most appropriate method under the OECD guidelines (OECD, 2020). The tribunal declined to uphold AVIC's claims of double taxation and procedural overreach. Stressed the significance of thorough transfer pricing documentation and functional analysis.

The decision has broader implications, renewing Kenya's commitment to minimizing base erosion and profit shifting (BEPS). This has sent a clear message to multinationals regarding their compliance with local tax laws and with OECD standards. The central insight of the case is that the tribunal considered the commercial rationale of intercompany transactions. AVIC's pricing did not reflect what independent parties would agree to. As such, the case suggests that tax authorities are actively using anti-abuse to test and challenge abusive transfer pricing by multinationals.

Case 12.4 Mis-declaration of Goods to Evade Customs Duties: A Story of a Chinese Businessman (2016)

The central figure had misdeclared goods in the 2016 case involving a China-based businessman. His actions led to a deeper understanding of the seriousness of importing goods into the United States, an apparent attempt to evade customs duties. According to reports from the Basel Institute on Governance (2016), the businessman was sentenced for undervaluing imported goods from China by more than $40 million, resulting in a significant case of tax evasion (2016).

The case is representative of misdeclaration—a practice that involves using tricks to defraud the government of its due revenue from duties on a particular importation, thereby obtaining otherwise unwarranted financial benefits. It involves intentionally undervaluing goods to lower the assessed customs duties, thereby reducing the government's financial obligations.

Mis-declaring goods is an activity, as described by the influential Basel Institute on Governance (2016), in which offenders deliberately and falsely manipulate the declared value of goods in customs declarations to evade authorities and avoid paying customs taxes. This illegal practice has also distorted trade and posed numerous challenges for customs in ensuring fair, just, and transparent international trade.

Case 12.5 Carousel VAT Fraud Scheme: EU-Wide Crackdown on VAT Fraud Syndicate Defrauding Spain (Spain, 2021)

Carousel fraud, also known as Missing Trader Intra-Community (MTIC) fraud, exploits the VAT-free movement of goods between EU member states. For instance, organized crime groups use a network of front companies in Spain and other EU member states to create a false impression of cross-border trading. Fraudsters typically submit documents purporting to describe fictitious sales and transactions to claim VAT refunds for goods that never left Spain.

The methodology (FATF, 2007) most commonly adopted in this case included:

Step 1: A company in Spain purchased goods VAT-exempt from another EU country.

Step 2: The company in Spain then sold the goods in Spain with VAT applied to a second company.

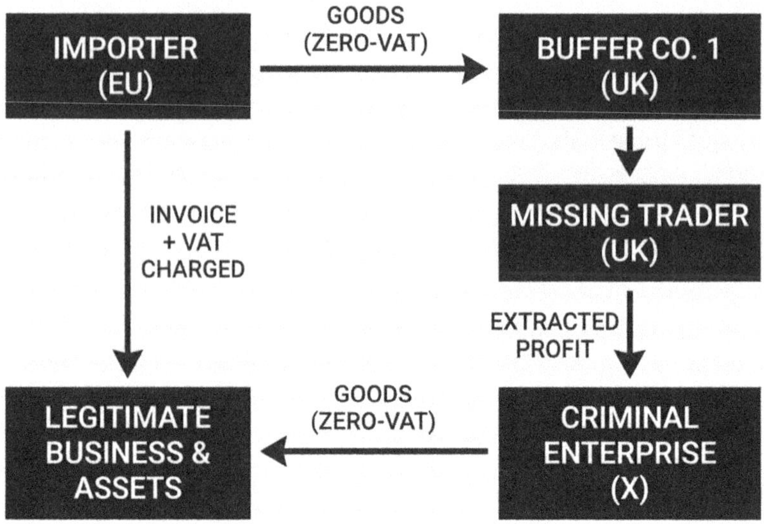

Figure 12.3 Spain's Carousel VAT Fraud Scheme (2021)

Step 3: The second company ("missing trader") disappeared after the transaction and failed to remit VAT to the Spanish authorities.

Step 4: The third company exported the goods (entirely fictitious) and filed a VAT refund claim.

Infrastructure: The syndicate produced several front companies and used forged trading documents to create what appeared to be legitimate cross-border trading activity.

Over €26.5 million was defrauded from the Spanish treasury (Ljubas, 2021). Two coordinated Europol-Eurojust operations took place simultaneously in five countries, resulting in the arrest of 22 suspects. Total seized assets comprise 16 luxury vehicles, 13 properties valued at €1.3 million, and bank accounts held by 33 financial institutions. Carousel fraud costs the EU approximately €40–60 billion per year, distorting tax systems and facilitating money laundering.

Key insights: This type of fraud exploited EU VAT arrangements intended to facilitate cross-border trade. There were no actual international shipments of goods—transactions were entirely fictitious. The scheme involved high-value goods and a rapid flow of funds through several jurisdictions. Authorities noted the use of a sophisticated infrastructure and a complex layering of financial transactions, which, as expected, effectively concealed the trail (Figure 12.3).

This flowchart illustrates a carousel VAT fraud scheme:

- Blue arrows represent the movement of goods (Zero-VAT).
- Red dashed arrows indicate invoicing with VAT, often used to create artificial tax liabilities.
- Black arrows show the extraction of illicit profits by the criminal enterprise.
- The "X" mark on the Missing Trader highlights its role in the fraudulent loop.

According to the UK National Crime Agency (NCA, 2019), carousel fraud is a significant problem for tax authorities worldwide. It compromises the integrity of the VAT system, weakens public finances, and distorts fair competition among legitimate businesses. Due to the complexity of carousel fraud schemes, which often span multiple jurisdictions and involve numerous participants, detection, and investigation can be challenging for law enforcement agencies.

The tax fraud ring operating in the UK is a potent reminder of the need to implement effective measures to combat carousel fraud and safeguard tax revenue. This further underscores the importance of close collaboration between law enforcement agencies, tax authorities, and international organizations to achieve effective results. Such a partnership is both beneficial and essential for intelligence sharing, the exchange of best practices, and the implementation of appropriate preventive measures.

Preventive measures against carousel fraud include enhancing risk assessment, improving data analysis capabilities, and implementing targeted enforcement actions. Tax authorities must reinforce scrutiny and auditing procedures, impose proper limits on registration and verification, and ensure transparency in supply chain transactions to reveal and deter fraudulent conduct.

Chapter Summary

International trade is a complex economic system that requires financing to facilitate the exchange of goods and services. It is primarily through the ICC that international trade is affected, as this body takes a vital interest in trade financing and has actively contributed to the development of rules and mechanisms for trade-finance dispute settlement. To comprehend this role, therefore, will require a comprehensive understanding of the global trade system and the role of banks and financial institutions in providing funding, as well as various methods of settlement, including open accounts, letters of credit, documentary collections, and cash-in-advance.

Trade financing instruments are vulnerable to manipulation, with a particular focus on the letter of credit. This knowledge should make us cautious and alert. Trade-based money laundering is a common practice in structured financing products, including pre-shipment finance, post-shipment finance, factoring, and buyer's credit. Export factoring is a commonly used structured financing product in international trade. However, fraud may occur during the accounting of exports. Export forfeiting is another structured financing product used in international trade. Understanding its characteristics, mechanisms, and methods for fraud prevention is crucial. Factoring and forfeiting are two different structured financing products used in international trade. It is essential to understand the critical differences between the two. Both factoring and forfeiting have vulnerabilities that must be addressed to frustrate fraud.

Simply put, buyer's credit refers to a short-term loan facility extended by an overseas lender, typically a financial institution or bank, to an importer. It may be among the most common structured financial instruments used in international trade, as it enables an importer to finance the procurement of goods or services from an exporter. Unfortunately, this method is often subject to abuse, as various techniques are employed to manipulate trade-financing instruments through misinvoicing, short shipping, and multiple invoicing.

End of Chapter: Discussion Questions

1 What is the role of the International Chamber of Commerce (ICC) in trade financing?
2 How do banks and financial institutions play a critical role in trade finance?
3 Can you explain the various methods of settlement in international trade?
4 What are some of the vulnerabilities in trade financing instruments?
5 How does trade-based money laundering occur in structured financing products?
6 What is export factoring, and how does it work?
7 What is the issue of fraud in export factoring?
8 Can you explain export forfeiting and its characteristics?
9 What are the critical differences between factoring and forfeiting?

10 What are the vulnerabilities in factoring and forfeiting?
11 Can you explain the buyer's credit, vulnerabilities, and protections?
12 What is misinvoicing, and how does it impact trade financing?
13 Can you explain the concepts of short shipping and multiple invoicing?
14 What other methods can be used to manipulate trade financing instruments?
15 What is the importance of understanding the modes, methods, and techniques of settlement and financing in international trade?

Bibliography

Academy of Tax Law. (2025, January 20). Kenya vs. AVIC international: Transfer pricing case. Retrieved from https://academyoftaxlaw.com/kenya-vs-avic-international-transfer-pricing-case.

Alvarez & Marsal. (2024). *Digital identity and invoice fraud risks: What it means for UAE businesses.* Alvarez & Marsal Thought Leadership. Retrieved from https://www.alvarezandmarsal.com/thought-leadership/digital-identity-and-invoice-fraud-risks-in-peppol-based-e-invoicing-belgium-s-case-and-what-it-means-for-uae-businesses

Barnes, J. G., & Byrne, J. E. (2003). Letters of credit: Autonomy, strict compliance, and the fraud exception. *University of Pennsylvania Journal of International Economic Law*, 24(3), 475–501.

Basel Institute on Governance (2016). Trade-Based Money Laundering: The Next Frontier in International Money Laundering Enforcement.

Bjerregaard, E., & Kirchmaier, T. (2019). *The Danske Bank money laundering scandal: A case study.* Copenhagen Business School Research Portal. https://research.cbs.dk/en/publications/the-danske-bank-money-laundering-scandal-a-case-study

Cazacu, A.-L. (2017). Transfer pricing and the manifestations of tax Evasion. *Journal of International Business and Economics*, 5(1), 114–118. https://doi.org/10.15640/jibe.v5n1a10.

Central Bank of the UAE. (2022). *Guidance for licensed financial institutions on risks related to Trade-Based Money Laundering (TBML) and Transshipment.* CBUAE Rulebook. https://rulebook.centralbank.ae/en/rulebook/guidance-licensed-financial-institutions-risks-related-trade-based-money-laundering-%E2%80%9Ctbml%E2%80%9D

Chandrasekhar, D. (n.d.). Trade-based money laundering: A case study. Compliance Alert. https://calert.info/details.php?id=1318

CheHashim, R., & Mahdzan, N. S. (2014). Fraud in letter of credit transactions: The experience of Malaysian bankers. *International Journal of Law, Crime and Justice*, 42(3), 224–236. https://doi.org/10.1016/j.ijlcj.2014.01.008

Cheng, Y., Tsang, K., & Chung, M. (2019). State ownership, policy missions, and commercial operation: A case study of the Agricultural Bank of China. *Journal of Financial Stability*, 28, 142–154. https://doi.org/10.1080/10971475.2018.1545366

Ellen, E. (1996). Fraud watch. DCI (ICC), Spring, 2(2), 2. Trade newsletter, ICC Banking Commission.

Faull, L. (2017, December 17). *Malabu OPL245 scandal: Nigeria sues JP Morgan for $875m over 'grossly negligent' payments to money launderer. Finance Uncovered.* https://www.financeuncovered.org/money-laundering/malabu-scandal-jp-morgan-nigeria-etete-opl245.

Financial Action Task Force (FATF). (2007). Laundering the proceeds of VAT carousel fraud. Retrieved from https://www.fatf-gafi.org/en/publications/Methodsandtrends/Launderingtheproceedsofvatcarouselfraudreport.html.

Financial Action Task Force. (2020). Trade-based money laundering. https://www.fatf-gafi.org/publications/methodsandtrends/documents/trade-based-money-laundering.html

Global Financial Integrity. (n.d.). Trade misinvoicing. Retrieved July 23, 2024, from Global Financial Integrity.

International Chamber of Commerce. (n.d.). About ICC. Retrieved from https://iccwbo.org/about-icc-2/

International Chamber of Commerce Academy. (n.d.). *Introduction to letters of credit and global trade rules.* Retrieved from https://academy.iccwbo.org/trade-finance/article/sanctions-and-letters-of-credit/

International Trade Administration. (n.d.). *The trade finance guide: A quick reference for U.S. exporters*. U.S. Department of Commerce. https://www.trade.gov/trade-finance-guide-quick-reference-us-exporters

Just Finance International. (2021, June 11). Decarbonizing danish export credits – a case study: A critical review of the climate footprint, environmental and social due diligence and transparency in the Danish Export Credit Agency. *Just Finance International*. https://justfinanceinternational.org/2021/06/11/decarbonising-danish-export-credits-a-case-study-a-critical-review-of-the-climate-footprint-environmental-and-social-due-diligence-and-transparency-in-the-danish-export-credit-agency/.

Kar, D., & Spanjers, J. (2014). Illicit Financial Flows from Developing Countries: 2003–2012. Global Financial Integrity. https://www.gfintegrity.org/wp-content/uploads/2014/12/Illicit-Financial-Flows-from-Developing-Countries-2003-2012.pdf

Krishna, R. (2018, February 15). PNB scam: Nirav Modi and Mehul Choksi defraud ₹11,400 crore. The Economic Times. https://economictimes.indiatimes.com

Kuo-Ellen, S. L. (2002). UCP needs to change.Journal of Money Laundering Control 5(3), 231–236.

Legal Consultant, UAE. (2024, May 22). Fraud case in Dubai punishment - Latest rules & help. https://legalconsultantuae.ae/blog/fraud-punishment-dubai

Ljubas, Z. (2021, May 20). Spain loses millions in a 'carousel fraud' case. Organized Crime and Corruption Reporting Project (OCCRP). Retrieved from https://www.occrp.org/en/news/spain-losses-millions-in-a-carousel-fraud-case.

Magazine, F. (2023). Living the Good life! Fraud-Magazine.com. https://www.fraud-magazine.com/article.aspx?id=4294969421

Mahender Singh Manral. (2022, December 16). CBI registers three more fraud cases against Mehul Choksi. *The Indian Express*. https://indianexpress.com/article/india/mehul-choksi-booked-fresh-cases-bank-loan-fraud-8328883/

Mukundan, P. (2008). Fraud with L/Cs - latest modus operandi. *Paper presented at the 2nd Annual International Conference on Letters of Credit*, ICC Austria, Vienna.

Mukundan, P. (2009). Trade finance frauds. *Paper presented at the 3rd Annual Conference on Letters of Credit*, ICC Austria, Vienna.

National Crime Agency (NCA) UK (2019). VAT fraud: tackling the problem. Retrieved from https://www.nationalcrimeagency.gov.uk/publications/vat-fraud-tackling-the-problem/.

Organization for Economic Co-operation and Development (OECD) (2017). Transfer pricing guidelines for multinational enterprises and tax administrations. Retrieved from https://www.oecd.org/tax/transfer-pricing/transfer-pricing-guidelines-for-multinational-enterprises-and-tax-administrations-2017/.

OECD. (2017). *OECD transfer pricing guidelines for multinational enterprises and tax administrations 2017*. OECD Publishing. https://doi.org/10.1787/tpg-2017-en

OECD. (2022). *OECD transfer pricing guidelines for multinational enterprises and tax administrations*. OECD Publishing.

Public Citizen. (2010). *Rapidly increasing criminal and civil monetary penalties against the pharmaceutical industry: 1991–2010*. Washington, DC: Public Citizen Health Research Group. https://www.citizen.org/article/pharmaceutical-industry-criminal-and-civil-penalties-1991-to-2010

Rajah, J. (2025, June 23). Rasmala Trade Finance Fund v Trafigura Pte Ltd [2025] EWHC (Ch) 901. UK Chancery Division Judgment.

Rafique, R. (2021). Preventive measures to mitigate the risk of fraud in letters of credit transactions in Malaysia. *UUM Journal of Legal Studies, 12*(1), 27–49.

Staff Reporter. (2020, March 12). SEBI fines Gitanjali Gems ₹50 million for lapses in disclosure in the PNB fraud. *Business Standard*. https://www.business-standard.com

Staff, R. (2020, February 27). India fines jewellery firm for withholding information in $2 bln bank fraud. Reuters. https://www.reuters.com/article/india-fraud-punjab-natl-bank-idUKL3N2AR4O1

Tax Foundation. (2015). Cigarette taxes and cigarette smuggling by State. https://taxfoundation.org/data/all/state/cigarette-tax-cigarette-smuggling-2015

United Nations Office on Drugs and Crime. (2019). Trade-based money laundering: Overview and case studies. https://www.unodc.org

United States Department of Justice. (2016, March 21). Miami man sentenced to 12 years in prison for role in multimillion-dollar scheme to defraud commercial lenders and U.S. Export-Import Bank.

https://www.justice.gov/opa/pr/miami-man-sentenced-144-months-prison-role-multimillion-dollar-scheme-defraud-commercial

US Department of Justice. (2013). Two individuals indicted for money laundering using shell companies and misinvoicing in international trade. https://www.justice.gov/usao-sdny/pr/two-individuals-indicted-money-laundering-using-shell-companies-and-misinvoicing

US Government Accountability Office. (2020, December). Report on the trade finance industry.

Wikipedia contributors. (2024). OPL 245 bribery affair. Wikipedia. https://en.wikipedia.org/wiki/OPL_245_bribery_affair

Wikipedia contributors. (2025, April 15). Punjab National Bank Scam. Wikipedia. https://en.wikipedia.org/wiki/Punjab_National_Bank_Scam

World Trade Organization. (2020). World trade report 2020: Government policies to promote innovation in the digital age. https://www.wto.org/english/res_e/booksp_e/wtr20_e/wtr20_e.pdf.

Zhang, Y. (1992). *Approaches to resolving the international documentary credit problem* (Doctoral dissertation, University of Sheffield). British Library EThOS. https://ethos.bl.uk/OrderDetails.do?uin=uk.bl.ethos.240311

Additional Learning Resources

Books

1 International trade and political conflict: Commerce, coalitions, and mobility. Michael J. Hiscox. (2002). Princeton University Press, 2002. www.degruyter.com
This book provides a comprehensive overview of international trade, covering topics such as the theory of trade, trade policy, and the impact of trade on economic growth. It also includes a chapter on trade finance.

2 Multinational Business Finance by David K. Eiteman, Arthur I. Stonehill, and Michael H. Moffett (2019). 15th ed. www.amazon.com.au
This book is a classic text on international trade finance, covering topics such as letters of credit, documentary collections, and trade terms. It also includes a chapter on the use of trade finance in international trade.

3 "International Business: The Challenges of Globalization (What is New in Management)." John J. Wild and Kenneth L. Wild. (2021). Pearson.
This 9th edition provides a comprehensive exploration of the complexities and opportunities of conducting business in a globalized world. It covers a wide range of topics, including cultural differences, political and legal environments, and economic factors, offering practical insights and real-world examples. The book conveys that understanding and effectively navigating the challenges of international business are crucial to success in today's interconnected global marketplace.

4 "International Finance" is prepared by Keith Pilbeam (2023) and published by Bloomsbury Publishing. The book provides insights into international finance, covering topics including global markets, exchange rates, and international investment.

Article

5 "The Hidden Cost of Trade Financing: How International Banking Regulations on Illicit Money are Disrupting International Trade," Julia C. Morse.
The article examines the adverse effects of banking regulations on illicit funds in international trade, highlighting the hidden costs associated with these regulations.

6 "Trade and trade finance in the 2008–09 financial crisis." Irena Asmundson, Thomas William Dorsey, Armine Khachatryan, Ioana Niculcea, and Mika Saito (2011).
The article examines the impact of the financial crisis on trade and trade finance during the years 2008–2009.

7 Trade-Based Money Laundering – With Special Focus on Trade Finance Instruments. Ramandeep Kaur Chhina. (2013, November). Paper presented at the 7th International Conference on International Law and Trade, Assumption University of Thailand, Bangkok, Thailand. Available at: https://napier-repository.worktribe.com/output/1038466/trade-based-money-laundering-with-special-focus-on-trade-finance-instruments
This paper sheds light on the intricacies of trade-based money laundering and its connection to trade finance instruments. The paper, presented at the 7th International Conference on International Law and Trade, emphasizes the need for a targeted approach in combating this form of illicit financial activity.

Documentary

8 "The China Hustle" is a documentary film directed by Jed Rothstein. It was released in 2017.
The film examines large-scale financial fraud, focusing on practices involving Chinese companies listed on U.S. stock exchanges. The film aims to inform viewers about this complex issue and shed light on the geopolitical implications of such fraud. While it may not be fueled by intense anger, "The China Hustle" is a slick and informative documentary that serves as a primer on global financial fraud.
9 Trump's Trade War (full documentary). (2019). pbs.org/frontline. Available at: https://tinyurl.com/tradewar1
This documentary examines the trade war between the United States and China and its impact on businesses and consumers worldwide. The documentary also discusses the role of trade finance in international trade.
10 The Dirty Money (2018). www.imdb.com
This documentary series examines the dark side of the global financial system, including the use of trade finance to facilitate money laundering. The series features interviews with experts and journalists who investigate financial crimes.

YouTube

11 "International Trade: What is it, How Does It Work?" (2019). Investopedia, a financial education website, prepared it. Available at: https://tinyurl.com/Intltrade1
The video provides an overview of international trade, covering its definition, types, and benefits.

13 Common Red Flags of Money Laundering Involving Trade

To effectively protect the global trade system, it is necessary first to identify financial crime. Moreover, to take a proactive stance in detecting illegal activities. Spotting the red flags of fraud, such as unusual payments, widely fluctuating prices, constantly changing shipping routes, or trade with high-risk jurisdictions, is the baseline of the fight against money laundering and other illegal activities. According to leading institutions combating money laundering, it is essential to maintain continuous vigilance and update systems through robust monitoring infrastructure to reduce risks and preserve the integrity of international trade (FATF, 2021; U.S. Department of the Treasury, 2020).

Uncovering the Hidden World of Money Laundering

Money laundering is a complicated affair. It entirely undermines the whole edifice and stability, and existence of financial institutions, allowing criminals to perpetrate unlawful activities such as corruption, tax evasion, or financing of terrorism. Methods employed by money launderers have been evolving rapidly, making it a constant challenge for governmental and regulatory bodies to combat this menace. However, indicators of money laundering must be understood, specifically in the context of trade-based money laundering (TBML). This knowledge enables the detection and assessment of potential TBML cases before resorting to measures that will monitor or effectively address such illegal practices.

The Rise of TBML

More recently, a new facet of finance has emerged: TBML, which poses a significant challenge to the global financial and trade systems. TBML is a method of choice for money launderers who inflate or create the appearance of trade transactions to move and conceal illicit funds. A UNODC report states that TBML is increasingly prevalent, particularly in cross-border trade, with estimates that it generates hundreds of billions of dollars annually (UNODC, 2021).

The Evolution of Red Flags in the Fight Against Financial Crime

Historically, since the early 1900s, some 20–30% of red flag indicators have been employed to spot financial crime. In 1909, the Association of Certified Public Accountants (AICPA) published a pamphlet that listed 12 warning signals to alert auditors. These red flags manifest as unusual transactions, unexplained discrepancies, and suspicious employee conduct.

i In the 1970s, the U.S. government decided to launch a full-fledged attack against white-collar financial crimes. Known for combating financial fraud, the Bank Secrecy Act requires institutions to report suspicious activity to various government agencies.

DOI: 10.4324/9781003477631-14

ii In 1977, the American Congress decided to fight perverted financial crimes on a grand scale. To cope with this, the Financial Crimes Enforcement Network was established. The network is designed to collect and analyze financial intelligence data related to money laundering and other financial crimes.
iii The applicability of red flags has gained increasing significance over time due to the complexity and ingenuity of financial crime, which has exponentially heightened its level of sophistication. In 2001, the Financial Action Task Force, an international body that sets standards in combating money laundering and related crimes, issued 40 red-flag indicators that financial institutions must consider and address.

There are some selected cases where red flags have made significant differences:

- In 2008, the Lehman Brothers, an elite investment bank, succumbed and filed for bankruptcy in the United States (U.S. Securities and Exchange Commission, 2010). The entity owed more than $630 billion, making it the most significant bank failure in U.S. history. It has long been suspected that it failed to recognize signals of impending financial difficulties.
- In 2015, wealthy individuals and businesses came to light through the Panama Papers scandal (International Consortium of Investigative Journalists, 2016) when it was found that they employed offshore entities to conceal their actual assets from taxation regimes where these assets belonged. Against this backdrop, financial institutions have either turned a blind eye to or failed to take appropriate measures to identify and respond to the red flags associated with the shell company scheme.
- In 2017, the Fédération Internationale de Football Association (FIFA) corruption scandal emerged over the awarding of lucrative contracts (U.S. Department of Justice, 2017). When higher authorities of the FIFA accepted huge bribes in exchange for awarding contracts. The inability of financial institutions to thoroughly investigate red flags regarding FIFA officials' involvement in corrupt practices was the primary cause of this scandal.

The application of red flags has evolved over the years as the sophistication of financial crime has expanded. In earlier times, red flags were straightforward. However, systematic complexity has become a new reality, and the sophistication and ingenuity of crimes have attracted greater attention. These warning signs now have the potential to indicate other dubious activities, namely, money laundering, fraud, corruption, or terrorist financing.

The evolution of red flags has itself been a significant contribution to the battle against financial crime. Identifying red flags and initiating an investigation would not only protect the business or financial institution from these pernicious threats but also protect governmental agencies from the involvement of criminal elements.

Red Flags of Money Laundering

The first step in identifying and stopping money laundering is recognizing the red flags that indicate potential criminal activity. Some of the common red flags of TBML include:

a Unexpected changes in the volume, value, or nature of trade transactions
b Utilization of shell companies, offshore accounts, or jurisdictions with weak AML regulations
c Inflated or artificially high prices of goods or services
d Unusual shipping or transportation arrangements, such as multiple stops or detours
e Payments made in round sums or a currency other than the one employed in the trade transaction

f Absence of transparency or verifiable information about the parties engaged in the transaction
g Complex and illogical corporate structures that contain shell companies or companies registered in high-risk jurisdictions
h Transactions that lack a clear business purpose or strategy
i Sudden or unexpected variations in the volume or value of trade transactions
j Transactions relating to goods or services that are commonly employed in TBML schemes
k The application of trade finance instruments, such as letters of credit, to move illicit or restricted goods
l The utilization of transfer pricing or other pricing schemes to diminish tax liabilities
m The fraudulent alteration of bills of lading to get payment for non-existent cargo
n Customer profile, including information acquired during the due diligence, indicates a history of trade fraud or criminal association.

It is also essential to note that warning signs or risk indicators vary by the specific business, industry, and clients involved. Therefore, compliance officers must consider all the facts and circumstances when evaluating whether a red flag or risk indicator exists.

It is essential to note that financial institutions are facing increasing pressure to take a more proactive role in monitoring trade to prevent TBML and other forms of financial crime. Compliance officers must report suspicious activity to assist law enforcement agencies in identifying, recognizing, and investigating TBML.

Numerous instances highlight red flags of money laundering directly linked to trade.

Oi Kar Wang Case: Overpriced Imports and Corporate Camouflage Were Used to Launder Funds Across Borders (Malaysia, 2019):

> One example is Oi Kar Wang, a Malaysian businessman suspected of using overpriced imports to launder money. It was established that trade-based money laundering syndicates were exposed through investigations conducted by the Malaysian Anti-Corruption Commission. In this case, it reveals the inflated value of imports through the misrepresentation of goods and the manipulation of shell companies to camouflage the bona fide owners of funds and goods.
>
> (Financial Times, 2019)

This method enabled him to

i move funds under the pretext of legitimate trade;
ii evade law enforcement scrutiny by taking advantage of the loopholes in financial oversight, acting as a cover for him, and
iii falsify documentation and trade records to justify suspicious financial flows.

The case contributed to:

a Exposing TBML Syndicates: The case arrived at a decision that allowed for the exposure of much larger networks of actors associated with trade fraud and financial crime.
b Regulatory Action: It prompted Malaysian authorities to tighten controls on documentation related to the importation of goods and beneficial ownership of entities involved in import transactions.
c International significance: International reports referenced the case as a typical example of TBML, establishing a need for cross-border communication and collaboration (Thanasegaran & Shanmugam, 2007).

Trade-Based Money Laundering in China: The Use of Fake Invoices in Trade Transactions:

This is a typical instance of TBML. Authorities in China have found that counterfeit invoices are being used to launder money through trade transactions. It is the practice of creating and using fictitious invoices to falsify trade records, thereby enabling the movement of illicit funds under the guise of legitimate trade (Thai 2018).

The revelation of such schemes constitutes a primary form of exploitation, turning trade transactions into money-laundering crimes. By utilizing forged invoices, criminals can conceal the true nature and origins of funds, making the detection and tracing of illicit transactions extremely challenging. Criminals embezzle and misrepresent the facts of trade records by forging invoices to transfer money to and from foreign countries illegally, thereby bypassing the scrutiny of AML regulations.

The significance of TBML generated through fictitious invoices is such that it undermines the integrity of international trade and poses a serious threat to the entire financial system. It not only facilitates the laundering of crime proceeds but can also misrepresent trade statistics and distort economic data or tax revenue. All these considerations have led governments and regulators to implement measures to tighten controls and mitigate TBML, particularly its use of fake invoices.

Law enforcement agencies, financial institutions, and trade stakeholders must collaborate to combat TBML, which is often facilitated by forged invoices. This demand has enhanced due diligence in verifying trade documents, scrutinizing invoice authenticity, and detecting and deterring the use of counterfeit invoices for money laundering.

With technological advancements, the game changers in the fight against TBML are high-tech, unique methods, such as advanced data analytics tools in tandem with artificial intelligence systems, which are efficient at detecting patterns and anomalies in trade transactions. This is a means of identifying suspicious practices and all possible activities arising from the premature use of fake invoices. Ultimately, modern technologies improve the capacity of law enforcement and institutions to detect and mitigate. Therefore, such examples demonstrate the way forward, showing that technology is needed to detect and prevent TBML, thereby instilling confidence in the effectiveness of new tools.

Case 13.1 Wirecard—Ignoring the indicators of financial fraud and money laundering

Wirecard AG is a German payment processing services firm. A towering figure and darling company in the fintech industry was once familiar. The company declined and was embroiled in a scandal. *The Financial Times* began publishing articles concerning the company's alleged fraud in June 2020. After a few months of allegations, it experienced a dramatic decline in its share price and the subsequent resignation of its CEO, Markus Braun. The company was forced to acknowledge that €1.9 billion of what it had reported as cash on the balance sheet was, in effect, missing. The Wirecard company declared insolvency in June 2020 (BBC News, 2020). It has become the figurehead of Germany's largest accounting scandal.

Background

The company primarily provided payment processing services to Internet retailers and other merchants. It enabled customers to make payments via multiple methods. Wirecard also included ancillary services in its customer service portfolio, such as transaction monitoring, fraud prevention, and risk assessment. Compliance solutions, such as AML checks and regulatory reporting, were also included. With corroborating evidence, the company's success was reflected in its share price, which rose from €10 in 2016 to around €190 in 2018, making Wirecard one of the 30 companies listed on the DAX, Germany's blue-chip stock index.

Allegations of Accounting Irregularities

In April 2019, Wirecard AG was embroiled in a controversy that escalated. This was primarily due to a series of articles published by the Financial Times, titled "The Wirecard Saga." They contended that Wirecard was engaging in revenue and profit margin manipulation. It was intended to misrepresent its financial health status. The central allegation was that Wirecard had manipulated its earnings by up to €1 billion. It has thus seriously jeopardized the company's economic credibility. The revenues were viewed as "suspiciously optimistic," thereby casting doubt on their veracity. Wirecard dismissed the allegations as "baseless" and announced that it had initiated legal action against *The Financial Times*.

Investigation articles were republished by *The Financial Times* in June 2020. The investigative articles ultimately accused Wirecard of massive accounting manipulations, inflating profits by €1.9 billion. The articles alleged that Wirecard had engaged in the so-called "round-tripping," whereby transactions were booked to inflate reported revenue from non-existent transactions. This technique should be viewed as a form of TBML, as the business intentionally obscures its financial accountability. Such actions were deliberately intended to mislead the public into believing that Wirecard was achieving higher profit margins than it actually did. While Wirecard continued to reject these charges, the Financial Times stood by its reporting.

The following months were marked by a sharp decline in its share price. This occurred because the company was unable to refute the allegations, and investors began to doubt its financial integrity. Wirecard eventually admitted that the €1.9 billion supposedly held in two local banks in the Philippines was nonexistent. The authorities leveled fraud and market manipulation charges against the company's CEO, Markus Braun, and Wirecard later filed for insolvency.

Another aspect that distinguished the Wirecard case from other financial fraud cases was that the company was a fintech firm. This further complicated fraud detection for regulators and auditors. This was a DAX-listed company with high expectations of upholding its reputation and, therefore, an enormous responsibility to maintain a substantial stock price. This added to the existing pressure on the company. Moreover, wire cards leveraged their role as payment processors to obscure fraudulent activities within their operations.

One major takeaway from the Wirecard scandal is that fintech firms, especially those experiencing rapid and unsustainable growth, should be scrutinized and held to strict standards. With the rapid evolution of the industry, it is now the responsibility of regulators and auditors to keep pace with contemporary developments and equip themselves with the necessary means, knowledge, and skills to detect and deter devastating fraud. This case underscores the importance of closely monitoring large cross-border transactions to prevent financial crime.

Another key takeaway from the Wirecard scandal is the importance of whistleblowers and robust regulatory oversight. On the other hand, the Financial Times reported receiving a whistleblower who, in 2016 statements, raised concerns about Wirecard's financial performance, including whether the information was reported to the appropriate law enforcement authorities and whether the whistleblower faced retaliation for disclosing it. The significance of whistleblower incentives to come forward and of their protection from retaliation thus reinforces the need to combat money laundering and other financial crimes. In the case of Wirecard, multiple red flags were either blatantly disregarded or not adequately addressed. This highlights the importance of robust internal controls and oversight within companies, as well as the critical need for effective regulatory oversight and enforcement to hold individuals and organizations accountable for their illicit activities.

To encapsulate the fraud story, the Wirecard case underscores the dangers of ignoring red flags of financial crime and the need for robust oversight and enforcement to hold individuals and organizations accountable for prohibited activities. It also calls for encouraging and protecting whistleblowers, who are instrumental in locating and stopping financial crimes. Whistleblowers are the discoverers and torchbearers working in the murky waters of corporate financial malfeasance. These are lessons that companies and regulatory authorities need to learn from the Wirecard incident to prevent similar occurrences.

Case 13.2 Luanda Leaks: Unmasking the Financial Empire of Isabel dos Santos (Angola, 2020)

Background

The story of Isabel Dos Santos, the former First Lady of Angola, depicts the dark side of executive authority. Power converges with corruption. It epitomizes extraordinary wealth, unrestrained power, and considerable controversy. Because of her reputation as one of Africa's richest women, Dos Santos was subjected to intense scrutiny and a thorough investigation. The scandal garnered overwhelming media coverage and became an issue of international significance. It was revealed to the public by the International Consortium of Investigative Journalists (ICIJ) in 2020.

The Trail of Leaks

The Luanda Leaks are a cluster of documents released to the public that revealed business transactions and wealth acquired by Dos Santos, allegedly siphoning more than $1 billion in public funds (Fitzgibbon, 2021). The documents, which included emails, contracts, financial statements, and other materials, totaled over 715,000 and were released by the ICIJ (Boghani, 2020). And other media partners, such as the BBC and Le Monde. It revealed how Dos Santos, through her connections with the Angolan government, amassed her fortune and became one of the wealthiest women in Africa.

The Business Empire

The leaked records uncovered a network comprising approximately 400 entities in 41 countries, many of which are located in secrecy jurisdictions such as Malta and Mauritius. Most of these businesses were registered in tax havens and engaged in dubious transactions. The companies were primarily engaged in telecommunications, banking, diamond mining, and the energy sector. Dos Santos used these companies to secure favorable deals and government contracts, thereby enabling her to evade taxes in Angola.

The Cost of Negligence

The Luanda Leaks revealed that several companies were associated with Dos Santos. They were primarily engaged in unethical and potentially illegal practices. Such practices were a considerable detriment to the Angolan people, most of whom live in dire poverty and wretched economic conditions. According to the ICIJ, Dos Santos and her associates misappropriated more than $1 billion in public funds. Unfortunately, some of the Western firms, such as PwC and Boston Consulting Group, were also involved and reaped millions while purportedly ignoring red flags.

The Aftermath

The release of the Luanda Leaks, a collection of over 715,000 secret financial and economic documents, provoked indignation and demanded accountability. The revelations surrounding the scandal about the malpractices of the daughter of the former Angolan president. It tells of her alleged involvement in money laundering and numerous financial improprieties. The Angolan government responded to the leaked information by launching an investigation into Dos Santos's business dealings and subsequently freezing her assets in the country. Also, her money laundering and other financial crimes were charged against her in Angola, Portugal, and the Netherlands. The U.S. government imposed sanctions in 2021 due to significant corruption. Dos Santos claims she has done nothing wrong and states that she is a victim of a political witch hunt.

The Lessons Learned

The Dos Santos case, revealed by the Luanda Leaks, is a sobering reminder of the importance of transparency and accountability across nearly all facets of business and government. The leaked documents have elucidated how Dos Santos utilized her government connections to amass exceptional wealth and engage in shady business practices. This case has become a litmus test for anti-corruption reforms in Angola under President João Lourenço (Mbale Nsongan, 2020). The case underscores the urgent need for stronger AML and anti-corruption laws, as well as greater transparency in business. This lesson is important to each of us in our professional lives.

To conclude, this compelling storyline provided an insightful account of the lives of the richest, most powerful, and most corrupt African women. The leaked documents created a stir and an uproar, with calls for accountability and for concrete actions to ensure transparency and anti-corruption measures in businesses and governments.

Combating TBML: Identifying Risk Indicators through Customer, Transaction, Shipment, and Payment Red Flags

TBML implies a sophisticated and ingenious technique for money laundering. It generally concerns the handling of cross-border payments associated with trade transactions and the movement of monetary proceeds from illicit operations. Financial institutions and regulatory agencies remain key players of substantial significance. It is vitally imperative to establish a set of red flags or risk indicators. The warning signs are generally employed to recognize suspicious practices and transactions. These red flags—customer, transaction, shipment, and payment—are crucial tools in our coordinated, systematic efforts to combat TBML.

Customer Red Flags or Risk Indicators

- i Sudden or significant changes in a customer's business qualities, character, and nature.
- ii A customer with a high volume of trade activity but limited financial resources.
- iii A customer is unwilling or unable to supply proper information about their business or dealings.
- iv A customer with a history of engaging in a range of suspicious practices, like sanctions violations or money laundering.
- v A Customer from a high-risk jurisdiction or connected with high-risk sectors of the industry.

Transaction Red Flags or Risk Indicators

- i Transactions concerning goods or services that do not match the client's expressed business activities.
- ii Transactions involving goods or services that are commonly used in money laundering or other illicit activities.

iii Transactions that involve goods or services that are over- or undervalued.
iv Transactions that involve multiple invoices for the same goods or services.
v Transactions where a customer makes multiple recurrent payments for a single sale of an item or a service within a specified period.
vi Transactions that involve a third party that is not adequately identified or is in a high-risk jurisdiction.

Shipment Red Flags or Risk Indicators

i Shipments that involve goods or services that are not consistent with a customer's stated business activities
ii Shipments that involve goods or services that are commonly used in money laundering or other illicit activities
iii Shipments that are over- or under-invoiced
iv Shipments that are sent to a third party that is not adequately identified or is located in a high-risk jurisdiction
v Shipments that are sent to a country that is known for money laundering or other illicit activities
vi Shipments sent to a country differ from the country of origin of the goods or services.

Payment Red Flags or Risk Indicators: Financial institutions and compliance officers play a crucial role in preventing TBML. Identifying these red flags is a key part of their responsibility. Payments that involve goods or services that are not consistent with a customer's stated business activities

i Payments involve goods or services that are ordinarily used in money laundering or other illegitimate activities.
ii Payments are made to a third party not adequately identified or located in a high-risk jurisdiction.
iii Payments are made to a country identified for money laundering or other unlawful activities.
iv Payments are made through a circuitous or complex routing.
v Payments are made through a bank or financial institution notorious for money laundering or other illicit activities.

These red flag indicators are not conclusive evidence of TBML. Instead, it suggests that the specific transaction or activity requires thorough scrutiny. The problem of TBML is a collaborative endeavor. Financial institutions and regulatory authorities must employ these indicators, along with other due diligence measures, such as know your customer (KYC) procedures. In the future, there could be several possibilities, for example, to fulfill the prerequisite AML compliance requirements. This development should foster a collective sense that everyone is responsible for combating TBML and that everyone should work together in this effort.

Example of TBML Red Flags: In 2018, a TBML investigation was initiated into a luxury car dealership in the U.S. Those luxury cars were meant to be sold to specific individuals as members of a drug trafficking organization. The investigation revealed several red flags, including:

i The dealership's customers had a high volume of trade activity but limited financial resources
ii The dealership's customer had a history of involvement in other suspicious activities
iii The dealership's customer was based in a high-risk jurisdiction
iv The dealership's transactions involved goods that were overvalued

v The deliveries made to the dealership were sent to a third party without proper identification and were supposedly located in a high-risk area.
vi The payments to the dealership were carried out through a bank known for money laundering.

In this instance, customers, transactions, deliveries, and payments involving the dealership raised multiple red flags indicating TBML activity. Investigations established that the luxury cars were bought with the proceeds of drug trafficking. These vehicles were then released to third countries for the laundering of criminal business proceeds. In this case, the recognition of red flags and the commencement of an investigation to prevent imminent TBML underscore the urgency and significance of the matter.

The case in point is only one possible scenario. In this regard, it is essential to acknowledge that all instances are uniquely diverse. Each case must be considered on its merits, and regulators must pay close attention and conduct a thorough analysis. Financial institutions and businesses must comply fully with all rules and regulations issued by regulatory authorities to prevent THML. This also includes performing due diligence measures, which involve KYC procedures. This must also be considered while monitoring transactions for indicators of suspicious activity. In addition to recognizing suspicious practices, financial institutions and businesses should maintain a robust compliance program to identify and prevent TBML. To this end, staff members should receive regular training on TBML and related regulations; internal controls and policies should be in place; and internal audits should be conducted regularly to ensure compliance. This would also involve reporting suspicious matters to the authorities.

To conclude, the discussion suggests that TBML is a significant concern, posing a substantial threat to the global financial system. Financial institutions and businesses must be alert to salient signs, risk indicators, and red flags associated with TBML and implement the necessary measures to detect and prevent misconduct. Key factors involved in considering TBML include the design and operation of customer transactions, ongoing monitoring, adherence to regulatory requirements, and the enforcement of robust compliance programs (Figure 13.1).

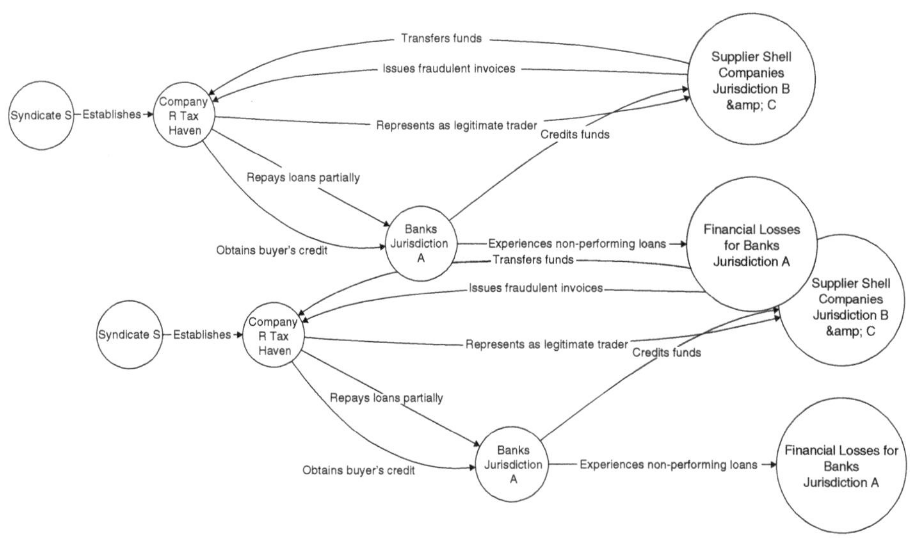

Figure 13.1 Composite Case Study: Criminal Syndicate S in Jurisdiction A

Legend:

- Syndicate S: Criminal syndicate orchestrating the TBML scheme.
- Company R (Tax Haven): Shell was established as a front for illicit activities in a tax haven jurisdiction.
- Supplier Shell Companies (Jurisdiction B & C): These are fictitious entities controlled by the syndicate and used to fabricate trade transactions.
- Banks (Jurisdiction A): Financial institutions where Syndicate S obtained high-value loans and conducted fraudulent trade transactions.
- Financial Losses for Banks (Jurisdiction A): Consequences of the TBML scheme, resulting in non-performing loans and financial losses for the banks.

This graph illustrates the flow of illicit funds and transactions within the TBML scheme, highlighting the interconnectedness of the entities involved and the detrimental impact on financial institutions in Jurisdiction A.

Introduction

This case study presents a fictional scenario of a criminal syndicate operating in Jurisdiction A that employs TBML to transfer funds illicitly. The syndicate, known as "Syndicate S," employs various techniques to conceal its illicit activities and evade detection by law enforcement and regulatory authorities. Financial institutions and compliance officers play a pivotal role in identifying and preventing such illicit activities.

The Scenario

Syndicate S incorporated a shell company, "Company R," in a tax haven jurisdiction. This company serves as a front for the syndicate's illegal activities.

Syndicate S set up multiple "supplier" shell companies in Jurisdictions B and C to further conceal their activities. These companies are also owned or controlled by the syndicate and exist solely on paper, with no business activity.

Syndicate S then opened accounts in more than ten banks in Jurisdiction A and applied for high-value loans. Company R represented itself as a legitimate cross-border trader to facilitate these loans.

Company R then proceeded to "purchase" goods from the supplier shell companies in Jurisdictions B and C, using counterfeit invoices to inflate the value of the goods being traded.

Company R has obtained buyers' credit from banks in Jurisdiction A to finance these fictitious trade transactions. The banks, in turn, credited the funds to the bank accounts of the supplier shell companies in Jurisdiction B and Jurisdiction C.

Upon receipt of the funds, the supplier's shell companies routed the money through a circuitous path to Company R and other accounts controlled by Syndicate S. This was done to conceal the funds' origin and to make it difficult for relevant authorities to trace them.

Company R then used a portion of the funds to repay the loans partially, further concealing the illicit nature of the transactions.

The forged transaction cycle resulted in outstanding non-performing loans for banks in Jurisdiction A, leading to financial losses.

This composite case study illustrates the complex and multifaceted nature of TBML. The syndicate utilized a network of shell companies, cross-border trade, and counterfeit invoicing to facilitate criminal fund transfers. They also exploited the relaxed AML regulations in the tax haven jurisdiction to conceal their activities and avoid detection. The criminal syndicate established a company, Company R, in a tax haven jurisdiction and multiple "supplier" shell companies in Jurisdiction B and Jurisdiction C. They then opened accounts in multiple banks in Jurisdiction A and applied for high-value loans, using Company R as a front for their cross-border trade activities.

Company R claimed to have purchased goods from supplier shell companies in Jurisdiction B and Jurisdiction C, and subsequently achieved buyer's credit from banks in Jurisdiction A to repay these supposed purchases. However, the criminal syndicate controlled the supplier shell companies, and the invoices for the supposedly purchased goods were forged.

The banks in Jurisdiction A credited the buyer's credit to the accounts of the supplier shell companies, which then transferred the funds through a circuitous route to Company R and other accounts controlled by the criminal syndicate. Part of the funds was used to repay bank loans partially. This counterfeit transaction cycle resulted in outstanding non-performing loans for the banks in Jurisdiction A.

The case study highlights the risks associated with TBML, where criminals use shell companies and complex ownership structures to facilitate cross-border money movements and conceal their operations. It also establishes that due diligence was insufficiently emphasized in the financial sector, with banks failing to verify the full identities of overseas counterparties before transferring funds, resulting in substantial losses.

Identifying Red Flags: A Composite Case Study of Criminal Syndicates in Jurisdiction A

The following is a composite case regarding Criminal Syndicate S in Jurisdiction A. Warning flags to consider include shell companies, specifically a shell company called R in a tax-haven jurisdiction, alongside one or more "supplier" shell companies established in different jurisdictions. This is a red flag, as shell companies with complex ownership structures in lax regulatory environments are common tactics used in money laundering and illicit financial activities.

- i High-value loans: Syndicate S applied for high-value loans from banks in Jurisdiction A, which could indicate that they were planning to use the loans for illicit purposes.
- ii Claims of cross-border trade: Shell Company R claimed to be a cross-border trader, purchasing goods from "supplier" shell companies in other jurisdictions. This is a red flag, as it could indicate that the transactions were fake and being used to launder money.
- iii Direct payments to related parties: The banks in Jurisdiction A made direct payments to the "supplier" shell companies without verifying their identities or the details of the trade transactions. This is a red flag, as it could indicate that the payments were being applied to launder money.
- iv Circuitous fund transfers: The "supplier" shell companies transferred funds to R and other accounts controlled by Syndicate S through a circuitous route. This is a red flag, as it could indicate that the transfers were being used to hide the origin of the funds and evade detection.
- v Non-performing loans: The fake transaction cycle caused outstanding non-performing loans for banks in Jurisdiction A, which could indicate that the loans were attained fraudulently and were being utilized for illicit purposes.

Financial institutions and regulatory agencies must exercise caution when these warning signs are present to identify and avoid TBML operations.

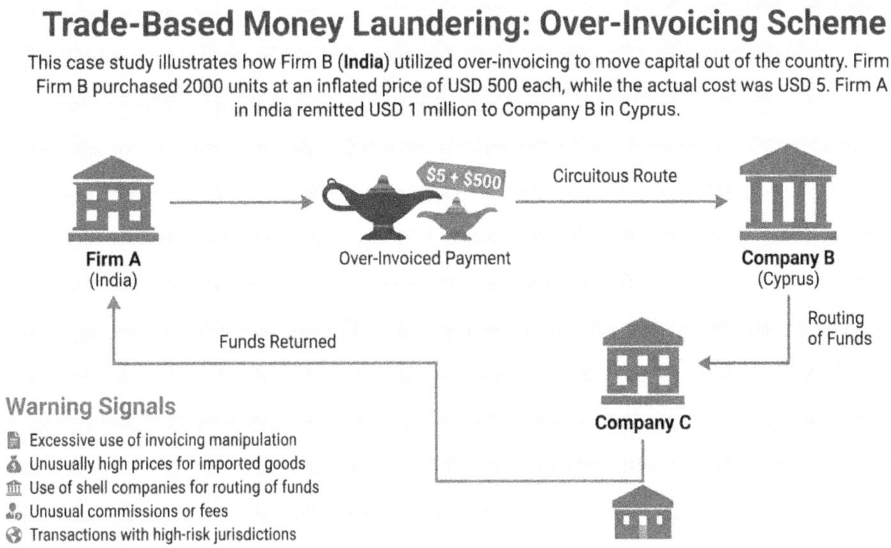

Figure 13.2 The Case Illustrates the Full Money Trail, Over-invoicing, and Circular Fund Repatriation

Illustrating the Modus Operandi of Over-Invoicing: A Case Study of Money Laundering Through Trade

This case study illustrates how a company (Firm A) in India used over-invoicing to transfer funds out of the country. The company (Firm B) in a foreign country purchased 2000 Aladdin lamps at a low price of USD 5 each but exported them to Firm A in India, mispricing them at a much higher value of USD 500 each. This resulted in Firm A in India remitting USD 1 million to Firm B in a foreign country.

Firm A could remit funds abroad by falsely inflating the value of the imported goods. In addition, the company continued to remit funds abroad by falsely overvaluing its exports and claiming fraudulent export incentives. The funds stashed abroad were then brought back into the country through a circuitous route with the assistance of an investment house based in Cyprus (Company B). Company B established a new company (Company C) to serve as a conduit for routing funds back to Firm A after deducting specified fees (Figure 13.2).

The warning signals in this case include:

i Excessive use of invoicing manipulation.
ii Unusually high prices for imported goods.
iii The use of shell companies for the routing of funds
iv Unusual commissions or fees associated with transactions.
v Transactions with a high-risk jurisdiction or countries with weak AML regulations

In this accompanying case, the company employed over-invoicing to move funds out of the country and stash them abroad. It then brought the funds back into the country through a circuitous route, utilizing the assistance of an investment house based in a high-risk jurisdiction. This emphasizes the need for financial institutions to scrutinize cross-border transactions closely and be wary of warning signs of over-invoicing.

Chapter Summary

Money laundering is recognized as a serious problem and occurs through trade as one of its means. Financial institutions and compliance officers play a crucial role in significantly deterring money laundering by identifying red flags or risk indicators. Your attentiveness and proactive approach can significantly contribute to combating TBML, underscoring your central role in this process.

End of Chapter: Discussion Questions

1. What red flags or risk indicators suggest potential TBML activity?
2. How can financial institutions and compliance officers spot potential TBML activity?
3. What is the role of customer red flags in preventing money laundering in trade?
4. What are some examples of transaction red flags in TBML?
5. What are shipment red flags, and how can they help identify TBML activity?
6. What are payment red flags in TBML, and how can they help prevent money laundering?
7. How can financial institutions use red flags for customers, transactions, shipments, and payments to detect TBML activity better?
8. What are the potential consequences of ignoring red flags in TBML?
9. How can financial institutions and compliance officers identify high-risk customers and transactions in TBML?
10. What measures can be taken to mitigate the risk of TBML?
11. How can financial institutions and governments work together to prevent TBML?
12. How can technology be used to detect better and prevent TBML?
13. What are some best practices for financial institutions to follow when identifying and mitigating TBML risk?
14. How can organizations keep up with the constantly evolving TBML landscape?
15. What is the role of international cooperation in combating TBML?

References

Association of Certified Public Accountants (AICPA). (1909). *Red flags for auditors*. AICPA.

Boghani, P. (2020, January 21). How the Luanda Leaks were reported: Q&A. *PBS Frontline*. https://www.pbs.org/wgbh/frontline/article/how-the-luanda-leaks-were-reported-qa-icij

Financial Action Task Force. (2021, March). Trade-based money laundering: Risk indicators. https://www.fatf-gafi.org/en/publications/Methodsandtrends/Trade-based-money-laundering-indicators.html.

Financial Times. (2019, August 23). Malaysian businessman accused of trade-based money laundering. Retrieved from https://www.ft.com/content/9c8f7de6-c2c2-11e9-a8e9-296ca66511c9

Financial Times. (2020, June 18). Wirecard scandal: How the FT uncovered the truth. Retrieved from https://www.ft.com/content/a26fbf7e-af48-11ea-aeb3-955839e06441

Fitzgibbon, W. (2021, December 9). US sanctions Angolan billionaire Isabel dos Santos for corruption. International Consortium of Investigative Journalists. https://www.icij.org/investigations/luanda-leaks/us-sanctions-angolan-billionaire-isabel-dos-santos-for-corruption

International Consortium of Investigative Journalists. (2016). Panama Papers: Exposing the rogue offshore finance industry. ICIJ. Retrieved from https://www.icij.org/investigations/panama-papers

International Consortium of Investigative Journalists (ICIJ). (2020). Luanda Leaks. https://www.icij.org/investigations/luanda-leaks/

Mbale Nsongan, P. (2020, January 25). The dos Santos scandal is a test for the fight against corruption in Angola. Africanews. https://www.africanews.com/2020/01/25/the-dos-santos-scandal-a-test-for-the-fight-against-corruption-in-angola

Regulation (EU) 2016/679 of the European parliament and of the council of 27 April 2016 on the protection of natural persons concerning the processing of personal data and on the free movement of such data, and repealing Directive 95/46/EC (General Data Protection Regulation), OJ L 119/1, art. 17.

Sancak, I. E. (2020, October 9). *The Wirecard scandal: The high-speed rise and fall of a FinTech Company and its implications for developed and developing economies.* Oxford Law Faculty Blogs. https://blogs.law.ox.ac.uk/business-law-blog/blog/2020/10/wirecard-scandal-high-speed-rise-and-fall-fintech-company-and-its

ThaiPBSWorld.(2018,October1).Fakeinvoicesareusedtolaundermoneythroughtradetransactions.Retrieved from https://www.thaipbsworld.com/fake-invoices-used-to-launder-money-through-trade-transactions/

Thanasegaran, H., & Shanmugam, B. (2007). International trade-based money laundering: The Malaysian perspective. *Journal of Money Laundering Control*, 10(4), 429–437. https://doi.org/10.1108/13685200710830916

UNCITRAL. (n.d.). *Legal aspects of smart contracts and artificial intelligence in international trade.* United Nations. Retrieved from https://uncitral.un.org/en/texts/ecommerce

U.S. Department of Justice. (2017, December 4). FIFA officials charged in corruption case. *United States Department of Justice*. Retrieved from https://www.justice.gov

U.S. Department of the Treasury, Office of Foreign Assets Control. (2019). *A framework for OFAC compliance commitments.* U.S. Department of the Treasury. https://www.treasury.gov/resource-center/sanctions/Documents/framework_ofac_cc

United Nations Office on Drugs and Crime. (2021). *Money laundering and terrorism financing through trade in cultural property and antiques*. Author.

U.S. Securities and Exchange Commission. (2010). Report of investigation: Lehman Brothers bankruptcy. SEC. Retrieved from https://www.sec.gov

Additional Learning Resources

Articles

1 Trade-based money laundering: development of the Â «red flagsÂ» system. M. G. Girich and A. D. Levashenko (2022). International Trade and Trade Policy 7(4):55–69;
Available at: https://www.researchgate.net/publication/357872795_Trade-based_money_laundering_development_of_the_red_flags_system
The authors discuss the development of a red-flag system for TBML. They propose a risk-based approach that considers the characteristics of the transaction, the parties involved, and the country of origin and destination. The system identifies ten red flags that may indicate TBML.

2 "Tackling money laundering in trade" by Joy Macknight (2019). Available at: https://www.thebanker.com/Tackling-money-laundering-in-trade-1575277503
The article discusses the challenges of tackling money laundering through trade. She argues that TBML is a complex and evolving threat and that traditional AML measures are not always practical. She calls for a more targeted AML approach that focuses on the specific risks posed by TBML.

3 The Trade-Based Money Laundering, Risk Indicators report was prepared by the Financial Action Task Force (FATF) and Egmont Group. (2021, March). Available at: https://www.fatf-gafi.org/en/publications/Methodsandtrends/Trade-based-money-laundering-indicators.html.
This report provides a comprehensive overview of the risks posed by TBML and identifies several red flags that businesses and financial institutions should be aware of. The report also guides how to mitigate the risks of TBML.

Films

4 "The Laundromat" is a 2019 American biographical comedy-drama film directed by Steven Soderbergh. It is based on the book "Secrecy World: Inside the Panama Papers Investigation of Illicit Money

Networks and the Global Elite" by Jake Bernstein. The film stars Meryl Streep, Gary Oldman, Antonio Banderas, and other notable actors. www.imdb.com
The film explores the Panama Papers scandal and the complex issue of how modern wealth-protection systems have created loopholes for money laundering. It is available for streaming on Netflix.

Documentaries

5 Dirty Money (2018-present). www.rottentomatoes.com
This documentary series investigates financial crime. Each episode focuses on a different case of money laundering, fraud, or corruption.
6 The Panama Papers (2016). www.rottentomatoes.com
This documentary film recounts the Panama Papers leak, which exposed the offshore financial dealings of the wealthy and powerful. The film features interviews with journalists and experts who investigated the leak.

YouTube

7 What is TBML | Trade-Based Money Laundering Explained | Risk Indicators | Techniques | KYC Lookup (July 2023). Available at: https://www.kyclookup.com/
This video explains TBML, including its definition, methods, challenges in detection, and ways to combat it. It also discusses the policy-making bodies involved in addressing TBML. The video focuses on criminal activity, AML, and risk indicators.
8 "Trade-based money laundering, The Financial Action Task Force (2021)." The video can be viewed on YouTube at the following link: https://www.youtube.com/watch?v=If-zOniF2Xc
This short video provides an overview of TBML, explaining what it is, the methods used, the challenges in detection, and how to combat it.

14 The Many Faces of TBML

Identifying and Understanding Different Typologies

The battle against money laundering, specifically through trade channels, is a dynamic and perpetual challenge. Criminal methodologies evolve to exploit new vulnerabilities in the global financial system. Similarly, a corresponding adaptation of detection and prevention strategies is imperative. This constant battle requires continuous self-control. Above all, a new level of collaboration among national governments, financial institutions, and international law enforcement agencies is required. It helps to mitigate sustained risks and safeguard the integrity of the economy (IMF, 2023; FATF, 2023).

Experts, policymakers, and global organizations have categorized several typologies of TBML:

1 "Trade-Based Money Laundering: Typologies and Case Studies (FATF, 2013)." This FATF report recognizes and discusses various types of trade-based money laundering (TBML), including over- and under-invoicing, misinvoicing, and counterfeit documentation. It also reviews TBML case studies across multiple sectors and countries.
2 "Trade-Based Money Laundering: A Threat Assessment (Europol, 2016)." Europol's research identified and analyzed various forms of TBML, including the use of shell companies, trade misinvoicing, and the misuse of trade finance instruments. The report also addresses the challenges that TBML presents to law enforcement and financial institutions.
3 "Trade-Based Money Laundering: An Overview of the Problem and Policy Responses" (UNODC, 2019). The report, compiled by the United Nations Office on Drugs and Crime, examines the nature, incidence, and policy measures to control TBML. It discusses and classifies various typologies of TBML schemes, ranging from the abuse of free trade zones and trade misinvoicing to misconduct in trade finance instruments. These documents survey various typologies of TBML and its facilitation of money laundering. They shed light on TBML's risks and challenges, thereby justifying effective countermeasures. The text complements a general understanding of TBML and its repercussions. The texts, which offer practical insights into the entire TBML issue, reinforce the need for robust mechanisms to avert and deter this criminal act.

Understanding TBML Typologies and Their Impact on Anti-money Laundering Efforts

TBML is a method by which criminals transfer and conceal illicit funds, primarily through international trade-facilitated channels. Beyond the common understanding, TBML is a relatively complex and dynamic form of illicit money movement that can undermine legitimate businesses and commerce. Compliance officers must be familiar with the various types of TBML and the

DOI: 10.4324/9781003477631-15

corresponding red flags or risk factors that may indicate suspicious activity, thereby enabling them to prevent TBML effectively.

One of the key typologies of TBML is overinvoicing. It is a practice wherein an entity manipulates the values of goods and services on invoices/claims. This scheme aims to remove money from the country, which is often routed through tax havens. For instance, a foreign entity would purchase goods valued at $10,000 from a government entity and export them to a third country at a fictitious price of $100,000. The $90,000 differential is outside the country and could be used for corruption or drug trafficking.

Another critical type is under-invoicing, which is precisely the opposite of over-invoicing. Under-invoicing is the methodology of intentionally charging a company a lower value for its goods or services. It will be compared with the actual value of those goods or services. Thus, it facilitates the transfer of funds from the country of origin. This method evades tax and customs duties and launders funds to make them appear to be legitimate business proceeds.

Another typology of TBML is misinvoicing, in which the company intentionally manipulates the value, quantity, and product description on invoices to repatriate funds from the country. Misinvoicing can enable a company to evade tax and customs duties, potentially laundering money by using it as alleged business proceeds.

A typology is also well known as round-tripping. This occurs when a company remits funds out of the country, often to a tax haven, through over- or under-invoicing, and then repatriates them as export proceeds. Round-tripping can be used to evade taxes and customs duties and to launder money by concealing it as legitimate business proceeds.

Another typology is extensively known as the Black-Market Peso Exchange (BMPE). This type enables the laundering of proceeds from drug trafficking and other illicit activities through a parallel exchange system that operates independently of the standard financial system (Weitz & Porter, 2013). In this scheme, criminal organizations sell their illicit funds to individuals or companies known as "peso brokers" at a discount in pesos. These peso brokers then use that money to purchase goods or services from normally operating firms that export and sell them for foreign currency.

TBML typologies often overlap; therefore, it is essential to remain aware of this co-occurrence. Moreover, depending on the typology embraced, indications of TBML red flags and risk factors will vary. Each TBML legitimacy case should consider the geographical location of such transactions, the volume of trade conducted, a proven history of trade fraud or money laundering in that location, and any existing trade linkages of a suspect nature to criminals.

TBML continues to evolve, and this threat requires that financial institutions remain vigilant against the latest methods perpetrators adopt. To effectively counter TBML, financial institutions must be aware of the latest typologies and trends associated with it. They must also continuously review and update their respective compliance programs to align with evolving industry standards and best practices.

Proactively monitoring red-flag alerts and suspicious activities may also enable the financial institution to detect TBML and prevent its execution. This protects financial institutions against future regulatory and reputational damage, offering more resilient avenues for an uncertain global economic system.

The battle against TBML is a shared responsibility, and some commitment from all stakeholders is necessary. These across-the-board stakeholders encompass financial institutions, regulatory bodies, law enforcement agencies, civil society organizations, governments, and the private sector in their inevitable roles.

Pooling resources and expertise can yield more effective strategies and solutions for combating TBML. It also prevents illegal actors from exploiting the global financial system. This requires a proactive approach emphasizing information sharing, transparency, and cooperation across borders and sectors.

Given the current challenges, it is essential to recognize that the fight against TBML is ongoing and requires sustained effort and consistent focus. Since the typologies of TBML evolve, we should remain vigilant and responsive to changes in our response. This involves staying abreast of the perpetrators' latest trends and techniques and continuously improving our compliance programs and risk management strategies. Ultimately, TBML's fighting aims to build a better and safer financial world. By collaborating and remaining committed to this aim, we can help ensure the safety of the global financial system and protect vulnerable communities from the consequences of financial crime.

Some common TBML typologies (Patel, 2023) include:

Over- and Under-invoicing: One of the most widespread forms of TBML is overstating the value of goods or services on an invoice to transfer funds from one location to another illicitly. Over-invoicing is the most common technique used when the numbers declared in export operations are overstated, either to pay less tax to the government or to facilitate money laundering. On the other hand, under-invoicing is the preferred method for reducing the value of imports, thereby avoiding the payment of customs duties and taxes.

Trade-Based Structuring: Under this type of TBML, in which the value of goods is broken down into multiple smaller transactions, entities should be relieved of certain obligations under anti-money laundering (AML) reporting requirements. This is often completed through multiple invoices or by breaking down a huge transaction into smaller parts.

Trade-Based Document Fraud: This form of TBML involves illicit profit obtained through the issuance of forged invoices. An example of cash flow manipulation is the issuance of counterfeit invoices for the delivery of intangible items or for the provision of nonexistent goods or services, or the manipulation of invoices for tangible goods or services to siphon off some of the profit.

Trade-Based Smuggling and Re-Exportation: This type of TBML employs fraud to move money across trade transactions. It can include smuggling, counterfeiting, and illegal re-exportation.

Trade-Based Smurfing: This TBML method uses numerous small, routine transactions to bypass AML reporting thresholds. It typically entails dividing a larger sum into smaller amounts to evade regulatory scrutiny.

Financial institutions must be well-versed in the various forms of TBML to detect and effectively disrupt them. A practical compliance framework is the backbone that supports comprehensive risk assessments, customer due diligence verification, and continuous transaction monitoring. The staff should receive the necessary training and tools to confidently recognize and report suspicious behavior, which is equally critical.

Mitigating and eliminating TBML effectively requires ongoing coordination among financial institutions, law enforcement, and government agencies. A thorough understanding of the methods and strategies employed by criminals and the implementation of a risk-based compliance approach are necessary. This involves keeping pace with emerging typologies and techniques while regularly evaluating and refining compliance measures to stay ahead.

It must be remembered that any red flags, suspicious practices, or dubious dealings observed must be brought to the attention of the competent relevant authority. This action can attract comprehensive, in-depth scrutiny. Reporting the issue is paramount in identifying, investigating, and preventing TBML. It supports the broader effort to combat money laundering and terrorist financing globally.

An Insight: Cracking Down on Money Laundering: A Pilot Project in Latvia Unveils the Most Common Typologies

Money laundering is an international crime that conceivably turns illicit proceeds into legitimate ones. It is crucial to the matter, concerns everyone, and requires urgent attention. In 2020, the Financial Intelligence Unit (FIU) in Latvia developed methodological materials to promote coherence and uniformity in understanding money-laundering typologies in the country.

The "Typologies and Features of Money Laundering" study identifies 19 money-laundering typologies in Latvia, with the most common predicate crimes committed using one or more of these methods. To help identify these typologies, the FIU divided the features of money laundering into six groups, ranging from customer information to transaction documentation. For example, typology 1 involves the transfer of funds across multiple accounts in different jurisdictions controlled by shell companies as part of a complex scheme. This typology comprises 25 features grouped into categories A, B, C, D, and F, with professional providers participating in the implementation of the scheme (Financial Intelligence Unit of Latvia [FIU Latvia], 2021, 2024).

The results of the pilot project, which aimed to establish a correlation between the features identified by the FIU and those confirmed by experts, were remarkable. In 6 criminal proceedings, experts identified between one and five typologies, with 14 types corresponding to 8 typologies developed by the FIU. The match value was calculated as a percentage for each typology and criminal proceeding, with the arithmetic mean of features used across all typologies. The pilot project's findings provide valuable insights into Latvia's most prevalent money-laundering typologies and can inform future AML efforts. The FIU's pilot undertaking may serve as a blueprint for other countries seeking to combat money laundering. The increasing prevalence of illicit financial activities compels financial institutions and law enforcement agencies to remain proactive in combating money laundering.

An Insight: The Dark Side of Global Trade: How Illicit Funds are Hiding in Plain Sight

With globalization, distances have shrunk for businesses, bringing countries closer together. However, it has widened avenues for criminals who increasingly rely on the financial system (UNODC, 2021). For example, TBML is a methodology in which illicit funds are disguised as proceeds of legitimate trade transactions.

Understanding Trade-Based Money Laundering

TBML is a money-laundering method that exploits vulnerabilities in international trade systems (FATF, 2020).

How it works: Criminals conceal their actual financial transactions by using false invoices, over-invoicing, under-invoicing, and other fraudulent methods.

The world is apprehensive about TBML, with international law enforcement and financial institutions now struggling with its ramifications. TBML is estimated to affect nearly 5% of global GDP; therefore, international collaboration to combat this issue is imperative.

A Closer Look at TBML Typologies

Mispricing: This involves artificially inflating or deflating the prices of goods to facilitate capital flows across borders.

Over- and Under-invoicing: Criminals manipulate invoice values to conceal the flow of illicit funds.

Shell Companies: Criminals use shell companies to create a complex web of trade transactions that are difficult to trace.

False Shipping Documents: Criminals use false shipping documents to conceal the true nature of their transactions.

Case 14.1 China's 2019 Crackdown on TBML Networks

TBML is arguably the most widespread and among the most challenging forms of financial crime because it is built on the legitimate international trade system. In 2019, Chinese authorities disrupted a significant TBML network that employed extensive trade diligence across China—including the trading corridors linked to the Belt and Road Initiative (BRI)—to conceal unlawful financial flows. This case examines the operations of these networks, regulatory responses, and their effects on China's monetary and trade environment.

China's growing economy and integration into the web of global trade have made it susceptible to financial crimes such as TBML. As the world's largest exporter and a central player in the global supply chain, China's trade system has been frequently exploited to facilitate the cross-border export of illicit funds. The BRI encourages global trade, thereby enhancing TBML schemes by enabling large volumes of trade through unrestricted supply chains (Global Financial Integrity, 2022). Before 2019, weaknesses in customs enforcement, financial diligence, and corporate diligence also made China vulnerable to TBML activity. The TBML networks identified in 2019 employed multiple sophisticated techniques to evade detection. Criminal organizations routinely falsify trade invoices by inflating export values and deflating import values to facilitate large-scale cross-border financial transfers, thereby masking the flow of illicit proceeds.

Criminal organizations used a complex network of front companies to simulate and disguise trade transactions. The front companies generally had no legitimate commercial purpose and were used solely to layer financial transactions and obscure the beneficial ownership of illicit proceeds. Specifically, banks processed TBML transactions without reasonable expectations of due diligence, thereby lending legitimacy to TBML transactions. Moreover, the sheer volume of trade flowing through BRI-related infrastructure provided cover for these activities.

In reaction to the risk represented by the 2019 findings, which indicated an increasing threat of TBML. The authorities in China coordinated a multi-agency approach to target TBML networks. It was an operation led by the People's Bank of China (PBOC) in collaboration with customs and financial regulatory authorities to enhance monitoring of cross-border transactions. This included a detailed scrutiny of trade documentation and customer profiles (Hogan, 2025). The authorities employed machine learning in conjunction with Regtech to identify suspicious trade patterns and financial flows. The use of these technologies enabled the analysis of extensive datasets to identify deviations consistent with invoice fraud or ghost shipments. Since TBML is inherently transnational, Chinese authorities have cooperated with multiple foreign agencies to track illicit flows and dismantle networks, leveraging different jurisdictions to freeze illicit funds derived from TBML scams.

The impact of the crackdown was quite huge. Numerous individuals and organizations faced criminal and civil charges, were convicted, and were ordered to pay restitution, forfeit property, and face imprisonment. The crackdown indicates the determination of the government to take TBML and AML seriously. Traditional financial institutions have been subject to strict AML compliance, notably enhanced customer due diligence requirements. The crackdown has also led to statutory changes to corporate transparency measures, including proposals for federally centralized beneficial ownership registries. The enforcement action crippled illicit supply chains leveraged by TBML actors through BRI funding mechanisms for major project development and supply chain logistics in reliant territories. It is critical to ensure that governments incorporate AML mechanisms in BRI-style trade initiatives.

The 2019 enforcement action demonstrated several key issues. The specific case demonstrated that large-scale trade initiatives, such as the BRI, could serve as conduits for crime, given the absence of regulatory safeguards to eliminate or mitigate risks within the scheme. If protective provisions are neglected, the risks of merging legitimate and illegitimate flows will continue to disfavor legitimacy. Financial crimes, in turn, could disrupt and impede global economic stability.

Chapter Summary

TBML manifests in multiple forms of criminal activity, including over-invoicing, under-invoicing, misinvoicing, round-tripping, and the BMPE. These strategies are designed to conceal illegal funds as legitimate profits from trade operations. Understanding these typologies and schemes is essential for detecting and thwarting TBML, which poses severe threats to the global financial system and national economies.

End of Chapter: Discussion Questions

1 Can you provide examples of different TBML typologies and how they work?
2 How do TBML typologies impact the global financial system and the economies of countries?
4 What is the significance of understanding TBML typologies in preventing and combating this illegal activity?
5 How have international organizations such as FATF, Europol, and UNODC responded to the issue of TBML?
6 What steps can countries and financial institutions take to prevent and detect TBML activities?
7 Can you explain the BMPE typology and its relevance in TBML?
8 How do governments and law enforcement agencies work together to combat TBML activities?

References

Europol. (2016). *Trade-based money laundering: A threat assessment*. Europol.

Financial Action Task Force. (2013). *Trade-based money laundering: Typologies and case studies*. FATF.

Financial Action Task Force (FATF). (2020). Trade-based money laundering. Retrieved from https://www.fatf-gafi.org/publications/fatfrecommendations/documents/trade-based-money-laundering/.

Financial Action Task Force. (2023). FATF report on the state of effectiveness and compliance with the FATF standards. https://www.fatf-gafi.org/en/publications/Assessments/General-Report-Standards-Compliance-Effectiveness-2023.html.

Financial Intelligence Unit of Latvia. (2021). *Typologies and indicators of money laundering* (2nd revised edition). Finanšu izlūkošanas dienests. https://fid.gov.lv/uploads/files/2021/FIU_Typologies%20and%20indicators%20of%20ML_2nd%20revised%20edition.pdf

Financial Intelligence Unit of Latvia. (2021). Typologies and indicators of money laundering: Methodological material (2nd revised ed.). FIU Latvia. Retrieved from https://fid.gov.lv/uploads/files/2021/FIU_Typologies%20and%20indicators%20of%20ML_2nd%20revised%20edition.pdf

Financial Intelligence Unit of Latvia. (2024). Typologies and indicators of money laundering: Methodological material (3rd revised ed.). Finanšu izlūkošanas dienests. https://fid.gov.lv/uploads/files/2023/Typologies%20nad%20Indicators%20of%20ML_3rd%20edition.pdf

Global Financial Integrity. (2022). China's Belt and Road Initiative Exacerbating illicit supply chains and trade-based money laundering. Retrieved from https://gfintegrity.org/press-release/chinas-belt-and-road-initiative-exacerbating-illicit-supply-chains-and-trade-based-money-laundering/.

Hogan, M. (2025). Chinese money laundering: A comprehensive analysis of methods, impacts, and countermeasures. Retrieved from https://www.linkedin.com/pulse/chinese-money-laundering-comprehensive-analysis-matthew-hogan-ms-krsre.

International Monetary Fund. (2023). Global financial stability report: Navigating the high-inflation era. https://www.imf.org/en/Publications/GFSR/Issues/2023/10/10/global-financial-stability-report-october-2023.

Patel, S. V. (2023). Money laundering and terrorist financing typologies that reduce financial crime risks (Doctoral dissertation, Walden University).

United Nations Office on Drugs and Crime. (2019). *Trade-based money laundering: An overview of the problem and policy responses*. UNODC.

Weitz, E., & Porter, C. W. (2013). Understanding and detecting the black-market peso exchange. *United States Attorneys' Bulletin*, 61, 29.

Additional Learning Resources:

Articles

1 He, P. (2010), "A typological study on money laundering", Journal of Money Laundering Control, Vol. 13 No. 1, pp. 15–32. Emerald Group Publishing Limited. Available at: https://www.emerald.com/insight/content/doi/10.1108/13685201011010182/full/html?fullSc=1
This paper provides a comprehensive analysis of various money laundering techniques, including trade-based money laundering, which criminal organizations and terrorist financiers use to move funds, obscure their origins, and integrate them into the formal financial system.

2 Trade-based money laundering: Responding to an emerging threat. Samuel McSkimming. (2010). Deakin Law Review, 15(1), 37–63.
This article discusses TBML, which has emerged as a significant threat in the global financial system, requiring prompt and effective responses. TBML involves exploiting international trade transactions to conceal the illicit origins of funds. As financial institutions and regulatory bodies grapple with this evolving challenge, it is crucial to implement robust measures and enhance international cooperation to combat TBML effectively.

Documentaries

3 The Dirty Money (2018), www.imdb.com
This documentary series explores the dark side of the global financial system, including the use of TBML to launder money. The series features interviews with experts and journalists who investigate financial crimes.

4 The China Hustle (2020). www.imdb.com
This documentary tells the story of a group of investors who uncovered a massive fraud scheme involving Chinese companies listed on U.S. stock exchanges. The film offers a glimpse into the world of international trade finance and the associated risks.

YouTube

5 "What are Smurfing and Structuring?" Available at: https://www.youtube.com/watch?v=f9E4N4EDmZo
The video provides an overview of smurfing and structuring in the context of AML practices. The video aims to educate viewers about these money-laundering techniques and their implications.

6 What is Round Tripping | Round Tripping Explained? Available at: https://www.youtube.com/watch?v=RM-5CgBJdr4
The video provides an overview of the concept of round-tripping in the context of money laundering and tax evasion. The video explains that round-tripping involves trading shell transactions or assets on a no-profit basis, or through mutual agreement, to boost earnings. The video aims to educate viewers about this money-laundering technique and its implications. This video was issued on YouTube on July 17, 2023.

15 Stopping Financial Criminals in Their Tracks

Profiling and AML Measures

A speech delivered by Therese Chambers, the Executive Director of Enforcement and Market Oversight at the UK's Financial Conduct Authority, depicted investigators of financial crimes poring over "complicated spider webs of transactions, meant to obfuscate the flow of money" and emphasized the role of pattern analysis in uncovering illicit activities. Profiling and transaction analysis are the methods used by law enforcement to disentangle complicated financial crime syndicates (Chambers, 2025). This discussion investigates profiling as a tool for detecting fraud and money laundering and demonstrates its effectiveness through several case studies.

Profiling as a Forensic Tool in Financial Crime

Criminal profiling has been predominantly used for violent crimes. It has been restructured and applied in the analysis of non-violent crimes such as fraud, embezzlement, and money laundering (Douglas & Olshaker, 2006; Ressler, Burgess & Douglas, 1988). In finance, it employs behavioral science, forensic psychology, and criminology to recognize patterns, motives, and behavioral characteristics of suspects. Research has shown that psychological profiling is of great benefit to banks and other financial institutions. Baldwin (2010) associated fraudulent activity with behavioral indicators such as risk-seeking, social manipulation, and disregard for rules. Once such behaviors have been identified, financial institutions can take preemptive measures to prevent misconduct from escalating into widespread abuse. Chappell's 2009 work applied this framework to anti-money laundering. He found that examining behavioral patterns can help identify types of money laundering involving complex transactions and shell companies. This aligns with Financial Action Task Force (FATF)'s advice to incorporate behavioral components into how businesses validate customer compliance mechanisms (FATF, 2023).

Profiling in Practice: Case Evidence

Case studies indicate that profiling is effective in financial crime investigations. For example, profiling was necessary in uncovering the Enron scandal. It also facilitated the identification of the principal offenders and the company's misconduct (Larkin, 2006). In the context of money laundering, profiling techniques have been employed to trace the involvement of numerous global banks by analyzing transaction data associated with illicit activities (Kamal, 2017). A well-known case is Operation Casablanca, a U.S. law enforcement endeavor focused on the money laundering activities of the Mexican drug cartels. Profiling techniques play a pivotal role

DOI: 10.4324/9781003477631-16

in identifying prominent individuals and organizations, and in integrating financial intelligence (FININT) and behavioral analysis to identify high-risk actors and delineate laundering methodologies (Bunker & Rosen, 2003; U.S. Treasury, 1998). The operation resulted in more than 100 indictments and the confiscation of more than $100 million. Thereby, it demonstrates the strategic value of integrating behavioral science with forensic accounting and AML compliance (Turvey, 2011).

The History of Criminal Profiling

Profiling has evolved from its exclusive use in violent crime investigations (e.g., the FBI's Behavioral Science Unit) to a tool for analyzing complex financial cases. Although its methodological strength has been questioned, its application to white-collar crime has brought about pattern analysis of both behavior and transactions as the primary consideration.

Integrating Profiling into a Comprehensive Approach to Detecting Money Laundering

Money laundering has become a significant concern for governments and financial institutions, which have been addressing and combating such practices worldwide for years. Emerging evidence suggests the need for a comprehensive approach to combating financial crime, employing investigative techniques such as economic analysis and intelligence gathering to provide a comprehensive understanding of individuals and/or organizations involved in illicit activities. Although profiling is not a panacea, it is a critical tool that pinpoints relevant individuals, locations, and modus operandi, and identifies motivations and how to approach them, thereby making law enforcement highly effective.

Validity of Assessment Procedures

Experts have seriously discussed the validity of various assessment procedures in criminal profiling. Some researchers have challenged the validity and reliability of psychological profiling in identifying and capturing criminals. Others believe that when used in combination, profiling and other investigative strategies may be practical tools for law enforcement agencies. Thus, it is crucial that profiling is conducted effectively and in accordance with applicable local laws and regulations governing such practices.

Implications for Financial Institutions and Regulators

This case study highlights the necessity of incorporating behavioral profiling into organizations' AML frameworks. Financial institutions should:

- Train compliance officers in examining behavioral risk indicators.
- Use profiling algorithms in transaction monitoring.
- Work with forensic psychologists when conducting high-risk investigations.

These policy initiatives provide additional early-warning detection capabilities and would support regulatory authorities in enforcing obligations within complex laundering environments (Figure 15.1).

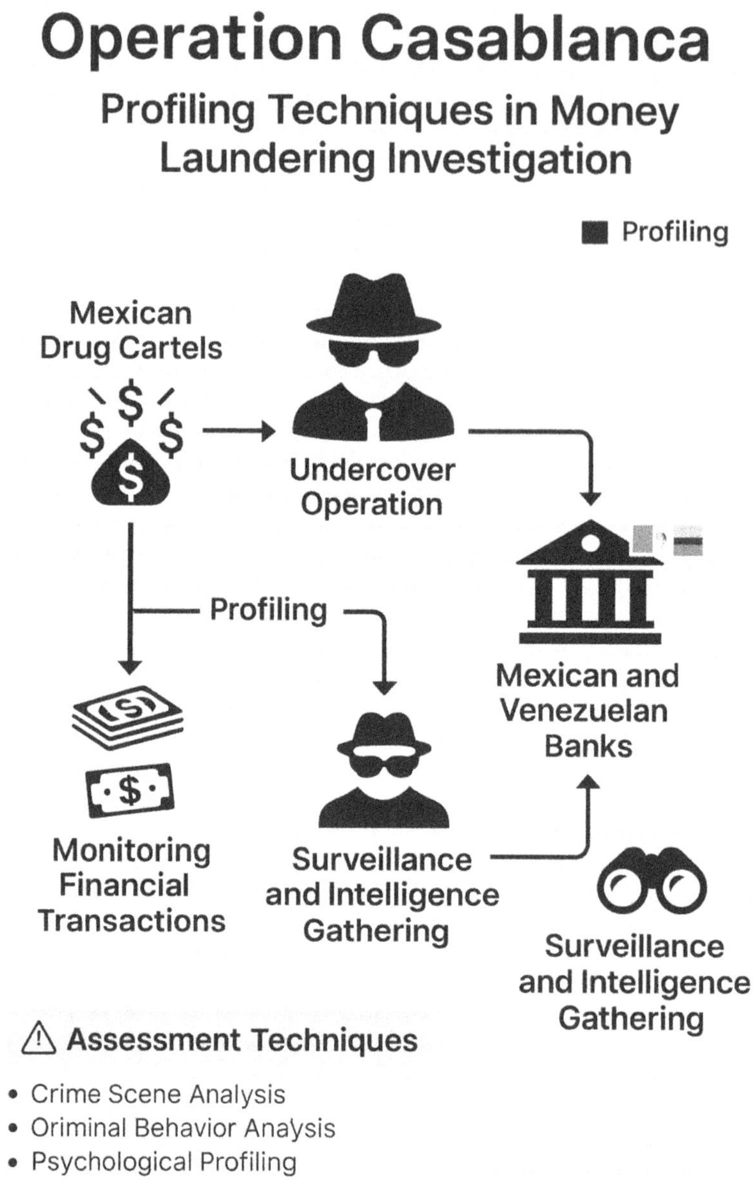

Figure 15.1 Operation Casablanca: Behavioral Profiling in Transnational Money Laundering Investigation

Approaches to AML Profiling

Various methods are used to profile money laundering activities. Each of these methods has distinct advantages and disadvantages (see Table 15.1). The rule-based methodology applies predefined thresholds to flag dubious transactions. However, it can be inflexible and may also cause false alarms, as in JPMorgan's 2012 fine for negligence in monitoring (Business Insider, 2012). Machine Learning (ML) methods, by contrast, use algorithms that detect recurring

Table 15.1 AML Profiling Approaches

Approach	*Methodology*	*Strengths*	*Limitations*	*Use Cases*
Rule-based	Predefined rules/ thresholds	Simple, interpretable	Rigid, high false positives	Legacy AML systems, regulatory compliance
Machine learning	Supervised/ unsupervised algorithms	Adaptive, scalable	Requires quality data, explainability issues	Large-scale transaction monitoring
Behavioral analysis	Time-series/ profile deviation tracking	Contextual, human-centric	May miss novel laundering patterns	Insider threats, customer risk profiling
Hybrid	Combines rules, ML, and behavior analytics	Balanced, reduces false alerts	Complex implementation	Tier-1 banks, fintech AML platforms
Graph ML	Network-based/ deep learning models	Detects hidden relationships	Computationally intensive	Shell company detection, cross-border schemes

patterns and outliers in transaction data. Besides, they help to improve the new data (Ajagbe, Majola, & Mudali, 2025). However, high-quality data are necessary, but there can be challenges with explainability. The Danske Bank issue, involving more than $230 billion in questionable transactions, is a salient example (Bjerregaard & Kirchmaier, 2019). Another approach is behavioral analysis, which observes the deviations from the customer's normal behavior and therefore chooses to think that there might be a case of suspected fraud (the methods of Danske Bank are cited in the case study, where they noticed some transactions characterized by high volume and round-off transactions from non-resident clients) (Odionu, Bristol-Alagbariya, & Okon, 2024). Network analysis investigates relationships among parties and thereby sheds light on hidden laundering rings. The case of Liberty Reserve, a digital currency that facilitated the laundering of over $250 million, was one such example (Financial Crime Academy, 2024). The hybrid strategy mixes the techniques; for instance, the rule-based system uses ML to balance the pros and minimize the cons. An example is Standard Chartered Bank, which uses a combined AML framework that includes rules for initial flagging and ML for detailed pattern analysis (Alexandre & Balsa, 2023). We identified new tools, including Graph ML, Federated Learning, Natural Language Processing (NLP), and Explainable AI (XAI). These emerging techniques are of great benefit to the team in relational intelligence, privacy-preserving collaboration, unstructured data analysis, and model transparency (Zhang et al., 2023; Yang et al., 2019; Ribeiro, Singh, & Guestrin, 2016) (Figure 15.2).

Case 15.1 HSBC Money Laundering Scandal

The 2012 HSBC money-laundering scandal significantly altered perceptions of the field and had a substantial impact on anti-money laundering. The consequences of its failures were several. Profiling was the primary technique used throughout the investigation. It was primarily HSBC's global business activities that facilitated the laundering of illicit funds. Included among them were $881 million in drug proceeds that the bank's Mexican

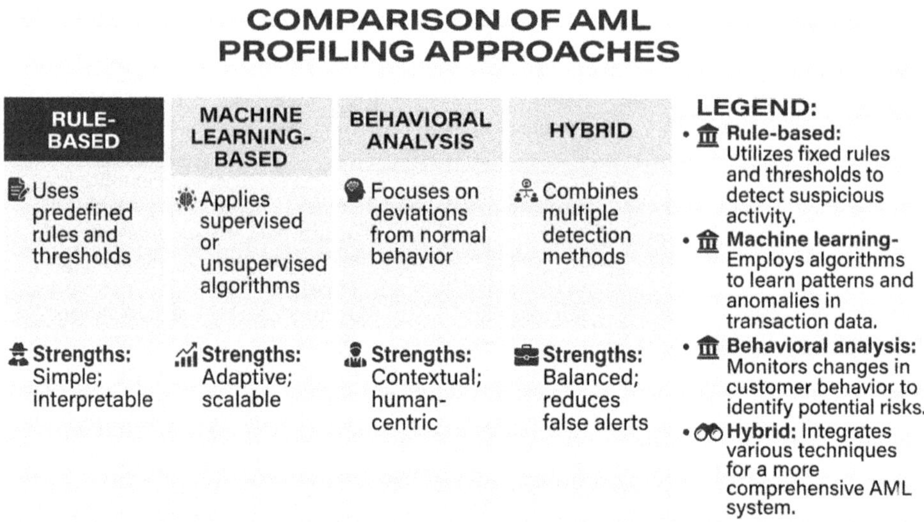

Figure 15.2 Comparison of AML Approaches

subsidiary handled and transactions involving sanctioned entities, such as Iran (U.S. Department of Justice, 2012). Profiling enabled the investigators to conduct the operation, which involved analyzing large volumes of transactional data, monitoring customer activities, and assessing departmental involvement. All of these pointed to underlying problems with CDD and transaction monitoring. Several deficiencies were identified in the bank's overall anti-money laundering measures. The management, however, was not blamed for the failures. The compliance culture was indeed weak (U.S. Senate Permanent Subcommittee on Investigations, 2012). To avoid indictment, the bank entered a Deferred Prosecution Agreement with the United States Department of Justice. A third-party compliance monitor was appointed to the bank, and the bank was obligated to pay a $1.9 billion fine (HSBC Holdings, 2013). At the core of this disastrous situation was the collapse of KYC, EDD, real-time monitoring, and ethical leadership principles. The case also elucidated the potent disclosures by insiders and investigative journalists. That have egregiously exposed financial malpractices (FATF, 2023; Interpol, 2022).

Ethical Considerations and Public Perception

The first considerations in profiling are privacy, bias, and discrimination, which are its main ethical problems. One argument against the use of profiling is that it may reinforce societal stereotypes. That in turn leads to the unjust targeting of minority groups based on race or ethnicity (Cole & Dioso-Villa, 2007; Gatowski, 2005). The collection and analysis of personal financial data can pose risks to individual privacy rights (Friedman, 2010). People are mostly on opposite sides of the fence. The overwhelming majority of surveys indicate that people are generally positive about the use of profiling in criminal investigations (Duff, 2008). However, concerns about bias and civil rights persist. Profiling, therefore, should be conducted openly, justly, and consistently within the law's purview. It comprises mechanisms to guard against discrimination and mistreatment (Starr & McCormick, 2013; Nesbit, 2016).

Chapter Summary

In short, profiling is a highly effective weapon in the fight against financial crimes, such as fraud and money laundering. Profiling methods and scrutiny of actions, behaviors, and trades can reveal not only the criminals but also the motivations for the crimes and, ultimately, the operations of their networks. Moreover, the use of AI methods, such as machine learning, enhances the effectiveness of detection systems. However, it is essential to adhere to ethical and legal standards when using the technology to thwart misuse and shield individuals' rights. The HSBC fiasco demonstrates that profiling exposes hidden structural failures. It also indicates that a bank may incur significant losses if it fails to implement appropriate AML controls. Moving forward, it is essential to maintain a balance between these two ends, whereby technological progress is utilized while ethical values are upheld. As a result, it effectively facilitates the prevention of financial crime.

End of Chapter: Discussion Questions

1. What are the benefits of profiling and anti-money laundering measures in stopping financial criminals?
2. How effective are these measures in detecting financial crimes, and what factors affect their effectiveness?
3. What are the ethical and legal considerations surrounding profiling and anti-money laundering measures in the fight against financial crimes?
4. What are the limitations of these measures, and how can they be improved to detect financial crimes better?
5. What role do technological advancements, such as artificial intelligence and machine learning, play in improving the effectiveness of profiling and anti-money laundering measures?
6. How do financial criminals adapt to these measures, and what strategies can be employed to stay ahead of them?
7. What challenges do law enforcement agencies face in implementing profiling and anti-money laundering measures, and how can they be addressed?
8. How does the international nature of financial crimes complicate the use of profiling and anti-money laundering measures, and what solutions are available?
9. What are the differences between traditional and financial criminal profiling, and how do they complement each other?
10. How can businesses and individuals be involved in the fight against financial crimes through anti-money laundering measures?
11. What are the potential consequences of not using profiling and anti-money laundering measures in detecting financial crimes?
12. How do financial institutions and regulatory bodies collaborate to ensure effective profiling and anti-money laundering measures?
13. How can the public know the value of profiling and anti-money laundering measures in detecting financial crimes?
14. How can financial institutions balance the benefits of a rule-based approach, which provides clear guidelines and is easier to explain to regulators, with the benefits of a machine learning-based approach, which can detect more subtle patterns and adapt to evolving money laundering tactics?
15. In what ways can a hybrid approach for profiling money laundering, combining both rule-based and machine learning-based approaches, help to address the limitations of each

approach and improve the accuracy of detecting money laundering activity? How can financial institutions ensure these approaches are used ethically and comply with data privacy regulations?

References

Ajagbe, S. A., Majola, S., & Mudali, P. (2025). Comparative analysis of machine learning algorithms for money laundering detection. *Discover Artificial Intelligence*, 5, Article 144. https://doi.org/10.1007/s44163-025-00144-7

Alexandre, C. R., & Balsa, J. (2023). Incorporating machine learning and a risk-based strategy in an anti-money laundering multi-agent system. *Expert Systems with Applications*, 217, Article 119500.

Baldwin, J. (2010). Behavioral indicators of fraud in financial institutions. *Journal of Financial Crime*, 17(3), 284–297.

Bjerregaard, E., & Kirchmaier, T. (2019). *The Danske Bank money laundering scandal: A case study*. Social Science Research Network.

Bunker, R. J., & Rosen, D. (2003). Combating criminal cartels: Lessons from Operation Casablanca. *Journal of Strategic Security*, 1(1), 45–62.

Business Insider. (2012). JP Morgan could be staring at a money laundering probe.

Chambers, T. (2025, December 4). *Teamwork: A smart way to tackle financial crime* [Speech transcript]. Financial Conduct Authority.

Chappell, D. (2009). Profiling money launderers: Behavioral insights and detection strategies. *Crime, Law and Social Change*, 52(1), 35–49.

Cole, S. A., & Dioso-Villa, R. (2007). Racial profiling and the Fourth Amendment. *Constitutional Commentary*, 24(2), 291–302.

Douglas, J. E., & Olshaker, M. (2006). *The cases that haunt us: Serial killers and their victims*. Pocket Books.

Duff, A. (2008). *Criminal profiling: Principles and practice*. Routledge.

FATF. (2023). *Guidance on digital transformation of AML/CFT systems*. Financial Action Task Force.

Financial Crime Academy. (2024). Liberty Reserve case study: Anatomy of a digital laundering empire.

Friedman, L. M. (2010). *Engineering privacy*. Yale University Press.

Gatowski, S. I. (2005). Developing guidelines for profiling terrorists. In R. Bull (Ed.), *Criminal profiling: Developing a practical science and practice* (pp. 223–242). Willan Publishing.

HSBC Holdings. (2013). HSBC Holdings plc Annual Report and Accounts 2012.

Interpol. (2022). Financial crime and anti-money laundering frameworks.

Kamal, A. (2017). Stopping financial criminals in their tracks: The benefits of profiling and anti-money laundering measures. *Journal of Financial Crime*, 24(3), 375–389.

Larkin, R. W. (2006). The art and science of criminal profiling: A review of the behavioral science unit. *Journal of Police and Criminal Psychology*, 21(1), 1–13.

Nesbit, J. C. (2016). Bias in criminal profiling: A review of the evidence. *Journal of Police and Criminal Psychology*, 31(1), 1–11.

Odionu, C. S., Bristol-Alagbariya, B., & Okon, R. (2024). Behavioral analytics in digital payments: A conceptual analysis of anti-money laundering techniques. *International Journal of Scholarly Research in Multidisciplinary Studies*, 5(2), 52–72.

Ressler, R. K., Burgess, A. W., & Douglas, J. E. (1988). *Sexual homicide: Patterns and motivations*. Lexington Books.

Ribeiro, M. T., Singh, S., & Guestrin, C. (2016). "Why should I trust you?": Explaining the predictions of any classifier. *Proceedings of the 22nd ACM SIGKDD International Conference on Knowledge Discovery and Data Mining* (pp. 1135–1144). San Francisco, CA: ACM. https://doi.org/10.1145/2939672.2939778

Starr, R. H., & McCormick, T. H. (2013). Criminal profiling and the Fourth Amendment: The constitutionality of using profiles to identify the perpetrators of terrorism. *Indiana Law Journal*, 88, 1433–1464.

Turvey, B. E. (2011). *Criminal profiling: An introduction to behavioral evidence analysis*. Academic Press.

U.S. Department of Justice. (2012). HSBC Holdings plc and HSBC Bank USA, N.A. admit to violations of anti-money laundering and sanctions laws.
U.S. Senate Permanent Subcommittee on Investigations. (2012). U.S. vulnerabilities to money laundering, drugs, and terrorist financing: The HSBC case history.
U.S. Department of the Treasury. (1998, May 20). Operation Casablanca continues its sweep (Press Release No. RR-2467). U.S. Department of the Treasury. https://home.treasury.gov/news/press-releases/rr2467
Yang, Q., Liu, Y., Chen, T., & Tong, Y. (2019). Federated machine learning: Concept and applications. *ACM Transactions on Intelligent Systems and Technology*, 10(2), 1–19.
Zhang, Y., et al. (2023). Graph-based anomaly detection for financial crime. *IEEE Transactions on Knowledge and Data Engineering*, 35(4), 789–804.

Additional Learning Resources

Book

1 "Criminal Profiling: An Introduction to Behavioral Evidence Analysis" by Brent E. Turvey. Published in 2011.
This book focuses on criminal profiling as an investigative and forensic process that helps solve crimes through an accurate understanding of the nature and behavior of criminals.

Films

2 The Wolf of Wall Street (2013), Directed by Martin Scorsese. With Leonardo DiCaprio, Jonah Hill, Margot Robbie, and Matthew McConaughey. https://www.imdb.com
This film tells the true story of Jordan Belfort, a stockbroker who engaged in massive securities fraud. The film provides a glimpse into the world of white-collar crime and the techniques that criminals use to evade detection.
3 Catch Me If You Can (2002). (USA), Director: Steven Spielberg. Adapted from: Catch Me If You Can. This film tells the true story of Frank Abagnale, a con artist who impersonated a doctor, a lawyer, and a pilot. The film shows how Abagnale exploited others' trust to commit financial crimes.
4 American Hustle (2013) is a crime drama film directed by David O. Russell and written by Eric Warren Singer and Russell.
The film is based on the FBI Abscam operation of the late 1970s and early 1980s, and stars Christian Bale, Amy Adams, Bradley Cooper, Jennifer Lawrence, and Jeremy Renner. The film tells the story of Irving Rosenfeld, a con man who is forced to work for FBI agent Richie DiMaso in a sting operation to catch corrupt politicians. Irving teams up with Sydney Prosser, a seductive con artist, and they set out to entrap a New Jersey mayor. However, the operation quickly spirals out of control, and the con artists find themselves in over their heads.

Documentaries

5 The Panama Papers: Behind the Scheme (Crime Documentary). Nov 14, 2019.
This documentary film recounts the history of the largest global corruption scandal. The film follows the hundreds of journalists who risked their lives to break the story, and it exposes the hidden world of offshore finance.
The film begins with the leak of millions of documents from the Panamanian law firm Mossack Fonseca. These documents revealed the secret offshore accounts of some of the world's most powerful people, including politicians, celebrities, and criminals. The journalists who broke the story faced threats and intimidation, but they persevered and exposed the truth. The Panama Papers scandal had a significant global impact. It has led to the resignations of several high-profile politicians and has raised awareness of the problem of offshore finance. The film *The Panama Papers: Behind the Scheme* is a significant and timely documentary that recounts one of the largest scandals of our time.

6 The Dirty Money (2018), www.imdb.com
This documentary series explores the dark side of the global financial system, including the use of TBML to launder money. The series features interviews with experts and journalists who investigate financial crimes. This Netflix series explores the world of financial crime, from money laundering to insider trading. Each episode focuses on a different case and shows how financial criminals operate.

Articles

7 "FATF/Egmont Trade-based Money Laundering: Trends and Developments" (2023). Fatf-Gafi.org. Available at: https://www.fatf-gafi.org/en/publications/Methodsandtrends/Trade-based-money-laundering-trends-and-developments.html
This report by the FATF provides insights into trade-based money laundering trends and developments, offering a comprehensive understanding of the subject.

8 "Criminal Minds: Profiling Architects of Financial Crimes" by Shazeeda A. Ali (2021). Journal of Financial Crime, 28(2), 324–344.
This article constructs a profile of a financial criminal, with particular emphasis on their psychological attributes, to determine whether such a profile can serve as a valuable tool for detecting perpetrators of financial crime and for implementing risk-reduction strategies.

YouTube Videos

9 "Confessions of Convicted Fraudsters" (2022). It is part of the content shared by the Association of Certified Fraud Examiners (ACFE) on their YouTube channel. Available at: www.acfe.com
This video features testimonials from two convicted fraudsters, who share their perspectives on the crimes they committed and offer insights into the loopholes they believe facilitated the fraud. The ACFE conducts interviews with convicted fraudsters to better understand their actions and the vulnerabilities in systems that enabled the fraud. The video provides valuable insights into fraudsters' mindsets and tactics, thereby raising awareness and improving fraud prevention measures.

10 "Financial crime detection: Understanding Customer Behavior is Just the Beginning" - a webinar by ACAMS. Available at: https://www.youtube.com/watch?v=PLyIo5osQlw
This video discusses the importance of understanding customer behavior in detecting financial crime, highlighting the role of data analytics and machine learning in profiling and detecting suspicious activity.

16 Understanding the Sanctions Regime

Types, Objectives, and Impact

Sanctions regimes are a key tool by which the world can resolve issues such as illicit finance, corruption, and human rights violations. However, their use and application still require careful, focused consideration. Sigal Mandelker, former Under Secretary for Terrorism and Financial Intelligence at the U.S. Treasury, remarked that "sanctions are a double-edged sword" (Mandelker, 2024, para. 1). Sanctions can be an effective tool. However, great care must be exercised in their application. That sanctions should be coupled with international cooperation and collaboration is intended to avoid adverse consequences. There is an immense risk of damaging the global financial system. Given these potential adverse repercussions, a thoughtful, joint effort to sanction is both urgent and essential.

A sanctions regime is the implementation of coercive measures by certain governments, international agencies, or groups of countries. The mechanism is to apply pressure on specific individuals, groups, or countries to fulfill some specific strategic goals. The objectives can attain peculiar political, economic, or security-oriented targets; for example, protecting human rights, combating terrorism, or inhibiting access to nuclear, chemical, or biological weapons.

Sanctions can be used to demonstrate the political, economic, or social power of a state or group of countries. They constitute concrete examples of both the use of mutually hostile measures as a standard of measurement and their deployment as punitive measures for noncompliance with international norms or law. The anticipated action can be used to induce behavioral change or to achieve specific policy objectives (LexisNexis, 2023). A sanctions regime typically combines arms embargoes, restrictions on cultural/sports/social contact, and financial and trade sanctions (partial or total) (Segall, 1999).

Institutions Are Empowered to Impose Sanctions

Various international, regional, and national organizations and institutions are empowered to impose sanctions. The United Nations (UN) is one of the best-known organizations that imposes sanctions. Under Chapter 7, the UN Security Council can impose sanctions on states and individuals (Sanctions | United Nations Security Council, 2023). Other international agencies could also have a sanctioning role: the EU, the African Union (AU), and the Organization of American States (OAS). However, national governments would have the independent authority to impose sanctions on persons and entities within their respective jurisdictions.

The main object of sanctions against a country is to deter or penalize specific acts or policies to effect change (LexisNexis, 2023). In this sense, one would have to consider that a specific sanctions regime might destabilize that country, in which case, political instability, tensions, or violence may erupt. An adequately designed sanctions regime should focus on the target state's elite—those with the power or ability to effect change in the afflicted state—rather than on the

DOI: 10.4324/9781003477631-17

nation as a whole. This avoids 'collateral' damage and consequences such as humanitarian crises, consolidation of authoritarian regimes, and the population's increased reliance on the ruling government (Segall, 1999).

Types of Sanctions

Sanctions are meant to impose constraints. They are inconsistently implemented across various forms, primarily financial, trade, and diplomatic sanctions. Financial sanctions typically involve measures such as freezing assets and blocking transactions. Trade sanctions are measures that typically impose restrictions on exports, imports, or the transfer of goods and services, as well as on various forms of exchange. In some cases, even diplomatic sanctions are effective against states rendered ineffective by travel prohibitions for specific purposes. Other means include withholding diplomatic recognition or contending that specific states should be excluded from certain international bodies.

Classifications

Financial sanctions are typically classified as innovative or comprehensive. Smart sanctions mean selective sanctions. Such sanctions are directed at specific individuals or entities; for instance, freezing the assets of a particular individual or entity constitutes a targeted sanction. It intends to minimize the impact on the general population. In contrast, comprehensive sanctions have the opposite effect and tend to hit the whole population of the target country. These may be in the form of a comprehensive trade embargo, restrictions on financial transactions, and bans on travel to and from the target country. It generally limits trade, transport, and communication with the target country.

Financial Sanctions

Financial sanctions are intended to limit access to financial resources and may include freezing assets and blocking transactions. In this context, it may involve specific individuals or entities linked to the target country or group, as well as the banning of financial transactions with such entities. These sanctions include the implementation of regulations issued by the U.S. Office of Foreign Assets Control (OFAC) and the EU's financial sanctions regimes (International sanctions, 2023). These are examples of financial sanctions.

Smart Sanctions

These restrictions are smart sanctions that seek to deny asset ownership by selectively targeting designated persons or entities rather than a country or segment of the population. Examples are travel bans, asset freezing, and prohibitions on entering into financial transactions (Ayad & Al-Daoudi, 2022).

Trade Sanctions

Trade sanctions are legal restrictions on trade with a specific country for foreign policy reasons. These sanctions are intended to reverse specific objectionable policies or punish a targeted nation. In the broader set of trade sanctions, economic sanctions restrict or prohibit economic activities, including investments or the withdrawal of foreign assistance (Snyder 2022).

Terrorism Sanctions

Sanctions against terrorism help restrict the funding and support for individuals, entities, or institutions viewed as terrorist groups under the aegis of the UN (U.S. Department of the Treasury, Office of Foreign Assets Control, 2022). Sanctions imposed by the resolution may include, but are not limited to, asset freezes, bans on financial transactions, travel bans, and other measures. There is no clear definition of terrorism. The UN does not have an unequivocal definition of the term 'terrorism'. This has led to broad interpretations of these measures, which have invariably resulted in gross and widespread human rights violations and abuses involving individuals and civil society actors (United Nations Sanctions Committee of the Legal Advisers on Public International Law, 2014).

Diplomatic Sanctions

Diplomatic sanctions seek to weaken international relations with the target state. These sanctions include a cutoff from diplomatic recognition, suspension from international organizations, and travel restrictions on senior officials. They are intended to isolate the target state diplomatically. An example of terrorism sanctions includes the UN's overwhelming measures against Al Qaeda and the Taliban, which restrict transactions with these designated terrorist organizations or individuals (ODU United Nations Society, 2020).

Dual-Use Goods

Dual-use goods are items with both civilian and military applications. The export of these goods is often restricted to block their use in developing weapons of mass destruction (WMD) or other military capabilities that can threaten international peace and security. For instance, certain chemicals and materials essential for nuclear weapons production are subject to dual-use controls (Colussi, 2016). Moreover, sanctions can be imposed on individuals or entities that are overtly suspected of human rights violations or terrorism. There are other sanctions options, including, but not limited to, travel bans, asset freezes, and other financial restrictions.

Examples of Sanctions

The UN sanctions regime against Iraq is a prominent example of economic statecraft (Office of Foreign Assets Control, 2023). Imposed in the aftermath of the 1991 Gulf War, these sanctions encompassed measures such as a comprehensive trade embargo, financial restrictions, and travel bans (Office of Foreign Assets Control, 2023). The primary objective was to compel Iraq's disarmament and dismantlement of its WMD program through economic pressure (Office of Foreign Assets Control, 2023). The regime's effectiveness remains a subject of debate, but it was ultimately lifted in 2003 following the U.S. invasion of Iraq.

The UN-mandated disarmament of Iraq's WMD program was at the core of the UN sanctions regime, which in effect was implemented only immediately after the Gulf War, in 1991. However, considerable effort was invested in this disarmament. Subsequent revelations of limited WMD stockpiles raise a question mark over the program's full extent and the effectiveness of inspections (Duelfer, 2004). The human cost of sanctions, including widespread hardship and resource depletion, further complicates the narrative (O'Connell, 2007).

Another source of economic sanctions (U.S. Department of State, 2023) is the United States' sanctions on Iran since 1979. The events unfolded from the inauguration of the Iranian

Revolution and the takeover of hostages at the U.S. Embassy in Tehran. The sanctions have been hectically pursued for several reasons, including Iran's active support for terrorism, human rights violations, and its nuclear and missile programs. They have also targeted the Iranian oil and banking industries, along with persons and organizations directly linked to the Iranian government.

The ongoing discussion about how effective the international community has been in persuading Iran to back off from its nuclear program is still very much alive. On the flip side, some contend that these efforts have stalled the advancement of the Iranian Nuclear Program (Sanger, 2016). Others note the program's potential long-term sustainability and possible negative impact on the Iranian people (Mendelsohn, 2019). Finally, those concerned about the program's economic fallout (particularly its effects on relative resource allocation and potential social hardship) remain in contention (Rezaian, 2020).

UN organizations, individual nations, and regional organizations possess the authority to enforce sanctions. The UN Security Council alone has the unique authority to impose sanctions globally. Every country can enforce rules, and the European Union functions as a regional bloc to take similar actions. Sanctions constitute a robust diplomatic mechanism that empowers states to target both states and specific individuals, entities, or organizations.

The United States and the European Union imposed rigorous sanctions on Russia, mainly because of its 2014 invasion of Crimea. Sanctions were the most effective mechanism for exerting pressure on the most powerful Russian tycoons. Others included were oligarchs and high-ranking government officials in the Kremlin (Council of the European Union, 2014; U.S. Department of the Treasury, 2014). These sanctions were to deprive the offenders of their property by freezing assets and imposing travel restrictions. The sanctions were directed at individuals who were compelled to participate in the annexation process or who violated human rights (Dalacoura, 2015).

Numerous scholars hold differing views on how these sanctions affect the Russian government and its broader population. Supporters claim that the sanctions have stunted Russia's economic growth, restricted its access to international financing, and diminished the political clout of specific individuals (Nolan, 2017). On the other hand, critics focus on Russia's ability to adapt and tap into alternative markets, implying that the overall impact may be limited (Dolgopyatov & Goldstein, 2018). The ongoing discussion also touches on the long-term effectiveness of the sanctions and the possibility of unintended effects on the broader Russian population (von Habsburg & Light, 2020).

The situation between Russia and Ukraine, which is still going on, and its immense implications have resulted in a firestorm of unimaginable economic sanctions against the Russian government, its aligned entities, and individuals (Congressional Research Service, 2024). The United States, the European Union, and other countries imposed these measures to compel Russia to withdraw its military operations and pursue a peaceful resolution (The White House, 2024). The sanctions list comprises several key measures, including account blockages, embargoes, and prohibitions on all monetary transactions (Council of the European Union, 2024). These performance measures and potential longer-term economic effects on Russia and the global economy remain under scrutiny (Faria & Obstfeld, 2024).

The economic effects of sanctions on targeted countries can be pretty complex. Although they aim to pressure governments, these sanctions often disrupt legitimate economic activities and can unfairly impact civilians (Dreher, 2009). Stringent financial restrictions and trade barriers can hinder honest business operations, resulting in job losses and reduced access to essential goods (Wallerstein, 2001). This economic hardship can further fuel social unrest and instability (Borden, 2016).

The effectiveness of sanctions can be undermined by the tactics employed by targeted individuals and entities (Goldstein et al., 2010). Sanctioned parties may exploit loopholes or utilize complex financial instruments and structures to circumvent the intended restrictions (Goldstein et al., 2010; Moody, 2023). This can lead to unintended consequences, including the perpetuation of illicit activities, such as trade-based money laundering (TBML; Pickering et al., 2012). When sanctioned countries face restrictions on the legal import of certain goods, criminal organizations may step in, offering these goods through TBML channels, thereby further undermining the intended effects of sanctions. This may include the use of front companies, shell entities, and third-party intermediaries to obscure the actual ownership and control of assets (Jersey Financial Services Commission, 2023; Moody's, 2023). Sanctions evasion may also encompass the misrepresentation of transactions, the omission of identifying information, and the provision of false documentation to sanctions authorities (Jersey Financial Services Commission, 2023). Consequently, maintaining the integrity and impact of sanctions regimes requires vigilant monitoring, robust due diligence, and the continuous adaptation of enforcement measures to address evolving evasion techniques (Central Bank of the UAE, 2021; Moody's, 2023).

The above discussion implies that sanctions regimes have enormous effects that transform the behaviors of governments and individuals. They help strengthen international peace and security conditions. Examining the potential adverse effects of these measures while constantly evaluating their effectiveness remains essential. Monitoring and implementing protective measures remain predominant because sanctions could escalate unlawful practices through TBML.

OFAC Sanctions, UN Sanctions, and EU Sanctions

Sanctions are measures that a government or international organization takes to achieve specific objectives, including counterterrorism, human rights policy, nonproliferation of WMD, and compliance with international standards (LexisNexis, 2023). Travel bans and financial constraints, including asset freezing and withdrawal of financial services, export and import controls, and suspension or withdrawal from international organizations, form some of the manifestations of sanctions (Council on Foreign Relations, 2015).

In the following paragraphs, we examine the various sanctions administered by the OFAC on behalf of the U.S. Treasury, the UN, and the European Union, and their impact on TBML.

OFAC Sanctions

The OFAC, a division of the United States Treasury Department's executive branch, implements and administers economic and trade restrictions to advance national security and foreign policy (Grecu, 2023; Cipriani et al., 2023). OFAC is most responsible for enforcing economic and trade sanctions against foreign countries, organizations, or individuals that it targets. While several sanctions can be established, country-based sanctions are the most common. Country-based sanctions impose complete or partial trade embargoes on a particular country (e.g., those against Cuba, Iran, North Korea, and Syria). Targeted sanctions restrict individuals whom they believe pose a threat to U.S. national security and foreign policy interests. Such individuals and entities would be added to the Specially Designated Nationals and Blocked Persons List (SDN). OFAC is also critical to maintaining compliance with internationally imposed sanctions lists, particularly for commercial banks that conduct domestic transactions (Grecu, 2023).

Financial sanctions, including those imposed by OFAC, have become increasingly instrumental in international diplomacy, notably in advancing democracy and human rights (Eland, 2018). The development of U.S. export control regulations, which emphasize the use of dual-use goods for national security purposes, further demonstrates the integration of economic measures into broader foreign policy approaches (Eland, 2018). The regulation of virtual assets through sanctions and compliance systems further underscores governments' comprehensive approach to combating illicit financial activities (Cipriani et al., 2023).

The U.S. government imposed sanctions on the Venezuelan government and its officials in 2019 under the authority of the OFAC (OFAC, 2024). The sanctions were imposed to deprive Maduro's government of its financial resources and to broaden the pressure exerted. It could be pressured to change its policies, which were seen as undermining democracy and human rights in Venezuela (Congressional Research Service, 2024). Under those sanctions, the government of Venezuela "blocks all property and interests in property of the government of Venezuela that come under U.S. jurisdiction and prohibits U.S. persons from any transactions with the Venezuelan government" (OFAC, 2024). The Venezuelan government freezes assets, imposes transaction restrictions, and exempts American companies and individuals from trading with specific individuals and entities in Venezuela.

OFAC also compiles and maintains the SDN list. It includes many groups, organizations, and countries that meet the criteria for U.S. sanctions. As soon as an individual or entity is put on the SDN list, all the assets under U.S. jurisdiction that belong to that person or entity are frozen. U.S. persons are generally barred from doing any financial transaction with them. In addition, the UN supports OFAC sanctions, enabling the United States to restrict activities involving entities, individuals, or countries that threaten global peace and security. The UN Security Council typically imposes punitive measures, such as economic sanctions, no-fly lists, and arms embargoes. Parties that engage in illegal activities such as terrorism, weapons proliferation, or human rights violations and are designated as blocked parties may be affected by UN sanctions.

The European Union also implements restrictive measures, such as asset freezes and travel bans. The EU Council applies these restrictions. They target individuals, organizations, and states that pose risks to EU security and stability, human rights, and international law. EU member states are accordingly required to comply with numerous measures outlined in decisions, regulations, and agreements.

At their core, the underlying reasons for such sanctions are to discontinue the proliferation of WMD. To break up material support for terrorism and its affiliates, and make sure that human rights are not violated. They can also be employed to curb unlawful practices such as drug trafficking, money laundering, and transnational organized crime.

Money laundering is a serious offense that corrupts the financial system and, consequently, the economy. Sanctions, in turn, are an indispensable means for states and international structures to pursue individuals and organizations directly or indirectly involved in illicit practices such as organized crime, terrorism, and the spread of WMD. Sanctions are an effective instrument for combating money laundering; for instance, the use of so-called smart sanctions can enhance their effectiveness in that endeavor.

These targeted sanctions confer on governments the authority to impose restrictions on the financial activities of individuals or entities while minimizing adverse effects on the public. For instance, authorities may impede access to their illicit wealth by freezing the assets of individuals on the sanctions list, thereby preventing them from using such wealth to fund their criminal activities. Moreover, restricting financial activity or cutting off financial services can limit their ability to transfer or conceal unlawful funds.

The OFAC is a fundamental component of the U.S. Department of the Treasury. The U.S. Department of the Treasury is often regarded as the core branch and the leading agency for administering and enforcing U.S. sanctions. These sanctions are potent strategic tools for achieving U.S. national security and foreign policy goals (Office of Foreign Assets Control, 2023). They target specific foreign countries, regimes, terrorists, international drug traffickers, and those who indulge in the proliferation of WMD. OFAC seeks to impose sanctions on individuals deemed to threaten U.S. foreign policy, national security, and the economy by freezing assets and impeding trade (Office of Foreign Assets Control, 2023). Collating and managing the SDN is a crucial tool in the OFAC's arsenal (Office of Foreign Assets Control, 2023). This SDN list regularly embodies individuals and entities implicated in unlawful operations. This comprehensive list is not limited to money laundering, organized crime, and terrorism. This updated SDN List is imperative for furthering U.S. foreign policy and promoting national security.

The UN adopts a hardline stance, imposing effective and crippling sanctions, as well as serious consequences, on individuals and organizations committing illegal acts. Most UN sanctions are imposed on states that violate international law and undermine established legal frameworks. The sanctions are also directed against governments that pose risks to global security and peace and that contribute to the prevention of conflict and instability. UN sanctions often involve a combination of severe measures, such as asset freezes or trade bans. The UN, through sanctions, exercises authority at the highest level. The highest level of authority within the UN framework is the UN Security Council (UNSC), which considers, reviews, and determines the primary impact of sanctions. Each member state must comply with these sanctions within its jurisdiction.

Regulation 36/2012 sets the framework for implementing and regulating the EU's sanctions, with no exceptions for any member state. Under this regime, specific sanctions, such as travel bans, financial restrictions, and asset freezing, are rigorously imposed.

In essence, sanctions can be a viable mechanism for addressing money laundering and other illicit practices. Governments and international bodies can substantially disrupt the movement of illicit funds by targeting specific individuals and entities and by enforcing strict financial regulations. This was intended to dismantle the wrongdoings and the ability to continue their criminal enterprises. However, sanctions should be applied to uphold the sanctity of human rights, not to inflict harm, and should avoid harming those not implicated in illegal actions.

Historical Context

The OFAC dates to 1950, when it was established to handle the impending Korean War. The OFAC was tasked with following the orders set by Harry S. Truman. The president determined that all Korean 'assets' be blocked in the United States. This was the first time the U.S. government had used its extensive authority to freeze a foreign country's assets and to prohibit transactions with individuals or entities in Korea.

Major Historical Involvements

Since its inception, OFAC has established itself as one of the most important agencies for initiating U.S. sanctions policy. In some of the roles that have been critical in the most pivotal moments of American history. The events were reckoned as the Cuban Missile Crisis, the Vietnam War, and the ongoing campaign against terrorism. The sanctions were issues of the international drug trade, the proliferation of WMD, and human rights violations that were addressed. In the same context, OFAC identified networks and individuals who brokered these transactions and also blacklisted them.

Licensing and Authorizations

Beyond enforcement, OFAC issues licenses and authorizations permitting certain transactions and activities that would otherwise be prohibited under sanctions regulations. For instance,

OFAC may allow a U.S. individual to export agricultural products to a sanctioned country or enable a foreign financial institution to process specific U.S. dollar transactions (U.S. Department of the Treasury, n.d.).

Case 16.1 Rami Makhlouf and JPMorgan Chase: Sanctions, Accountability, and Compliance Failures (U.S. Department of Justice, 2013; U.S. Senate Permanent Subcommittee on Investigations, 2013)

One interesting example is Rami Makhlouf, a successful business magnate in Syria. He had extensive influence on the nation's economy. As a cousin of President Bashar al-Assad, he had evident connections to the regime. His significant financial and political clout and influence have raised concerns among international regulators. In 2008, the OFAC characterized and designated Makhlouf as an SDN due to his participation and backing of the Syrian regime. Subsequently, he was named for participating in corrupt activities. The sanctions suspended the U.S. accounts owned by Makhlouf and prohibited U.S. citizens from conducting business with him. In 2011, the authority extended this designation to Makhlouf's mobile phone company, Syriatel, for the profits directed to the Syrian regime.

The Makhlouf case illustrates the U.S. government's countermeasures, specifically the use of sanctions against individuals and organizations that aid hostile or corrupt regimes. The case also highlights the necessity of exercising due diligence for companies doing business in a country on the U.S. sanctions list to avoid huge fines. In another equally crucial case, JPMorgan Chase was affected by a 2013 enforcement action (U.S. Department of Justice, 2013). OFAC stated that the bank violated the embargoes on Cuba, Iran, Sudan, and Burma by facilitating more than $1.1 billion in prohibited transactions through the U.S. financial system. The bank appeared to have no suitable instruments to ensure compliance with the mandatory compliance rules. JPMorgan agreed to pay a $536 million civil penalty and execute better compliance measures as part of the agreement (OFAC, 2023).

To summarize our discussion, OFAC is usually the principal enforcer of U.S. sanctions and imposes economic and trade-restrictive measures against designated parties. In her speech, the Director of OFAC, Andrea Gacki, said, "The mission of OFAC is to protect the financial system from shady actors and to further the U.S. national interest, security, and foreign policy goals by the use of economic sanctions and other measures" (Gacki, 2021).

Case 16.2 Danfoss FZCO and the Sanctions Web: Unravelling Iran-Linked Evasion Networks Through Dubai's Engineering Sector (United Arab Emirates, 2013–2017) (U.S. Department of Justice, 2013)

Danfoss FZCO is a UAE-based subsidiary of the Danish multinational Danfoss A/S, which exclusively specializes in engineering solutions. The entity distributes components to various industries, including air conditioning, heating, and ventilation. In 2013, it was immensely engaged in a sanctions evasion scheme involving Iran, Syria, and Sudan. This case study will examine exclusively the criminal network employed, how the scheme operated, the estimated loss, the fate of the perpetrators, and the lessons learned from sanctions enforcement in the Danfoss case.

A Notorious Criminal Network Involved

Danfoss FZCO was found to have violated international sanctions against Iran through a complex network of intermediaries and shell companies. The firm instructed customers in sanctioned jurisdictions from 2013 to 2017 to send payments to a U.S.-based financial institution account in the UAE, thereby violating multiple OFAC sanctions programs (OFAC, 2022; Gorny, 2023). The OFAC concluded Danfoss FZCO engaged in the facilitation of 225 apparent violations, leading to a $4.38 million settlement (OFAC, 2022) & (Iran Watch, 2022). The company's Iranian business partners included Reza Ebadzadeh, Ali Faraji, and Zoltan Komaromi. The three individuals were also implicated in the UAE-based company MultiMate (UANI, 2023). The U.S. Department of Justice (DOJ) referred to the network as the "Danfoss Network."

The Discovery of the Scheme

The scheme came to a glaring light when the DOJ began an investigation in 2012. The probe found that Danfoss FZCO had been supplying U.S.-manufactured components to its Iranian partners, thereby circumventing the U.S. embargo on Iran. It also found that the company had established a sophisticated network of shell companies and intermediaries to procure components from U.S. vendors and export them to Iran via the UAE.

Mechanics of the Scheme

Danfoss FZCO's scheme to circumvent U.S. sanctions against Iran relied on a sophisticated network of shell companies and intermediaries. Iranian customers would order U.S.-origin goods, prohibited under the embargo, through Danfoss FZCO. To conceal the illicit nature of such deals, Danfoss FZCO employed a network of shell companies and intermediaries to purchase the products from American suppliers and resell them to Iran via the United Arab Emirates (U.S. Department of Justice, 2023).

Financial Loss Estimate

The Danfoss case cost a tremendous amount of money, estimated at $13.7 million. This cost was incurred by U.S.-based suppliers who unwittingly sold their goods to Danfoss FZCO, which were then exported to Iran. This substantial financial cost underscores the practical implications of sanctions evasion and the need for effective compliance procedures.

The Fate of the Perpetrators

The DOJ charged Danfoss FZCO and its Iranian business partners, Reza Ebadzadeh, Ali Faraji, and Zoltan Komaromi. Danfoss FZCO consented to pay a $3.3 million fine to settle the serious allegations in 2018. Reza Ebadzadeh and Ali Faraji were indicted and pleaded guilty to conspiracy charges arising from their involvement in the 1977 International Emergency Economic Powers Act (IEEPA). The law is the IEEPA. Ebadzadeh was sentenced to 24 months, while Faraji was sentenced to 12 months. Zoltan Komaromi's actions sent a warning signal. They reflected the gravity of such behavior and underscored the necessity to enforce sanctions.

Economic Implications of Sanctions Evasion

The Danfoss case focuses on the substantial economic consequences of sanctions evasion. In this situation, U.S.-based suppliers lost an estimated $13.7 million due to the illicit scheme. The evasion weakened the effectiveness of global sanctions in suppressing Iran's operations and raised concerns about the importance of stringent compliance measures. The economic effects of sanctions evasion in the Danfoss case underscore the importance of vigilance and robust compliance measures in the financial industry. The Danfoss case offers critical lessons about the effectiveness of sanctions enforcement. It focuses on the enforcement of sanctions and sound supply chain due diligence. It emphasizes coordination between law enforcement authorities and private industry to combat sanctions evasion effectively.

The Danfoss case highlights the importance of enforcing strict sanctions. It underlines the significance of due diligence in supply chain management, encompassing thorough customer vetting and transaction monitoring to detect potential sanctions breaches. It also emphasizes the importance of collaboration between law enforcement agencies and the private sector to enable all parties to combat sanctions evasion as part of an effective and integrated effort.

The Danfoss FZCO case elucidates the complexities and pitfalls of enforcing international sanctions (OFAC, 2022). It underscores the imperative of decisive enforcement actions, due diligence, and cooperative efforts between the government and industry to ensure the integrity of global sanctions frameworks (Sanctions.io, 2022). This case prevents incidents like the Danfoss case, which focuses on the exposé. U.S. entities encountered by foreign companies, including non-U.S. entities, while conducting commercial transactions with the U.S. financial system involving sanctioned countries, areas, or individuals (OFAC, 2022). The case concerns entities' obligation to maintain effective, risk-based sanctions compliance programs. Training essential personnel, including senior management, is crucial for identifying and referring potential violations to the proper compliance personnel. The Danfoss case also highlights the importance of adhering to OFAC guidance and advisories to enhance sanctions compliance efforts (OFAC, 2022).

Ultimately, the case of Danfoss FZCO is a poignant reminder to companies to take sanctions compliance seriously. It emphasizes the importance of cooperation with sanctions regimes to ensure the integrity of sanctions worldwide, positioning the audience to feel responsible for upholding the system's integrity.

Case 16.3 Evading Sanctions and Export Controls Using Cryptocurrency—the Iurii Gugnin and Evita Scheme

Introduction

The geopolitical scenario in which the circumstances surrounding the Evita operation were further characterized by intensifying international sanctions against Russia related to its invasion of Ukraine. This case exemplifies the growing complexity of illicit finance schemes that exploit the blurred line between traditional and digital finance, enabling the movement of substantial amounts of value across borders with reduced risk of detection. The Evita case is specifically notable, considering the large amount of value (over $500 million) and the involvement of sanctioned Russian entities after the 2022 Ukrainian invasion. The sanctions applied were targeted against several major Russian financial institutions, including, but not limited to, PJSC Sberbank, PJSC VTB Bank, PJSC Sovcombank, and JSC Tinkoff Bank, all of which are implicated in the Evita case (U.S. Department of Justice, 2025; U.S. Attorney's Office, Eastern District of New York, 2025). By 2023, these sanctions had placed a tremendous burden on Russian financial institutions, creating incentives for creative evasion mechanisms and the use of evolving financial instruments, including cryptocurrencies.

Background and Context

Iurii Gugnin (also referred to as Iurii Mashukov and George Goognin), a 38-year-old Russian citizen and New York resident, organized Evita Investments Inc. and Evita Pay Inc. as complementary platforms for processing cryptocurrency-based payments for use in all retail transactions. As founder, president, treasurer, and compliance officer of Evita, Gugnin exercised full authority over the financial, operational, and regulatory aspects of both companies. The consolidated authority was essential to the execution and facilitation of the alleged conduct. Gugnin was the only person who had made it easy for him to implement his determination to comply and to override any internal controls.

Evita's corporate structure concealed illegal activity while presenting an outward appearance of legitimacy. As stated in the court papers, Evita described itself as a global provider of cryptocurrency payments, offering services that included "avoiding sanctions through stablecoins." This type of marketing suggests that the company, at least to some extent, believed it was legitimately disclosing its ability to evade sanctions in its advertisements, including to clients seeking to circumvent international restrictions. The entity operated in both the cryptocurrency ecosystem (through exchanges and wallets) and the traditional financial system (through U.S. bank accounts), thereby functioning as an intermediary between the two systems.

Methodology and Mechanics of the Scheme

TRANSACTIONAL ARCHITECTURE

Gugnin's operation employed a sophisticated methodology to transfer value across borders while maintaining the concealment of the transactions' origins, destinations, and purposes. The operation worked in stages, utilizing specific characteristics of cryptocurrency—specifically stablecoins—to evade detection by financial institutions.

The primary mechanism involved receiving cryptocurrency (primarily Tether/USDT) from foreign clients, many of whom held funds at banks sanctioned by the Russian government. Digital assets were transferred to cryptocurrency wallets controlled by Evita and converted to U.S. dollars or other fiat via bank accounts in the United States. The exchange effectively laundered the funds by obscuring their sources and disrupting the audit trail that would have linked the ultimate beneficiaries to their origins. Between June 2023 and January 2025, Gugnin utilized this mechanism to potentially transfer approximately $530 million through the U.S. financial system (TRM Labs, 2025).

CONCEALMENT STRATEGIES

To maintain the appearance of legitimacy, Gugnin employed multiple misrepresentations targeting banks and regulators. He consistently lied to banks and cryptocurrency exchanges, denying that Evita had engaged in business with Russian entities or had any business dealings with sanctioned entities. These misrepresentations were all material because, had Gugnin been truthful in his disclosures, his access to the U.S. financial system would have been terminated immediately, and he would have drawn the scrutiny of regulators.

Gugnin also engaged in document manipulation to conceal the involvement of sanctioned parties. He regularly obfuscated invoices by digitally "whiting out" the names and addresses of his Russian customers, creating the appearance of legitimate business transactions with non-sanctioned entities. In addition, Gugnin secured a money transmitter license from the state of Florida by making materially false statements about Evita Pay's business activities, then used this fraudulently obtained license to induce a cryptocurrency exchange to process transactions on his behalf (Table 16.1).

Table 16.1 Evita's Money Laundering Methodology

Stage	*Mechanism*	*Purpose*
Initial entry	Receive cryptocurrency (primarily USDT) from sanctioned Russian entities	Introduce illicit funds into the financial system
Conversion	Transfer digital assets through multiple cryptocurrency wallets	Obscure transaction trail and source of funds
Layering	Convert cryptocurrency to fiat currency through U.S. bank accounts	Create an appearance of legitimate business activity
Integration	Make payments through Manhattan bank accounts on behalf of foreign clients	Provide clean funds to sanctioned end-users

ENABLING TECHNOLOGY ACQUISITION

Beyond mere financial transactions, Gugnin's operation facilitated the acquisition of sensitive technology by Russian end-users in violation of U.S. export controls. According to the indictment, Gugnin facilitated payments by foreign customers to procure sensitive electronics, including an export-controlled server designed by a U.S. technology company (U.S. Department of Justice, 2025). Gugnin also laundered funds from a Moscow-based supplier to purchase parts for Rosatom, Russia's state-owned nuclear technology company.

This feature of the scheme demonstrates that financial facilitation can directly assist activities with national security implications. Gugnin facilitated a payments channel that bypassed both economic sanctions and export control regulations, enabling Russian entities to acquire technologies otherwise unavailable due to national security restrictions. This case illustrates the intersection of financial crime and technology transfer controls, underscoring the need for a joint strategic response to address both within integrated enforcement mechanisms.

Legal and Regulatory Compliance Failures

Bank Secrecy Act Violations

In these instances, Gugnin failed to implement the recommended anti-money laundering (AML) protections under the Bank Secrecy Act while maintaining the pretense that Evita was a compliant money services business. Even though he purported to the banks and cryptocurrency exchanges regarding strict AML and know your customer requirements in practice, he entirely ignored them. Most significantly, Gugnin failed to establish Evita's purported AML program and never filed any suspicious activity reports with FinCEN as required by the statute.

These compliance failures were not merely negligent; they demonstrated a deliberate choice to evade detection of illicit activity. The BSA sets forth a regime of preventive measures to identify and report suspected shady activity, thereby creating key gatekeeping functions that Gugnin routinely undermines. Moreover, as the compliance officer for Evita, he held positions that were multiplicative violations of the law and authority, thereby ensuring inadequate control over the flow of illicit funds (U.S. Department of Justice, 2025; Internal Revenue Service, 2025).

Evasion of Sanctions and Export Controls

Gugnin's conduct constituted a straightforward, unequivocal breach of the IEEPA (U.S. Department of Justice, 2025). This law confers legal authority on many U.S. sanctions programs. Specifically, Gugnin's arrangement of a transaction involving sanctioned Russian banks, including PJSC Sberbank, PJSC Sovcombank, PJSC VTB Bank, and JSC Tinkoff Bank, violated prohibitions against facilitating transactions related to the services of a sanctioned entity. In addition, instituting his own accounts at two sanctioned Russian banks, JSC Alfa-Bank and PJSC Sberbank, while physically present in the United States, facilitated prohibited transactions with persons who remained subject to sanctions imposed and enforced by U.S. law enforcement and regulatory authorities (Table 16.2).

When considered a whole, the export control aspect of the scheme further enhanced its legal repercussions. Gugnin's role in facilitating the acquisition of sensitive U.S. technology by Russian end users constituted a breach of U.S. export controls enforced by the Bureau of Industry and Security (BIS), an agency of the Department of Commerce (Export Compliance Daily, 2025). The violations, by definition, involved financial crimes and therefore also presented a national security component that increased the risk posed by Gugnin's conduct, elevating it from regulatory offenses to more serious crimes (Figure 16.1).

Table 16.2 Legal Charges Against Iurii Gugnin

Charge Category	*Specific Violations*	*Maximum Penalties*
Financial fraud	Wire fraud, bank fraud, conspiracy to defraud the United States	20–30 years per count
Sanctions evasion	Violations of the International Emergency Economic Powers Act (IEEPA)	20 years per count
Money laundering	Operation of an unlicensed money transmitting business, money laundering conspiracy	20 years per count
Compliance failures	Failure to implement an AML program, failure to file SARs	10 years per count

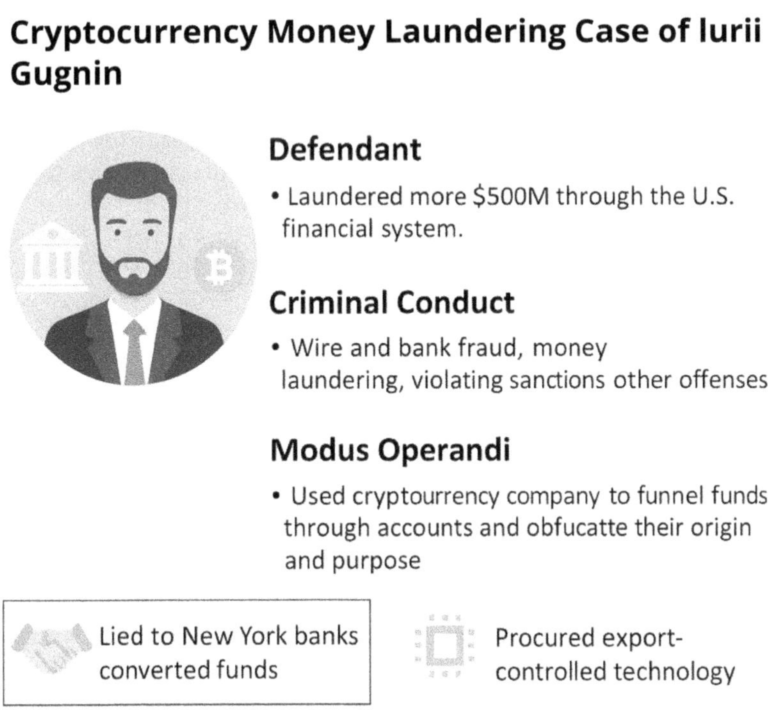

Figure 16.1 Cryptocurrency Laundering Exposed: The Iurii Gugnin–Evita Network

Economic and National Security Implications

Financial System Vulnerabilities

Gugnin's large-scale operation—$530 million being moved through the U.S. financial system over approximately 19 months. This demonstrates critical systemic vulnerabilities at the interface of traditional finance and cryptocurrency ecosystems (TRM Labs, 2025; CoinTelegraph, 2025). The case illustrates how bad actors can exploit jurisdictional gaps across regulatory regimes by utilizing cryptocurrency to initiate transactions and subsequently transfer the value to professionals and businesses within the insulated U.S. financial system, thereby converting the cryptocurrency into fiat currency immediately.

This fraudulent service degraded the integrity of financial institutions that unknowingly processed transactions for sanctioned entities. By deceiving banks about the nature of his business and the origins of funds, Gugnin subjected these institutions to sanctions violations for facilitating sanctions evasion. This case illustrates the challenges financial institutions face in detecting illicit activity when counterparties systematically deceive, for example, by providing false information about payments and obscuring payment trails.

National Security Implications

The national security ramifications of the Evita scheme reach beyond the financial sphere to encompass technology transfer and strategic advantage. By allowing Russian actors to access sensitive U.S. technology, including export-controlled servers and components used by a Russian state-run nuclear technology company (Rosatom). Gugnin was potentially enhancing the capabilities of critical competitors and adversaries.

The case unfolded against the backdrop of worsening and strained relations between Russia and Western countries. This invasion occurred during the deepening crisis of 2022, when Russia entered a war against Ukraine. One of the most effective ways to constrain Russia's ability to engage in battle is to use. This was also essential to limit the development of sophisticated military capabilities that have been through sanctions and export restrictions. Evasion of these actions through cryptocurrency channels thus directly undermined attempts to limit Russian aggression and ensure international security.

Conclusion and Implications

Case Resolution and Legal Proceedings

Iurii Gugnin is charged with a multi-count felony indictment that describes a variety of illegal activities. The most prominent of these are wire fraud, bank fraud, money laundering, and conspiracy to commit fraud against the United States, among others. Moreover, he knowingly and willfully engaged in the unlicensed operation of a money transmission business. He also miserably failed to adhere to the financial institution's anti-money laundering protocols. The allegations would demonstrate a scheme of extreme financial fraud. If found guilty of bank fraud, Gugnin would face up to 30 years in prison; 20 years for wire fraud; sanctions violations; and 10 years for any violations involving a deficiency in an effective AML program. Gugnin was arrested in New York when the indictment was unsealed in June 2025 and was arraigned and detained in custody until trial (U.S. Department of Justice, 2025; U.S. Attorney's Office, Eastern District of New York, 2025).

The prosecution of Gugnin demonstrates that cryptocurrency-based sanctions evasion is of heightened interest to U.S. authorities. This specific case was conducted as part of the Disruptive Technology Strike Force (U.S. Department of Justice, 2025). This is a joint initiative between the Department of Commerce and the DOJ. The strike force is an interagency law enforcement initiative that concentrates on targeting illicit actors, protecting supply chains, and preventing authoritarian regimes and hostile nation-states from obtaining critical technology.

Theoretical and Policy Implications

The Evita case exemplifies the evolving sophistication of sanctions evasion strategies that utilize cryptocurrency. In contrast to earlier iterations of cryptocurrency-based money laundering, which primarily employed privacy coins or mixing services. The primary currency used in this operation was Tether (USDT), a stablecoin pegged to the U.S. dollar at a 1:1 ratio. Bad actors using an infrastructure of stablecoins constitute a sophisticated form of leveraging the liquidity and stability of these currencies. By contrast, the less-regulated status of these assets relative to traditional financial instruments is advantageous.

From a policy perspective, the case highlighted the need for a more coordinated framework and protocols among regulators in the financial market, national security agencies, and cryptocurrency intermediaries. The DOJ has stated that it will take a closer look at cryptocurrency-enabled crime, as illustrated by the National Cryptocurrency Enforcement Team (NCET); however, NCET was reportedly dissolved in April 2025 (Steptoe LLP, 2025) as part of a policy adjustment that focuses on punishing individual bad actors rather than entire bad actor platforms.

The case highlights the ongoing substantive tensions that arise at the intersection of digital asset innovation and regulation. Although the Trump administration has signaled a clear intent to approve "responsible growth and use of digital assets" (Steptoe LLP, 2025) and is shifting away from previous administrations' focus on central bank digital currencies, the Evita case highlights the ongoing risks posed by the insufficient regulation of cryptocurrency ecosystems.

Future Research Opportunities

The Evita case offers several promising avenues for future research at the intersection of finance, technology, and security studies. First, researchers might consider the comparative effectiveness of regulatory mechanisms for overseeing cryptocurrencies by examining how various jurisdictions address innovation-related concerns and the associated risks of illicit finance. Second, the case invites an exploration of the differences that exist between types of cryptocurrencies, stablecoins specifically, concerning their exploitation, as well as whether regulatory or technical constraints can either (1) dampen the risk of misuse or (2) impede legitimate use cases. Scholars could ultimately analyze the continued viability of traditional finance as the industry integrates with cryptocurrency infrastructure, where exploitative potential may be inferred; they could then design mechanisms to protect financial integrity and national security.

In a nutshell, Iurii Gugnin and Evita Investments highlighted a complex challenge of evasion from sanctions—and more broadly, illicit finance through cryptocurrency—and how technological innovation can outpace regulatory frameworks, providing opportunities for bad actors to undermine national security and the integrity of the financial system. As cryptocurrency continues to evolve and traditional finance interfaces with cryptocurrency structures, regulators, financial institutions, and law enforcement will need to adapt in parallel to address emerging threats.

Chapter Summary

These tough sanctions regimes are stringent measures imposed on individuals or entities that threaten international peace and security. Sanctions can take the form of financial, trade, or diplomatic measures. Financial sanctions typically comprise "smart" and "comprehensive" sanctions. The restriction of economic resources and access to support is expected as a sanction toward designated terrorist organizations. In addition, dual-use goods with civilian and military applications may be subjected to stringent sanctions. The institutions that impose these sanctions are the UN, the European Union, and the U.S. government's OFAC. Any sanction regime, however, can also indirectly facilitate illegal activities, such as TBML.

End of Chapter: Discussion Questions

1. What are the objectives of the sanction regime?
2. Who are the institutions empowered to impose sanctions?
3. What are the different types of sanctions?
4. What are smart sanctions and comprehensive sanctions?
5. How do sanctions impact the targeted individuals, entities, or organizations?
6. Why are terrorism sanctions imposed?
7. How are dual-use goods controlled through sanctions?
8. What are the potential unintended consequences of sanctions regimes?
9. How does TBML challenge the sanctions regime?
10. What is the role of the UN in imposing sanctions?
11. What is the role of the U.S. government's OFAC in imposing sanctions?
12. What is the impact of sanctions on the global economy?
13. Can sanctions be effective in achieving their intended objectives?

References

Ayad, M., & Al-Daoudi. (2022). Smart sanctions as an alternative to international economic sanctions within the framework of public international law. *RIMAK International Journal of Humanities and Social Sciences*. https://doi.org/10.47832/2717-8293.18.30

BBC News. (2024, February 22). *US targets Russia with more than 500 new sanctions.* Retrieved from https://www.bbc.com/news/world-us-canada-68380251

Borden, S. (2016). Sanctions and unintended consequences. *Strategic Studies Quarterly*, 10(3), 86–106.

Bouchet-Saulnier, F. (2023). *Sanctions (diplomatic, economic, or military).* The Practical Guide to Humanitarian Law. Retrieved from https://guide-humanitarian-law.org/content/article/3/sanctions-diplomatic-economic-or-military/

Central Bank of the UAE. (2021). 3.1. Sanctions evasion. *CBUAE Rulebook.* https://rulebook.centralbank.ae/en/rulebook/31-sanctions-evasion

Cipriani, M., Goldberg, L. S., & La Spada, G. (2023). Financial sanctions, SWIFT, and the architecture of the international payments system. *Social Science Research Network.* https://doi.org/10.2139/ssrn.4336483

CoinTelegraph (2025). How a Russian national allegedly laundered $530M in crypto via Tether. Available at: https://cointelegraph.com/news/how-a-russian-national-allegedly-laundered-530m-in-crypto-via-tether (Accessed: 24 August 2025)

Colussi, I. A. (2016). International trade sanctions related to dual-use goods and technologies. *Athens Journal of Law*. https://doi.org/10.30958/AJL.2-4-3

Congressional Research Service. (2024). Russia-Ukraine War: Sanctions and other economic measures. https://crsreports.congress.gov/product/details?prodcode=R45415

Council of the European Union. (2014, March 17). The Council adopts restrictive measures in light of the situation in Ukraine. https://www.consilium.europa.eu/media/29224/141707.pdf
Council of the European Union. (2024, June 14). Council adopts the tenth package of sanctions against Russia over its aggression against Ukraine. https://oeil.secure.europarl.europa.eu/oeil/spdoc.do?i=60725&j=0&l=en
Council of the European Union. (n.d.). *EU restrictive measures (sanctions): How and when the EU adopts restrictive measures*. European Council. https://www.consilium.europa.eu/en/policies/sanctions/
Council on Foreign Relations. (2015). What are economic sanctions? Retrieved from https://www.cfr.org/backgrounder/what-are-economic-sanctions
Dalacoura, K. (2015). The targeted sanctions on Russia and the evolving landscape of international financial regulation. *Journal of International Banking Law & Regulation*, 30(4), 197–212.
Dolgopyatov, C., & Goldstein, I. (2018). The myth of Russian economic isolation: Evidence from trade data. *Carnegie Endowment for International Peace*.
Dreher, A. (2009). The macroeconomics of economic sanctions. In T. Sandler & K. Hartley (Eds.), *Handbook of defense economics* (Vol. 2, pp. 853–865). Elsevier.
Duelfer, C. (2004). The Report of the Iraq Survey Group. Retrieved from https://nsarchive2.gwu.edu/NSAEBB/NSAEBB394/docs/80-09-17%20CIA%20Alert%20Memo%20Iran-Iraq.pdf
Eland, I. (2018). Economic sanctions as tools of foreign policy. https://doi.org/10.4324/9780429493935-3
Export Compliance Daily (2025) Russian citizen violated sanctions, export controls through illegal operation of crypto company. Available at: https://exportcompliancedaily.com/article/2025/06/11/russian-citizen-violated-sanctions-export-controls-through-illegal-operation-of-crypto-company-2506100048?BC=bc_684d65f09ef9a (Accessed: 24 August 2025)
Faria, L., & Obstfeld, M. (2024, May). The global economic impact of the Russia-Ukraine war. *National Bureau of Economic Research*. https://www.nber.org/papers/w30247
Gacki, A. (2021, January 27). OFAC's role is to safeguard the financial system and promote national security. *Remarks at the New York University School of Law*, New York. Retrieved from https://www.treasury.gov/press-center/speeches/Pages/jl0547.aspx
Ghodoosi, F. (2015). The sanctions theory: A frail paradigm for international law? *Harvard International Law Journal*, 55, 348–439. Retrieved from https://journals.law.harvard.edu/ilj/wp-content/uploads/sites/84/Ghodoosi-Article.pdf
Goldstein, A., Pinker, S., & Drezner, D. W. (2010). The effectiveness of economic sanctions. *International Security*, 34(4), 189–193.
Gorny, T. J. (2023, January 17). The Danfoss OFAC sanctions violations case. Sanctions.io. https://www.sanctions.io/blog/the-danfoss-ofac-sanctions-violations-case.
Grecu, L. (2023). Importance of OFAC sanctions in the anti-money laundering compliance process of commercial banks. https://doi.org/10.53486/9789975359030.57
Habsburg, A. von, & Light, M. (2020). Sanctions and unintended consequences: The case of Russia. *International Affairs*, 96(2), 381–400.
Internal Revenue Service (2025). Founder of cryptocurrency payment company charged with evading sanctions and export controls, defrauding financial institutions, and violating the bank secrecy act. Available at: https://www.irs.gov/compliance/criminal-investigation/founder-of-cryptocurrency-payment-company-charged-with-evading-sanctions-and-export-controls-defrauding-financial-institutions-and-violating-the-bank-secrecy-act (Accessed: 24 August 2025).
Iran Watch. (2022, December 30). OFAC settles with Danfoss A/S for $4,379,810 related to apparent violations of the Iran, Syria, and Sudan sanctions programs. https://www.iranwatch.org/library/governments/united-states/executive-branch/department-treasury/ofac-settles-danfoss-4379810-related-apparent-violations-iran-syria-sudan.
Jersey Financial Services Commission. (2023). Sanctions obligations and sanctions evasion techniques. https://www.jerseyfsc.org/industry/international-co-operation/sanctions/sanctions-obligations-and-sanctions-evasion-techniques/
Kirilakha, A., Felbermayr, G., Syropoulos, C., Yalcin, E., & Yotov, Y. V. (2024). *The global sanctions database: Mapping international economic restrictions*. GSDB Project Platform. https://www.globalsanctionsdatabase.com/

LexisNexis. (2023). LexisNexis. *Lexisnexis.com*. https://internationalsales.lexisnexis.com/glossary/compliance/sanctions
Mandelker, S. (2024). Remarks on economic sanctions and global financial integrity. U.S. Department of the Treasury. Retrieved from https://home.treasury.gov/news/press-releases.
Masters, J. (2019). *What are economic sanctions?* Council on Foreign Relations. https://www.cfr.org/backgrounder/what-are-economic-sanctions
Mendelsohn, S. (2019, April 10). The Iran Deal: A flawed but necessary agreement. *The Stimson Center*. https://www.stimson.org/2023/a-common-sense-policy-on-iran/
Moody's. (2023). Sanctions compliance and sanctions evasion - increased enforcement and evolving tactics. https://www.moodys.com/web/en/us/kyc/resources/insights/sanctions-compliance-sanctions-evasion-increased-enforcement-evolving-tactics.html
Nolan, P. (2017). The sanctions effectiveness debate. *The Peterson Institute for International Economics Policy Brief* (PB17–13).
O'Connell, P. (2007). The human cost of sanctions. *International Affairs*, 83(1), 1–23.
Office of Foreign Assets Control. (2008). Designation of Rami Makhlouf as SDN under Executive Order 13460. https://www.treasury.gov/press-center/press-releases/pages/hp858.aspx
Office of Foreign Assets Control. (2011). Expansion of Syrian sanctions to Syriatel Mobile Telecom. https://www.treasury.gov/press-center/press-releases/pages/tg1212.aspx
Office of Foreign Assets Control. (2022, December 30). Settlement agreement between the U.S. *Department of the Treasury's Office of Foreign Assets Control and Danfoss A/S*. https://ofac.treasury.gov/recent-actions/20221230_33
Office of Foreign Assets Control. (2023). Overview and history of OFAC. *U.S. Department of the Treasury*.
Office of Foreign Assets Control. (2023, March 23). Office of foreign assets control | U.S. *Department of the Treasury*. https://ofac.treasury.gov/
Office of Foreign Assets Control. (2024). Venezuela-Related Sanctions. https://ofac.treasury.gov/sanctions-programs-and-country-information/venezuela-related-sanctions/
Sanctions | United Nations Security Council. (2023). Un.org. https://www.un.org/securitycouncil/sanctions/information
Sanger, D. E. (2016, January 16). How Iran outfoxed the West. *The New York Times*. https://www.nytimes.com/2024/04/15/us/politics/iran-israel-nuclear-deal-biden.html
Segall, A. (1999). Economic sanctions: Legal and policy constraints. *International Review of the Red Cross*, 81(836), 763–784. Retrieved from https://www.cambridge.org/core/journals/international-review-of-the-red-cross/article/economic-sanctions-legal-and-policy-constraints/E9AD0668ED333F6EE6C9356007A6F164
Snyder, M. (2022). Economic sanctions. https://doi.org/10.1093/wentk/9780197530313.003.0002
United Nations Security Council. (n.d.). *Subsidiary organs: Security Council sanctions committees*. United Nations. https://www.un.org/securitycouncil/sanctions/information
U.S. Department of State. (n.d.). *Economic sanctions policy and implementation*. Bureau of Economic and Business Affairs. https://www.state.gov/economic-sanctions-policy-and-implementation/
U.S. Department of the Treasury. (2009, December 16). *U.S. Treasury Department announces joint $536 million settlement with Credit Suisse AG*. U.S. Department of the Treasury Press Center. https://home.treasury.gov/news/press-releases/tg452
U.S. Department of the Treasury. (2014, March 20). Treasury sanctions Russian officials and entities for activities in Ukraine. https://home.treasury.gov/news/press-releases/jl2629
U.S. Department of the Treasury. (n.d.). *Sanctions programs and country information. Office of Foreign Assets Control*. https://ofac.treasury.gov/sanctions-programs-and-country-information
U.S. Department of the Treasury. (n.d.). Frequently asked questions. Retrieved from https://www.treasury.gov/resource-center/faqs/Sanctions/Pages/faq_compliance.aspx
U.S. Department of the Treasury, Office of Foreign Assets Control. (2022). Global terrorism sanctions regulations. *Federal Register*, 87(126), 39337–393391. https://www.federalregister.gov/documents/2022/07/01/2022-13969/global-terrorism-sanctions-regulations
U.S. Department of Justice. (2013, November 19). Justice Department, federal and state partners secure record $13 billion global settlement with JPMorgan for misleading investors about securities containing toxic mortgages. Office of Public Affairs. Retrieved from https://www.justice.gov/archives/opa/pr/justice-department-federal-and-state-partners-secure-record-13-billion-global-settlement

U.S. Senate Permanent Subcommittee on Investigations. (2013). JPMorgan Chase compliance failures in sanctions enforcement. Washington, DC: U.S. Government Printing Office.
United Nations Sanctions - Committee of Legal Advisers on Public International Law. (2014). Committee of Legal Advisers on Public International Law.
Wallerstein, M. (2001). Economic sanctions: An overview. In D. Cortright & G. A. Lopez (Eds.), *The sanctions decade: Assessing UN strategies in the 1990s* (pp. 19–37). Lynne Rienner Publishers.
The Washington Post. (2023, January 10). *How Iran's crumbling economy fueled the Mahsa Amini protests*. The Washington Post.
The Washington Post. (2026, May 13). *Soaring inflation and plummeting economy test Iran's ability to absorb blockade pressure*.

Additional Learning Resources

Books

1 "Economic Sanctions Reconsidered" by Gary Clyde Hufbauer, Jeffrey J. Schott, and Kimberly Ann Elliott, Columbia University Press. (2017). Columbia University Press; CUP. https://cup.columbia.edu/book/economic-sanctions-reconsidered/9780881324129
This book examines the rich experience of sanctions in the 20th century to derive lessons for their more effective use in the 21st century. It provides a comprehensive analysis of the effectiveness of economic sanctions and their impact on targeted countries.
2 "12 Sanctions policy" by Piet Eeckhout. Pages 501–548; Published: May 2011. https://doi.org/10.1093/acprof:oso/9780199606634.003.0012.
This book offers an excellent case study of the evolving interactions between external policies under the Treaty on the European Union (TEU) and the Treaty on the Functioning of the European Union (TFEU), with a focus on the EU's sanctions policies.
3 "Economic Sanctions Reconsidered: Supplemental Case Histories" by Gary Clyde Hufbauer. Peterson Institute, 1990.
This book provides supplemental case histories to the landmark study "Economic Sanctions Reconsidered," offering additional insights into the use and effectiveness of economic sanctions.

Articles

4 "United Nations Sanctions Regimes and Selective Security" by Marijn Kruiper (2019).
This article examines the impact of economic sanctions on Haiti. It presents critical findings that may be of value to those responsible for establishing measures to prevent and detect financial crime.
5 "The Dark Side of Economic Sanctions: Unveiling the Plight of Women from Myanmar/Burma-A Minor Field Study in Myanmar and Thailand" by Lina Sturfelt (2009). muep.mah.se.
This article examines the plight of women in Myanmar (Burma) and the impact of economic sanctions on their lives.

Documentaries

6 "The Importance of Effective Economic Sanctions" (2018) - TEDx Talk by Robert J. Ward, Jr. https://www.youtube.com/watch?v=kgqz2K4lKwo
In this TEDx Talk, Robert J. Ward, Jr., an attorney with 30 years of experience, discusses the importance of effective economic sanctions in addressing global issues.
7 "Explainer: What are United Nations sanctions?" - United Nations video. https://www.youtube.com/watch?v=wgS-aNJVEK4
This video explains United Nations sanctions, their purpose, and their impact.

17 Understanding the Importance of Know Your Customer and Combating Financing of Terrorism in the Banking Industry

Overview of KYC and CFT

Know your customer (KYC) and combating the financing of terrorism (CFT) are basic regimes set forth by the legal framework to counter money laundering (ML) and terrorist financing (TF). KYC broadly encompasses the identification and verification of customer identity. It also evaluates exposure to money laundering or terrorist financing and comprehends the nature of the underlying funds. In this way, financial institutions can detect and prevent illegal activities. CFT, on the other hand, caters to restricting the usage of the economic system for the financing of terrorists. CFT procedures would include the identification, freezing, and immediate reporting of terrorist assets to relevant authorities.

Governments and banks across the world have enforced and put into practice various anti-money laundering measures to deter illegal practices. These measures are aimed at preventing, detecting, and punishing money laundering. It also obligates banks to authenticate customer identities, monitor transactions, and notify the authorities of any suspicious activity. Highlighting the essential nature of these controls, the International Monetary Fund (IMF, 2022) has remarked that "by implementing strong know-your-customer (KYC) and combating the financing of terrorism (CFT) procedures and by performing customer due diligence and transaction monitoring for suspicious activities, banks are the first line of defense in protecting the integrity of the global financial system" (para. 4).

A Definition of KYC and CFT

"KYC and CFT are the two sides of the same coin and are complementary in nature (para. 7)," said the Financial Action Task Force (FATF, 2021). The FATF is a global intergovernmental organization. The body develops and enforces global guidelines to combat money laundering and terrorist financing. It is the process of combating unlawful financial activities. The FATF has strongly emphasized that KYC rules and strategies for CFT are mutually supportive. The FATF has also underlined the mutually reinforcing nature and character of CFT efforts and KYC measures (FATF, 2018, p. 8). Conversely, robust CFT controls, such as targeted financial sanctions and monitoring suspicious transactions, complement KYC by disrupting the flow of funds to terrorist organizations (FATF, 2018).

KYC stands for "know your customer," a practice used to identify and verify customers of financial institutions. Banks and other financial institutions must comply with laws on money laundering and terrorist financing. KYC primarily mitigates the risk that illicit clients will use KYC-verified entities as conduits for such operations.

DOI: 10.4324/9781003477631-18

CFT is a subset of KYC. One type of KYC and its implicit principles. It is a specific part that prohibits money laundering. CFT is perhaps the most widely used and vital process in the financial sector, enabling the identification of customers and the assessment of their exposure to terrorist financing activities. Financial institutions, including banks, should use CFT effectively to comply with AML and CFT regulations. According to the U.S. Securities and Exchange Commission (SEC), every new customer must provide a detailed account of their financial position before their investment or banking account is activated (Know Your Client (KYC): What It Means, Compliance Requirements, 2023).

The customer identification program, customer due diligence (CDD), and enhanced due diligence are among the essential KYC requirements (Know Your Customer: Quick Reference Guide, 2016).

The IMF is concerned that money laundering and terrorism financing can harm its members' economies (Anti-Money Laundering/Combating the Financing of Terrorism (AML/CFT)—Topics, 2023).

B Significance of KYC and CFT

KYC and CFT are imperative for several apparent reasons. Firstly, the technology employed in such systems helps banks satisfy their regulatory and statutory obligations to prevent money laundering and the financing of terrorism (CGAP, 2009; FATF, 2012). Secondly, robust KYC and CFT controls are primary tools for financial institutions to prevent money laundering and mitigate potential penalties or reputational damage by complying with anti-money laundering standards (FATF, 2012; IIBF, 2019).

Secondly, KYC and CFT measures enable financial institutions to effectively address financial and legal risks arising from their use in money laundering or terrorist financing schemes (FATF, 2012; Barclays, n.d.). Through the processes of verifying customer identities, monitoring transactions, and reporting suspicious activities, financial institutions can protect both their operations and the broader financial system against breaches of integrity (FATF, 2012; IIBF, 2019).

Thirdly, predictably, the confirmed use of KYC and CFT measures by a collective would have a different impact on the promotion of financial and energy security (FATF, 2012; CGAP, 2009). Identifying and stopping criminals through these financial services controls helps ensure the safety and continuity of the financial system, which is of utmost significance for economic development and financial inclusion (FATF, 2012; IIBF, 2019).

C Examples of the importance of KYC and CFT

Case 17.1 HSBC's $1.9 Billion Fine in 2012

In 2012, the United States held HSBC, a global conglomerate and credible institution, liable for egregious failures in its anti-money laundering program. The bank also breached sanctions against Cuba, Sudan, and Iran. The international bank was fined $1.9 billion. The case highlighted deficiencies in HSBC's internal controls and compliance mechanisms.

Key Issues

Failure in Anti-money Laundering (AML) Program:

- HSBC did not maintain an effective AML program.
- There were significant gaps in KYC and CFT controls.
- These gaps allowed illegal activities to go undetected and unreported.

Breach of U.S. Sanctions:

- HSBC facilitated transactions with countries under U.S. sanctions.
- The bank's internal policies and procedures were insufficient to thwart these infractions.

Consequences:
Financial Penalty:

- U.S. regulators penalized HSBC $1.9 billion, a relatively high figure considering the nature and scope of egregious breaches.

Reputational Damage:

- This case has substantially tarnished HSBC's reputation, compelling regulators, investors, and customers to doubt the bank's compliance and operational integrity.

Regulatory Oversight:

- After the settlement, HSBC encountered heightened regulatory supervision. It was also required to significantly reform its AML and sanctions compliance programs.

Operation Car Wash

Lessons Learned

Importance of Robust AML Programs:

- Banking institutions necessitate strong AML programs with efficient KYC and CFT controls that can identify and obstruct illegal activity.

Compliance with Sanctions:

- Strict compliance with global sanctions is imperative. Banks should ensure that their procedures and policies can thwart sanctioned transactions.

Corporate Governance and Oversight:

- Robust corporate governance and regulatory mechanisms are essential. They help ensure regulatory compliance and maintain the integrity of financial systems.

Continuous Improvement:

- Compliance programs must be constantly examined and improved to keep up with progressive regulatory expectations and emerging exposures.

The HSBC case underscores the importance of maintaining effective AML programs and adhering to global sanctions. It focuses on the severe consequences of noncompliance and the necessity for ongoing attention and innovation in compliance infrastructure at financial institutions.

The U.S. Department of Justice (DOJ) specifically stated that HSBC's inability to enforce an effective AML program was a key factor. The bank flagrantly disregarded implementing the U.S. sanctions, which "were directly the result of inadequate policies, procedures, and controls" (U.S. Department of Justice, 2012).

Case 17.2 Bangladesh Bank Heist (Federal Reserve Bank of New York, 2016)

In 2016, hackers launched a sophisticated and nuanced cyberattack against the Bangladesh Bank. The hackers breached the account associated with the Federal Reserve Bank of New York and stole $81 million. The attack exploited vulnerabilities in Bangladesh Bank's KYC and combating the financing of terrorism controls (Federal Reserve Bank of New York, 2016; Reuters, 2016).

Key Issues:

Weak KYC and CFT Controls:

- Bangladesh Bank's inadequate KYC and CFT procedures failed to detect and avert fraudulent transactions.
- The bank's lack of proper CDD and insufficient transaction monitoring allowed the hackers to move funds undetected.

Exploitation of the SWIFT Network:

- Hackers attacked the SWIFT network that banks use to exchange secure financial messages.
- Having infiltrated the bank's systems, the hackers were able to make fake transfer requests to the Federal Reserve Bank of New York.

Inadequate Security Features:

- According to the Federal Reserve Bank of New York, Bangladesh Bank's systems' weak security
- Features facilitated the attack.
- The bank's security was not adequately protected against advanced, more intricate cyberattacks.

Consequences:

Financial Loss:

- Bangladesh Bank lost $81 million, of which only a portion was eventually recovered.

Reputational Damage:

- The incident significantly tainted the reputation of the Bangladesh Bank. It also raised concerns about the security of other financial institutions employing the SWIFT network.

Enhanced Regulatory Scrutiny:

- The incident led regulators to focus on strong cybersecurity controls and sound KYC and CFT controls within financial institutions.

Lessons Learned:

Significance of Strong Cybersecurity Measures:

- Financial institutions must institute robust cybersecurity measures to ward off advanced cyberattacks.
- Regular security audits and maintenance are necessary to make resilient banking systems.

Enhanced KYC and CFT Controls:

- Comprehensive KYC and CFT processes are essential to expose and inhibit illegal operations
- Frequent monitoring and CDD are a must to recognize suspicious transactions.

Secure Use of Financial Messaging Networks:

- Financial institutions are required to deploy security measures to ensure the safety of financial messaging networks, such as SWIFT.
- Training and educational events for your employees could be an effective initiative in mitigating the issue of the wrong people trying to gain access to sensitive zones illegally.

Collaboration and Information Sharing:

- Cooperation between the financial institutions and the regulatory agencies will assist in detecting and stopping cyberattacks.
- Making threats and vulnerability information available may assist institutions in better securing their defenses.

The Bangladesh Bank heist also underscores the importance of implementing proper cybersecurity protocols, effective CFT and KYC controls, and secure use of financial messaging systems. It signals the severe risk of falling behind in these sectors and the absolute necessity of sustained vigilance and development to preserve the integrity of financial institutions.

According to the Federal Reserve Bank of New York, "The attack was made possible by the nature of the targeted financial institution's systems, which had inadequate security features" (Federal Reserve Bank of New York, 2016). The bank's lack of proper CDD and transaction monitoring was cited as a major factor in the hack's success.

KYC and CFT Requirements for Banks

Financial institutions' key KYC and CFT measures are meant to stop money laundering and terrorist financing. These measures ensure that financial institutions understand customers and financial transactions comprehensively, enabling them to identify and prevent illegal activities.

Why do these Requirements Need to be Fulfilled?

KYC and CFT norms have been established to combat financial crimes, including money laundering and terrorist financing. Money laundering involves transforming illegal funds into legitimate ones. Conversely, terrorist financing is the provision or collection of funds with knowledge that they will likely be used to commit terrorist acts. Both activities have dire consequences, including funding organized crime and terrorism, and shaking the bedrock stability of the international financial system.

Financial institutions are prime targets of these activities, as they are often used as conduits for illicit funds. Therefore, they must implement robust KYC and CFT controls to identify and prevent such suspicious activities.

How to Comply

There are many tangible steps financial institutions can take to comply with KYC and CFT obligations:

i Customer Due Diligence: CDD is a basic process that financial institutions leverage to mitigate their risk of money laundering and terrorist financing (Jumio, 2024). It outlines a series of activities focused on verifying a customer's identity, assessing their risk profile, and understanding the nature and purpose of their business relationship (ComplyAdvantage, 2024). A comprehensive view enables institutions to identify suspicious transactions and submit reports to the relevant authorities to halt criminal activity (Swift, 2024).
ii Transaction Monitoring: This oversees financial transactions to spot and report suspicious activity. Financial institutions should implement systems to identify and flag unusual transactions that may indicate money laundering or terrorist financing.
iii Banking institutions confront various types of exposures. They should maintain a broad risk management framework to identify and mitigate exposure to money laundering and terrorist financing. The framework states that risk management must include reviewing customer and transaction data and training staff about suspicious activity.

    i Reporting: Financial institutions can be held legally accountable for reporting suspicious activities to the relevant authorities. Reports such as Suspicious Activity Reports and the freezing of terrorist assets constitute these obligations.

Risk Management and Customer Identification Procedures

i Risk management and customer identification processes are integral to an institution's compliance with KYC and CFT requirements. They enable financial institutions to identify and understand money laundering and terrorist financing exposures and to take the requisite steps to mitigate them.
ii Risk Assessment: Exposures come in many dimensions. Financial institutions should conduct periodic and systemic assessments of their potential exposure to money laundering and terrorist financing risks. Such assessments should include reviews of the institution's clients, products, services, geographical area, and policies and procedures.
iii Customer Identification: Financial institutions are expected to implement strict procedures for customer identification. The procedures aim to verify customers' identities accurately. They would include collecting and authenticating all required personal information to confirm their name, address, and identification.

The HSBC case elucidates the essence of KYC and CFT regulations. The HSBC case elucidates the essence of KYC and CFT regulations. In 2012, U.S. regulators imposed a $1.9 billion fine on the global conglomerate for blatant deficiencies in its AML program. The bank allegedly breached stringent sanctions against Sudan, Iran, and Cuba (U.S. Department of Justice, 2012). Enabled in part by the failure of KYC and CFT controls, this case is a dramatic example of the costs a financial institution can incur when it fails to comply with KYC/CFT regulations (U.S. Department of Justice, 2012).

The 2016 Bangladesh Bank heist highlights the risks associated with weak 'know-your-customer' measures and the challenges of combating and controlling the financing of terrorism. The hackers detected and exploited the bank's configuration of money laundering and terrorist financing controls. They secured around $81 million from the bank's account at the Federal Reserve Bank of New York (FRBNY, 2016). The analysis concluded that multiple CDD failures, including inadequate transaction monitoring, had enabled a cyberattack on the bank to facilitate money laundering. This reinforces the significance of KYC/CFT frameworks. It helps establish barriers to cybercrime, specifically in the areas of money laundering and terrorist financing activities (FRBNY, 2016) (U.S. Department of Justice, 2012).

Understanding the Importance of KYCC and RFIs in Preventing Trade-Based Money Laundering

To combat trade-based money laundering (TBML), financial institutions must implement robust know your customer's customer (KYCC) and red flag indicator (RFI) systems to identify and mitigate suspicious transactions.

Implementing KYCC

KYCC identifies a customer's ultimate beneficial owner (UBO), enabling banks to assess the ultimate source of funds and identify any undue risk of money laundering. KYCC is crucial for identifying TBM; otherwise, banks can identify only the customer, not the customer's UBO engaging in TBM. A case in point is Al Rayan Bank PLC (Al Rayan), which was sanctioned and reprimanded by the Financial Conduct Authority (FCA) for failing to implement thorough anti-money laundering procedures, or at a minimum, treating KYC as a requirement. Al Rayan enabled funds to flow through its bank and into the UK between April 1, 2015, and November 30, 2017, without conducting adequate checks on its customers' Sources of Wealth and Funds. The fact that Al Rayan had not checked its customers' UBOs further amplified the risk of exposure to money laundering and other financial crimes. This case demonstrates that the consequences of failing to implement adequate KYC and CFT procedures are severe; sanctions and reputational damage can significantly affect the bank's business.

Utilizing Red Flag Indicators to Combat TBML

RFIs can serve as warning signs or objective indicators of suspicious activities. Indicators may include large and frequent cash deposits, illogical transactions, and transactions that do not align with the customer's prior activity. Banks and other financial institutions can use RFIs to detect TBML activities and identify potential money laundering risks. For instance, HSBC was penalized $1.9 billion by the DOJ for not having an effective AML Program. The DOJ determined that HSBC did not use RFIs to identify and report suspicious transactions, including those facilitated by TBML. By not using RFIs, HSBC facilitated large-scale money laundering. This also included drug traffickers' ability to move their drug trafficking proceeds through the entire U.S. financial system. The HSBC case remains a potent reminder that watchfulness and an effective AML Program are essential for using RFIs to monitor and report questionable activities. This essentially helps to protect the bank from reputational and financial harm.

Ultimately, the discussion reveals that financial institutions must have robust KYCC and use RFIs to detect and stop TBML. Doing so will protect them and the financial system from the adverse impact of money laundering and financial crimes.

Examples and Cases of KYC and CFT in the Banking Industry: Conclusion and Future Outlook

KYC and CFT will constantly evolve. Technology will become increasingly essential, shaping future regulations and our capacity to address financial crimes. We need to remain at the forefront of these developments, innovate, and adapt to shape a brighter future and the integrity of our financial systems.

Illustrative Cases

1 The Danske Bank case is a prominent example of the consequences of failures in KYC and CFT controls. The bank was found to have engaged in significant money laundering involving multiple billions of dollars. It ultimately resulted in substantial fines and subsequent reputational damage (Danske Bank, 2019). According to their report, in September 2018, Danske Bank discovered that its Estonian branch had been used to launder funds on a massive scale from Russia and other former Soviet Union states between 2007 and 2015 (Danske Bank, 2019). They noted that the bank had failed to implement adequate KYC procedures and to continue monitoring clients and suspicious transactions, thereby facilitating the processing of illicit funds with impunity (Danske Bank, 2019). This incident underscores the importance of robust KYC/CFT controls for the continued legal and ethical operations of our financial institutions (FATF, 2012).
2 HSBC was probably the most famous case. The HSBC Holdings case is the largest globally recognized bank. In 2012, HSBC Holdings faced severe repercussions from U.S. federal regulators due to a notable breakdown in compliance and its anti-money laundering systems. HSBC knowingly did not detect, or entirely disregarded, that they were laundering money for the Colombian Norte del Valle cartel and the Sinaloa Cartel. In essence, HSBC agreed to pay $1.9 billion in penalties, plus an additional civil monetary penalty of $665 million. This significant penalty underscored the need for HSBC to implement corrective measures to close the gap and enhance its AML processes (HSBC Holdings, 2012). The bank's activities were specifically egregious, leading to the laundering of over $881 million for the aforementioned drug cartels. While HSBC made some attempts to reinforce its AML practices, it was still criticized for failing to implement an effective remedy to address money laundering (HSBC Holdings, 2012).
3 Another well-known case is Standard Chartered. In 2012, the bank faced substantial legal implications arising from money laundering involving sanctioned Iranian entities. The bank decided to pay $667 million in a settlement of charges that it breached U.S. sanctions by processing transactions for Iranian, Sudanese, and Libyan clients. The commonality with Standard Chartered was that it obscured around 60,000 transactions valued at $250 billion from regulators (Reuters, 2012).

In addition to these examples, other cases in which banks failed to comply with KYC and AML regulations led to the banks being accused and fined. In 2013, JPMorgan Chase faced accusations of failing to report suspicious financial transactions. The bank agreed with the government to pay $1.7 billion in fines, signaling a strict financial backlash against noncompliance (New York Times, 2013). It became clear that strong internal controls and alert monitoring systems are indispensable. It is not enough to respond to noncompliance; we must anticipate incidents and ensure that those systems remain operational.

BNP Paribas faced similar issues in 2014 when it processed transactions for customers in embargoed countries, including Sudan and Iran. The bank agreed to pay penalties totaling $8.9

billion (Financial Times, 2014), underscoring the consequences of noncompliance with international regulatory standards.

In the cases of JPMorgan Chase and BNP Paribas, the regulatory fines for noncompliance were so large that the banks had to pay substantial sums, thereby weakening their financial position and damaging their reputations. It is not only the monetary loss but also the risk that regulatory noncompliance can adversely affect the general public's perception of the bank. If this occurs, one can foresee a lack of customer trust and a substantial decline in the bank's stock price. The violation of KYC and AML regulations could implicate the bank and its leaders in legal proceedings. As a result, this can require the bank to engage in protracted litigation, incur substantial financial penalties, and face the possible imprisonment of executive staff found guilty of negligence or complicity.

Let us take the previous cases as examples. It is clear that the inability to comply with KYC and AML requirements, which has affected banks and financial institutions, can have devastating repercussions. In addition to incurring substantial fines and unavoidable penalties, noncompliance is dangerous for banks. They lose the support of authorities, clients, and the public, which may significantly undermine the brand's confidence and loyalty.

To summarize, the two things in the banking industry, Know Your Customer and Combating Financing of Terrorism, are needed. Because they enable banks to identify their clients and detect suspicious activities associated with money laundering or terrorist financing. Actual incidents and cases, for example, from HSBC, Standard Chartered, JPMorgan Chase, and BNP Paribas, reveal the importance of adhering to KYC and CFT rules and the severe sanctions that can be imposed for noncompliance.

The banking sector's outlook depends on KYC and CFT protocols remaining relevant and adapting to emerging exposures. Banks and financial institutions must remain vigilant and comply with the requirements of KYC and CFT laws to avoid penalties, legal fees, and reputational harm.

Outlook

i The increasingly stringent laws and regulations governing KYC and CFT for banks are expected to evolve within the coming years. To meet compliance, the mechanism for adapting to such enhancements will require an even more advanced use of technology and systems within financial institutions.

ii The trend of using artificial intelligence and machine learning in KYC and CFT processes is increasingly being adopted in the financial industry. With the assistance of these advanced technologies, financial institutions are expected to shift from merely analyzing large datasets to applying sophisticated techniques. This helps identify and disrupt activities related to money laundering or terrorism financing.

iii The acceleration of the "blockchain" technology will likely occur convincingly in the coming years. This is because, while blockchain is secure and decentralized, it could change how records are kept and transactions are authenticated. Transparency and immutability can be formidable deterrents to money laundering and terrorist financing. Some experts claim that, in the future, blockchain will provide an even greater value proposition for know your customer and for countering the financing of terrorism.

iv Besides technological improvements, governments and financial institutions should step up their participation in fighting money laundering and terrorism financing. This cooperation encompasses information sharing, intelligence, joint development, and the development of new rules and laws.

KYC and CFT are the banking industry's strategic foundations. Therefore, banks must remain fluid and flexible, able to adapt to these changes. They must also regulate while protecting their consumers and economy from the pernicious effects of money laundering and terrorist financing.

Case 17.3 Al Rayan Bank PLC's AML Failures and Fines (UK, 2019)

Understanding the Importance of Adequate Anti-Money Laundering Measures in the Banking Industry

Al Rayan Bank PLC is one of the leading Islamic banks, specifically in the UK. This bank takes pride in being a classic instrument of Islamic finance. Its commitment is to offer Sharia-compliant financial products and services. The bank meets a wide range of banking needs for both individuals and businesses. It offers a wide range of products, including home loans and savings accounts. Masraf Al Rayan, a leading Islamic bank, acquired the bank. It was integrated into its portfolio as an important component in 2019.

Despite severe criticism for failing to implement essential controls to avert money laundering and the financing of terrorism, the Financial Conduct Authority (FCA) and the Prudential Regulation Authority (PRA, 2019) simultaneously conducted a joint review of the bank's anti-money laundering and counter-terrorist financing measures in 2019. The review results confirmed that the bank was at a high risk of being used by criminals for money laundering. The report, therefore, suggests that Al Rayan was not just the potential source of terror financing but also money laundering by criminals.

In 2016, the Financial Conduct Authority (FCA) in the UK imposed a £3.5 million fine on Al Rayan. The fine was imposed due to serious gaps in its AML and CFT controls. Between April 2015 and November 2017, the bank permitted the laundering of funds without conducting the necessary checks and controls. They failed to assess the sources of their customers' wealth and funds, a crucial step in combating financial crime. Furthermore, Al Rayan's employees did not receive sufficient training in AML and CFT. To make matters worse, the bank failed to conduct proper due diligence on its correspondent banking relationships.

Due to subsequent failures and lapses, Al Rayan failed to assess the risk of money laundering within its business. The tremendous concerns included the possibility of their accounts being used for funding terrorist operations. The banking regulatory bodies criticized Al Rayan for not having robust AML procedures. It lacked appropriate controls, governance, and organizational frameworks that were not well-suited to monitoring and protecting the efficient functioning of risk management within the bank.

The FCA's director of Enforcement and Market Oversight, Tracey McDermott, explicitly stated, "Banks play a crucial role in combating financial crime. It is essential that they have the right systems and controls in place to identify and assess the money laundering risks they face" (McDermott, 2016).

Regulators identified a significant deficiency in Al Rayan's poor CDD procedures. The FCA and PRA specifically noted that the bank failed to conduct adequate CDD for several customer categories. This comprised high-risk individuals and politically exposed individuals. The bank also failed to implement regular surveillance of its clients. It was to ensure that their activity aligned with their risk profiles. Such an inadequate CDD procedure and the lack of ongoing monitoring exposed the bank to significant risks of money laundering and terrorist financing.

Moreover, the regulators identified deficiencies in Al Rayan's transaction-monitoring systems. The bank lacked effective systems for flagging and reporting suspicious transactions.

The institution also allowed illicit activity to go undetected. Al Rayan's failure to regularly review the systems inhibited assurance of their continued effectiveness. Shocking deficiencies were apparent in transaction monitoring, which substantially increased costs associated with money laundering and terrorist financing vulnerabilities.

The FCA fined Al Rayan Bank PLC £4.023 million for systemic breaches. It was imposed for serious flaws and gaps in its AML control mechanisms (FCA, 2023). The investigative findings reveal that between April 2015 and November 2017, Al Rayan permitted its clients to transfer funds within the UK. The transfer of funds was processed without verifying the customers' sources of funds. This failure to perform CDD heightened the bank's money laundering and financial crime risks (FCA, 2023).

According to the FCA press release (2023), it was also emphasized that Al Rayan was not only aware of these deficiencies in their AML controls but had also failed to take any tangible steps to implement practical changes to address them, despite the FCA's prior concerns (FCA, 2023). The seriousness of Al Rayan's AML shortcomings is evidenced not only by the FCA's findings and subsequent action but also by the duty of financial institutions to maintain a rigorous AML infrastructure and associated risk-mitigation measures to reduce the likelihood and severity of further exposure to economic crime. Moreover, due to these AML failures, the FCA found that the bank lacked sufficient staff training in handling large deposits, thereby increasing its exposure to money laundering and other financial crimes. During the FCA's 2017 visit to Al Rayan, the bank voluntarily agreed to refrain from onboarding any further high-risk customers. The bank is no longer required to prevent the onboarding of high-risk customers following improvements to its systems and controls. However, a few restrictions have been lifted. The bank remains subject to limited restrictions until further improvements are implemented.

In conclusion, the failings at Al Rayan Bank PLC underscore the importance of maintaining robust AML controls and providing targeted staff training to prevent money laundering and other financial crimes. Banks must remain alert to their substantial obligations under AML laws and take the necessary and concrete steps to comply.

Insight: Risk-Based Approach Guidance for the Banking Sector by FATF

FATF is regarded as a strong and effective body for combating money laundering and terrorist financing internationally (FATF, 2023). The FATF's "Risk-Based Approach Guidance for the Banking Sector" will be an invaluable resource for banks and financial institutions. It is mainly designed to implement adequate AML/CFT regulations strictly. The guidance also emphasizes the importance of adopting a risk-based approach as an integral part of addressing the weaknesses identified in each institution.

The FATF framework promotes the identification, evaluation, and understanding of ML/TF vulnerabilities by FIs. It is directly linked to their customers, products, services, and geographic footprints. The level of risk provides the base for building and implementing risk-based AML/CFT policies, procedures, and controls. FIs with higher inherent exposures may also require more onerous CDD requirements or transaction monitoring.

The FATF guidance also underscores the continuing need for customer and transaction monitoring. Regular reviews help ensure your AML/CFT controls remain effective. This may primarily lead to the recognition of emerging threats. Moreover, the guidance requires establishing and emphasizing the importance of staff training, education, and awareness programs. Ensure that employees have been adequately trained to identify, locate, and notify the relevant authorities of any illegal activity. Without exception, this is a primary prerequisite for the adoption process of the AML/CFT program. The guidance also recognizes the value of FIRs in delivering intelligence on financial transactions, profiles, and activities. It may relate to emerging threats of money laundering, terrorist financing, or other illicit financial practices.

An essential FATF document, 'Risk-Based Approach Guidance for the Banking Sector,' represents a major step forward for banks and other financial institutions. The chief purpose of this guidance is to enhance and strengthen clients' AML/CFT obligations and, where necessary, mitigate the sprawling threats of ML/TF. By adopting a risk-based approach and emphasizing continuous monitoring and staff training, FIs can help create a safer, more secure financial system.

Danske Bank and the Estonian Branch Scandal: Triggering Global Investigations and a $2 Billion U.S. Settlement (Denmark, Estonia, Russia, and the USA, 2018)

Danske Bank is the largest and most viable financial institution in Denmark. It has acknowledged conspiring to commit bank fraud and has agreed to forfeit $2 billion as part of a settlement with the DOJ. The bank was to resolve a long-standing investigation into billions of dollars in payments linked to illegal activities (Finance Magnates, 2023). This is the United States' first action against a Danish bank. The DOJ has been central to one of the largest money laundering scandals in history (Finance Magnates, 2023).

Background

The Danske Bank scandal originated in 2007 at the bank's Estonian branch and is a momentous event in the financial industry. The branch's attraction of high-risk clients from Russia and other countries, along with its provision of minimal oversight for large fund transfers, facilitated the estimated €200 billion ($212 billion) in illicit funds that flowed through the U.S. financial system by 2016. This was enabled by weak AML control mechanisms that permitted clients to use shell companies and obscure ownership (U.S. Department of Justice, 2022; Skadden, Arps, Slate, Meagher & Flom LLP, 2022).

Discovery of the Scandal

The DOJ reported, based on internal audits, whistleblower reports, and regulatory information, that Danske Bank was informed of the illegal transactions by at least February 2014. The bank acknowledged that the AML program at its Estonian branch fell short of its standards, a fact prosecutors emphasized.

Investigation and Consequences

Danske Bank has been grappling with a money laundering scandal for nearly five years. On October 4, 2018, it announced that it would set aside approximately $1.9 billion to cover investigations by the DOJ, the SEC, and the Danish Special Crime Unit. Investors also sued Danske Bank's former CEO, Thomas Borgen, although a Danish court found him not liable in November 2019 in connection with the scandal.

The bank's settlement with the DOJ marks the first U.S. action against Danske Bank regarding the money laundering scheme. Court filings indicate that the bank acknowledged defrauding U.S. banks between 2008 and 2016. It had processed high-risk non-resident customers, mostly Russians, through its office in Estonia. Danske Bank agreed to a $2 billion forfeiture. It also entered into a deferred prosecution agreement with the DOJ. The bank also amicably reached settlements with the Danish Financial Supervisory Authority (DFSA) and the SEC. To settle the prospective investigation, the bank agreed to pay the DFSA $150 million and the SEC $500 million.

Precautions and Takeaways

The Danske Bank scandal is a sobering reminder of financial institutions' need for sturdy AML and KYC policies and procedures. With flimsy and vulnerable AML controls, employees at the bank's branch in Estonia could conceal the nature of various illicit transactions by utilizing shell companies. This failure enabled billions of dollars in illicit funds to flow through the U.S. financial system.

Strengthening AML and KYC Controls

The case highlights the urgent need for rigorous AML and KYC controls. Control mechanisms are reviewed regularly to ensure they are updated more often to reflect evolving vulnerabilities. By continually reviewing and updating their processes, institutions will remain agile and cope with newly identified threats. Financial institutions and banks must take concrete steps in CDD to identify risks. This includes red flags that help identify money laundering. Active transaction monitoring is crucial for detecting suspicious or anomalous activity. The customer's due diligence process should also be regularly updated. The urgency of these actions cannot be overstated in the fight against financial crime.

Improving Internal Controls and Risk Management

Danske Bank should consider reinforcing its internal controls and risk management processes. These help to spot and mitigate potential money laundering risks. Methods include deploying advanced technologies, such as analytics, to identify and analyze suspicious transactions. However, the bank also must strengthen its governance and compliance processes. These clarify lines of responsibility and accountability for the AML program. They also bolster the bank's compliance function, enabling it to identify and investigate potential money laundering.

Collaboration with Regulators and Law Enforcement

Collaborating with regulators and law enforcement is crucial, necessary, and urgent for Danske Bank. This demonstrates full cooperation with ongoing investigations. The bank is required to be transparent with regulators and take tangible steps to address the concerns that arise during the investigation.

The Danske Bank case is essential for understanding the significance of an anti-money laundering perspective. It is widely regarded as essential in the financial services sector. The bank's sincere efforts to recognize and prohibit money laundering were unsuccessful. This case has triggered substantial economic losses and irreparable damage to the bank's brand reputation. Danske Bank must implement pragmatic measures to prevent a recurrence of this situation. Various measures are crucial, such as adopting stringent anti-money laundering measures, maintaining up-to-date customer data, and maintaining communication with regulators.

Chapter Summary

KYC and CFT processes are essential for financial institutions to verify their customers' identities. This is all the more important for curbing money laundering and the financing of terrorism.

KYC is a broader process, whereas CFT is more defined. Financial institutions must undertake CDD transaction monitoring seriously. It must use risk-based methods to determine and comply with legal and regulatory responsibilities. The institution must also report and take action against suspicious activity to the appropriate authorities. Understanding KYCC and using RFIs are equally crucial in combating TBML.

End of Chapter: Discussion Questions

1. What is the difference between KYC and CFT processes?
2. Why are KYC and CFT important for financial institutions?
3. What are the legal and regulatory requirements for preventing money laundering and terrorist financing?
4. What is CDD, and how does it help with KYC and CFT?
5. How does transaction monitoring help prevent money laundering and terrorist financing?
6. What is the role of risk management in KYC and CFT?
7. Why is it essential for financial institutions to report suspicious activities?
8. Can you explain the purpose of KYCC in preventing TBML?
9. How can RFIs help combat TBML?
10. How can financial institutions comply with KYC and CFT requirements?

Bibliography

Abdel-Qader, A. (2018, September 21). *Finnish regulator probes local Ties to Danske's money-laundering case.* Finance Magnates. Retrieved from https://www.financemagnates.com/institutional-forex/regulation/finnish-regulator-probes-local-ties-to-danskes-money-laundering-case/

Barclays. (n.d.). Importance of KYC. Retrieved from https://www.barclays.in/content/dam/barclays-in/documents/download-forms/kyc/Importance_of_KYC.pdf

ComplyAdvantage. (2024). What is customer due diligence (CDD)? Retrieved from https://comply-advantage.com/

Consultative Group to Assist the Poor (CGAP). (2009). AML/CFT: Strengthening financial inclusion and integrity. Retrieved from https://www.cgap.org/sites/default/files/CGAP-Focus-Note-AML-CFT-Strengthening-Financial-Inclusion-and-Integrity-Oct-2009.pdf

Danske Bank. (2018, September). *Report on the non-resident portfolio at Danske Bank's Estonian branch.* Bruun & Hjejle. Retrieved from https://danskebank.com/-/media/danske-bank-com/file-cloud/2018/9/report-on-the-non-resident-portfolio-at-danske-banks-estonian-branch.pdf

Federal Reserve Bank of New York. (2016). Statement on the Cyber Attack against the Central Bank of Bangladesh. Retrieved from https://www.newyorkfed.org/newsevents/news/banking/2016/an160310

Financial Action Task Force (FATF). (2012). International standards on combating money laundering and the financing of terrorism & proliferation. Retrieved from https://www.fatf-gafi.org/media/fatf/documents/recommendations/pdfs/FATF%20Recommendations%202012.pdf

Financial Action Task Force (FATF). (2018). Anti-money laundering and counter-terrorist financing measures - Pakistan. Retrieved from https://www.fatf-gafi.org/media/fatf/documents/reports/mer-fsrb/APG-Mutual-Evaluation-Report-Pakistan-2019.pdf

Financial Action Task Force. (2021). Guidance on the risk-based approach to KYC and CFT. https://www.fatf-gafi.org/publications/fatfrecommendations/documents/rba-guidance.html.

Financial Action Task Force. (2023). Guidance on digital transformation of AML/CFT systems. Paris: FATF. Retrieved from https://www.fatf-gafi.org/en/publications/Methodsandtrends/Trade-based-money-laundering-trends-and-developments.html

Financial Conduct Authority. (2023, January 11). *FCA penalizes Al Rayan Bank PLC for anti-money laundering failures.* Press Releases. https://www.fca.org.uk/news/press-releases/fca-penalises-al-rayan-bank-plc-anti-money-laundering-failures

Financial Conduct Authority. (2023, January 11). *Final notice: Al Rayan Bank PLC (Reference No. 229148).* Enforcement Division. Retrieved from https://www.fca.org.uk/publication/final-notices/al-rayan-bank-plc-2023.pdf

Financial Conduct Authority. (2023). Risk-based approach guidance for the banking sector. Retrieved from https://www.fatf-gafi.org/en/publications/Risk-based-approach/Risk-based-approach-guidance-banking-sector.html.

Financial Times. (2014, July 1). BNP Paribas agrees to an $8.9 billion settlement over sanctions violations. Retrieved from https://www.ft.com/content/bnp-paribas-settlement.

Indian Institute of Banking & Finance (IIBF). (2019). Master Circular on Know Your Customer (KYC) norms/Anti-Money Laundering (AML) standards/Combating Financing of Terrorism (CFT)/Obligation of banks and financial institutions under Prevention of Money Laundering Act (PMLA), 2002. Retrieved from https://www.iibf.org.in/documents/kyc-aml-cft-pmla.pdf

International Monetary Fund. (2023). Anti-Money Laundering/Combating the Financing of Terrorism (AML/CFT) - Topics. Retrieved from https://www.imf.org/external/np/leg/amlcft/eng/aml1.htm

Jumio. (2024). What Does CDD (Customer Due Diligence) Mean for Banks and Financial Companies? Retrieved from https://www.jumio.com/use-case/kyc-aml-compliance/

New York Times. (2013, November 19). JPMorgan Chase to Pay $1.7 Billion in Settlement Over Madoff. Retrieved from https://www.nytimes.com/2013/11/20/business/jpmorgan-chase-settlement.html

PricewaterhouseCoopers (PwC). (2016). Know Your Customer: Quick Reference Guide. Retrieved from https://www.pwc.com/gx/en/financial-services/publications/assets/pwc-anti-money-laundering-2016.pdf

SWIFT. (2024). What is Customer Due Diligence (CDD)? Retrieved from https://www.swift.com/your-needs/financial-crime-cyber-security/know-your-customer-kyc

U.S. Department of Justice. (2012, December 12). *Historic settlement with HSBC Bank leads to nearly $2 billion in forfeitures & penalties.* https://www.justice.gov/archive/usao/wvn/news/2012/december/hsbc.html

U.S. Department of Justice. (2012, December 11). HSBC Holdings Plc. and HSBC Bank USA N.A. Admit to Anti-Money Laundering and Sanctions Violations, Forfeit $1.256 Billion in Deferred Prosecution Agreement. Retrieved from https://www.justice.gov/opa/pr/hsbc-holdings-plc-and-hsbc-bank-usa-na-admit-anti-money-laundering-and-sanctions-violations

U.S. Department of Justice. (2012, December 11). *HSBC Holdings Plc. and HSBC Bank USA N.A. admit to anti-money-laundering and sanctions violations and forfeit $1.256 billion under a deferred prosecution agreement.* Office of Public Affairs. Retrieved from https://www.justice.gov/archives/opa/pr/hsbc-holdings-plc-and-hsbc-bank-usa-na-admit-anti-money-laundering-and-sanctions-violations

U.S. Department of Justice, Office of Public Affairs. (2022, December 13). Danske Bank pleads guilty to fraud on U.S. banks in a multi-billion-dollar scheme to access the U.S. financial system [Press release]. https://www.justice.gov/archives/opa/pr/danske-bank-pleads-guilty-fraud-us-banks-multi-billion-dollar-scheme-access-us-financial

U.S. Department of the Treasury. (2012, December 10). *Treasury department announces $227 million settlement with Standard Chartered Bank for sanctions violations.* U.S. Treasury Press Center. https://home.treasury.gov/news/press-releases/tg1791

U.S. Securities and Exchange Commission. (2023). Know Your Client (KYC): What It Means and Compliance Requirements

Willkie Farr & Gallagher LLP. (2023, January 11). *FCA imposes £4 million penalty on Al Rayan Bank for inadequate AML safeguards.* Willkie Compliance Concourse. https://complianceconcourse.willkie.com/articles/news-alerts-2023-01-january-20230111-fca-imposes-4-million-penalty-on/

Additional Learning Resources

Books

1 "Combating Money Laundering and Terrorist Financing: A Comprehensive Guide to Compliance" by Peter Lilley (2016)
This book provides a comprehensive guide to understanding and implementing effective measures for combating money laundering and terrorist financing in the banking industry.

2 "Anti-Money Laundering and Counter-Terrorist Financing" by Mark Pieth and Gemma Aiolfi (2014)
This book explores global efforts to combat money laundering and terrorist financing, offering insights into regulatory frameworks, best practices, and the challenges faced by the banking industry.

Articles

3 Know Your Customer: Quick Reference Guide. (2016). https://www.pwc.com/gx/en/financial-services/publications/assets/pwc-anti-money-laundering-2016.pdf
This quick-reference guide by PwC provides an overview of the importance of KYC in the banking industry, highlighting global differences and the guide's contents.
4 Schott, P. A. (2006). *Reference guide to anti-money laundering and combating the financing of terrorism (2nd ed. and supplement on Special Recommendation IX)*. The World Bank and the International Monetary Fund. Retrieved from https://documents1.worldbank.org/curated/en/558401468134391014/pdf/350520Referenc1Money01OFFICIAL0USE1.pdf
This reference guide from the World Bank provides insights into anti-money laundering and the financing of terrorism, including the importance of understanding customers' relationships with other borrowers.

Websites

5 International Monetary Fund (IMF) - Anti-Money Laundering/Combating the Financing of Terrorism (AML/CFT) (2023). Imf.org. https://www.imf.org/external/np/leg/amlcft/eng/aml1.htm
The IMF provides resources and information on the economic consequences of money laundering and the financing of terrorism.
6 FDIC | Banker Resource Center: Anti-Money Laundering/Countering the Financing of Terrorism (AML/CFT). (2023). Fdic.gov. https://www.fdic.gov/resources/bankers/aml-cft/
The FDIC provides information and resources on AML/CFT to promote financial transparency and deter misuse of the financial system.

18 Understanding Financial Intelligence Reports about Trade-Based Money Laundering

Trade-based money laundering (TBML) has been recognized as a profound challenge to the integrity and viability of the global financial system. Practical and robust mechanisms are required to detect and disrupt unlawful activities. Among these, the financial intelligence reports (FIRs) play a central role. According to Cohen (2016), who served as Under Secretary for Terrorism and Financial Intelligence at the U.S. Department of the Treasury, combating TBML requires a global collaboration. It still requires a joint effort by financial institutions and law enforcement agencies to monitor international trade transactions, analyze behavioral patterns, and uncover complex money laundering schemes. To successfully communicate high-level financial intelligence, three components are required: sustained enhancement of analytical capabilities, closer international relationships, and continuous evolution of all three essential elements to combat this crime. (see, for example, FATF, 2020).

This chapter provides a comprehensive overview of FIRs on TBML, including their definitions, analyses, interpretations, and formats.

FIRs are flexible and versatile reports. They can be viewed and used from various perspectives, including those of academics, practitioners, policymakers, bankers, and analysts.

From an academic perspective, FIRs are analytical reports that provide intelligence on transactions and activities potentially related to money laundering, terrorist financing, funding, and other illegal financial activities (Shazeeda, 2020). These reports are produced after extensive scrutiny of the economic data and information to provide intelligence on the possible nature and scope of financial crime and any current methodologies for preventing and detecting these crimes (Shazeeda, 2020).

FIRs are valuable tools for practitioners, such as Financial Intelligence Units (FIUs) and law enforcement, to detect, investigate, and disrupt the flow of illegally generated funds. They provide practitioners with the information and support to take explicit action, and, more notably, to act against financial crime. They represent practitioners' hope and confidence in combating money laundering and terrorist financing (FATF 2020).

From a policymaker's perspective, FIRs are not simply reports; they are important sources of information for developing and refining anti-money laundering and counter-terrorist financing (AML/CFT) policies and regulations (FATF 2020).

From the perspective of bankers and other financial institutions, FIRs are regarded as invaluable resources. They are meant to enhance the applications of AML/CFT compliance programs. They can uncover and flag suspicious transactions through these reports. It demonstrates a proactive approach and an unwavering commitment to combating financial crime (ACAMS 2022). The industry may further reassure the audience by analyzing FIRs to evaluate the effectiveness of AML/CFT initiatives within the financial sector and with regulatory bodies. It also helps to investigate any emerging trends in financial crimes (ACAMS, 2022).

DOI: 10.4324/9781003477631-19

By exploring deeper into the multifaceted values of FIRs, we may gain a comprehensive insight into their indispensable role in combating financial crime:

Academic Insights

For academics, FIRs are not just dusty forms of paperwork, more specifically reports, but a treasure trove of data for research on money laundering and terrorist financing. These reports offer a rich source of information (2023). By analyzing. These reports enable researchers to identify emerging trends and typologies in illegal financial activity:

- Identify emerging trends and typologies in illicit financial activity (Egmont Group, 2023).
- Critically evaluate the effectiveness of existing AML/CFT regulations and compliance frameworks (FATF, 2023).
- Formulate and evaluate new strategies for preventing, detecting, and investigating financial crimes (Levi, 2017).

Practitioner's Perspective

From the practitioner's perspective, financial institutions and investigators rely on FIRs as a critical tool for identifying and investigating suspicious activity (Egmont Group, 2023). These reports will assist the financial investigators in:

- Discovering patterns and red flags that might reveal money laundering or terrorist financing (Wolters Kluwer, 2023).
- Filing Suspicious Activity Reports (SARs) to alert authorities about potential financial crimes (Egmont Group, 2023).
- Launching targeted investigations based on the intelligence gleaned from FIRs (UNODC, 2023).

FIRs are based upon a sound foundation. The solid support it confers to financial institutions and law enforcement agencies. The reports contain both information and analysis regarding potential money laundering or terrorist financing activities, without losing sight of their vital role in combating illicit finance. The benefits of financial intelligence, often derived from Bank Secrecy Act (BSA) reporting control, which Financial Crimes Enforcement Network (FinCEN) oversees, should not be underestimated (FBI, 2018). While these reports often rely on STRs submitted by financial institutions, they have undergone rigorous analysis by a specialized unit or a government-agency-developed FIU. FinCEN supports BSA and regulatory functions, as well as law enforcement and interagency collaboration on domestic and international financial crime (Terrorism & Financial Intelligence, 2020).

Constructing a profile of a financial criminal will involve understanding the criminal's modus operandi. Developing an adequate approach will help avert further crimes. This process, in which you serve as a pivot, will involve collecting and analyzing data from various sources, such as financial transactions, communication records, and other relevant information. By recognizing the behavioral patterns of financial criminals, law enforcement and regulatory bodies will design strategies to combat financial crime (Shazeeda, 2020). FIRs are the first steps, a crucial weapon; thereafter, they bring in crucial tools to investigate and disrupt financial crimes. They provide key documents in the fight against money laundering and terrorist financing. Your dedicated work with FIRs is instrumental in this fight.

Underscoring the urgency and significance of our collective efforts. Policymakers and Regulators:

Policymakers and regulatory bodies, as the driving force behind change, utilize FIRs to evaluate the strengths and weaknesses of existing AML/CFT frameworks (FATF, 2023). This information allows them to:

- Identify areas requiring regulatory reform or improvement (UNODC, 2023).
- Develop targeted AML/CFT policies that address emerging threats and vulnerabilities (FATF, 2023).
- Monitor the effectiveness of implemented regulations and adapt them as needed (Egmont Group, 2023).

One thing policymakers need to understand about FIRs is that they must be used to detect and prevent financial crimes. In this way, FIRs constitute a source of knowledge that may be beneficial for combating money laundering and terrorist financing. They also help shape policy and the legislative environment.

Financial Institution's Perspective

Those working in financial institutions and banks might refer to FIRs as a means of satisfying the regulatory standards. FIRs help the bank easily identify its customers and their reputational risks (Know Your Customer: Quick Reference Guide, 2016). However, the bank can still use FIRs to meet legal compliance requirements and fulfill its ethical commitment to prevent money laundering. Similarly, they can detect any money laundering or terrorist financing threats identified by FIRs and develop a response plan accordingly.

Analyst's Perspective

Analysts consider FIRs an information resource that can be employed for many tasks, such as evaluating and understanding the nature of financial crimes and detecting and prosecuting criminals. They help understand emerging trends and patterns (Shazeeda, 2020). The authors mentioned above also indicate that analysts can apply the latter to evaluate the risk level and the movement of funds associated with illegal activities. This process also shapes the path for strategic and tactical decisions and resource allocation.

The outcome of this discussion is that FIRs are critical in detecting and mitigating financial crime. FIRs provide practical intelligence that informs policymakers, bankers, analysts, and academics. The main spheres are policy development, risk management, research, and verification of the financial system, coupled with the financial system's productivity and creativity. It helps in protecting the integrity and viability of the financial system. The elements of practical intelligence in FIRs present a sense of empowerment to the audience to perform their respective roles in combating financial crime. FIRs are crafted and collated with the highest level of rigor through sophisticated economic analysis techniques, such as data mining, pattern analysis, and risk profiles.

Analysis and Interpretation of Financial Intelligence Reports

FIRs are a vital source for detecting and disrupting TBML activities (FATF, 2020). When analyzing FIRs, analysts closely examine suspicious financial transactions that exhibit characteristics commonly associated with TBML, such as over- or under-invoicing, round-tripping, and mismatched trade descriptions (UNODC, 2022). To interpret FIRs, it is essential to understand the nature of the transactions, the parties involved, and their associated risks and exposures (Egmont Group, 2021).

Moreover, financial institutions and compliant professionals employ FIRs as an effective tool to support their TBML identification and prevention efforts (ACAMS, 2023). FIRs provide an additional layer of insight, enabling entities to gain a deeper understanding of trade finance customers and transactions and to enhance customer due diligence, transaction monitoring, and suspicious activity reporting (ACAMS, 2023). Embedding financial intelligence within an institution's AML/CFT framework is a strategic measure to enhance the detection and mitigation of TBML (FATF, as highlighted in 2020).

The Crucial Role of Financial Intelligence Reports in the Fight Against TBML

FIRs are helpful tools for analysis and interpretation. AML experts, law enforcement agencies, and regulatory bodies often create them. They recognize and analyze suspicious and nuanced monetary transactions. They also help investigate financial crimes, such as money laundering and terrorist financing, with a primary focus on TBML. FIRs are a universal source of valuable TBML intelligence based on trade data. As a result, they almost always provide implicit details that reveal patterns and meaningful relationships. It may also identify suspicious practices, such as over-invoicing, under-invoicing, or misclassification of goods.

The primary objective of FIRs is to assist stakeholders in informed decision-making in the fight against financial crime. FIRs provide AML experts, law enforcement, and regulators with the information necessary to evaluate transactions and associated risks involving individuals or entities. By reviewing financial data and transaction patterns, FIRs are designed to recognize potential criminal activity. They also provide evidence to support investigations and the prosecution of financial crimes, thereby tangibly supporting each stakeholder in their decisions.

FIRs accomplish their purpose by leveraging sophisticated analytical tools and techniques. It embodies various methods, including data mining, pattern recognition, and predictive analytics. The multiple tools enable AML analysts and law enforcement to quickly sift through enormous amounts of financial data. This helps identify patterns and relationships in suspicious activity that would otherwise remain undiscovered.

Importance of Intelligence in FIRs

The significance of intelligence in FIRs lies in its ability to uncover and provide insights into complex financial crimes. If not adequately addressed, that might otherwise go undetected for a long time. Intelligence can offer law enforcement an array of insights, perspectives, and backgrounds into complex financial crimes, including:

- The identity of the perpetrators (FBI, 2018, p. 3).
- The perpetrators' modus operandi (Terrorism & Financial Intelligence, 2020, p. 5).
- The financial networks utilized by the perpetrators (FinCEN: AMLA Implementation and Beyond, 2022, p. 7).
- The assets acquired through criminal activity (Shazeeda, 2020, p. 9).

In addition to focusing on insights, perspectives, and backgrounds into complex financial crimes, intelligence can also be applied to:

- Prohibit financial crimes from happening in the first place (Shazeeda, 2020, p. 11).
- Uncover and disrupt criminal networks (Schott, 2004, p. 13).
- Recover stolen assets (Brun et al., 2021, p. 7).
- Hold criminals accountable for their crimes (Brun et al., 2021, p. 8).

Reviewing financial records may expose covert links or relationships among people, groups, and transactions. It can also provide an overall picture of a criminal network and the means and methods it employs. In turn, this overall picture reveals stakeholders with the knowledge and capabilities to address financial criminal activity. FIRs are employed strategically by AML professionals, law enforcement, and regulatory bodies to evaluate risks linked with specific financial transactions, persons, or entities. The intelligence contained in FIRs can help identify potential criminal activity and assist in investigating and prosecuting economic crimes.

Intelligence is key to understanding how financial criminals operate and conceal their actions and intentions. FIRs can demonstrate the frequency of suspicious behaviors that may not be immediately evident, such as repeated references to shell companies, known associates, personal identities, and their shared risk profiles, or the consistently complex structure of funds and transactions.

FIRs eventually provide the requisite insight to perpetrators' associates, enabling them to determine their own associated risk and develop an appropriate response. Importantly, FIRs safeguard the integrity of the legal system and uphold the rule of law by disrupting the activities of financial criminals. Ultimately, timely FIR action protects economic systems, examples of abuse, and the affected communities.

The following are the significant sections discussed in the FIRs:

I Background Information
II Methodology
III Case Studies
IV Risk Assessment
V Recommendations

These sections present a comprehensive overview of the essential components that must be included in the FIRs to analyze and combat TBML effectively.

Essential Components of FIRs

Background Information: Renders an introduction to financial crime and its impact on the global economy. It will confirm the regulatory framework and international standards for combating financial crimes.

Methodology: This section outlines the analytical techniques used to detect financial crimes, covering transaction monitoring, network analysis, and entity profiling. It also lists some of the data sources employed to analyze transactional financial data, such as bank statements, wire transfers, and public records.

Case Studies: This section presents real-life financial crime cases and describes how they were detected and investigated. This will assist AML experts in understanding the mechanisms of economic crime and the red flags to recognize the issue.

Risk Assessment: Analyzes risk variables within a specific region, sector, or country. It takes into account variables such as the size and value of financial transactions, the variety of financial products, corruption levels, and the enforcement of regulatory policy.

Recommendations: Furnish actionable recommendations to AML practitioners, policymakers, and regulators on how they can better counter financial crime, including updating their transaction monitoring systems, facilitating interagency collaboration, and supporting public-private partnerships.

Limitations of FIRs

One key limitation of FIRs is that they are always constrained by the data available at the time of analysis (FATF, 2022). Financial crimes are often complicated and continually evolving. Hence, it may not be possible to include all relevant information in one report (UNODC, 2023). During economic crime investigations, FIRs may also be constrained by data quality and accessibility, which can vary across jurisdictions and even within financial institutions (Egmont Group, 2021).

Moreover, FIRs cannot always convey a complete picture of the overall scope and scale of financial crime. Criminals employ various ways to obfuscate their activities, including multi-layered financial structures, cross-border transactions, and emerging technologies (FATF, 2022). These factors can make it challenging for analysts to uncover and understand all illicit flows solely from the content of FIRs (UNODC, 2023).

Another limitation is that FIRs tend to be retrospective, focusing on transactions, events, and activities that occurred in the past (Egmont Group, 2021). This complicates stakeholders' ability to proactively find and respond to emerging threats and vulnerabilities in the financial system. However, FIRs can prepare stakeholders to deal with emerging threats (2022). To address this issue, some jurisdictions are exploring the use of predictive analytics to enhance their efforts. They conduct ongoing monitoring to enhance the timeliness and forward-looking nature of financial intelligence (ACAMS, 2023).

In addition, the effectiveness of FIRs may likewise be constrained by the capacity and resources of agencies and institutions that generate and act upon this intelligence (UNODC, 2023). The lack of training, technology, and coordination among actors could limit the effectiveness and utility of FIRs (Egmont Group, 2021).

Despite the above limitations, FIRs remain a useful and informative source. They are inevitably an essential component of the fight against financial crimes. FIRs typically provide critical information and intelligence for a range of stakeholders (FATF, 2022). Continual efforts are needed to mitigate these limitations and enhance the quality, timeliness, and usefulness of FIRs. Thus, an effective global response to money laundering, terrorist financing, and other illicit financial flows can be achieved both individually and collectively (ACAMS, 2023).

How FIRs Fulfill the Purpose

FIRs provide actionable intelligence on potential financial crimes, including money laundering and terrorist financing. They fulfill this objective by employing analytical methods and data sources to identify red flags and plausible patterns indicative of potential criminal activity. The recommendations presented in FIRs help strengthen AML efforts and obfuscate financial crimes.

Choosing the Right Format for Effective Reporting

FIRs, also known as SARs, are crucial tools in combating money laundering. SARs must be compliant with applicable laws and regulations. The format of SARs varies by jurisdiction. Hence, it is essential to obtain validation from the appropriate authorities that your SAR complies with the law. Money laundering has become increasingly sophisticated; financial institutions, law enforcement agencies, and regulators must have accurate and timely information to address the problem.

Structured and Unstructured Formats

There are two primary, fundamentally different formats of financial intelligence reporting—structured and unstructured. The structured format is often based on standardized templates and codes, such as the FATF guidelines for reporting suspicious transactions. In contrast, the unstructured report relies on narrative reporting and typically provides a detailed description of suspicious transactions by financial institutions. Both formats have advantages and disadvantages, and the format used will depend on the organization or agency producing the report.

Models of Financial Intelligence Reports

The second dimension is that financial intelligence reporting formats vary. One of these models is the SAR model, which dominates in America. Other parts of the world have the STR model, which is pretty much the same. Both models provide a uniform framework that financial institutions would adopt when reporting suspicious activities. Hence, this ensures the same accuracy and consistency in the reporting.

Choosing the Right Format

Selecting among the available formats is crucial for FIRs. For this reason, it ensures their effectiveness. For example, in narrative reports, the most comprehensive form provides the most comprehensive analysis of the financial activities under investigation. Statistical reports, by contrast, primarily analyze quantitative data to identify trends in financial transactions. Visual reports, such as graphs or figures, can help present complex financial data in a more digestible format.

To conclude, FIRs are valuable in combating money laundering. Hence, amending suspicious transactions in the relevant formats and models would prove crucial to their effectiveness. As criminal activities become increasingly sophisticated, the timing and precision of information are critical to thwarting money laundering. Thus, the appropriate structure and model for FIRs could enable financial institutions, law enforcement agencies, and regulatory organizations to combat money laundering effectively.

Structure of Financial Intelligence Reports

The format of FIRs may vary depending on the target audience and purpose. However, some common elements should be encompassed in every report, such as:

Title page: The title page should include the report's name, date, author(s), and the organization's logo or name.

Table of Contents: A table helps readers quickly navigate the report.

Executive summary: The executive summary concisely overviews the report's key findings, conclusions, and recommendations.

Introduction: The introduction should provide a background on the issue being addressed in the report.

Main body: Present the report's findings and analysis. This section should be well-organized, with clear headings and subheadings.

Conclusion: The conclusion should summarize the report's findings and recommend future actions.

Appendices: The appendices may include additional data or supporting documents.

Guiding Principles for Effective Writing

FIRs are enhanced and made more evidence-based by these guiding principles when addressing suspected money laundering activities. Some of them are:

Clarity and Concise: Reports should be unambiguous and concise, with all relevant information presented logically and organized. Extraneous information should be avoided.

Timeliness: Reports should be prepared and submitted on time to enable early identification and remediation of potential money laundering activities.

Objectivity: Reports must be objective and should be free from bias. Finally, any information contained in reports must be supported by evidence.

Relevance: Reports should be concise and focused on direct relationships to potential money laundering, without embodying any speculation or conjecture.

Confidentiality: Reports should be kept confidential and shared only with appropriate detailing of persons or authorities.

Financial Intelligence Reports in Money Laundering Detection

Financial intelligence reports help overwhelmingly in exposing and disrupting successful money laundering operations. By informing the public and authorities about suspicious financial activities, such reports form the backbone of efforts to maintain the integrity of the economic system.

The Russian Laundromat Case

The Russian Laundromat is an exemplary case of financial intelligence being applied in practice. Between 2010 and 2014, it laundered 20.8 billion dollars through a network of shell companies. This complex scheme involved routing funds through various jurisdictions to obscure their origins and facilitate their integration into the legitimate financial system (Hylén, 2021).

The Role of the Financial Intelligence Unit of Moldova

Moldova's FIU performed a critical role in uncovering this underground network. While identifying suspicious behavior and analyzing patterns associated with money laundering, the FIU played a crucial role in providing data to other regulatory bodies. The resulting relationship and information exchanges led to the eventual shutdown of the network, demonstrating that international collaboration in combating financial crimes is indispensable (Panevski et al., 2021).

Recent Developments

Over the last few years, technological advancements have further boosted the capabilities of FIUs. The use of artificial intelligence and machine learning has not only facilitated more sophisticated data analysis but has also enabled more accurate detection and swifter resolution of money laundering crimes. These technological innovations are significant deterrents to global financial crime (Mahalakshmi et al., 2022).

Case 18.1 Recovering Funds from Corruption in Malaysia's 1MDB Sovereign Wealth Fund

The United States Department of Justice (DOJ) has taken significant steps to recover more than $1 billion in funds obtained through corruption. This was about Malaysia's sovereign wealth fund, 1Malaysia Development Berhad (1MDB). In a July 2016 statement, the DOJ first announced its intention to follow up and take action regarding these misappropriated assets (DOJ, 2016).

The FinCEN of the United States is a rockstar in this entire effort, releasing reports that revealed the identities of transactions and commonalities among the money laundering schemes connected to 1MDB. This prompted inquiries by the relevant countries' regulatory bodies, which, in turn, led to criminal charges against those involved in the corruption network (Chin, 2016).

The DOJ's Kleptocracy Asset Recovery Initiative was launched in 2010 to help facilitate these recovery and reclamation operations. The initiative partners with several Federal law enforcement agencies. It included the FBI, the IRS, and the Department of Homeland Security in the recovery of funds stolen by corrupt foreign officials (Congressional Research Service, 2016).

In the case involving 1Malaysia Development Bhd (1MDB), the DOJ was attempting to recover a wide array of assets. The loot included residential and commercial real estate, a private jet, art, and even the rights to the Hollywood movie *The Wolf of Wall Street*. To establish federal jurisdiction and trace the root of the misappropriated funds, the department is using records provided by multiple U.S. and foreign financial institutions (DOJ, 2020). These undertakings to stem cross-border corruption and recover stolen assets line up with the stated public international law policies of the United States. To keep its unflinching commitment to the United Nations Convention Against Corruption, of which it is a state party.

The following is a sample format of an FIR:
Report Identification
Report number
Date of report
Author of the report
FIU or other reporting entity
Subject of Report
Name of individual or entity under investigation
Description of suspicious activity

Background

Relevant background information, such as the individual's or entity's financial history, business activities, and relationships

Suspicious Activity

A detailed description of the suspicious activity, including the date, time, amount, and method of payment

Assessment

The author's assessment of the suspicious activity, including whether it is likely to be related to money laundering, terrorist financing, or other financial crimes

Recommendations

Any recommendations for further action, such as additional investigation or reporting to the law enforcement.

Below is an illustration of an actual FIR:
Report Number: 2023–07–13-001
Date of Report: 2023–07–13
Author of Report: John Smith
FIU: Financial Intelligence Unit of the United States
The subject of the Report: John Doe

Background: John Doe is a 45-year-old male who lives in New York City. He is a self-employed financial consultant.

Suspicious Activity: On July 12, 2023, John Doe deposited $100,000 in cash into his bank account in a single transaction. John Doe did not furnish any documentation to support the source of the funds.

Assessment: The deposit of $100,000 in cash into John Doe's bank account is suspicious because it is a large sum of cash, and John Doe has not provided any documentation to substantiate the source of the funds. This activity is consistent with money laundering.

Recommendations: The FIU recommends that law enforcement investigate John Doe to determine the source of the funds and whether he is engaged in money laundering.

Note: *The format and content of financial intelligence reports may vary by jurisdiction and reporting entity. However, the above format is a general guideline applicable to most reports.*

To recap the core points, intelligence reports can be crucial tools for discovering suspected instances of money laundering. They help, even disrupting the flow of illicit funds. By adhering to the principles of clarity, timeliness, objectivity, relevance, and confidentiality, financial institutions and regulators can develop reports that provide sound evidence in combating money laundering.

An Insight: The National Defense Authorization Act: A Critical Tool in U.S. Defense Policy

Purpose and Role

The National Defense Authorization Act (NDAA) is a notable piece of legislative action. The United States Congress passed this annual Act. The legislation establishes budget allocations and policies for national security and defense operations (Investopedia, 2022). The NDAA establishes policies and priorities for the Department of Defense and is considered one of the most crucial pieces of legislation for enhancing the United States' national security.

Jurisdiction

The NDAA authorizes a broad range of national security matters, including defense appropriations, military personnel, weapons systems, and national security policy (Morrison & Foerster, 2022). It is one of the exclusive "must-pass" bills that Congress considers every year. To pass it, it is frequently attached as an amendment to unrelated legislation.

Current Status

The House of Representatives approved H.R. 7900, the FY NDAA, on July 13, 2024. This bill is estimated to cost $923.3 billion for national defense in the next fiscal year (U.S. Senate Armed

Services Committee, 2024). The Senate is expected to proceed with the NDAA by considering S. 4543 in the coming weeks.

Impact on TBML/AML

The NDAA is a legislative act that can have an immense impact on trade-based and AML initiatives. The House, in the FY 2023 NDAA, passed an amendment, commonly known as the ENABLERS Act. This would regulate lawyers as "financial institutions" under the BSA (Commercial UAV News, 2023). If the amendment is a critical part of the final draft of the NDAA. Then, the lawyers are legally obligated to disclose private and other sensitive customer information to the government. This would necessitate extensive obligations for suspicious activity reporting, due diligence, AML, BSA account identification, and validation. The American Bar Association has expressed profound concerns that such provisions could potentially compromise the attorney-client privilege and confidentiality. This would considerably affect the relationship and deter clients from consulting with attorneys. The ABA has urged Congress not to include the provisions of the ENABLERS Act in the final NDAA bill.

The NDAA has also substantially affected the United States' jurisdiction. It delegated legal authority to the Department of Defense to perform various tasks. These consist of the detention and questioning of suspected terrorists, military commissions, and the use of force against foreign countries and terrorist organizations. The NDAA has at times been controversial, particularly its provisions regarding civil liberties and human rights.

Lately, the NDAA has been engaged in various aspects of AML and countering the financing of terrorism. One of these is the 2021 NDAA, which reinforces provisions against money laundering. The bill also obligates businesses to reveal the identities of their beneficial owners. Some threats and vulnerabilities are intricate and have multiple contributing aspects, making them difficult to counter. This is a necessary component of a larger plan. It invariably underscores the requirement to stem terrorism and curb money laundering.

The NDAA is a primary piece of legislation that tremendously affects the U.S. Department of Defense's funding, policy-making, and activities. It has jurisdictional and global breadth. NDAA and its corresponding provisions possess far-reaching implications for national security and defense policy. The NDAA appropriated funds for military operations, military construction, and defense activities involving the Department of Energy. It prescribes military personnel strengths for each fiscal year. Its AML and terror financing provisions are tied to the growing recognition of the role of financial intelligence in national security tasks.

Chapter Summary

The FIRs are crucial evidence for regulatory bodies conducting TBML investigations. It is through FIRs that law enforcement officers obtain intelligence that can be used at various stages of the investigation and to identify TBML, or at the very least, to curb the problem.

FIRs are characterized by the presence of at least five elements: a definition of the TBML phenomenon, identification of different risks, and investigative leads. Even in practice, the appropriate choice of form will benefit the FIRs. The presentation and the use of words in the document must have specific characteristics, such as simplicity, and it must be easy to read, understand, and concise.

End of Chapter: Discussion Questions

1 How can FIRs assist in detecting and combating TBML?
2 What are the essential components of FIRs, and how do they contribute to the effectiveness of FIRs?

3. How can the limitations of FIRs be addressed to enhance their effectiveness in detecting TBML?
4. What are the guiding principles for effectively writing FIRs?
5. How can law enforcement agencies choose the correct format for FIRs to ensure adequate reporting and maximum impact in detecting TBML?

References

ACAMS. (2017). *Using data analytics to identify AML risk.* Acams.Org. Association of Certified Anti-Money Laundering Specialists. Retrieved from https://www.acams.org/en/opinion/using-data-analytics-to-identify-aml-risk?

ACAMS. (2022). *Moving from a compliance-driven to an intelligence-led approach to anti-money laundering and countering the financing of terrorism.* ACAMS Thought Leadership Papers. https://www.fdic.gov/media/166131

Ali, S. A. (2021). Criminal minds: Profiling architects of financial crimes. *Journal of Financial Crime*, 28(2), 324–344. https://doi.org/10.1108/jfc-11-2020-0221 https://www.semanticscholar.org/paper/Criminal-minds%3A-profiling-architects-of-financial-Ali/45d95c0abbc0694c93776f97e0204ac98b37aeb1

Basel Institute on Governance. (2024). *The Basel AML Index: Assessing global money laundering and terrorist financing risks.* https://baselgovernance.org/basel-aml-index

Brun, J. P., Sotiropoulou, A., Gray, L., Scott, C., & Stephenson, K. (2021). *Asset recovery handbook: A guide for practitioners* (2nd ed.). World Bank. https://openknowledge.worldbank.org/server/api/core/bitstreams/a7946020-2a53-5441-8bea-c53db046f620/content

Chin, J. (2016). The 1MDB Scandal and the Role of Financial Intelligence Units. *Journal of Financial Crime*, 23(4), 789–805.

Commercial UAV News. (2023). The potential impact of the 2024 national defense authorization act on the commercial UAV industry. https://www.commercialuavnews.com/regulations/the-potential-impact-of-the-2024-national-defense-authorization-act-on-the-commercial-uav-industry.

Congressional Research Service. (2016, August 15). DOJ brings forfeiture action to seize and return $1 billion embezzled Malaysian government assets. https://sgp.fas.org/crs/misc/malaysian.pdf

Egmont Group. (2021). Egmont group strategic plan 2021–2025. https://egmontgroup.org/en/content/egmont-group-strategic-plan-2021-2025

Egmont Group. (2023). The Egmont group of financial intelligence units. https://egmontgroup.org/

FATF. (2020). Guidance on financial intelligence units. https://www.fatf-gafi.org/media/fatf/documents/reports/Guidance-Financial-Intelligence-Units.pdf

FATF. (2020). Trade-based money laundering. https://www.fatf-gafi.org/media/fatf/documents/reports/FATF-Trade-Based-Money-Laundering-Report.pdf

FATF. (2022). Opportunities and challenges of new technologies for AML/CFT. https://www.fatf-gafi.org/media/fatf/documents/reports/Opportunities-Challenges-of-New-Technologies-for-AML-CFT.pdf

FATF/Egmont Trade-based Money Laundering: Trends and Developments. (2023). Fatf-Gafi.Org. Retrieved from https://www.fatf-gafi.org/en/publications/Methodsandtrends/Trade-based-money-laundering-trends-and-developments.html

Federal Bureau of Investigation. (2018). Combating money laundering and other forms of illicit finance. https://www.fbi.gov/news/testimony/combating-money-laundering-and-other-forms-of-illicit-finance

Federal Financial Institutions Examination Council. (n.d.). *Bank Secrecy Act/Anti-Money Laundering examination manual.* FFIEC Infobase. https://bsaaml.ffiec.gov/docs/manual/01_Introduction/01.pdf

Financial Action Task Force. (2023). International standards on combating money laundering and the financing of terrorism & proliferation: The FATF recommendations. FATF/OECD. Retrieved from https://www.fatf-gafi.org/en/publications/Fatfrecommendations/Fatf-recommendations.html.

Financial Crimes Enforcement Network. (2022). The Financial Crimes Enforcement Network (FinCEN): Anti-Money Laundering Act of 2020 implementation and beyond. https://crsreports.congress.gov/product/pdf/R/R47255

Hylén, L. (2021). *Dark, Dirty, and Secret. A Qualitative Study on Russia's Financial Active Measures.*
Know Your Customer: Quick Reference Guide. (2016). https://www.pwc.com/gx/en/financial-services/publications/assets/pwc-anti-money-laundering-2016.pdf
Levi, M. (2017). Assessing the trends, scale, and nature of economic cybercrimes: Overview and issues. *Crime, Law and Social Change*, 67(1), 3–20. https://doi.org/10.1007/s10611-016-9645-3
Mahalakshmi, V., Kulkarni, N., Kumar, K. P., Kumar, K. S., Sree, D. N., & Durga, S. (2022). The role of artificial intelligence and machine learning in the financial services industry is to generate competitive intelligence. *Materials Today: Proceedings*, 56, 2252–2255.
Panevski, D., Peráček, T., & Rentková, K. (2021). Analysis of the practices of financial intelligence units (FIUs) and other anti-money laundering agencies within the EU. *Developments in Information & Knowledge Management for Business Applications: Volume*, 2, 241–269.
Schott, P. A. (2006). *Reference guide to anti-money laundering and combating the financing of terrorism* (2nd ed.). World Bank. Retrieved from https://openknowledge.worldbank.org/entities/publication/4547038a-d3e2-5b37-9448-f9960a6d841e
Shazeeda, A. (2020). Fighting financial crime: failure is not an option. *Journal of Financial Crime*, 27(1), 1–23. https://doi.org/10.1108/JFC-04-2019-0050
Terrorism and Financial Intelligence. (2020, June). U.S. Department of the Treasury. https://home.treasury.gov/about/offices/terrorism-and-financial-intelligence
The Egmont Group. (n.d.). *About the Egmont Group of Financial Intelligence Units.* Retrieved from https://egmontgroup.org/about/
United Nations Office on Drugs and Crime. (2022). The UNODC-WCO Container Control Programme: Disrupting illicit trade and transnational organized crime. https://www.unodc.org/unodc/en/drug-trafficking/container-control-programme.html
United Nations Office on Drugs and Crime. (2023). *The Global Program against Money Laundering, Proceeds of Crime and the Financing of Terrorism (GPML)*. United Nations. https://www.unodc.org/unodc/en/money-laundering/global-programme-against-money-laundering/.html
U.S. Department of Justice. (2020, July 1). The U.S. Seeks to Recover Approximately $96 Million Traceable to Funds Allegedly Misappropriated from Malaysian Sovereign Wealth Fund 1MDB. https://www.justice.gov/opa/pr/us-seeks-recover-approximately-96-million-traceable-funds-allegedly-misappropriated-malaysian
U.S. Department of Justice. (2016, July 20). The united states seeks to recover more than $1 billion obtained from corruption involving Malaysian sovereign wealth fund. https://www.justice.gov/opa/pr/united-states-seeks-recover-more-1-billion-obtained-corruption-involving-malaysian-sovereign
U.S. Senate Armed Services Committee. (2024). National defense authorization act executive summary. https://www.armed-services.senate.gov/imo/media/doc/fy25_ndaa_executive_summary.pdf.
Wolters Kluwer. (2023). *Financial crimes compliance solutions*. US Regulatory Consulting. https://www.wolterskluwer.com/en/solutions/us-regulatory-consulting/financial-crimes-compliance

Additional Learning Resources

Books

1 Money laundering and illicit financial flows: following the money and value trails. John A Cassara (2020).
This book explores the various forms of money laundering and illicit financial flows, including TBML. It provides a comprehensive overview of criminal money laundering methods and offers recommendations to enhance the effectiveness of anti-money laundering efforts.
2 Reference Guide to Anti-Money Laundering and Combating the Financing of Terrorism by The World Bank (2013).
This guide provides an overview of anti-money laundering and counter-terrorism financing measures. It offers guidance on implementing these measures and provides examples of best practices.
3 Criminal Intelligence (2012). "Manual for Analysts. 2011." United Nations. UNODC. Viitattu 28

This manual guides the collection, analysis, and dissemination of criminal intelligence. It offers insights into the methods analysts use to evaluate information and intelligence and provides examples of best practices.

Article:

4 "Financial intelligence and financial investigation: opportunities and challenges." Ben Scott and Mark McGoldrick. (2018). Journal of Policing, Intelligence and Counter Terrorism, 13(3), 301–315. https://www.tandfonline.com/doi/abs/10.1080/18335330.2018.1482563
The authors explore the role of financial intelligence in detecting and preventing financial crimes, including money laundering and terrorist financing. The article provides insights into the methods employed by criminals to launder money and offers recommendations for improving the effectiveness of anti-money laundering efforts.

5 Financial intelligence: Uses and teaching methods (Innovative approaches from subject matter experts). Anne Walton (2013). Journal of Strategic Security, 6(3), 393–400.
The article examines the applications and pedagogical approaches to financial intelligence. The author discusses the importance of financial intelligence in detecting and preventing financial crimes, including money laundering and terrorist financing. The article provides insights into innovative approaches used by subject matter experts to teach financial intelligence.

19 Combating Trade-Based Money Laundering

Strategies for Future Preparedness

Money laundering poses immense challenges that are not restricted to a region, territory, or a nation. Instead, it is a persistent issue that requires nations to collaborate meticulously. It also comprises intelligence sharing and enforcement mechanisms that transcend borders (UNODC, 2023). This perspective is thoroughly aligned with the views of the UN Secretary-General António Guterres. He is serving for a second term. Guterres has called on the global community to join efforts to combat widespread financial crimes.

Current Challenges in Detecting TBML

The degree of sophistication in the structuring and commingling of illegal and legal trading activities: Trade-based money laundering (TBML) schemes are often designed to evade detection by obscuring the proceeds of crime through the disguise of legitimate trade transactions. This creates obstacles for financial institutions in discovering suspicious activity and reporting it to the relevant authorities (FICO, 2021; Shuftipro, 2020).

A complex network of relationships exists among transactions that may appear innocent at first glance. Criminals often utilize multiple shell companies and intermediaries to conceal the true nature of their transactions. Making it more challenging to trace the funds and identify the ultimate recipients of the illicit activity (FICO, 2021). In addition, non-documentary trades pose an even greater challenge and a more effective method of obscuring money. Because banks have limited information about transactions, it is impossible to determine whether they are suspicious (FICO, 2021).

Lack of Digitalization and Updated Tools

The absence of digitalization and modern tools for analyzing financial or trade data is a key challenge hindering the identification of TBML (FATF, 2020; GTR, 2022; ShuftiPro, 2022; FICO, 2022). As technology advances, criminals may exploit newly available technologies. They can continue to develop increasingly sophisticated TBML methods. Public authorities and financial institutions must pursue digitalization and improve tools for analyzing financial or trade data. Such institutional investments will enable public authorities and financial institutions to keep pace with TBML methods in their investigations and examinations of suspicious, potentially illegal activity (FATF, 2020; GTR, 2022; ShuftiPro, 2022; FICO, 2022).

Real-Life Example: PDVSA TBML Scheme

The case of Petroleos de Venezuela SA (PDVSA) concerns a state-owned oil company that was allegedly used to facilitate TBML. While there are many examples of TBML, the PDVSA

DOI: 10.4324/9781003477631-20

case was an actual instance of TBML being used as a guise. This real-life case of TBML elucidates the challenges and complexities in combating TBML (GTR, 2022; ShuftiPro, 2022; FICO, 2022). In December 2019, the U.S. Department of the Treasury's Office of Foreign Assets Control made a public announcement regarding the oil giant PDVSA. It was disclosed that Nicolas Maduro had exclusively and intentionally engaged in a shell network of front companies to evade U.S.-imposed sanctions. OFAC identified more than 200 individuals and entities, as well as transactions totaling more than $11 billion, associated with the conspiracy. This case demonstrates how TBML can be used to evade sanctions and how challenging it is to uncover a web of covert operations (FATF, 2020; GTR, 2022; ShuftiPro, 2022; FICO, 2022).

The Digitalization Dilemma in Anti-money Laundering

Financial institutions encounter an increasingly uphill battle against money laundering: the past is no longer a reliable guide to the future. A notable example is HSBC. The British bank received massive sanctions in 2012. It was one of the largest money laundering scandals implicated in the largest drug cartel in Mexico. The bank found itself utterly embroiled in a money laundering scandal. HSBC was fined nearly $1.9 billion. The bank had transferred $881 million in drug proceeds through its U.S. banking operation (U.S. Department of Justice, 2012). This incident demonstrated the lax enforcement of anti-money laundering regulations and the bank's reliance on outdated technologies. This contributed to its inability to conduct its operations and detect and report suspicious activity.

The scandal was a wake-up call for HSBC. The intention was loud and clear. To take corrective measures to strengthen its compliance programs and avoid repetition. Moreover, the bank's violations were not isolated incidents. They were represented by systemic failures in the bank's control mechanisms. HSBC should not be singled out for its utter failure. Instead, it is indicative of broader problems in the banking industry. Notably, several large banks have been fined substantial amounts for facilitating illegal transactions involving criminal organizations and sanctioned governments (Investopedia, 2023).

The HSBC case underscores the importance of robust, credible money laundering controls. It suggests that financial institutions should allocate their resources judiciously to modern controls and technologies. That will certainly assist in the detection and reporting of suspicious activity. Failing to apply the rules properly can have heavy financial and reputational ramifications, as HSBC learned the hard way (South China Morning Post, 2023; International Consortium of Investigative Journalists, 2020).

Strategies for Future Preparedness

Various strategies can be implemented to enhance future preparedness for the challenges posed by TBML.

I Information Sharing Across Institutions
   One of the most significant strategies for future preparedness is sharing information across institutions. By providing information on trends, methods, and frameworks used in TBML crimes. Proper steps taken by financial institutions and government officials can effectively prevent crime. For instance, in 2019, Financial Crimes Enforcement Network (FinCEN) issued a combined statement. In this regulatory action, the relevant agencies were the Federal Reserve Board, the Office of the Comptroller of the Currency, and the Securities and Exchange Commission. They intended to pursue and combat illegal activities. The declaration seeks to reinforce information sharing systems, enabling institutions to identify

emerging trends and typologies associated with financial crime more effectively (Financial Crimes Enforcement Network, 2019).

II Consolidation of Data

Another critical strategy is to recognize that TBML data mining involves multiple sources. This is possible using data from both customs and the freight community. It facilitates the detection of TBML techniques such as over- and under-invoicing. They are mainly used to transfer illicit payments. On 24 October 2019, U.S. Customs and Border Protection and the Department of Homeland Security announced a collaborative partnership. Joint efforts sought to consolidate trade data and communicate it effectively to improve detection of TBML (U.S. Customs and Border Protection, 2019).

III Pooling Data across Stakeholders

Pooling data across stakeholders, including financial institutions, government bodies, and private-sector entities, is crucial for robust analytics and TBML detection. By pooling data, stakeholders can more effectively identify recurring trends and patterns in TBML and develop more effective strategies to address the accelerating problem.

IV Employee Awareness

A supportive factor in curbing TBML is employee awareness. Financial institutions can mitigate TBML exposure by educating employees at all levels about associated risks and red flags. They can also prepare the employees to recognize and report their suspicious behavior. This is achieved by continuous training and updates on TBML trends and typologies. As employees become acquainted with various financial crimes, they should be trained to recognize and respond appropriately.

V Role of Technology

Technology holds considerable promise for impeding TBML through data and transaction analysis (Acuity Knowledge Partners, 2023). The improper use of technology can also create vulnerabilities (Tookitaki, 2023). However, the potential of technology to reformulate TBML should not be overlooked. It also raises some hope for a secure financial space. Its improper use can, conversely, create vulnerabilities (Tookitaki, 2023). For example, digital currencies, fintech, and blockchain technologies promise efficiency but also enable alternative methods for transferring and laundering illicit funds (Acuity Knowledge Partners, 2023). Financial organizations must understand these new technologies and adjust reporting policies and procedures to counter the financing of terrorism. This continuous adaptation is essential to improve TBML and keep pace with the evolving tactics it entails.

Digital currencies (e.g., Bitcoin and Ethereum) have gained popularity lately. One main reason is that they lack centralization, which creates a perceived anonymity. However, they also provide criminal entities with a substantial opportunity to launder illicit proceeds undetected. A study was conducted by the European Union Agency for Law Enforcement Cooperation (Europol). This study suggests that criminals are increasingly using virtual currency platforms to launder money. Financial institutions must remain current with technological change and adapt their AML and CFT processes accordingly.

1 Fintech enterprises, such as online marketplaces and peer-to-peer lending platforms, have been targets of TBML due to a lack of AML and CFT procedures in traditional financial institutions. This provides money launderers with an effective means of moving illicit proceeds through these services. Financial institutions are primarily responsible for assessing organizational integrity. They cooperate with and comply with the legislation they implement, including effective anti-money laundering and counter-terrorist financing measures.

2 Blockchain technology is the foundation of cryptocurrencies. There are numerous advanced methods of using this technology for TBML. Notably, blockchain transparency can readily expose money launderers who obtain illicit funds from illegal activities (Economist, 2018). On the other hand, black coats can mix clean with dirty funds by leveraging blockchain mechanisms, for example, by using the same blockchain addresses associated with criminals involved in drug or human trafficking, making it more challenging to investigate and solve crimes through blockchain. This necessitates that banks and financial institutions update their AML and CFT processes using advanced technologies to combat emerging threats of money laundering and shadow financing.

The Role of Blockchain in Trade Automation

Blockchain technology can significantly disrupt traditional trade processes by reducing costs and enhancing efficiency. It is not merely a ledger; it is an immutable, transparent ledger encompassing all transactions in a trade network, thereby exposing more fraudulent activity in areas where banks have limited visibility and control. Automating trade processes and real-time visibility into the movement of goods can help spot and prevent TBML (ICC, 2019).

Impediments and Challenges:
Blockchain's potential to automate trade is considerable, but many barriers must first be overcome. Blockchain technology may automate many operational steps in a trade, thereby achieving cost savings and improved transparency. A fabulous issue is the prevalence of divergent national laws that are unsupportive of digitization and lack standards. Other issues include connectivity and digital islands (platforms that are not yet connected), which impede system interoperability. Other critical issues are data privacy, data security, and regulatory compliance (World Bank, 2019).

Solutions and Recommendations

To accelerate digital trade integration and combat TBML. Developing a framework that incorporates the interests of shareholders, the government, and the broader trade community is crucial for effective trade facilitation and automation. This integration includes: (1) a unified legal and regulatory system, (2) promoting liaison and partnerships among stakeholders, and (3) educating and training all people connected in the trade. Moreover, it is also essential to promote the implementation of standards and rules for blockchain-based trade systems. This measure will benefit security, interoperability, and regulatory compliance.

In sum, blockchain technology has enormous potential to disrupt the trade industry. It has the potential to streamline and automate processes. It leads to improved security and transparency, as well as lower expenses. However, for introducing blockchain to operate successfully in trade, a close liaison among governments, stakeholders, and the trade community is required. It is also crucial to address hurdles such as regulatory and legal obstacles, interoperability issues, and connectivity challenges. Moreover, it is essential to devote greater effort to the research and development of blockchain technology to gain a comprehensive understanding of its capabilities in trade (Pw C, 2018).

Chapter Summary

Addressing TBML in the international trade finance community and combating the risk of TBML are serious concerns. This depends on collective action by all relevant stakeholders. There are many complications in identifying TBML, arising from the real-world challenges and intricacies of trade finance transactions. It also called for meaningful information sharing with institutions. In response to these constraints, potential solutions include data integration, information sharing among stakeholders, and enhanced employee awareness. Moreover, technology alone can be essential in TBML; for example, digital currency and fintech entities may be involved in facilitating TBML effectively and synthetically. Blockchain technology, the foundation of digital currencies, is related to TBML but is also enormously significant in the context of trade automation and may pose obstacles and challenges.

End of Chapter: Discussion Questions

1. What are the current challenges in detecting TBML?
2. How can information sharing across institutions help in combating TBML?
3. What is the role of employee awareness in preventing TBML?
4. What is the significance of digital currencies in TBML?
5. How can fintech companies be vulnerable to TBML?
6. What is the role of blockchain technology in trade automation and TBML?
7. What are the impediments and challenges of using blockchain technology in trade finance?
8. How does the consolidation of data help in detecting TBML?
9. How important is pooling information across stakeholders in deterring TBML?
10. What are some other strategies for future preparedness in combating TBML?

References

Acuity Knowledge Partners. (2023, June 14). Trade-based money laundering: How it works and ways to combat it. https://www.acuitykp.com/solutions/kyc-and-client-due-diligence/

Board of Governors of the Federal Reserve System, Federal Deposit Insurance Corporation, Financial Crimes Enforcement Network, National Credit Union Administration, & Office of the Comptroller of the Currency. (2018, December 3). *Joint statement on innovative efforts to combat money laundering and terrorist financing [Policy Statement].* https://www.fincen.gov/sites/default/files/2018-12/Joint%20Statement%20on%20Innovation%20Statement%20%28Final%2011-30-18%29_508.pdf

Europol. (2019). *Internet Organized Crime Threat Assessment (IOCTA) 2019 [Landing Page Portal].* European Union Agency for Law Enforcement Cooperation. Retrieved from https://www.europol.europa.eu/publications-events/main-reports/internet-organised-crime-threat-assessment-iocta-2019

FICO. (2021, March 24). Challenges in countering trade-based money laundering. FICO Decisions Blog. https://www.fico.com/blogs/challenges-countering-trade-based-money-laundering

FICO. (2022). Challenges in countering trade-based money laundering.

Financial Action Task Force. (2020). Trade-based money laundering: Trends and developments.

Financial Crimes Enforcement Network. (2018, December 3). *Joint statement on innovative efforts to combat money laundering and terrorist financing*. U.S. Department of the Treasury. https://www.fincen.gov/news/news-releases/joint-statement-innovative-efforts-combat-money-laundering

Global Trade Review. (2022). Going digital: Banks and authorities face a shifting TBML threat.

International Chamber of Commerce. (2019, July 1). *ICC digital initiatives that will equip businesses for the next century of global trade*. https://iccwbo.org/news-publications/news/icc-digital-initiatives-that-will-equip-business-for-the-next-century-of-global-trade/

International Consortium of Investigative Journalists. (2020). HSBC moved vast sums of dirty money after paying a record-breaking fine for money laundering. https://www.icij.org/investigations/fincen-files/hsbc-moved-vast-sums-of-dirty-money-after-paying-record-laundering-fine/

Investopedia. (2023, September 19). HSBC's Money Laundering Scandal. https://www.investopedia.com/stock-analysis/2013/investing-news-for-jan-29-hsbcs-money-laundering-scandal-hbc-scbff-ing-cs-rbs0129.aspx

Office of the Comptroller of the Currency. (2018, December 3). *Agencies issue a joint statement on innovative industry approaches (News Release No. 2018-130).* U.S. Department of the Treasury. https://www.occ.gov/news-issuances/news-releases/2018/nr-occ-2018-130.html

PwC Asia Pacific Customs and Trade. (2018, September). *Blockchains without borders*. Trade Intelligence, 2018(09), 1–4. Retrieved from https://customs.pwc.com/en/publications/assets/pdf/trade-intelligence-201809.pdf

ShuftiPro. (2020, October 13). Trade-based money laundering - Challenges, detection, and prevention. https://shuftipro.com/blog/trade-based-money-laundering-challenges-detection-and-prevention/

ShuftiPro. (2022). Trade-based money laundering - Challenges, detection, and prevention.

South China Morning Post. (2023, January 1). How HSBC laundered money for Mexican drug cartels, paid a US$1.9b fine, and hardly anyone noticed. https://www.scmp.com/magazines/post-magazine/books/article/3185472/how-hsbc-laundered-money-mexican-drug-cartels-paid

The Economist. (2018). Blockchain technology: The great chain of being sure about things. https://www.economist.com/leaders/2018/01/18/blockchain-technology-the-great-chain-of-being-sure-about-things

Tookitaki. (2023, February 22). *Trade-based money laundering explained*. Tookitaki Compliance Hub. https://www.tookitaki.com/compliance-hub/trade-based-money-laundering-explained

United Nations Office on Drugs and Crime. (2023). *Transnational organized crime: The globalized illegal economy*. https://www.unodc.org/toc/en/crimes/organized-crime.html

U.S. Customs and Border Protection. (2019). *CBP and DHS announce partnership to combat trade-based money laundering*. Department of Homeland Security. https://www.cbp.gov/newsroom/media-releases/trade

U.S. Department of Justice. (2012). HSBC Holdings Plc. and HSBC Bank USA N.A. Admit to Anti-Money Laundering and Sanctions Violations, Forfeit $1.256 Billion in Deferred Prosecution Agreement. https://www.justice.gov/opa/pr/hsbc-holdings-plc-and-hsbc-bank-usa-na-admit-anti-money-laundering-and-sanctions-violations

U.S. Government Accountability Office. (2020). *Trade-based money laundering: The U.S. government has worked with partners to combat the threat, but could strengthen its efforts (Report No. GAO-20-333)*. Washington, DC: GAO. https://www.gao.gov/assets/gao-20-333.pdf

World Bank. (2019). Unlocking the Potential of Trade Digitization. https://openknowledge.worldbank.org/handle/10986/31320

Additional Learning Resources

Article

"Global Developments in Trade-Based Money Laundering" by Herbert G. (2022). https://doi.org/10.19088/k4d.2022.165. Available at: https://opendocs.ids.ac.uk/opendocs/bitstream/handle/20.500.12413/17742/EIR_55_Trade-Based_Money_Laundering.pdf?sequence=1

The resource provides an overview of the latest developments in TBML.

The article discusses the challenges and innovative solutions for combating this type of financial crime. It offers insights into the methods used by criminals to launder money through trade transactions and provides recommendations for improving the effectiveness of anti-money laundering efforts.

Report

Trade-based Money Laundering: Trends and Developments. (2020). Available at: https://www.fatf-gafi.org/content/dam/fatf-gafi/reports/Trade-Based-Money-Laundering-Trends-and-Developments.pdf

This report was published by the Financial Action Task Force (FATF). It provides insights into the trends and developments in TBML. The report offers risk indicators and analysis to help combat this form of financial crime. It serves as a useful resource for policymakers, law enforcement agencies, and financial institutions in understanding and addressing TBML.

Trade-Based Money Laundering: A Global Challenge. The report was published in February 2023 by Global Financial Integrity (GFI), Fedesarrollo, Transparency International Kenya, and the Advocates Coalition for Development and Environment (ACODE). Available at: https://gfintegrity.org/report/trade-based-money laundering-a-global-challenge/

The report provides an in-depth analysis of TBML, a type of money laundering that uses international trade transactions to conceal the proceeds of crime.

20 The Battle Against Financial Crime

A Comparative Study of Anti-Money Laundering Regulations in Islamic Banking Systems of the UAE, Malaysia, Sudan, and Pakistan

Given the serious nature of financial crime, the global financial system's stability and integrity continue to be challenged, among which money laundering is the most threatening, albeit sophisticated. Christine Lagarde, the former managing director of the International Monetary Fund (IMF), noted that it has already shifted the implementation of effective countermeasures from a regulatory obligation to a strong critical requirement for public trust in the financial sector (FATF, 2020). This chapter presents a comparative study of anti-money laundering (AML) regulations in the Islamic banking systems of the United Arab Emirates, Malaysia, Sudan, and Pakistan, focusing on their frameworks, challenges, and efficacy in combating illicit financial flows.

AML regulations are crucial for regulating economic crimes (namely, terrorism financing, drug trafficking, and other unlawful activities) worldwide. This issue is particularly relevant to Islamic banking systems, which rely on their AML frameworks to foster confidence and, ultimately, stability in financial services (Investopedia, 2023). Whether AML regulations are effective in combating economic crime is a topic of ongoing debate. Some contend that they constitute excessive restrictions on financial freedom, whereas others argue that they are a legitimate means of curbing illicit money flows. This debate offers an interesting perspective on AML regulations in Islamic banking systems (Investopedia, 2023). This discussion compares AML frameworks in Islamic banking systems. The selected countries are the UAE, Malaysia, Sudan, and Pakistan, and their assessment of the effectiveness of combating financial crime.

Islamic Banking Systems in the UAE

The UAE is ranked among the fastest-growing economies globally. Islamic banking provides a primary source of fuel for the engine of economic growth (Britannica, 2023). In 2020, the country's Central Bank reported that Islamic banks' assets surged to AED 1.03 trillion (approx. USD 280 billion). Moreover, it held a 39% market share (Central Bank of the UAE, 2021). The UAE has a robust AML framework. The mechanism facilitates the curbing of Money Laundering and the combating of the Financing of Terrorism (AML/CFT) in accordance with the 2018 Law (Central Bank of the UAE, 2018). The UAE's implementation includes strict AML regulations to safeguard the country's financial system and deter money laundering and the financing of terrorism.

The UAE Central Bank and the FATF govern the UAE's AML regulations. The Central Bank establishes requirements for all financial institutions, including Islamic banks, to extend comprehensive AML frameworks. It broadly covers customer due diligence (CDD) and suspicious transaction reporting (STR) (Central Bank of the UAE, 2021). The FATF has also issued numerous recommendations to address AML in the Islamic finance industry, including, but not

DOI: 10.4324/9781003477631-21

limited to, the requirement to create an AML risk assessment framework, implement customer identification measures, and adopt a CDD and STR system (FATF, 2018).

Islamic Banking Systems in Malaysia

Malaysia is another key player and has been rapidly developing a thriving Islamic finance industry. The Central Bank of Malaysia reported the results for the banking sector, which held a sizeable market share of 47.6% in 2020. The total value of banking assets was MYR 697.2 billion (around $167 billion) (Bank Negara Malaysia, 2021). Similarly, Malaysia, like the UAE, has undertaken ongoing initiatives and rigorously established and adopted AML policies to combat financial crime effectively.

In Malaysia, numerous laws directly impact Islamic banking and the prevention of money laundering. The bulk of the country's AML statutes are governed and implemented by the Anti-Money Laundering, Anti-Terrorism Financing, and Proceeds of Unlawful Activities Act of 2001 (Bank Negara Malaysia, 2001). Bank Negara Malaysia (BNM) requires all financial institutions to engage in robust AML policies and procedures. It also includes internal policies and procedures taken to comply with CDD and STR (Bank Negara Malaysia, 2021). The FATF is the international standard-setting body responsible for regulating and controlling AML activities. It also recommends specific guidelines in its standards for the Islamic finance industry. The AML regulations comply with FATF recommendations. This demonstrates a cohesive approach to policy compliance and implementation in fighting money laundering and terror financing. The strategy provides reassurance in combating global financial crime (FATF, 2018).

Islamic Banking Systems in Sudan

Sudan is a key country with an expanding Islamic finance sector. The accessibility of Islamic banking for clients is improving. The Central Bank of Sudan reported that Islamic banking assets represented a 40% market share in 2020. The total banking assets are valued at SDG 43.7 billion (around SDG 1.4 billion) (Central Bank of Sudan, 2021). While Sudan has an AML framework in place to deter financial crime, it is substantially weaker than those in the UAE or Malaysia.

The Central Bank of Sudan and the IMF monitor and audit Sudan's AML regulations. The Central Bank expects all financial institutions, including Islamic banks, to establish AML policies and procedures, including CDD measures and STR systems (Central Bank of Sudan, 2021). The IMF has also published guidance and best practices for AML/CFT in Islamic finance institutions (Kyriakos-Saad et al., 2016). At the same time, countries are actively seeking to adopt and implement AML regulations within their Islamic banking systems. Many of them lack a subjective assessment of the effectiveness of AML regulations in Islamic banking systems. According to a study conducted by the Middle East and North Africa Financial Action Task Force (MENA FATF), Malaysia had the most robust AML framework among the countries surveyed. In comparison, Sudan had the lowest (Trade-Based Financial Crime -Middle East and North Africa: A Reference Guide for the Anti-Financial Crime Community, 2022).

The Dubai Financial Services Authority (DFSA) in the UAE has outlined AML regulations with strict guidelines for the financial services sector. It has implemented various measures to prevent financial crime and money laundering, including the establishment of a dedicated Anti-Money Laundering Unit (AMLU) and risk-based AML supervision (DFSA, 2021). However, a follow-up report by the FATF identified gaps and weaknesses in the UAE's AML system and urged improvements (FATF, 2019).

Bank Negara Malaysia (BNM), the Central Bank of Malaysia, has taken critical actions to ensure the deployment of the AML framework. This includes the introduction of AML/CFT policies under which financial institutions are required to conduct CDD and STR to mitigate money laundering risk (BNM, 2021). Further, Malaysia has a strong AML/CFT legal framework. It has also established a National Coordinating Committee on Anti-Money Laundering and Counter Financing of Terrorism (NCC-AML/CFT) to coordinate the efforts of the agency cohort (BNM, 2021).

The Central Bank of Sudan has stipulated the AML regulations. However, their efficacy has been scrutinized due to the limited capacity and resources available to the Central Bank and other regulatory agencies (CBOS, 2024). A recent FATF report noted that Sudan has made responsible progress in its AML/CFT efforts. However, considerable work remains to achieve full compliance with international standards (FATF, 2021).

Islamic Banking Systems in Pakistan

The State Bank of Pakistan (SBP) has implemented AML regulations aligned with international standards. The State Bank requires all financial institutions to implement AML policies and procedures and adopt CDD measures. Recognizing and prohibiting money laundering activity is imperative (State Bank of Pakistan, 2020).

SBP has AML regulations for Islamic banks, but enforcement is even more challenging (SBP, 2021). The Asia/Pacific Group on Money Laundering (APG) report stated that Pakistan needs to take appropriate measures to address deficiencies in the AML/CFT framework. This requires a stronger legal framework and enhanced regulatory capacity (APG, 2019).

The FATF noted that the UAE is committed to implementing AML measures (FATF, 2019). Transparent and robust AML/CFT standards have been implemented. The UAE government has also instituted various relevant governmental agencies. The primary tasks involved implementing and supervising the AML regulations. The Central Bank of the UAE has also established a specialized unit, the Anti-Money Laundering and Suspicious Transactions Unit (AMLSCU) (FATF, 2019).

In Malaysia, the Central Bank of Malaysia has formally established AML regulations to align with national standards. The Central Bank also requires all financial institutions to institute AML policies and procedures. It is further obligated to conduct due diligence on clients to identify and prevent money laundering (Central Bank of Malaysia, 2020).

Conversely, Sudan has faced numerous challenges in implementing its AML framework in recent years, owing to political and economic constraints. In the face of these formidable challenges, the Central Bank of Sudan has continually sought to ensure compliance with AML regulations. It further requires adopting CDD and establishing STR requirements (Central Bank of Sudan, 2021).

Key players debate the effectiveness of AML legislation within Pakistan's Islamic banking industry. Some experts contend that it has been successful, whereas others suggest that loopholes remain and require continued prudent handling (Malik, 2020; Akhtar, 2018).

One of the primary obstacles to evaluating the effectiveness of AML regulations in the Islamic banking sector is the potential disparity in their application across financial institutions. This inconsistent application can result in discernible differences in the legislation's overall effectiveness. Despite these obstacles, it is concluded that the AML legislation has effectively curbed money laundering within Pakistan's Islamic banking community.

There is potential for improvement, and the current state of AML regulations in Islamic banking is not without its hurdles (Hassan, Hussain, & Sajid, 2021). Yes, the problem is being addressed, and the enforcement mechanisms have been considerably reinforced. For the future of financial compliance, this possibility ought to inspire optimism and hope. The efficacy of AML regulations in Pakistan's Islamic banking system can be improved by identifying gaps and ensuring they are consistently addressed across the sector. Continued efforts to strengthen the regulatory authorities' framework and bolster their capabilities will be essential to further lowering the vulnerabilities of money laundering in this sector (Khan, 2022).

To summarize, there is ongoing discussion regarding the effectiveness of AML regulations. Despite strenuous efforts made to incorporate them into Islamic banking systems in the United Arab Emirates, Malaysia, Sudan, and Pakistan. Malaysia has the strongest AML framework among the countries surveyed, while Sudan has the weakest. The limited capacities, meager resources, and weak legal frameworks of regulatory bodies are among the major challenges that Sudan, Pakistan, and the UAE continue to face in meeting international AML/CFT standards.

Trade-Based Money Laundering: Emerging Trends and Countermeasures

Trade-based money laundering is challenging to detect and deter due to the complexity of international trade networks and the involvement of multiple actors and jurisdictions. We will examine recent advances and countermeasures for combating TBML.

Global Financial Impact of TBML

According to Global Financial Integrity, five Central Asian countries—China, India, Indonesia, Malaysia, and Thailand—are among the top global destinations for significant financial outflows due to TBML (GFI). The adverse impacts on affected countries, particularly in Africa and Latin America, are well documented. There is no doubt that this massive flow of money has significantly affected the health and development of the population, underscoring the urgent need for action (GFI, 2020).

The Financial Stability Oversight Council: Safeguarding U.S. Financial Stability

The Wall Street Reform and Consumer Protection Act of 2010 established the entity, the Financial Stability Oversight Council (FSOC). The latter's primary role was to monitor and mitigate threats to the U.S. financial system. Thus, it helps maintain the new regulation and protects the financial sector (Dodd-Frank Wall Street Reform and Consumer Protection Act, 2010). The Dodd-Frank Act (2010). Responded to the financial crisis and aimed to reform regulations to avert future meltdowns. Maintaining its core values is still essential. The Secretary of the Treasury chairs the Council, which combines the expertise of federal and state financial regulators. This seeks to recognize potential threats to financial stability, address evolving issues, and promote market discipline (Dodd-Frank Wall Street Reform and Consumer Protection Act, 2010).

The Council's annual report discusses its operations, key financial market and regulatory developments, and potential vulnerabilities to the financial system. The suggestions are intended to preserve investor trust and enhance the effectiveness and stability of financial markets. A 2015 report examined weaknesses in the financial system and concluded that they remained moderate overall. However, the report also identified specific areas where the risk had an adverse impact and contributed to economic shocks. Financial reforms have been implemented to strengthen regulatory standards for financial institutions and enhance consumer protections. The report concludes by advocating for sustained action to combat TBML and protect financial systems (FSOC, 2015).

Mandate and Responsibilities

The FSOC's essential responsibilities are specified by the Dodd-Frank Act (Dodd-Frank Wall Street Reform and Consumer Protection Act, 2010):

i Recognizing exposures to the United States' financial stability that may stem from large, systemically significant bank holding companies, nonbank financial companies, or external factors.
ii Encouraging market discipline by eliminating expectations that the government will protect companies against losses upon failure.
iii Responding to evolving threats to the stability of the U.S. financial system.

To fulfill its mandate, the Council is authorized to gather information from relevant regulatory agencies. It suggests tracking foreign and domestic regulatory developments and submitting them to either Congress or the Federal Reserve (DF Act, 2010). Moreover, the FSOC is empowered to recognize certain nonbank enterprises that the Federal Reserve should scrutinize for their potential impact on monetary stability, as well as those whose activities are potentially risky (DF Act, 2010).

Promoting Transparency and Accountability

The FSOC pledges to be open and transparent in its operations, thereby fostering confidence and assurance. Each year, the FSOC reports to Congress on the state of the American financial system (DF Act, 2010). Every voting member must verify that the government is exercising reasonable efforts to promote financial stability. The DF Act further outlines additional measures to be undertaken (DF Act, 2010).

The FSOC is essential to preserving the stability of the American financial system and averting future financial crises because it recognizes risks, promotes market discipline, and reacts to evolving threats (DF Act, 2010).

Dealing with Transaction Monitoring in Banks: An Urgent and Costly Challenge

Banks worldwide are under tremendous pressure to counter money laundering and fraud, as evidenced by the staggering $180 billion spent globally in 2019 on technology and human capital to this end (Napier, 2023). This massive investment, a staggering $180 billion worldwide in 2019, underscores the severity of the issue and the need for more effective measures. It is a considerable investment, but its returns have been poor, with false-positive rates favorably above 95% (Napier, 2023). This implies that of 100 transactions flagged as suspicious, only 5 are actually suspicious.

In the United States, only 0.1% of the flagged suspicious transactions have resulted in money laundering (Napier, 2023). This alarmingly low percentage underscores that transaction monitoring practices impose costs on banks and make no meaningful contribution to the identification or deterrence of financial crimes.

How the COVID-19 Pandemic Impacted TBML

The COVID-19 pandemic has enormously changed the approach many countries take to combating TBML and terrorist financing. The FATF is an international policy-making and standard-setting body that has examined the issue and published a series of reports since May 2020. The reports demonstrate that criminals will exploit the crisis state (FATF, 2020).

Emerging Threats and Vulnerabilities

The reports highlighted the targeting of government organizations engaged in combating COVID-19 with malware, ransomware, and phishing attacks (FATF, 2020). These and other similar threats and vulnerabilities are also emerging risks of money laundering and terrorist financing that could result in:

i Criminals circumventing CDD;
ii More exploitation of online financial services, including virtual assets, to move and conceal illicit funds;
iii Exploitation of economic stimulus efforts and insolvency schemes so that both natural persons and legal persons can conceal illicit proceeds and launder money;
iv More use of the unregulated financial sector, which will create more opportunities to launder illicit proceeds;
v Misuse and misappropriation of domestic and international aid/donations and emergency funding;
vi Criminals and terrorists exploiting COVID-19 and the economic decline that goes with it to move into new target lines of business that are cash-intensive and high-liquidity businesses in developing countries (FATF, 2020).

Recommended Policy Responses

In this context, the FATF encouraged stakeholders to maximize the use of FinTech (financial technology), Regtech (regulatory technology), and Suptech (supervisory technology). The reports recommend that Anti-Money Laundering/Countering the Financing of Terrorism (AML/CFT) policy responses can facilitate the rapid and efficient implementation of measures to address TBML and terrorist financing during the epidemic (FATF, 2020).

International Cooperation

TBML transactions are typically transnational. They entail a sophisticated puzzle constructed by launderers, with front businesses registered in one country but fund transfers and goods shipments occurring in another jurisdiction. Therefore, determining the offense's jurisdiction is always challenging. Thus, international collaborative efforts, such as effective information exchange and joint investigations that lead to accurate prosecutions, can act as a deterrent (UNODC, 2020).

Payment Methods and TBML Risk

Among trade payment methods, documentary credits and collections, in which banks can review trade-related documents, are considered considerably less vulnerable to TBML exposure than open accounts. The major problem is that Open Account provides a legitimate settlement process that must be considered, as it is readily accessible and easy for all parties to use. Although there is an enhanced risk of TBML with open accounts, it is worth noting that most global trade by value is conducted through open accounts. This severely complicates the obligations of regulating, enforcing, and investigative authorities.

A practical approach to combat TBML is to raise awareness of TBML among both public authorities and the commercial sector. Studies have revealed that the understanding of TBML and its issues is severely limited among these groups. This lack of awareness is one of the challenges in addressing TBML. Broadly speaking, this can be addressed through education and training initiatives, awareness campaigns for public authorities and commercial-sector organizations, and targeted campaigns for both public authorities and businesses, all of which can help.

Another key countermeasure is the advancement of effective and efficient trade-related risk management systems. Banks and financial institutions should deploy comprehensive risk management systems that proactively mitigate risks associated with TBML and the exposures linked to it. Advancing risk management systems will require the use of sophisticated technologies, such as artificial intelligence (AI) and machine learning, and the adoption of effective internal policies and procedures.

In brief, TBML is a complex, multilayered, and global challenge that requires multifaceted responses. It is imperative to improve awareness and understanding of TBML among public authorities, the commercial sector, and the broader public. Banks and other financial institutions should implement effective trade-related risk management systems to facilitate the detection and prosecution of TBML. Strengthening international liaisons and knowledge sharing is also necessary.

Combating TBML: Tremendous Challenges and Innovative Solutions

The trade finance process and record structure are often centered on paper-based documentation, which creates a profound challenge for detecting and addressing TBML.

The Challenge of Unstructured Data in Trade Finance Documents

The International Chamber of Commerce (ICC) estimates that an enormous amount of trade finance documentation is in circulation at any given time. This is reckoned to number around 4 billion pages (ICC, 2023). Documentation is necessary to facilitate international trade. It contains many key documents, including certificates of origin, bills of lading, insurance documents, bills of exchange, and letters of credit.

The ICC's Digital Standards Initiative (DSI) has identified seven core trade documents that can be digitized. This is a testament to the significance of digital transformation in global trade processes. They include bills of lading, commercial invoices, and certificates of origin (Hoffman, 2023). The DSI advocates digitizing all trade documents to improve efficiency and reduce errors (Hoffman, 2023). However, a further challenge is that trade finance documents often contain unstructured data and free-form text. Although the unstructured format of this information facilitates automated processing and compliance screening, it also reduces processing efficiency and may affect financial vulnerabilities.

Adapting to the Digital Trade Era: Challenges and Opportunities

The World Trade Organization released the book *Adapting to the Digital Trade Era: Challenges and Opportunities*, edited by Maarten Smeets, in 2021 (WTO, 2021). It examines the impact of digitalization on international trade and the challenges and opportunities that arise in this evolving context.

The Digitalization of Trade

This book discernibly explores how digitization, specifically the accelerating development of digital technologies such as the Internet, e-commerce, and blockchain, will dramatically transform the engagement of businesses and governments in international business. It discusses the potential benefits of digitization, including greater efficiency, lower costs, and improved transparency across many trade processes (WTO, 2021).

Challenges and Opportunities

However, the publication examines the complex features of the digital trade era. These can be both baffling and challenging, including operationalizing international regulatory cooperation, balancing digital divides, and addressing potential data privacy and security risks. Despite its challenges, the book also explores new opportunities for digitalization, including expanded market access, integration into global value chains, and greater opportunities for small and medium-sized enterprises to engage in international trade (WTO, 2021).

Recommendations for Policymakers

The book offers valuable insights and practical recommendations to help policymakers, trade negotiators, and other stakeholders navigate the obstacles of the digital trade era (WTO, 2021). It underlines the significance of international cooperation, the development of uniform regulations, and investment in digital infrastructure and skills to ensure that the benefits of digitalization are widely shared (WTO, 2021).

The growth of digital trade has presented policymakers with evolving opportunities and challenges, including how to address and mitigate emerging trade barriers and to validate the security of digital transactions (WTO, 2021). Since the challenges posed by trade-based money laundering have surface-level associations with threat finance, many initiatives and projects have been developed to improve the efficiency of trade finance processes and structures.

i The Potential of Blockchain in Indian Logistics: The Case of I LOGNET
I LOGNET (Indian Logistics Network), an initiative of the Indian Ministry of Commerce, is a promising example of blockchain's potential in logistics (Movers International Pvt. Ltd., 2024). I LOGNET breaks the reliance on paper-based documents in transportation and instead is built on blockchain-based digital document management and exchange platforms that are secure, transparent, and structured to facilitate the digital generation and transfer of trade documents, thereby enhancing security while reducing time and cost. The project synchronizes with both large and small businesses through training and global implementation. Overall, I LOGNET appears to present a unique solution given the necessary components of a transportation solution—collecting and managing transport documentation for various capacities and types of documents (e.g., bill of lading, certificates of origin, etc., for various ports for various shipping companies) (Movers International Pvt. Ltd., 2024).

i The SPUNTAC project was initiated in 2017 by the Italian Banking Association (Associazione Bancaria Italiana, ABI) and coordinated by the ABI Lab, a research and innovation entity, to use blockchain technology to advance visibility and reconciliation of transactional data in the framework of the Italian banking scenario. This initiative involves 13 Italian banks building on the Hyperledger Fabric blockchain. The SPUNTAC project's name is an acronym for Sistema di Pagamenti elettronici su Tecnologie Abilitanti di tipo Blockchain (Electronic Payment System on Blockchain-Enabled Technologies). It aims to pioneer the implementation of blockchain technology in the Italian banking ecosystem. Most Italian banks regularly employ the SPUNTAC system. SPUNTAC has demonstrated the applicability and advantages of blockchain in banking functions. Beyond its primary goals, the SPUNTAC project is currently investigating the potential of a digital Euro (Osato Avan-Nomayo, 2021). The exploration of a digital Euro aligns with widespread European Union efforts into central bank digital currencies (CBDCs). It has the potential to transform finance in Italy and beyond (European Central Bank, 2022).

ii Spunta Banca Distributed Ledger Technology (DLT): Revolutionizing Interbank Reconciliation with Distributed Ledger Technology
Spunta Banca DLT is a project sponsored by ABI and managed by ABI Lab that aims to redesign the interbank process using DLT (Spunta Project: DLT per La Spunta Interbancaria - ABI Lab, 2023).

Streamlining Interbank Transactions

With the Spunta Banca DLT application, banks can efficiently identify and resolve discrepancies in interbank transactions by relying on shared data that both banks are confident is secure. Banks can conduct their due diligence through the application, interact directly, and share standardized processes and communications to address any issues that may arise. The innovative contract technology automatically provides transaction feedback, mitigates potential operational risk, and accelerates the transaction process by maintaining a clear record of actions. The application features a user-friendly interface designed to enhance usability (Spunta Project: DLT per La Spunta Interbancaria - ABI Lab, 2023).

Successful Implementation and Adoption

The success of the Spunta Banca DLT project is apparent. We have completed technical performance tests simulating 200 million transactions (equivalent to a full year of transactions). The application has been in production since October 1, 2020, with 97 banks (Spunta Project: DLT per La Spunta Interbancaria – ABI Lab, 2023).

Collaborative DLT Infrastructure

For the successful implementation of Spunta Banca DLT, ABILabChain acts as the underlying distributed ledger technology infrastructure. The ABILabChain is a shared resource that provides a flexible environment for generating ideas and executing projects in the field of distributed applications. In such an environment, ABILabChain offers a reliable method for distributing specific products. It is shared among Italian banks on a DLT platform, thereby increasing efficiency. It also promotes collaboration among Italian banks to achieve efficiency, attract investors, and collectively reach their goals (Spunta Project: DLT per La Spunta Interbancaria - ABI Lab, 2023).

Collaborative Governance and Stakeholder Engagement

ABI Lab, the prestigious research and innovation center approved by ABI, is part of the highly qualified team working on the project. Moreover, 97 banks, representing 91% of the banking industry's workforce, are actively involved in this undertaking. The project's carefully decentralized governance structure, which maintains a cooperative approach to implementation and decision-making, comprises 18 banks and banking groups. With this explicit framework, the lab is committed to a development-friendly approach throughout. It will contribute to the project's success by shaping its mission and ensuring its completion (Spunta Project: DLT per La Spunta Interbancaria - ABI Lab, 2023).

Transformative Potential of DLT in Banking

Spunta Banca DLT marks a major milestone in the evolution of interbank processes, offering banks a secure, efficient, and transparent solution. The project's completion, coupled with the participation of multiple banks, provides compelling evidence of DLT's potential to transform the banking sector. The project primarily examines how DLT can radically transform conventional banking processes. It also creates new opportunities for operational efficiency, enhanced security, and improved transparency in the industry (Spunta Project: DLT per La Spunta Interbancaria - ABI Lab, 2023).

iii Enhancing Transparency in Commodity Trade Finance through Blockchain
In Singapore, a consortium of 14 banks, led by DBS and Standard Chartered Bank, has developed a proof of concept (POC) for the Trade Finance Registry (Finextra, 2019). This innovative solution is a blockchain-based POC that enables banks to identify duplicate financing for the same cargo (Finextra, 2019).

The Trade Finance Registry

The Trade Finance Registry seeks to enhance transparency in commodity trade and the use of bank finance for lending. In Singapore, it will serve as a safe, secure central repository of information for housing transactions that banks finance. The registry will utilize blockchain technology to provide a decentralized, tamper-resistant platform for recording and validating trade finance transactions (Finextra, 2019).

Benefits of the Blockchain-based Solution

The blockchain-based Trade Finance Registry offers several vital benefits (Finextra, 2019):

a Better detection of duplicate financing: The registry allows banks to quickly recognize and impede the same cargo being pledged as collateral for duplicate financing transactions, thereby mitigating fraud risk (Finextra, 2019).
b Enhanced transparency: The blockchain-based platform's secure and transparent attributes amplify the visibility of trade finance activity, which helps create trust among stakeholders (Finextra, 2019).
c Streamlined lending practices: As a centralized and trusted source of trade finance data, the registry can help banks make more informed lending decisions and manage overall risk more effectively (Finextra, 2019).

Collaborative Approach

The Trade Finance Registry was an example of how well Singaporean banks' collaborative efforts have worked. A consortium of banks collaborated to leverage blockchain technology, offering a solution that could enhance the integrity and efficiency of the trade finance ecosystem, which is a positive sign for the future (Finextra, 2019).

Singapore is recognized as a global trade hub, an essential transit point for trade worldwide. This is in everyone's interest, as the collaborative bank efforts are a strong positive impetus for the future fight against TBML.

Other Global Initiatives Include

iv Streamlining Trade Finance: The eTradeConnect Platform
eTradeConnect is a trade finance platform that utilizes blockchain technology to enhance process efficiency, eliminate redundant operations, and combat fraud in trade finance transactions. The project commenced in 2018 with the assistance of the Hong Kong Monetary Authority (HKMA) and is financed by a consortium of 12 of Hong Kong's largest banks (Hong Kong Economic and Trade Office, 2018).

Technological Foundation and Objectives

This platform is built on Hyperledger Fabric and uses smart contracts to automate various trade finance processes. Its primary goal is to provide a secure and efficient channel for trade finance transactions, minimizing fraud and errors (Hong Kong Economic and Trade Office, 2018).

Benefits and Expectations

The adoption of eTradeConnect is expected to alter trade finance processes significantly. This initiative is designed to simplify procedures and reduce the time and costs associated with trade transactions (Hong Kong Economic and Trade Office, 2018).

ETradeConnect marks a big step forward for trade finance. Blockchain technologies hold considerable promise for improving security by minimizing fraud risk and optimizing efficiency through automated processes, keeping the future of trade finance looking bright.

v The Rise and Fall of the We. trade Blockchain Platform
The We. trade project was a trade finance blockchain platform created by a consortium of 12 central European banks, including CaixaBank, Deutsche Bank, HSBC, and UniCredit (IBM, 2021; Blockdata, 2023). The platform was announced in October 2018 to create a transparent, secure, and simplified trading environment for businesses and banks (IBM, 2021).

Leveraging Blockchain Technology

The We. trade platform leveraged two blockchain platforms: Hyperledger Fabric and R3 Corda for DLT, consensus, and smart contracts. These blockchain-based features improved the efficiency, security, and transparency of trade finance processes (Blockdata, 2023).

Collaborative Approach and Early Success

The impact of collaboration through the we trade platform demonstrated that a European banking consortium and IBM could work together as technology partners (IBM, 2021). At that time, the we. trade platform had onboarded 15 member banks across 16 countries, and the logistics and insurance sectors were exploring opportunities (IBM, 2021).

Challenges and Shutdown

Despite a positive launch, we trade faced several challenges, leading to its cessation of operations in March 2023 (FinTech Futures, 2022). The challenges of integrating multiple blockchains, the need for broad adoption, and the development of various regulations governing trade finance may have contributed to the platform's closure (Blockdata, 2023).

Lessons Learned

The rise and fall of the we trade platform provides a rich case study, offering crucial lessons on the challenges and prospects of delivering blockchain-enabled trade finance solutions within a highly regulated financial ecosystem. The project demonstrated the potential of blockchain technology to enhance the efficiency of trade finance operations. The project equally highlighted the challenges of institutionalization and regulation (Trade Finance Global, 2022).

vi The TradeIX project is a blockchain-based trade finance platform developed by a consortium of banks and technology companies in the United States. It aims to improve efficiency and reduce fraud in international trade finance. The platform is built on R3's Corda and leverages smart contracts to automate the trade finance process. The TradeIX project, also known as Marco Polo, is a consortium that aims to enhance efficiency in international trade finance through blockchain technology. The network aims to establish real-time connectivity and greater transparency in trading relationships while reducing barriers to capital access (Palmer, 2019). TradeIX is a technology company that has developed an application-enabled trade finance platform-as-a-service. TradeIX bundles its trade finance platform with applications and licenses the service to banks as their trade finance transactional solution. Banks partner with TradeIX by either joining Marco Polo, using it directly, or integrating it with their existing platform (Morris, 2018).

vii Establishing a Pan-European Blockchain Network: The European Blockchain Services Infrastructure

The European Blockchain Services Infrastructure (EBSI) is part of a project coordinated by the European Commission to design a blockchain infrastructure across Europe for use by public authorities and businesses (European Commission, 2024).

Blockchain Platforms Utilized

Various blockchain platforms are central to EBSI's implementation. Many European banks and financial institutions extensively use Corda, a private blockchain especially designed for regulated businesses (European Commission, 2024). Hyperledger Fabric is recognized for its flexibility, and numerous companies and organizations have adopted it for various purposes (IOTA, 2022). EBSI intends to establish a unified European digital infrastructure to enhance innovation, efficiency, and effectiveness across the public and private sectors.

viii Komgo: Revolutionizing Commodity Trade Finance with Blockchain
Komgo was established in 2028 in Geneva, Switzerland. It is a consortium of 15 central banks, trade, and oil giants that has created a blockchain-based trade finance platform to digitize and streamline commodity trade finance (Consensys, 2018; Komgo, 2024).

Tackling the Challenges in Commodity Trade Finance

The commodity trade finance industry has confronted numerous challenges. Some of the issues include miscommunication, security vulnerabilities, manual processes, fraud, and notably slow verification times (Consensys, 2018). Komgo was designed to address these issues by leveraging blockchain technology to enhance transparency, security, and efficiency in trade finance transactions (Consensys, 2018; Ledger Insights, 2019).

Key Features and Benefits

Komgo's blockchain-based platform offers various key features and benefits (Consensys, 2018; Komgo, 2024; Ledger Insights, 2019):

a Reinforced Transparency: Komgo is a single source of truth, allowing authorized participants to transact and share information securely and efficiently in a digital environment.
b Better Security: Komgo's blockchain-based architecture eliminates the risk of information being corrupted or lost, and access to information is tightly controlled.
c Greater Efficiency: Komgo improves operations by automating processes, lessening manual tasks, and eliminating delays caused by third-party intermediaries.
d Cost Savings: Komgo is expected to enable a 20–50% reduction in operational costs and a 30–40% rise in cash-flow benefits across the production chain (Komgo, 2021).

Collaborative Approach and Expansion Plans

Komgo was developed in collaboration with 15 founding shareholders, including central banks, trading companies, and oil companies (Consensys, 2018; Ledger Insights, 2019). The platform leverages JPMorgan's Quorum, a blockchain-based system, and direct connectivity to the VAKT blockchain for post-trade processing, thereby maximizing efficiency in trade settlement (Ledger Insights, 2019). Komgo is primarily focused on utilizing the platform for the energy sector. However, the platform's monetized sharing spans a wide range of commodity sectors, including agribusiness and metals, further transforming the trade finance sector (Ledger Insights, 2019). While the impact of blockchain on trade finance is significant, the $28.5 trillion global trade market still relies on traditional, predominantly paper-based processes to support cross-border trade (Blockdata, 2022).

Leveraging Technology to Combat TBML

The battle against trade-based money laundering has increased reliance on modern technical tools. Governments and regulatory authorities are rapidly implementing measures to leverage emerging technology in this pursuit.

Singapore Customs created a blockchain-based system to detect TBML activity (ZDNet, 2019). The blockchain system uses AI to analyze trade data, identify suspicious behavior patterns, and facilitate the sharing of real-time information with other government agencies. To enhance the effectiveness and security of trade finance, the HKMA has also launched a POC for a blockchain-based trade finance platform (CoinDesk, 2018).

AI technology and vessel-tracking systems are essential for improving TBML detection and prevention. This next-generation technology provides a strong defense against illicit activities

(Acuity Knowledge Partners, 2022). By integrating vessel-tracking data with trade data and other relevant information, AI can more readily identify and flag suspicious activity, thereby alerting banks and regulators in real time.

Blockchain technology provides a secure, transparent record of all transactions and dealings, enabling the tracking of goods and money across borders (Acuity Knowledge Partners, 2022). Moreover, technologies such as machine learning, data analytics, and network visualization offer numerous benefits. It will assist financial organizations and regulators in identifying complex transaction networks, visualizing cross-border money flows, and detecting suspicious activity.

Combating TBML: A Multifaceted Approach

The Significance of International Trade

International trade plays a major role in globalization and business development. It determines a country's ranking as a global economic leader (KPMG, 2020). A nation becomes a leading contender in the global economy through successful international trade engagement. Financial powerhouses such as the United States and China are seeking to strengthen trade ties with countries with stronger AML compliance records. Countries that present a framework for enacting checks and balances to address potential trade vulnerabilities are attractive partners. Regulators worldwide, particularly in the United States, will not tolerate money laundering and sanction violations; they will impose heavy, multi-billion-dollar fines. Banks must balance the growth of their traded finance services by volume and value while also preventing illicit funds from entering their systems. The potential adverse financial and reputational consequences of failing to develop adequate controls and establish parameters are significant and must be avoided at all costs. Banks need to support the development of a new risk assessment to detect, identify, and report suspected money laundering transactions. Client onboarding, due diligence on counterparties, invoice fraud detection, goods movement monitoring, and other risk assessment evidence must be automated (KPMG, 2020).

A Collaborative Approach to Compliance

By adopting a collaborative approach that integrates financial crime and compliance, enhanced information sharing, and emerging technologies such as AI and machine learning (ML), Internet of things (IoT), and blockchain, we can stay ahead of TBML activity. Optical Character Recognition (OCR) enables the scanning of unstructured data, thereby increasing the volume and depth of big data. AI and ML algorithms analyze and process large volumes of data, enabling significant improvements in detection and compliance processes. The technology also yields substantial savings by reducing false positives and minimizing manual review. Better detection can be achieved through derivative centralized processing and data pooling. It is imperative to prioritize data protection to ensure the security of personal data and prevent misuse. While continuing to encourage stakeholders and financial institutions to share information, blockchain technology is expected to be the preferred platform for the upcoming digital trade ecosystem (KPMG, 2020).

The Role of Blockchain Technology

a Blockchain technology is poised to become the preferred platform for the future digital trade ecosystem. This is because it is widely accepted and impartial. However, implementation delays are more likely to arise from gradual changes in global legal frameworks. Some good projects have been completed in parts of Asia and developing countries. However, leading trading countries in the West are miles behind. The transition would be approximately five years, with a hybrid ecosystem period before complete digitization in the most significant trading countries (KPMG, 2020).

b TradeIX is a blockchain-powered trade finance platform that automates trade finance processes and boosts efficiency and transparency through state-of-the-art contract technology. This is a shining example of the helpful application of blockchain technology in the trade finance sector. Its decentralized structure eliminates the need for intermediaries and reduces the risk of errors and fraud. All parties are guaranteed equal access to information (TradeIX, 2022).

c According to "the Marco Polo Network," an industry source that has successfully mastered blockchain technology, the challenge has undoubtedly been game-changing (Marco Polo Network, 2019). In 2017, TradeIX and consortium partners from several banks launched the Marco Polo project—an open-account trade finance platform—built on R3's Corda blockchain framework. The pilot focused on elements of the working capital cycle, with 70 organizations from various industries and banks across more than 25 countries participating. Notably, the solution they worked on was Receivables Finance. This solution aims to optimize working capital, minimize credit exposure, and boost liquidity (Marco Polo Network, 2022). As the network launches on R3's Corda, members are gearing up for production.

d Giving another instance, the Contour project, a blockchain-based platform, proves instrumental in trade finance document flow management (Contour, 2022). The R3-based platform is digitizing trade finance documentation to automate the issuance of letters of credit. ING, Standard Chartered, and HSBC support the project. Following a 2019 pilot with 12 banks, the platform is now progressing toward production.

However, it is crucial to remember that blockchain technology is not a panacea and cannot be applied invariably in all trade finance scenarios (Komgo, 2022). "Not all issues necessitate a complex and costly technical infrastructure for resolution," said Guy de Pourtales, CTO at Komgo (Komgo, 2022). Consequently, an extensive assessment of the requirements must be conducted prior to deciding to adopt blockchain technology.

Training and Education

The battle against TBML is not a technological issue; training and education play a paramount role. By equipping professionals with the necessary skills and knowledge, we can enable them to analyze financial and trade data effectively, detect anomalies, and initiate investigations and legal proceedings in TBML cases. This highlights the need for extensive training modules that emphasize the value of trade and financial information in combating criminal operations and that provide appropriate analytical methodologies (KPMG, 2020). Such methods may cover:

a Comparing domestic and overseas import/export data to reveal discrepancies in different areas, including the Harmonized Tariff Schedule, country of origin, producer, trader, ultimate consignee, unit price, commodity, period, and port of discharge/loading (KPMG, 2020).

b Accessing financial information gathered by the FIU should be examined to spot patterns of transactions involving currency remittances, financial institution deposits, suspicious transaction reports, and parties involved (KPMG, 2020).

c Reviewing the physical cross-border movement of goods to detect discrepancies between shipping documents and the real cargo. Empowering trade finance professionals with the knowledge and skills necessary to identify and respond to TBML risks is essential (KPMG, 2020). This entails providing training on sector-specific risk considerations and on comprehensive AML and compliance. In addition, schools should integrate trade-based money laundering and the application of new technologies into their curricula (KPMG, 2020). This way, they ensure that prospective professionals are well-equipped to address this threat effectively.

To conclude, TBML is an emerging issue that requires multifaceted approaches to address. The tremendous value of global trade and the necessity of robust compliance systems make it imperative that nations, financial institutions, and companies collaborate to address this pressing concern effectively. Blockchain technology can essentially connect different parties and create a decentralized network. It also offers an immutable, tamper-evident, and distributed electronic ledger of transactions. In this way, blockchain is significantly reshaping the global trade finance sector by enhancing its effectiveness, transparency, and security. However, acknowledging that the solution is a combination of technology and other tools becomes the first and foremost step in implementing blockchain in trade finance. Moreover, it is noteworthy that industry players and the regulator should focus on developing and delivering relevant training programs to bring TBML initiatives to fruition.

An Insight: Digitizing the Shipping Industry

The shipping industry remains essential to the global trade system, transporting goods worldwide. However, the sector continues to face significant challenges in efficiently detecting and preventing TBML. Among these is the observation that the industry relies too heavily on paper-based processes, whereas trade finance relies on numerous data sources and entities. A study by the ICC in Paris estimates that more than 4 billion pages of documents are used in global trade operations at any given time (ICC, 2022). The document pile is generally disorganized and unstructured, with documents frequently using non-standard formats. Therefore, automated systems often struggle to recognize and trigger alerts for potential TBML indicators. Therefore, the ICC, recognizing the gravity of the issue, has advocated compliance with the instructions of the standard trade documents. The ICC's Uniform Customs and Practice for Documentary Credits (UCP) and the Uniform Rules for Demand Guarantees (URDG) are among its initiatives to establish standard practices in trade finance (ICC, 2019).

Harnessing Technology to Combat TBML in the Shipping Industry

Greater cooperation and collaboration among stakeholders worldwide will be required to combat TBML in shipping effectively. One option is to use the IoT and blockchain technology in this context.

Blockchain-Based Digital Bunkering Platforms

By leveraging these advanced technologies, it is possible to closely and incrementally monitor the bunkering process—the marine fuel supply chain. This helps to create a bunker delivery note (BDN) that can be stored and shared with approved agencies in a controlled environment. For instance, the Singapore government's Infocomm Media Development Authority (IMDA) provides a blockchain-enabled digital bunkering platform (IMDA, 2022). The platform's goal is to promote transparency and efficiency in the bunkering process. The platform will provide stakeholders with immediate access to bunker delivery notes, enabling them to execute, share, and validate sensitive information. In leveraging this technology, the platform significantly minimizes the risk of TBML and other fraudulent activities.

Collaborative Efforts and Information Sharing

To combat TBML, stakeholders, including financial institutions, regulators, and customs agencies, must collaborate. Greater action sharing among stakeholders will help identify TBML threats and respond accordingly (Regulation Asia, 2022). The COSMIC initiative, an abbreviation of Suspicious Transaction Reporting and Information Exchange, led by the Monetary Authority of Singapore, is a good example of how entire sectors can network to combat financial crimes.

Can Customs Play a More Significant Role?

Customs are not considered cooperative or powerful as they were in the last century. However, it remains necessary to trace the passage of goods across borders and to provide the required trade documents, such as the Bill of Entry and the Shipping Bill. However, in the current containerized shipping environment, customs authorities face several challenges in identifying TBML. The complexity and volume of containerized trade make it more difficult to detect illegal activity. Physical inspection and verification of all container contents are not realistic enforcement measures, given the large number of sealed containers that customs will release with accompanying paperwork, which would cause significant delays and backlogs.

Customs departments can combat TBML through the strategic use of non-intrusive inspection (NII) technologies, such as the Vehicle and Cargo Inspection System (VACIS). These state-of-the-art machines have been developed to identify and detect an array of illicit items, including nuclear material, drugs, guns, and other contraband. Additionally, they are suitable for examining the tailgates of selected containers. We must acknowledge the United States, which has been utilizing these machines as a proactive measure to enhance the effectiveness of crime prevention. However, it is important to recognize that this technology has limitations, especially when handling the massive volume of containers at a port. The technology does not function properly at high volume, and additional precautions are required to ensure that the area is exclusive to staff and security units. Therefore, customs departments are more inclined to deploy a risk-based inspection approach, in which they randomly select containers for further investigation or rely on suspicion or prior information of smuggling. With this approach, the authorities have ample opportunities to meet the necessary security requirements and facilitate legal trade without impediment (U.S. Customs and Border Protection, 2023).

Combating TBML: A Multifaceted Approach

The United Nations Office on Drugs and Crime states that the battle against TBML must be multi-pronged, encompassing a variety of measures and approaches (UNODC, 2020). NII technologies are essential to customs enforcement and should be used alongside other risk-based methodologies to detect and identify TBML effectively. The report further underlined that implementing NII technologies can be complex in specific environments (e.g., busy ports and ports with substantial traffic). This highlights the value of using NII as a targeted tool and the most effective ways to maximize its effectiveness within NII technologies (UNODC, 2020).

Customs Department's Toolkit for Combating TBML

In addition to NII technologies, customs departments can employ a variety of other measures to combat TBML, covering:

i Risk-based targeting: Recognizing and focusing on high-risk transactions or entities.
ii Data analytics: Utilizing data to spot patterns and recognize TBML relationships, trends, and indicators.
iii Intelligence gathering: Collecting, classifying, and analyzing data and relevant information about TBML operations.
iv International collaboration: Collaborating with other countries to share information and coordinate enforcement efforts (UNODC, 2020).

If customs authorities employ a variety of measures, they can substantially reduce the risk that criminals will use trade finance for money laundering. However, by taking a proactive approach to combating crime, customs authorities send a powerful message that such crime is unacceptable. Effective detection and prevention measures will enable law enforcement to reduce criminal activity and protect communities.

Leveraging Data Analytics and Blockchain Technology to Combat TBML

Data analytics provides a highly effective method for addressing TBML. By using data analytics, customs departments can systematically review data from transport documents and invoices to categorize containers for secondary examination. This method is highly beneficial for improving the accuracy and efficiency of TBML activity detection. For example, the UK Border Force uses data analytics to identify high-risk containers for inspection, thereby recovering millions of pounds' worth of illegal drugs, tobacco, and other counterfeit products (Blockdata, 2022).

Blockchain Technology for Enhancing Transparency

Blockchain technology is another tool customs authorities can use to combat TBML effectively. Blockchain innovation provides a secure, transparent platform for document exchange, making it the most viable option for customs departments (Blockdata, 2022). As a result, customs departments can also enhance their efficiency and accuracy in detecting TBML activities. For instance, in Singapore, a consortium of 14 banks, led by DBS and Standard Chartered Bank, has developed a POC for the Trade Finance Registry that utilizes blockchain technology (Blockdata, 2022). The registry's priority is to ensure the transparency of traded commodities and to improve lending practices by creating a secure central database for trade transactions financed by local banks.

The Rise of Electronic Bills of Lading and Digital Trade Networks

Major container shipping companies are increasing their use of electronic bills of lading (eBLs) to significantly enhance the digital trade sector. eBL issuance is expected to be 50% electronic in five years and 100% electronic in ten years, respectively. This is excellent news for blockchain trade networks such as Contour, GSBN, and TradeWaltz, whose stated aim is to digitize, manage, and streamline the trade finance process, to minimize transaction processing time and costs, and to improve transparency and security (Blockdata, 2022).

AI for TBML Detection

In addition, AI can be a valuable asset for customs departments in identifying and recognizing TBML (Blockdata, 2022). Customs departments can benefit from examining large volumes of data to identify patterns or misalignments that may indicate TBML operations. For example, Singapore's Customs and Excise Department has created an AI platform to detect trade-based money laundering (Blockdata, 2022). This cutting-edge platform will use advanced ML algorithms to analyze and identify suspicious trading transactions and assess their integrity.

The Way Forward: Leveraging Blockchain Technology for Improved Customs Operations

Implementation of Emerging Technologies

Blockchain technology has recently emerged as a transformative tool across sectors such as finance, supply chain management, logistics, and government. Customs operations are a ripe area for improving efficiency, security, and transparency through the use of this technology (European Commission, 2024).

Benefits of Blockchain for Customs Operations

Blockchain technology delivers numerous benefits for customs operations. It establishes a secure, tamper-proof ledger of transactions that enables customs administrations to verify the validity and accuracy of transaction information for the respective shipment, thereby minimizing the risk of fraud and inaccuracy. Complete and accurate visibility within the blockchain also helps ensure compliance with trade laws and regulations. It protects the company from actions such as attempting to smuggle goods or launder illicit funds (European Commission, 2024).

Blockchain in Customs Modernization: Global Cases

Many customs agencies worldwide are implementing blockchain technology to modernize their operations. One, Singapore Customs, developed a blockchain-based system for tracking and validating shipping documents in conjunction with the Singapore Shipping Association and Deloitte. Dutch Customs is also at the forefront of launching the "Blockchain for European Trade" (BET) project to improve the monitoring of goods across the European Union (IOTA, 2022).

Collaborative Efforts against TBML

To counter TBML effectively, the most appropriate approach is a collaborative effort among departments, including customs, financial institutions, and international organizations. Customs departments should use advanced analytical and inspection technologies (e.g., NII devices such as VACIS and data analytics) to identify high-risk containers and detect TBML. Collaboration with law enforcement and/or other entities with criminal intelligence capabilities (e.g., financial intelligence unit) further reinforces efforts to combat TBML (Ledger Insights, 2023).

Interpol's Arsenal against TBML: Information Sharing and Technological Innovation

Interpol is pivotal for combating TBML by providing member states with an effective range of tools and services. The Interpol Illicit Arms Records and Tracing Management System (iARMS) is a notable example that elucidates this point. The iARMS initiative enables member countries to exchange information on illicit arms trafficking, which often follows the same pathways as TBML activities (UNODC, 2020). Moreover, Interpol's Project Container demonstrates the organization's commitment to combating TBML through innovation and technology. Project Container enables customs and law enforcement authorities to disable and stop the illicit movement of goods within shipping containers, a more common avenue for TBML operations, through the collaboration of technology and the coordination of global efforts (Interpol, 2023). This is critical, given that more than 420 million containers are moved by sea each year, transporting 90% of the world's cargo (Container Control, 2021).

With the advent of a new era in customs operations enabled by blockchain technology. Nurturing a secure, transparent, and efficient environment is a powerful deterrent to TBML, ultimately facilitating seamless trade globally. Suppose customs collaborates with like-minded organizations and evaluates the planned investment in this technology judiciously. If so, they can unlock significant potential to improve productivity, enhance transparency, and foster sustainable global trading practices.

Insight: Blockchain-Based Digital Bunkering: Singapore's Pioneering Transformation

The maritime bunkering industry, traditionally reliant on manual processes and paper-based documentation, has long faced inefficiencies, fraud risks, and regulatory challenges. Blockchain technology—a decentralized, immutable ledger system—has emerged as transformative, particularly in Singapore, the world's largest bunkering hub. By digitizing and securing bunkering transactions, blockchain enhances transparency, efficiency, and trust across the supply chain.

This case study explores how Singapore has pioneered blockchain-based digital bunkering, its key functionalities, and the tangible benefits achieved through its implementation.

How Blockchain Revolutionizes Bunkering?

1 Ensuring Transparency and Traceability

- Blockchain creates a single, tamper-proof record of every bunkering transaction, accessible to authorized stakeholders (suppliers, shipowners, regulators).
- Singapore's Maritime and Port Authority (MPA) mandates e-Bunker Delivery Notes (e-BDNs) via blockchain, eliminating discrepancies in fuel quality and quantity (MPA, 2025).
- Real-time verification via QR codes reduces disputes and enhances accountability (SSA Singapore, 2024).

2 Automating Documentation and Reducing Fraud

- Traditional paper-based BDNs are replaced with smart contract-driven e-BDNs, minimizing human error and manipulation (Mumtaz, Bergey, & Letch, 2024).

- Fraud prevention: Blockchain's cryptographic security prevents fuel adulteration and false invoicing, saving millions in losses (SpectraFuels, 2024).

3 Enhancing Operational Efficiency

- Automated compliance reporting reduces administrative burdens.
- Singapore's digital bunkering initiative is projected to save 40,000 person-days annually and $300,000 in compliance costs (MPA, 2025).

Singapore's Blockchain Bunkering Success

1 World's First Mandatory e-BDN System (2025)

- Singapore became the first port globally to enforce default e-BDN adoption in April 2025.
- The MPA's centralized verification system allows instant authentication by banks, regulators, and vessel operators (MPA, 2025).

2 Smart Contracts for Seamless Transactions

- Ethereum-based smart contracts automate bunkering records, ensuring real-time data sharing between suppliers and clients (Temasek Polytechnic, 2023).
- Example: A blockchain pilot by a Singaporean bunker supplier reduced transaction disputes by 30% (S&P Global, 2021).

3 Strengthening Singapore's Bunkering Leadership

- Blockchain adoption has reinforced Singapore's reputation as the most trusted bunkering hub, attracting more maritime businesses (SpectraFuels, 2024).
- The Singapore Shipping Association (SSA) reports a 20% increase in stakeholder confidence due to digital bunkering (SSA, 2024).

Singapore's leadership in blockchain-based digital bunkering demonstrates how technology can streamline maritime operations, reduce fraud, and enhance regulatory compliance. By mandating e-BDNs and integrating smart contracts, Singapore has set a global benchmark for secure,

Table 20.1 Key Benefits of Blockchain Bunkering

Feature	*Impact*
Decentralized ledger	Tamper-proof records prevent fraud and disputes, ensuring auditability.
e-BDNs	Faster, error-free documentation with QR verification for real-time tracking.
Smart contracts	Automated invoicing, payments, and compliance reduce manual errors and improve efficiency.
Regulatory integration	Real-time reporting aligns with MPA and IMO standards, ensuring compliance.
Transparency & Traceability	End-to-end visibility minimizes transaction disputes and facilitates audits under GAAP and IFRS.
Risk management	Cryptographic security reduces the risk of unauthorized access and ensures data integrity.
Automated reconciliation	Streamlined financial reporting accelerates settlement cycles for bunker fuel suppliers and buyers.
Fraud prevention	Immutable records prevent falsified fuel specifications, reducing losses.
Environmental tracking	Supports carbon credit validation and sustainability initiatives.

efficient bunkering. As other ports adopt similar frameworks, Singapore's model serves as a blueprint for digital transformation in the maritime sector.

Chapter Summary

This section outlines the AML rules in place across four Islamic banking systems worldwide: the UAE, Malaysia, Sudan, and Pakistan. The UAE and Malaysia strictly enforce AML laws, whereas Sudan is developing AML regulations. However, their implementation is less stringent: Pakistan has AML laws, but it needs to strengthen enforcement to make them more effective and secure. Trade-based money laundering is a form of money laundering characterized by its transnational and complex nature, which makes it particularly vulnerable to detection. This chapter has been enriched with estimates of the global financial and banking dimensions of TBML, as well as the pandemic's effects. Payment methods also play a critical role, and changes in these methods have been identified as a key driver of enhanced TBML risk. The trade finance challenge posed by the predominance of document-based processes is highlighted, underscoring the difficulty of detecting TBML in paper-based transactions. Customs administrations ensure that products cross borders legally and issue the corresponding documents. However, like others, they have been finding it challenging to identify TBML cases. The benefits of easy, fast, and less costly customs transactions facilitated by blockchain technology have been explained.

End of Chapter: Discussion Questions

1. What are the Islamic banking assets of the UAE, Malaysia, Sudan, and Pakistan?
2. What is the market share of Islamic banking assets in Malaysia and Sudan?
3. How do Pakistan's AML regulations compare to international standards?
4. What are the challenges of detecting TBML?
5. Which payment methods are less prone to TBML risk?
6. What is most of the global trade conducted for in terms of value?
7. What are the challenges of detecting TBML in the trade finance process?
8. What is the role of customs departments in detecting TBML?
9. What are the limitations of the physical opening and checking of all containers' contents by customs departments?
10. What emerging technology can revolutionize customs operations?
11. How can blockchain technology be used in customs operations?
12. How does international cooperation act as a deterrent against TBML?

References

ACAMS. (2023). Transaction monitoring best practice guide. Napier.ai. https://www.napier.ai/post/transaction-monitoring-acams

Acuity Knowledge Partners. (2022). Trade-based money laundering: How it works and how to combat it. https://www.acuitykp.com/blog/trade-based-money-laundering-how-it-works-and-how-to-combat-it/

Akhtar, S. (2018). Challenges in implementing anti-money laundering regulations in Pakistan's Islamic banking industry. *International Journal of Islamic Banking and Finance*, 8(1), 23–36.

APG (2019). Mutual Evaluation Report - Pakistan. Asia/Pacific Group on Money Laundering. Retrieved from https://www.fatf-gafi.org/content/dam/fatf-gafi/fsrb-mer/APG-Mutual-Evaluation-Report-Pakistan-October%202019.pdf.

Bank Negara Malaysia. (2001). Anti-Money Laundering, Anti-Terrorism Financing, and Proceeds of Unlawful Activities Act 2001. Retrieved from https://www.bnm.gov.my/anti-money-laundering-and-counter-financing-of-terrorism.

Blockdata. (2022). Leveraging technology to combat trade-based money laundering. https://www.blockdata.tech/blog/general/leveraging-technology-to-combat-trade-based-money-laundering.

Blockdata. (2023, March 8). we. Trade: A blockchain-based trade finance platform. https://www.blockdata.tech/profiles/we-trade

BNM (2021). Anti-Money Laundering and Counter Financing of Terrorism Policy. Bank Negara Malaysia.

Central Bank of Malaysia. (2020). Anti-Money Laundering and Counter Financing of Terrorism (AML/CFT) Policy. https://www.bnm.gov.my/index.php?ch=en_regulation&pg=en_regulation&ac=3147&bb=file

Central Bank of Sudan. (2021). Anti-Money Laundering (AML) and Combating the Financing of Terrorism (CFT).

Central Bank of the UAE. (2021). Annual Report 2021. Retrieved from https://www.centralbank.ae/media/0q2ogybl/cbuae-annual-report-2021-prl_en.pdf.

CoinDesk. (2018, November). The Hong Kong monetary authority is launching a blockchain trade finance platform. Retrieved from https://www.coindesk.com/hong-kong-monetary-authority-launches-blockchain-trade-finance-platform

Consensys. (2018). Komgo: Blockchain case study for commodity trade finance. https://consensys.io/blockchain-use-cases/finance/komgo

Container Control. (2021). United Nations: Office on Drugs and Crime. https://www.unodc.org/unodc/es/urban-safety/container-control.html.

Contour. (2022). Contour: Transforming trade finance. https://www.contour.network/.

DFSA (2021). Anti-Money Laundering (AML) and Counter Financing of Terrorism (CFT). Dubai Financial Services Authority.

Dodd-Frank Wall Street Reform and Consumer Protection Act, Pub. L. No. 111–203, 124 Stat. 1376 (2010). https://www.govinfo.gov/content/pkg/PLAW-111publ203/pdf/PLAW-111publ203.pdf

European Central Bank. (2022, November 8). Digital euro. European Central Bank. https://www.ecb.europa.eu/paym/digital_euro/html/index.en.html.

European Commission. (2024). EBSI: Europa. Eu. https://ec.europa.eu/digital-building-blocks/sites/display/EBSI/Home

Financial Action Task Force. (2018). FATF Guidance for a risk-based approach: Islamic banking sector. Retrieved from https://www.fatf-gafi.org/media/fatf/documents/reports/RBA-Islamic-Banking.pdf.

Financial Action Task Force. (2019). Mutual evaluation report - United Arab Emirates. https://www.fatf-gafi.org/publications/mutualevaluations/documents/mer-united-arab-emirates-2019.html

Financial Action Task Force. (2020). COVID-19-related money laundering and terrorist financing: Risks and policy responses. https://www.fatf-gafi.org/media/fatf/documents/COVID-19-AML-CFT.pdf

Financial Action Task Force. (2021). Sudan: Mutual evaluation report. https://www.fatf-gafi.org/media/fatf/documents/reports/mer4/MER-Sudan-2021.pdf.

Financial Stability Oversight Council. (2015). Trade-based money laundering: An evolving threat to financial systems. https://www.treasury.gov/initiatives/fsoc/studies-reports/Documents/Final%20TBML%20Report%20-%20August%202015.pdf

Finextra. (2019). Singapore consortium claims breakthrough in DLT payments project. https://www.finextra.com/newsarticle/31156/singapore-consortium-claims-breakthrough-in-dlt-payments-project

FinTech Futures. (2022, June). Blockchain-based trade finance platform we trade shuts shop. https://www.fintechfutures.com/2022/06/blockchain-based-trade-finance-platform-we-trade-shuts-shop/

Global Coalition to Fight Financial Crime MENA Chapter, & MENA Financial Crime Compliance Group. (2022, October). *Trade-based financial crime - Middle East and North Africa: A reference guide for the anti-financial crime community.* GCFFC Publications. https://gfintegrity.org/wp-content/uploads/2022/10/TBFC-in-MENA-Report-English.pdf

Global Financial Integrity. (2020). Trade-based money laundering: The threat to the world's financial systems. https://www.gfintegrity.org/wp-content/uploads/2020/03/TBML-Report-2020.pdf

Hassan, S. S. U., Hussain, M. A., & Sajid, S. (2021). The effectiveness of anti-money laundering legislation in Islamic banking in Pakistan: Experts' opinion. *Journal of Money Laundering Control*, 24(1), 135–149. https://doi.org/10.1108/JMLC-02-2021-0014

Hoffman, C. (2023). Trade Finance Global. https://www.tradefinanceglobal.com/posts/icc-dsi-7-key-trade-documents-digitisation/.

Hong Kong Economic and Trade Office. (2018). Launch of eTradeConnect and collaboration with us. Trade. https://www.hketosf.gov.hk/ehk/ehongkong93/etradeconnect.htm

IBM. (2021). we. trade innovation | IBM. https://www.ibm.com/case-studies/wetrade-blockchain-fintech-trade-finance

IBM. (2021). we. trade: Blockchain facilitates international commerce.

ICC. (2022). ICC Global Survey on Trade Finance. https://iccwbo.org/publication/icc-global-survey-on-trade-finance/.

ICC. (2019). ICC Banking Commission. https://iccwbo.org/publication/icc-banking-commission-opinions/.

IMDA. (2022). Blockchain-based digital bunkering platform. https://www.imda.gov.sg/programme-listing/blockchain-based-digital-bunkering-platform.

Investopedia. (2023). Anti-Money Laundering (AML): What It Is, Its History, and How It Works. Retrieved from https://www.investopedia.com/terms/a/aml.asp.

International Chamber of Commerce. (2023). Trade finance survey 2023. https://iccwbo.org/global-insights/global-trade/trade-and-supply-chain-finance/.

Interpol. (2023). Project Container. https://www.interpol.int/en/Crimes/Maritime-crime/Project-Container.

IOTA. (2022). EBSI. https://www.iota.org/solutions/ebsi

Khan, S. (2022). Strengthening anti-money laundering regulations in Pakistan's Islamic banking sector. *Policy Perspectives*, 19(1), 45–60.

Kim, K., Lim, S., Lee, C., Lee, W., Jeon, H., Jung, J., & Jung, D. (2022). Forecasting liquefied natural gas bunker prices using an artificial neural network for procurement management. *Journal of Marine Science and Engineering*, 10(12), 1814. https://doi.org/10.3390/jmse10121814

Komgo. (2021). Komgo: Transforming trade finance through blockchain technology. Komgo SA. Retrieved from https://www.komgo.io.

Komgo. (2022). Komgo: Digitizing commodity trade finance. https://www.komgo.io/.

Komgo. (2024). Komgo | Trade finance platform & solutions. https://www.komgo.io

KPMG Taseer Hadi & Co. (2020, April). *Framework for managing risks of trade-based money laundering and terrorist financing.* KPMG International. https://assets.kpmg.com/content/dam/kpmgsites/pk/pdf/2020/04/Framework%20for%20managing%20Risks%20of%20Trade%20Based%20AML%20CFT%20%20SBP.pdf.coredownload.pdf

Kyriakos-Saad, N., Vasquez, M., Chady El Khoury, & Arz El Murr. (2016). Islamic Finance and Anti-Money Laundering and Combating the Financing of Terrorism (AML/CFT). IMF Working Paper WP/16/42; February 2016. https://www.imf.org/external/pubs/ft/wp/2016/wp1642.pdf.

Ledger Insights. (2019, January 3). Commodities trade finance blockchain Komgo goes live. VAKT relationship clarified. https://www.ledgerinsights.com/komgo-commodities-trade-finance-blockchain/

Ledger Insights. (2023, February 24). *Enterprise blockchain trade finance network Marco Polo is insolvent.* Retrieved from https://www.ledgerinsights.com/marco-polo-blockchain-trade-finance-insolvency/

The Marco Polo Network. (2019). Marco Polo: The world's leading trade finance network [Archived Web Page]. TradeIX. Preserved by the Internet Archive on December 20, 2019. https://web.archive.org/web/20191220131448/

Trade Finance Global. (2019). *Marco Polo: Innovative blockchain trade finance project revealed.* TFG Compliance Portal. Retrieved from https://www.tradefinanceglobal.com/posts/marco-polo-finance-innovative-blockchain-trade-finance-project-revealed/

Malik, A. (2020). Evaluating the effectiveness of anti-money laundering regulations in Pakistan's Islamic banking sector. *Journal of Islamic Finance*, 10(2), 45–57.

Maritime and Port Authority of Singapore (MPA). (2025). Digital Bunkering Initiative. https://www.mpa.gov.sg.

Movers International Pvt. Ltd. (2024, June). Movers International Pvt. Ltd. - Lognet Global Logistics Network, Logistic Partners. https://www.lognetglobal.com/specialty/warehouses/members/45198

Morris, N. (2018, June 20). Trade finance blockchain consortia: How they differ. Ledger Insights - Blockchain for Enterprise. https://www.ledgerinsights.com/trade-finance-blockchain-consortium/

Mumtaz, U. U., Bergey, P., & Letch, N. (2024). Assessing the role of blockchain technology for marine bunkering operations – A case study of task technology fit. *Marine Policy*, 159, 105909. https://doi.org/10.1016/j.marpol.2023.105909

Osato Avan-Nomayo. (2021, January 6). Italian Banking Association launches experimental digital euro project. Cointelegraph; Cointelegraph. https://cointelegraph.com/news/italian-banking-association-launches-experimental-digital-euro-project.

Palmer, D. (2019, September 19). Bank of America joins Marco Polo blockchain trade network. CoinDesk. https://www.coindesk.com/markets/2019/09/19/bank-of-america-joins-marco-polo-blockchain-trade-network/

Regulation Asia. (2022). A radical Re-think on combating trade-based money laundering. https://www.regulationasia.com/a-radical-re-think-on-combatting-trade-based-money-laundering/.

S&P Global Commodity Insights. (2021, March 23). *Digital bunkering is gaining traction on both cost and environmental grounds.* Shipping Market Insights. https://www.spglobal.com/commodity-insights/en/news-research/blog/shipping/032321-digital-bunkering-environment-blockchain-marine-fuel

SpectraFuels. (2024). Examining the impact of blockchain technology on the efficiency and functionality of marine bunkering operations. https://spectrafuels.com/examining-the-impact-of-blockchain-technology-on-the-efficiency-and-functionality.

SSA Singapore. (2024). FAQ on Digital Bunkering in Singapore. https://www.ssa.org.sg/wp-content/uploads/2024/06/vJuneSMW-FAQ-on-Digital-Bunkering-1.pdf.

State Bank of Pakistan. (2020). Anti-Money Laundering and Counter Financing of Terrorism (AML/CFT) Regulations. Retrieved from https://www.sbp.org.pk/pages/Anti-Money-Laundering-and-Counter-Financing-of-Terrorism-AML-CFT-Regulations.html.

State Bank of Pakistan. (2021). Anti-Money Laundering and Combating the Financing of Terrorism (AML/CFT) regulations for Islamic banking institutions. SBP. Retrieved from https://www.sbp.org.pk.

State Bank of Pakistan Exchange Policy Department. (2025). *Revised framework for managing risks of trade-based money laundering and terrorist financing (FE Circular No. 8 Annex)*. SBP Corporate Documents. https://www.sbp.org.pk/epd/2025/FECL8-Annex.pdf

Sudan Efforts on Anti-Money Laundering and Combating the Financing of Terrorism Report | CBOS. (2024). Cbos.gov.sd. Retrieved from https://cbos.gov.sd/en/content/sudan-efforts-anti-money-laundering-and-combating-financing-terrorism-report.

Temasek Polytechnic. (2023). Blockchain for the Bunkering Industry: Technology Overview. Overview.https://www.tp.edu.sg/content/dam/tp-web/files/research-and-industry/research-and-technology/Blockchain%20for%20the%20Bunkering%20Industry.pdf.

Thompson, F. (2021, October 20). Singapore to counter trade-based money laundering with a new platform. *Global Trade Review.* https://www.gtreview.com/news/asia/singapore-to-counter-trade-based-money-laundering-with-new-platform/

Trade IX. (2022). TradeIX: Powering the future of trade finance. https://tradeix.com/.

Trade Finance Global. (2022). we. trade enters the trough of disillusionment: What this means for the digitalization of trade finance. https://www.tradefinanceglobal.com/posts/we-trade-enters-the-trough-of-disillusionment-what-this-means-for-the-digitalisation-of-trade-finance/

Unger, B. (2007). *The scale and impacts of money laundering*. Edward Elgar Publishing. https://doi.org/10.4337/9781781007624

United Arab Emirates - Oil, Trade, Investment | Britannica. (2023). In Encyclopedia Britannica. https://www.britannica.com/place/United-Arab-Emirates/Finance.

U.S. Customs and Border Protection. (2022, October). *Trade News Snapshot: Increasing the focus on trade-based money laundering (Vol. 4, Issue 5)*. https://www.cbp.gov/trade/snapshot/volume-4-issue-5

World Trade Organization. (2021). Adapting to the digital trade era: Challenges and opportunities. https://onlinebookshop.wto.org/

Additional Learning Resources

Article

1 Money laundering in selected emerging economies: is there a role for banks? By Sulaiman Abdullah Saif Alnasser Mohammed (2020). Journal of Money Laundering Control. Retrieved from https://www.emerald.com/insight/content/doi/10.1108/JMLC-12-2019-0096/full/html

This article explores the role of banks in money laundering in emerging economies. The study examines factors including Islamic banks' performance, the legal environment, the financial crisis, and bank size in relation to anti-money laundering efforts. The research provides insights into the challenges and potential solutions for combating money laundering in these economies.

2 Do Islamic banks gain from corruption and money laundering (ML)? by Kinza Aish, M. Kabir Hassan, Qamar Uz Zaman, Sadaf Ehsan, Khurram Abbas, and Ijaz Hussain Shah (2022) published in the Journal of Money Laundering Control, 25(4), 909–929. https://doi.org/10.1108/JMLC-09-2021-0094.
This article explores the relationship between Islamic banks and corruption and money laundering. The study examines whether Islamic banks benefit from corruption and money laundering and offers insights into the challenges and potential solutions to combating money laundering in Islamic banking systems.

3 Mohamad Abdul Latif, A., & Abdul-Rahman, A. (2018). Combating money laundering in Malaysia: Current practice, challenges, and suggestions. *Asian Journal of Accounting and Governance*, 10, 109–122. http://dx.doi.org/10.17576/AJAG-2018-10-11. Retrieved from https://www.ukm.my/ajag/article/combating-money-laundering-in-malaysia-current-practice-challenges-and-suggestions/
The article examines current practices, challenges, and recommendations for combating money laundering in Malaysia. The study provides insights into Malaysia's AML/CFT regulatory framework and offers recommendations to enhance the effectiveness of anti-money laundering efforts.

4 The effectiveness of anti-money laundering legislation in Islamic banking of Pakistan: experts' Opinion by Syed Saqlain Ul Hassan, Mohammad Azam Hussain, and Saima Sajid (2021) published in the Journal of Money Laundering Control. Retrieved from https://www.emerald.com/insight/content/doi/10.1108/JMLC-02-2021-0014/full/html
This article explores the effectiveness of anti-money laundering legislation in Islamic banking in Pakistan. The study investigates experts' opinions on the effectiveness of current anti-money laundering legislation. It offers insights into the challenges and potential solutions to combating money laundering in Islamic banking in Pakistan.

5 Compatibility of Islamic Finance and Anti-Money Laundering Laws: A Myth or Reality? by Nasir, M. A. (2018) published in the IIUM Law Journal, 26(1), 55. Available at: https://heinonline.org/HOL/LandingPage?handle=hein.journals/iiumlj26&div=5&id=&page=
The article explores the compatibility of Islamic finance and anti-money laundering laws. The study investigates the challenges and potential solutions for combating money laundering in Islamic banking systems in Pakistan. The research provides insights into the AML/CFT regulatory framework in Islamic banking and offers recommendations to enhance the effectiveness of anti-money laundering efforts.

Working Paper

6 Islamic Finance and Anti-Money Laundering and Combating the Financing of Terrorism (AML/CFT)" is an IMF working paper by the International Monetary Fund (2016). WP/16/42. Retrieved from https://www.imf.org/external/pubs/ft/wp/2016/wp1642.pdf
The paper provides an overview of the key characteristics of Islamic financial institutions and products. It discusses what money laundering and terrorist financing are and how the FATF standards address these issues in the context of Islamic finance.

Book Chapter

7 The Relevance of Maqasid al-Shariah to Anti-Money Laundering and Terrorism Financing by Maruf Adeniyi Nasir (2020) published in the Handbook of Research on Theory and Practice of Global Islamic Finance (pp. 179–194). IGI Global.
This chapter explores the relevance of Maqasid al-Shariah (the purposes of Islamic Shariah) to anti-money laundering and terrorism financing. The chapter discusses how the principles of Maqasid al-Shariah can be applied to combat money laundering and terrorist financing in Islamic finance.

Epilogue

The Multi-faceted Approach to Combating Trade-Based Money Laundering

Trade-based money laundering (TBML) is a pervasive threat to the global financial system, with criminals exploiting the complexity of international trade to launder illicit funds. In recent years, several emerging trends and developments in TBML have significant implications for trade and financial systems. In this section, we examine these trends and their potential consequences.

Trend 1: Increase in TBML Cases

According to a recent report by the United Nations Office on Drugs and Crime (UNODC), TBML is on the rise, with criminals using more sophisticated methods to launder their money. The report reveals that TBML has become the most common method of money laundering, accounting for up to 80% of all illicit financial flows globally. The total value of illegal funds laundered through TBML is estimated to range from $800 billion to $2 trillion annually.

Trend 2: Use of Digital Technologies

Another trend in TBML is the increasing use of digital technologies to facilitate illicit trade. Criminals are using e-commerce platforms, social media, and other digital tools to commit illegal activities. This trend is particularly concerning because digital transactions are difficult to trace, thereby facilitating money laundering.

Trend 3: Collaboration between Criminal Networks

There is a growing trend in TBML that involves criminal networks collaborating. This collaboration facilitates these criminals' movement of illicit funds across borders and their laundering. Such a trend is highly alarming, as it poses a greater challenge for law enforcement agencies in detecting and disrupting TBML activities.

Trend 4: Increased Focus on Technology

Technology has become a crucial tool for TBML detection and prevention. Financial institutions are leveraging advanced analytics, artificial intelligence (AI), and machine learning to analyze trade transactions, identify red flags, and detect suspicious activity. According to a report by Accuity (Accuity 2019). A financial crime compliance solutions provider, 80% of respondents reported plans to invest in AI and machine learning to enhance TBML detection capabilities. The use of blockchain technology is gaining popularity in combating TBML, as it provides a secure and transparent record of trade transactions.

DOI: 10.4324/9781003477631-22

For example, SWIFT, the global financial messaging network, launched its Sanctions Screening service, which uses AI to scan billions of financial messages to detect potentially illicit activity. Similarly, the US Treasury's Office of Foreign Assets Control (OFAC) has launched a new tool that uses machine learning to analyze trade data for sanctions compliance.

Trend 5: Emerging Threats from Cryptocurrencies

Cryptocurrencies have emerged as a significant new threat in TBML. Criminals can use cryptocurrencies to move illicit funds anonymously across borders, making them an attractive option for money launderers. According to a report by Chainalysis(Chainalysis, 2013) in 2020, a blockchain analysis company reported that the value of illicit cryptocurrency transactions associated with TBML exceeded $500 million. The UNODC suggests that the increasing use of cryptocurrencies in TBML could be a significant challenge for law enforcement agencies.

Recent high-profile cases involving cryptocurrencies, such as the use of Bitcoin to fund the WannaCry ransomware attack, have heightened concerns about their use in TBML. In response, regulators are intensifying scrutiny of cryptocurrency exchanges and other virtual asset service providers to ensure compliance with anti-money laundering (AML) regulations.

Trend 6: Heightened Regulatory Scrutiny

Regulators are increasing their focus on TBML. The Financial Action Task Force (FATF) has recently updated its guidance on TBML, including new measures to prevent the misuse of trade transactions for illicit purposes. The revised FATF guidance places significant responsibility on financial institutions to ensure that their customers' trade transactions are not being used for illegal purposes. In addition, countries are strengthening their laws and regulations related to TBML. For example, in 2020, the US Congress introduced the Trade-Based Money Laundering Enforcement Act, which aims to improve the detection and prevention of TBML.

Impact on TBML and Global Trade

The impact of these trends and developments on TBML is massive. The increased focus on technology will lead to more effective detection and prevention of TBML. However, the emergence of cryptocurrencies as a new threat could make it more challenging to track and prevent illicit trade-based transactions. Heightened regulatory scrutiny will also make it more difficult for money launderers to use trade transactions for illegal purposes.

The impact of TBML on global trade is enormous. TBML can distort trade flows, inflate prices, and reduce the competitiveness of legitimate businesses. The use of TBML can result in a loss of tax revenue for governments, undermining their ability to fund critical public services. It can also fuel corruption and financial crimes, such as money laundering and terrorist financing.

Moreover, the use of TBML can damage the integrity and reputation of the financial system, as banks and other financial institutions may unwittingly facilitate or be used to facilitate TBML. This can result in reputational damage, regulatory scrutiny, and potential legal liabilities for financial institutions. It can also erode trust among customers, investors, and other stakeholders and harm the broader economy.

Potential Benefits

Despite the challenges posed by TBML, the latest trends and developments offer potential benefits. The increased focus on technology will lead to more effective detection and prevention of TBML, reducing its impact on global trade. The emergence of technologies such as blockchain could also create opportunities to enhance trade transparency and mitigate the risk of TBML. Heightened regulatory scrutiny will help to create a more level playing field for legitimate businesses, reducing the competitive advantage of those involved in TBML.

Challenges to Combat TBML

Lack of International Cooperation: TBML often involves multiple jurisdictions, making it challenging to coordinate a response. Some countries may have weak or nonexistent laws and regulations governing TBML, thereby facilitating criminal exploitation of these gaps.

Complexity of Trade Transactions: International trade transactions can be complex and involve multiple parties, making it difficult to detect and trace TBML. Criminals can employ various techniques to conceal their activities, such as misclassifying goods or using fraudulent invoices.

Insufficient Resources: Governments and financial institutions may lack the resources and expertise needed to combat TBML effectively. This can include a lack of skilled personnel, advanced technology, and analytical tools.

Complex Nature of TBML: TBML is a complex and constantly evolving form of money laundering. Criminals use various techniques to disguise their transactions, making detection and prevention challenging.

Lack of Standardization: There is a lack of standardization in TBML-related procedures and regulations, which impedes coordination of efforts to combat the problem.

Opportunities to Combat TBML Globally

Enhanced Collaboration: Increased collaboration between governments, law enforcement agencies, and the private sector is vital to combat TBML. Such cooperation can facilitate the sharing of information and intelligence, thereby enabling the identification of suspicious transactions and the entities behind them.

Technology Advancements: The development of technologies and innovative solutions, such as AI, machine learning, and blockchain, can enhance the detection and prevention of TBML. These technologies can aid in identifying patterns of behavior and transactions indicative of TBML and provide a more secure and transparent trading platform.

Strengthening Regulations: Stronger regulations to prevent TBML can be implemented at the national and international levels. These regulations can include mandatory due diligence procedures, reporting requirements, and sanctions against countries and individuals found to be involved in TBML.

Regulatory Improvements: Implementation of recommendations by FATF, and initiatives to oblige crypto-asset service providers to collect and make accessible information about the originator and the beneficiary of crypto-asset transfers.

Extending Whistleblower Reward Schemes: Schemes that provide financial rewards to whistleblowers have become increasingly popular in recent years across domains such as combating tax evasion and economic crimes. The U.S. government removed a $150,000 cap on rewards for money laundering whistleblowers, making them eligible to receive up to 30% of the fines paid by financial institutions.

Digitalization, the Internet of Things, and the Blockchain: Manual processing of trade documentation impedes the detection of issues because it requires a single reviewer to determine whether activity deviates from historical patterns. Progress has been made with the introduction of digitalization, the Internet of Things (IoT), and the blockchain. Digitalization can improve trade documentation by automating data collection and processing, enabling the detection of anomalies and issues that may not be identified through manual review. IoT can provide real-time data on the location and condition of goods being traded, reducing the risk of fraud or tampering. The blockchain can enhance the transparency and traceability of trade transactions, facilitating the identification of issues and the prevention of fraud. Together, these technologies have the potential to transform trade documentation, increase efficiency, and reduce risk.

Data Sharing and Big Data

Improving data sharing among financial institutions and across sectors involved in trade can make fraud exponentially harder to commit. Data sharing enables different actors to triangulate information, creating a more comprehensive view of trade transactions. Since 2005, the U.S. government has pioneered the concept of trade transparency units that enable the mutual sharing of detailed trade data with selected governments worldwide. The use of big data analytics can also help identify suspicious patterns, reducing the need for manual review.

Collaboration and Standardization

Collaboration is critical to combating TBML. Governments, international organizations, and the private sector must work together to develop effective solutions. Standardization of processes and procedures is also imperative, as it reduces the potential for inconsistencies and errors.

Challenges Ahead

Despite the progress made in combating TBML, significant challenges remain. Limited resources, the complex nature of TBML, and the lack of standardization present obstacles to effective enforcement. Addressing these challenges will require a concerted effort from all stakeholders to combat TBML effectively.

To wrap up the discussion, the multi-faceted approach to combating TBML requires the integration of technology, regulations, and collaboration. While progress has been made, there is still a long way to go. By working together and leveraging innovative solutions, it is possible to make significant strides in combating TBML.

References

Accuity. (2019). 2019 Survey: The Financial Crime Compliance Landscape.

Chainalysis. (2021). Cryptocurrency and the fight against trade-based money laundering. Retrieved from https://go.chainalysis.com/rs/503-FAP-074/images/Cryptocurrency_and_the_Fight_Against_Trade-Based_Money_Laundering.pdf.

Cobham, A., & Janský, P. (2020). *Estimating illicit financial flows: A critical guide to the data, methodologies, and findings.* Oxford University Press. https://library.oapen.org/bitstream/handle/20.500.12657/37433/9780198854418.pdf

The Anti-Money Laundering Act (AMLA) was enacted in January 2021 and introduces significant changes to the U.S. AML regime. Some of the key changes include introducing new mechanisms to enhance information sharing and cooperation, expanding the scope of the Bank Secrecy Act (BSA) to cover businesses providing services involving value that substitutes for currency, promoting international cooperation, and strengthening enforcement tools to deter money laundering and other financial crimes. AMLA also revised the BSA whistleblower provisions and requires the identification of beneficial owners of certain legal entities. The implementation of AMLA involves rulemaking, with some rulemakings already in progress, while others appear to be delayed.

The U.S. Congress passed the Corporate Transparency Act (CTA) as part of the Anti-Money Laundering Act (AMLA) in January 2021. The CTA requires certain entities to report their beneficial ownership information to the U.S. Treasury's Financial Crimes Enforcement Network (FinCEN), which will maintain a nonpublic database of such information.

Index

Note: *Italic* page numbers refer to figures, **bold** page numbers refer to tables.

For Product Safety Concerns and Information please contact our EU representative GPSR@taylorandfrancis.com
Taylor & Francis Verlag GmbH, Kaufingerstraße 24, 80331 München, Germany

www.ingramcontent.com/pod-product-compliance
Ingram Content Group UK Ltd.
Pitfield, Milton Keynes, MK11 3LW, UK
UKHW050230200926
475702UK00020B/2950

* 9 7 8 1 0 3 2 7 6 2 2 1 0 *